Recent Advances in Chaos, Fractal and Complex Dynamics in Nonlinear Systems

Recent Advances in Chaos, Fractal and Complex Dynamics in Nonlinear Systems

Guest Editors

Zhouchao Wei
Liguo Yuan

MDPI

Basel • Beijing • Wuhan • Barcelona • Belgrade • Novi Sad • Cluj • Manchester

Guest Editors

Zhouchao Wei
School of Mathematics
and Physics
China University of
Geosciences (Wuhan)
Wuhan
China

Liguo Yuan
College of Mathematics
and Informatics
South China Agricultural
University
Guangzhou
China

Editorial Office
MDPI AG
Grosspeteranlage 5
4052 Basel, Switzerland

This is a reprint of the Special Issue, published open access by the journal *Mathematics* (ISSN 2227-7390), freely accessible at: https://www.mdpi.com/journal/mathematics/special_issues/Chaos_Fractal_Complex_Dynamics.

For citation purposes, cite each article independently as indicated on the article page online and as indicated below:

Lastname, A.A.; Lastname, B.B. Article Title. *Journal Name* **Year**, *Volume Number*, Page Range.

ISBN 978-3-7258-4781-5 (Hbk)
ISBN 978-3-7258-4782-2 (PDF)
https://doi.org/10.3390/books978-3-7258-4782-2

Contents

About the Editors

Zhouchao Wei

Zhouchao Wei is a professor at the School of Mathematics and Physics, China University of Geosciences (Wuhan). He completed his integrated master's and doctoral studies at South China University of Technology from 2006 to 2011 and conducted his postdoctoral research in Mechanics at Beijing University of Technology from 2014 to 2017. He has also undertaken academic visits to the University of Oxford and Lodz University of Technology in Poland. His research interests include high-dimensional complex dynamical systems, bifurcation and chaos theory, non-smooth dynamical systems, and the structural vibration of ships. In recent years, he has published multiple papers in international SCI journals such as *Chaos, Physica D, Journal of Nonlinear Science, Ocean Engineering, EPL,* and *Nonlinear Dynamics,* with some of these recognized as ESI highly cited papers. He also serves as an editorial board member for several SCI journals and as a guest editor for multiple international Special Issues.

Liguo Yuan

Liguo Yuan, Ph.D., is currently an Associate Professor at the College of Mathematics and Informatics, South China Agricultural University. He also serves as a reviewer for the American journal *Mathematical Reviews* and as the deputy head of the Mathematics department of his institution. He has previously attended the University of California, Merced and Anhui University as a visiting scholar. He has published 51 papers and has a h-index and i10-index of 13 and 14, respectively. His research interests include chaos and bifurcation, fractal interpolation, fractional-order time-delay equations, and swarm intelligence optimization algorithms.

mathematics

MDPI

Article

Complex Periodic Mixed-Mode Oscillation Patterns in a Filippov System

Chun Zhang * and Qiaoxia Tang

School of Mathematical Science, Huaiyin Normal University, Huaian 223300, China; qxtang@hytc.edu.cn
* Correspondence: czhang@hytc.edu.cn

Abstract: The main task of this article is to study the patterns of mixed-mode oscillations and non-smooth behaviors in a Filippov system with external excitation. Different types of periodic spiral crossing mixed-mode oscillation patterns, i.e., "cusp-F^-/fold-F^-" oscillation, "cusp-F^-/two-fold/two-fold/fold-F^-" oscillation and "two-fold/fold-F^-" oscillation, are explored. Based on the analysis of the equilibrium and tangential singularities of the fast subsystem, spiral crossing oscillation around the tangential singularities is investigated. Meanwhile, by combining the fast and slow analysis methods, we can observe that the cusp, two-fold and fold-cusp singularities play an important role in generating all kinds of complex mixed-mode oscillations.

Keywords: mixed-mode oscillations; tangential singularity; spiral crossing oscillations; external excitation

MSC: 34C15; 34C05; 37G10; 37G18

1. Introduction

As a typical non-smooth dynamic system, the Filippov system reflected in the mathematical model can be expressed as discontinuous differential equations whose right-hand side is discontinuous [1]. The main motivation for studying the Filippov system comes from the fact that non-smooth factors in many practical engineering systems can be described by this kind of model, such as mechanical systems with friction [2], switched electronic systems [3], discontinuous control systems [4] and others [5,6]. Generally, a Filippov system always has a switching surface which connects two types of flows. When the trajectory touches the switching surface, the system is redefined, which can cause the qualitative changes in the system's dynamics, such as boundary equilibrium bifurcations, multiple collision and non-smooth periodic orbit bifurcations [7–10]. Especially, the system may exhibit various types of special phenomena on the switching surface, such as sliding motion and fold, cusp, two-fold, fold-cusp tangential singularities [11,12].

On the other hand, many important practical engineering problems also involve coupling of different time scales [13–16]. This type of system may cause mixed-mode oscillations, which are formed by a relatively large excursion and nearly harmonic small amplitude oscillation during every evolution period. For example, Abdelouahab et al. [17] studied the existence of mixed-mode oscillations and canard oscillations in the neighborhoods of Hopf-like bifurcation points based on the global and local canard explosion search algorithm. Liu et al. [18] found that the folded surface and critical manifold both play an important role in the existence of mixed-mode oscillations at the folded saddle in the perturbed system. Ma et al. [19] explored the evolution mechanism of different mixed-mode oscillation patterns caused by the pitchfork bifurcation and related delay behaviors in a van der Pol–Duffing system with parameter excitation. Yu et al. [20] studied the singular Hopf bifurcation conditions and MMO behaviors in the parametric perturbed BVP system and investigated the mechanisms of two different types of MMOs using a generalized fast-slow analysis method. Chen et al. [21] explored multiple fast-slow motions, including "periodic bursts with quasi-periodic spiking", "torus/short transient" mixed mode oscillations, "pitchfork/long transient" periodic mixed mode oscillations, amplitude-modulated and irregular oscillations from numerical method. It can be seen that the behaviors of the mixed-mode oscillation can be produced by many factors, such as different kinds of bifurcation structures [22,23], delay behaviors [24,25], and hysteresis loops [26,27]. However, most of the results about mixed-mode oscillations are made for smooth systems. When the non-smooth vector field contains multiple time scale couplings, mixed-mode oscillations may also observed. For example, Simprson et al. [28] investigated a piecewise-smooth linear FitzHugh–Nagumo system and showed that the piecewise-smooth linear model may exhibit MMO more easier than the classical FitzHugh–Nagumo model which contains a cubic polynomial as the only nonlinear term. Wang et al. [29] found that the delayed C-bifurcation leads to different types of transitions between multiple attractors, and explained the mechanism of mixed-mode oscillations in a typical Chua's system with external excitation and a piecewise resistor. Even so, up to now, the influences of a non-smooth vector field on the vibration of mixed modes are rarely studied.

This paper investigates the mixed-mode oscillations and non-smooth dynamical behaviors in a piecewise nonlinear system with external excitation, focusing on the effects of the tangential singularities on the mixed-mode oscillations. For this purpose, we continue to analyze a realistic model in the literature [30], focusing on the effect of the external excitation. The basic circuit model with the external excitation is presented in Figure 1, where $E > 0$ stands for the voltage source and R represents a resistive load. The voltage v_{out} across R is the system output.

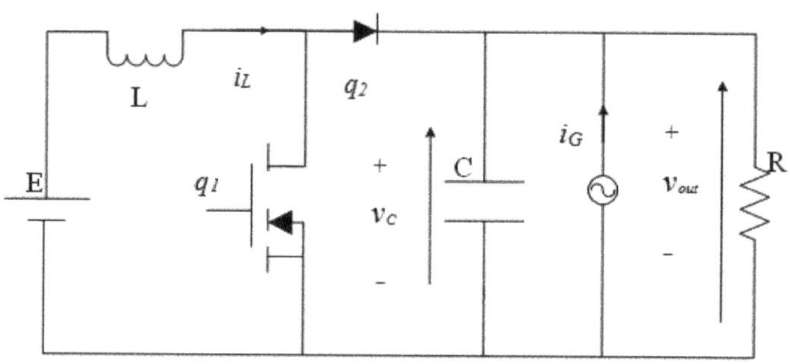

Figure 1. The basic circuit with a periodic excitation.

The structure of the paper is set up as follows. The differential equation model of the circuit is established and the stabilities of the equilibrium and tangential singularities conditions of the fast subsystem are given in Section 2. Then, three new mixed-mode oscillation patterns, i.e., "cusp-F$^-$/fold-F$^-$" oscillation, "cusp-F$^-$/two-fold/two-fold/fold-F$^-$" oscillation and "two-fold/fold-F$^-$" oscillation are reported and the associated evolution mechanism are presented in Section 3. In Section 4, we present a brief conclusion of the paper.

2. Hybrid Model

2.1. Mathematical Model

Considering the inductor current i_L and the voltage v_C as state variables, the circuit described in Figure 1 can be written as

$$\begin{aligned} L\frac{di_L}{d\tau} &= (E - i_L r_L)(q_1 + q_2) - i_L r_{DS} q_1 - (V_{D0} + \frac{i_L r_C + v_C}{r_C + R} R) q_2 + i_G cos(\Omega\tau), \\ C\frac{dv_C}{d\tau} &= \frac{R}{r_C + R} i_L q_2 - \frac{1}{r_C + R} v_C, \end{aligned} \tag{1}$$

where q_1 and q_2 are either 0 or 1 and not simultaneously equal to 0 or 1, $i_G > 0$ is the excitation amplitude and $\Omega = o(\varepsilon)$ is the excitation frequency. The voltage output v_{out} is given by v_C, i.e.,

$$v_{out} = \frac{r_C R}{r_C + R} i_L q_2 + \frac{R}{r_C + R} i_L v_C. \tag{2}$$

Considering that $r_L \neq 0$ and $r_{DS} = 0, V_{D0} = 0, r_C = 0$, thus $v_{out} = v_C$ and the above model can be simplified as follows

$$\begin{aligned} L\frac{di_L}{d\tau} &= (E - i_L r_L)(q_1 + q_2) - v_C q_2 + i_G cos(\frac{\omega}{\sqrt{LC}}\tau), \\ C\frac{dv_C}{d\tau} &= i_L q_2 - \frac{v_C}{R}, \end{aligned} \tag{3}$$

By using the dimensionless transformation

$$x = \frac{i_L}{E}\sqrt{\frac{L}{C}}, y = \frac{v_C}{E}, t = \frac{\tau}{\sqrt{LC}}, \alpha = \frac{1}{R}\sqrt{\frac{L}{C}}, \beta = r_L\sqrt{\frac{C}{L}}, \omega = \sqrt{LC}\Omega, A = i_G,$$

the model (3) can be expressed in the form

$$\begin{aligned} \dot{x} &= (1 - \beta x)(q_1 + q_2) - y q_2 + A cos(\omega t), \\ \dot{y} &= x q_2 - \alpha y, \end{aligned} \tag{4}$$

where the new parameters are $\alpha > 0, \beta > 0, w > 0$. According to Ponce and Pagano [30], a new differential equation $\dot{z} = w(x - z)$ was introduced, and the sliding control scheme can be defined as

$$q_2 = 1 - q_1 = \begin{cases} 0, & if\ h(\mathbf{x}) > 0, \\ 1, & if\ h(\mathbf{x}) < 0, \end{cases} \tag{5}$$

where $\mathbf{x} = (x, y, z), h(\mathbf{x}) = y - y_r + k(x - z)$, and $y_r > 1$ is the normalized voltage and $k > 0$. It can be seen that the system with the above sliding mode scheme is obtained by connecting two vector fields

$$F^+(\mathbf{x}) = \begin{bmatrix} 1 - \beta x - y + \delta \\ x - \alpha y \\ w(x - z) \end{bmatrix}, F^-(\mathbf{x}) = \begin{bmatrix} 1 - \beta x + \delta \\ -\alpha y \\ w(x - z) \end{bmatrix}, \tag{6}$$

according to the sign of $h(\mathbf{x})$, where $\delta = A cos(\omega t)$. h defines the discontinuity manifold $\Sigma = \{\mathbf{x} \in \mathbb{R}^3 : h(\mathbf{x}) = 0\}$, and dividing the whole state space into two regions: one is $S^+ = \{\mathbf{x} \in \mathbb{R}^3 : h(\mathbf{x}) > 0\}$, and the other is $S^- = \{\mathbf{x} \in \mathbb{R}^3 : h(\mathbf{x}) < 0\}$.

Since the excitation frequency $\omega = O(\varepsilon)$ is much less than the natural frequency, the extraneous excitation term evolves very slowly with the change of time, which indicates that the whole system has two time scales. Thus, the system can be thought of as the coupling of two subsystems, one is a slow subsystem, which is a piecewise-smooth dynamical system (6), and the other is a fast subsystem written as $\delta = A cos(\omega t)$. Furthermore, the main characteristics of the whole system is determined by the fast subsystem, while the slow subsystem plays a moderating role in the behaviors of the whole system. Therefore, we first study the stability and bifurcation dynamics of the fast subsystem, by considering δ as a modulation parameter.

The equilibrium points for the vector fields F^+ and F^- are

$$E^+ = \left(\frac{\alpha(\delta+1)}{\beta\alpha+1}, \frac{\delta+1}{\beta\alpha+1}, \frac{\alpha(\delta+1)}{\beta\alpha+1}\right), E^- = \left(\frac{1+\delta}{\beta}, 0, \frac{1+\delta}{\beta}\right),$$

respectively. E^+ is a stable node (for $\beta > \alpha+2$ or $\beta < \alpha-2$) or stable focus (for $\alpha - 2 < \beta < \alpha + 2$) since the associated eigenvalues have a negative real part, namely

$$\Big(-\frac{1}{2}(\alpha+\beta) - \frac{1}{2}\sqrt{(\alpha-\beta)^2-4}, -\frac{1}{2}(\alpha+\beta) + \frac{1}{2}\sqrt{(\alpha-\beta)^2-4}, -w\Big).$$

Because $h(E^+) = \dfrac{1+\delta}{\alpha\beta+1} - y_r$, E^+ is an admissible stable equilibrium if $\dfrac{1+\delta}{\alpha\beta+1} > y_r$, while if $\dfrac{1+\delta}{\alpha\beta+1} = y_r$, E^+ is a boundary equilibrium, else E^+ is a virtual stable equilibrium. E^- is always a admissible stable node since the associated eigenvalues are real and negative, namely $(-\beta, -\alpha, -w)$, and $h(E^-) = -y_r < 0$.

2.2. Tangential Singularities

Since the fast subsystem in Equation (6) is a piecewise-smooth dynamical system, the type of contact between the smooth vector fields $F^\pm$ and the switching surface $\sum$ can be explained by the Lie derivatives $\mathcal{L}_{F^\pm}h(\mathbf{x}) = \langle \nabla h, F^\pm \rangle$ where $\langle\cdot,\cdot\rangle$ and ∇h denote the canonical inner product and the gradient of switching boundary function h, respectively. The m-order Lie derivatives are defined as $\mathcal{L}^m_{F^\pm}h = \langle \nabla \mathcal{L}^{m-1}_{F^\pm}h, F\rangle, m = 2, 3, \cdots$.

The point $\mathbf{x} \in \sum$ is called tangential singularity (i.e., the orbit from $\mathbf{x}$ is tangent to $\sum$) if $\mathcal{L}_{F^+}h(\mathbf{x}) \cdot \mathcal{L}_{F^-}h(\mathbf{x}) = 0$. A point $\mathbf{x} \in \sum$ is called double tangency point (i.e., the trajectory of the smooth vector fields $F^\pm$ from $\mathbf{x}$ is both tangent to $\sum$) if $\mathcal{L}_{F^+}h(\mathbf{x}) = \mathcal{L}_{F^-}h(\mathbf{x}) = 0$. The tangential sets corresponding to $F^\pm$ are given by the space lines:

$$\begin{aligned}
T^+_\delta &= \Big\{\mathbf{x} : h(\mathbf{x}) = 0, \mathcal{L}_{F^+}h(\mathbf{x}) = 0\Big\} \\
&= \Big\{(x,y,z) : x = -\frac{(-w+k+\alpha)y}{-1+k\beta} - \frac{-k\delta+wr-k}{-1+k\beta}, y = y, \\
&\qquad z = -\frac{(k^2+k\alpha-k\beta+1-kw)y}{k(-1+k\beta)} - \frac{-k^2+k\beta r-k^2\delta+kwr-r}{k(-1+k\beta)}\Big\} \\
T^-_\delta &= \Big\{\mathbf{x} : h(\mathbf{x}) = 0, \mathcal{L}_{F^-}h(\mathbf{x}) = 0\Big\} \\
&= \Big\{\mathbf{x} : x = \frac{(w-\alpha)y}{k\beta} + \frac{-wr+k+k\delta}{k\beta}, y = y, z = \frac{(-\alpha+\beta+w)y}{k\beta} \\
&\qquad + \frac{k+k\delta-wr-\beta r}{k\beta}\Big\}.
\end{aligned}$$

It is well known that tangential singularities are important for the understanding of dynamical behaviors at a switching boundary and they form the boundaries dividing the switching surface $\sum$ into a crossing region and a sliding/escaping region:

Crossing regions are defined by $\sum^{c+} = \Big\{\mathbf{x} \in \sum : \mathcal{L}_{F^+}h(\mathbf{x}) > 0, \mathcal{L}_{F^-}h(\mathbf{x}) > 0\Big\}$ and $\sum^{c-} = \Big\{\mathbf{x} \in \sum : \mathcal{L}_{F^+}h(\mathbf{x}) < 0, \mathcal{L}_{F^-}h(\mathbf{x}) < 0\Big\}$;

The sliding region is defined by $\sum^{s} = \Big\{\mathbf{x} \in \sum : \mathcal{L}_{F^+}h(\mathbf{x}) < 0, \mathcal{L}_{F^-}h(\mathbf{x}) > 0\Big\}$;

The escaping region is defined by $\sum^{e} = \Big\{\mathbf{x} \in \sum : \mathcal{L}_{F^+}h(\mathbf{x}) > 0, \mathcal{L}_{F^-}h(\mathbf{x}) < 0\Big\}$.

In the 3-dimensional dynamical system, two important types of generic tangential singularities that are encountered on smooth portions of $\sum$ are as follows:

A point $\mathbf{x}$ is a fold point about the smooth vector field F^+ if $\mathbf{x} \in \sum, \mathcal{L}_{F^+}h(\mathbf{x}) = 0$, while $\mathcal{L}^2_{F^+}h(\mathbf{x}) \neq 0$, and the gradient vectors of $h(\mathbf{x})$ and $\mathcal{L}_{F^+}h(\mathbf{x})$ are linearly independent. Moreover, $\mathbf{x}$ is a cusp point with respect to the vector field F^+ if $\mathbf{x} \in \sum, \mathcal{L}_{F^+}h(\mathbf{x}) = \mathcal{L}^2_{F^+}h(\mathbf{x}) = 0$, while $\mathcal{L}^3_{F^+}h(\mathbf{x}) \neq 0$, and the gradient vectors of $h(\mathbf{x})$, $\mathcal{L}_{F^+}h(\mathbf{x})$ and $\mathcal{L}^2_{F^+}h(\mathbf{x})$ are linearly independent [31].

With the same method, fold and cusp point related to the smooth vector field F^- can also be defined. Moreover, it is possible for a point $\mathbf{x} \in \sum$ to be a double tangency point. When $\mathbf{x} \in \sum$ is a fold point, the cusp point with respect to the vector fields $F^\pm$, $\mathbf{x}$ is called a two fold, two-cusp singularity, respectively. If $\mathbf{x} \in \sum$ is a fold singularity with respect to one vector field and a cusp singularity with respect to the other one, we call $\mathbf{x}$ as a fold-cusp singularity [32].

The next result summarizes the conditions of the tangential singularities which will be covered in this paper according to the parameter β, w, δ and fixing $y_r = 2.0, k = 1.0, \alpha = 1.0$.

The double tangency point $\mathbf{x}_D$ is given by $T^+_\delta \bigcap T^-_\delta$, i.e.,

$$\mathbf{x}_D = \left\{ \frac{-\delta + 2w - 1}{-\beta - 1 + w}, \frac{-\delta + 2w - 1}{-\beta - 1 + w}, \frac{2(-\delta + w + \beta)}{-\beta - 1 + w} \right\}. \tag{7}$$

The point $\mathbf{x}_D$ is a two-cusp singularity if $\beta = -w + 1$ and $\delta = 3 - 2w$ or a fold-cusp singularity if $\beta \neq -w + 1$ and $\delta = -\dfrac{2w^2 - 3w - 2\beta^2 w + \beta w - \beta + 1}{\beta w + 1 - \beta - w}$ (fold for F^+, cusp for F^-) or $\delta = 1 + 2\beta$ (cusp for F^+, fold for F^-). In the other case, the point $\mathbf{x}_D$ is a two-fold singularity.

A straightforward calculation shows that the point $\mathbf{x}_{CF^+} = (x_{CF^+}, y_{CF^+}, z_{CF^+})$ with

$$\begin{aligned} x_{CF^+} &= \frac{3 - 4w - \beta + \beta w\delta - \beta\delta - \beta w - 2w\delta + 2w^2 + 3\delta}{3 - \beta^2 + 2\beta - 3w - 2\beta w + \beta^2 w + w^2}, \\ y_{CF^+} &= \frac{3 + 2\beta^2 w - 5w - \beta + 2w^2 - \beta\delta - 2\beta w - w\delta + 3\delta}{3 - \beta^2 + 2\beta - 3w - 2\beta w + \beta^2 w + w^2}, \\ z_{CF^+} &= \frac{2\beta^2 - 2\beta\delta + \beta w\delta - 6\beta + \beta w - 3w - 3w\delta + 2w^2 + 6\delta}{3 - \beta^2 + 2\beta - 3w - 2\beta w + \beta^2 w + w^2}, \end{aligned} \tag{8}$$

and the point $\mathbf{x}_{CF^-} = (x_{CF^-}, y_{CF^-}, z_{CF^-})$ with

$$\begin{aligned} x_{CF^-} &= \frac{2w - 1 + \beta\delta + \beta - \delta}{(\beta - 1)\beta}, \\ y_{CF^-} &= \frac{2\beta w}{\beta w + 1 - \beta - w}, \\ z_{CF^-} &= \frac{3\beta w + 1 - 3\beta - 3w + 2\beta^2 + \beta w\delta + \delta - \beta\delta - w\delta + 2w^2}{\beta(\beta w + 1 - \beta - w)}, \end{aligned} \tag{9}$$

are cusp points related to F^+ and F^-, respectively, due to the fact that $\mathcal{L}^2_{F^+}h(\mathbf{x}_{CF^+}) = 0, \mathcal{L}^3_{F^+}h(\mathbf{x}_{CF^+}) = -(2\beta - \delta + 1)w \neq 0$ and $\mathcal{L}^2_{F^-}h(\mathbf{x}_{CF^-}) = 0, \mathcal{L}^3_{F^-}h(\mathbf{x}_{CF^-}) = -2\beta w \neq 0$.

3. Mixed-Mode Oscillation and Its Mechanism

Based on the results of the analysis of the equilibria and the tangential singularities of Equation (6), we find that mixed-mode oscillations are obtained when the whole system undergoes a transformation between the fast system and slow system connected by the different types of tangential points on the switched surface.

In the following discussion, the parameters $\alpha = 1.0, w = 0.01, \beta = 0.32, y_r = 2.0, k = 1.0$ are always fixed and the excited frequency is fixed at $\omega = 0.01$. We study the evolution of the mixed-mode oscillation dynamics and the associated mechanism of the non-smooth behaviors at the switching boundary when the amplitude A is changed.

Note that E^+ is an admissible stable focus if $\delta > 1.64$, a boundary stable focus if $\delta = 1.64$ or a virtual stable focus if $\delta < 1.64$, while E^- is always a admissible stable node for the fixed parameters. A typical trajectory of the fast system is shown in Figure 2 for $\delta = 0.54$. The trajectory locally wraps around the singularity until the trajectory in the open region S^- meets with or is near to the tangential sets $T^-_{0.54}$ and then moves to the admissible stable node E^-.

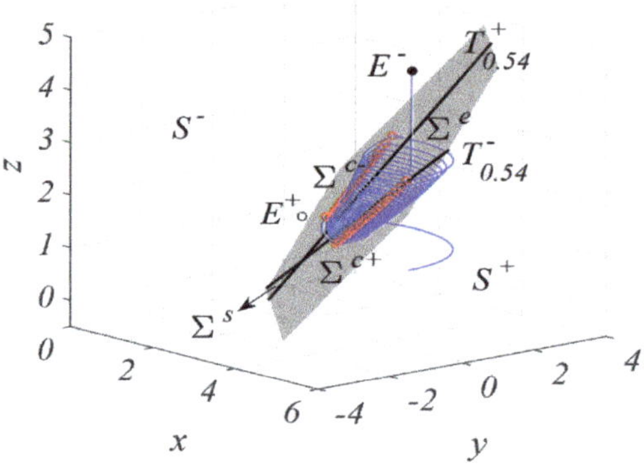

Figure 2. E^+ is a virtual stable focus; E^- is an admissible stable note. A typical orbit of the fast subsystem is shown: trajectories locally wrap around the tangential sets for $\delta = 0.54$.

3.1. Cusp-F^-/Fold-F^- Periodic Spiral Crossing Oscillation

As shown in Figure 3a, a periodic mixed-mode oscillation can be obtained when the amplitude is fixed at $A = 0.92$. It is seen that the periodic mixed-mode oscillation can be divided into two parts (seen in Figure 3b), i.e., the spiral crossing oscillation and the periodic oscillation which are connected by the tangential singularities.

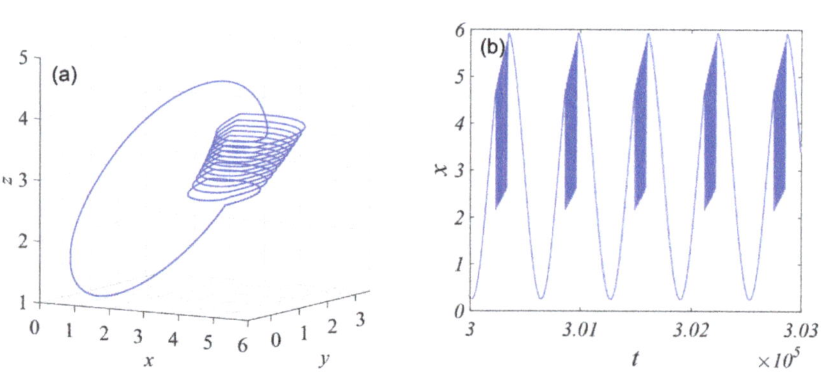

Figure 3. A typical mixed-mode oscillation pattern for $A = 0.92$. (**a**) Phase portrait; (**b**) time series of the mixed-mode oscillation.

To explain the mechanism of this mixed-mode oscillation, Figure 4a shows the overlap of the phase portraits of different amplitudes, while Figure 4b shows the transformed phase portrait and tangential singularities with the variation of the parameter δ. The green line in Figure 4b refers to the two-fold singularities, the black line denotes the cusp singularities with respect to the vector field F^-, while the black point corresponds to the fold-cusp singularity.

As is shown in Figure 4a, the limit cycle (the gray orbit) with $A = 0.91$ is completely in the open region S^- and does not meet the switching boundary $\sum$ when it oscillates around the admissible stable node E^- in counter-clockwise direction. When $A = 0.92$, the limit cycle (the blue orbit) contact with the switching surface $\sum$ at $P = (4.7357, 0.0079, 2.7357)$ with $\delta = 0.53925$. Based on Equation (9), the point P is the cusp singularity with respect to F^-(seen in Figure 4b), which means that the trajectory in the open region S^- is tangent to the switching boundary $\sum$ at P and then crosses through the switching surface $\sum$ to the open region S^+ governed by the vector field F^+. Since E^+ is the virtual stable focus under the parameter conditions, the trajectory inevitably contacts with the switching surface $\sum$ at the point P_1 in $\sum^{c-}$ when it scrolls down to the stable focus E^+, then returns to the open region S^- governed by the the admissible stable node E^-.

In the process of moving from the the point P_1 to the stable E^-, the trajectory may contact with the switching boundary again at P_2 in the crossing region $\sum^{c-}$, which may cause the trajectory to scroll down to the virtual stable focus. In this way, the trajectory may spiral around the switching surface $\sum$ from the cusp singularity P until the trajectory in the open region S^- meets with or is near to the tangential sets T_{δ}^-, causing the trajectory to return back to the point P along the limit cycle in open region S^-. We can refer to such mixed-oscillation formation as the cusp-F$^-$/fold-F$^-$ periodic spiral crossing oscillation.

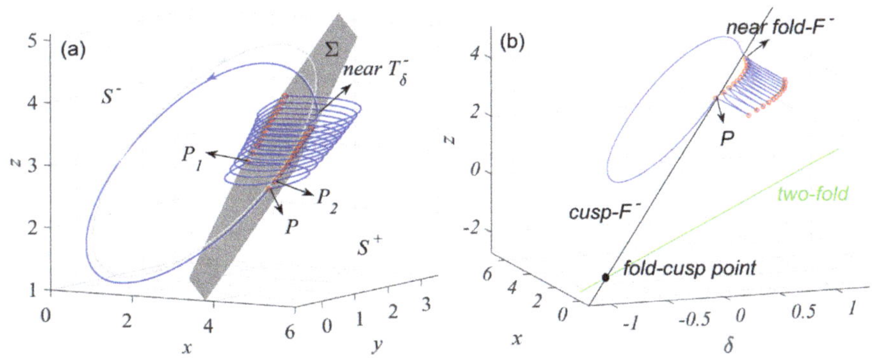

Figure 4. (**a**) Stable limit cycles with $A = 0.91$ (the gray orbit) and $A = 0.92$ (the blue orbit); (**b**) overlap of the tangential singularities branches and transformed phase portrait on the (δ, x, z).

3.2. *Cusp-F$^-$/Two-Fold/Two-Fold/Fold F$^-$ Periodic Spiral Crossing Oscillation*

When A increases from 0.92, the mixed-mode oscillation obtained in Equation (6) may exhibit some interesting behaviors. For example, Figure 5 shows a group of mixed-mode oscillation patterns in Equation (6) with increasing values of A for fixed $A = 1.35$ and $A = 1.7$. It can be seen that the spiral crossing oscillation in the mixed-mode oscillation (see Figure 5a) may be divided into two parts, i.e., the left and right spiral crossing oscillation parts (see Figure 5b) with the increase of the parameter A. The corresponding phase portraits are shown in Figure 5c,d. We may find that the left trajectories may spiral around the boundary $\sum^s$, while the right trajectories may spiral around the boundary $\sum^e$.

The phenomenon can be also understood by the analysis of the contact between the orbit and the tangential singularities. As shown in Figure 6, when the parameter A increases from 0.92 to 1.437, the trajectories of the cusp-F$^-$/fold-F$^-$ periodic spiral crossing oscillation may get to the two-fold singularity at $\delta = 1.437$, which imply that spiral crossing trajectories may split into two parts, i.e., the left trajectories spiraled around the boundary $\sum^s$, and the right trajectories spiraled around the boundary $\sum^e$, connected by two two-fold points (see in Figure 6b). We can refer to such mixed oscillation formation as the cusp-F$^-$/two-fold/two-fold/fold F$^-$ periodic spiral crossing oscillation.

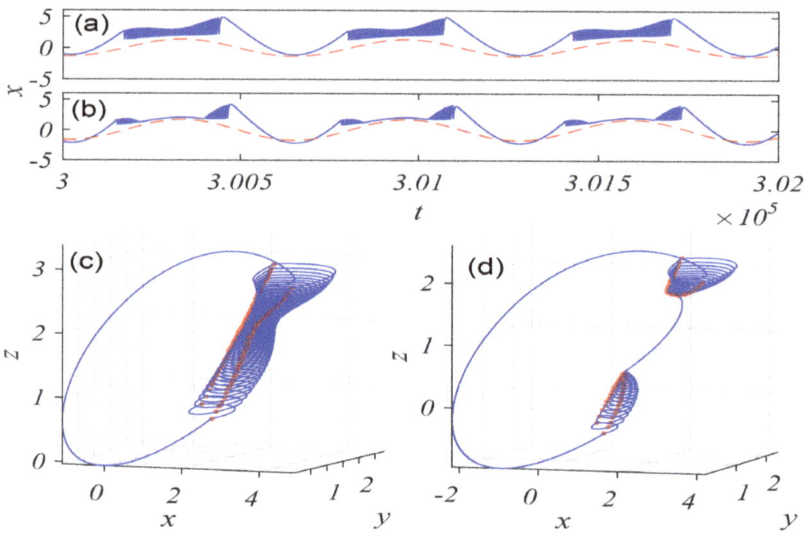

Figure 5. Tangential singularities-induced mixed-mode oscillation patterns in Equation (6), where $Acos(\omega t)$ (the dashed line) is overlayed to give a clear view that the frequency of the periodic mixed-mode oscillation is equal to ω. (**a**,**c**) $A = 1.35$; (**b**,**d**) $A = 1.7$.

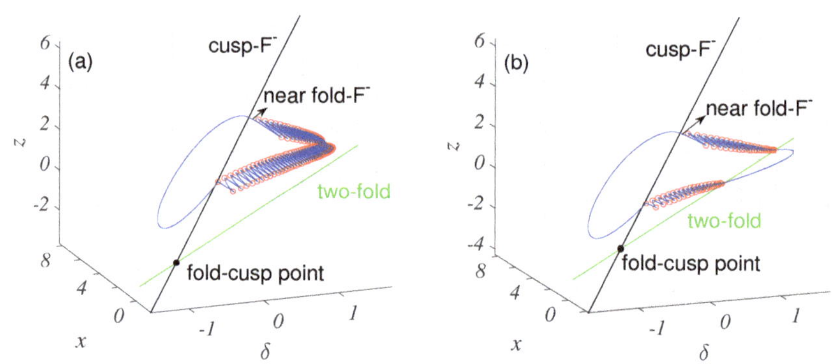

Figure 6. Overlap of the tangential singularities branches and transformed phase portrait on the (δ, x, z). (**a**) $A = 1.35$; (**b**) $A = 1.7$.

3.3. Two-Fold/Fold-F^- Periodic Spiral Crossing Oscillation

By a further increase of parameter A, the left spiral crossing oscillation around the boundary $\sum^s$ may gradually disappear, and only the right spiral crossing oscillation is left, which still wraps around the boundary $\sum^e$, as shown in Figure 7a for $A = 2.80$. The corresponding phase portrait is presented in Figure 7b.

The mechanism analysis is obtained by the overlap of the phase diagram on the space of (δ, x, z) with the tangential singularities with the change of the parameter δ, as presented in Figure 7c. The mechanism can be explained simply. When A increases through 2.25, the point P where the limit cycle of the vector F^- intersects the boundary Σ may pass through the fold-cusp singularity (fold respect to F^+ and cusp respect to F^-, shown in Figure 7c) along the cusp F^- singularity at $\delta = -0.8737$, causing the trajectory to pass through the boundary Σ and experience a sharp turn down to the two-fold point. The trajectories of the cusp-F$^-$/two-fold/two-fold/fold F$^-$ periodic spiral crossing oscillation may become unstable at $A = 2.25$, causing the left spiral crossing oscillation part to disappear (shown in Figure 5d) and evolve to a new mixed-mode oscillation pattern seen in Figure 7b. We can refer to such mixed oscillation formation as the two-fold/fold-F^- periodic spiral crossing oscillation.

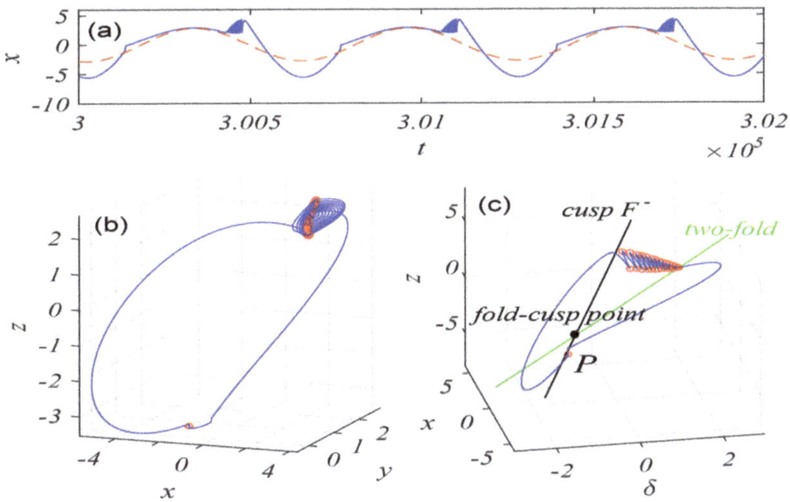

Figure 7. A typical mixed-mode oscillation pattern for $A = 2.80$. (**a**) Time history; (**b**) phase portrait; (**c**) transformed phase portrait.

4. Conclusions

This article studies mixed-mode oscillation dynamics in a Filippov system with external excitation. When the amplitude of the excitation is changed, three new mixed-mode oscillation patterns, i.e., "cusp-F$^-$/fold-F$^-$" oscillation, "cusp-F$^-$/two-fold/two-fold/fold-F$^-$" oscillation and "two-fold/fold-F$^-$" oscillation are first reported. By regarding the excitation term as a bifurcation parameter, the stabilities of the (admissible and boundary) equilibrium and the conditions of different types of tangential points, such as cusp, two-fold and fold-cusp singularity, are explored. With the decrease of the excitation amplitude, when the excitation term passes through the two-fold point, the periodic spiral crossing oscillation may become unstable and a periodic oscillation with two (left and right) spiral crossing trajectories is created. When the excitation term passes through the fold-cusp point, the left spiral crossing trajectory of the periodic oscillation may suddenly disappear and only the right spiral crossing trajectory is left. Besides, the results proposed in this paper are advantageous to understand the mixed-mode oscillation in non-smooth dynamical systems. Our further work will focus on the effect of the different behaviors of mixed-mode oscillation caused by various switched scheme and the potential applications on Filippov system.

Author Contributions: Formal analysis, C.Z.; methodology, C.Z. and Q.T.; writing—original draft preparation, Q.T.; writing—review and editing, C.Z. All authors have read and agreed to the published version of the manuscript.

Funding: This work is supported by the National Natural Science Foundation of China (Grant Nos. 11502091 and 11801209).

Institutional Review Board Statement: Not applicable.

Informed Consent Statement: Not applicable.

Data Availability Statement: Not applicable.

Acknowledgments: We would like to express our deep thanks to the anonymous referees for their valuable comments.

Conflicts of Interest: The author declares no conflict of interest.

References

1. Filippov, A.F. Differential Equations with Discontinuous Righthand Sides. In *Mathematics and Its Applications*; Soviet Series; Arscott, F.M., Ed.; Springer: Dordrecht, The Netherlands; Kluwer Academic: Boston, MA, USA, 1988.
2. Polekhin, I. On Montions without falling of an interted pendulum with dry friction. *J. Geom. Mech.* **2018**, *10*, 411–417. [CrossRef]
3. Meo, S.; Toscano, L. On the existence and uniqueness of the ODE solution and its approximation using the means averaging approach for the class of power electronic converters. *Mathematics* **2021**, *10*, 1146. [CrossRef]
4. Baier, R.; Braun, P.; Grune, L.; Kellett, C.M. Numerical calculation of nonsmooth control lyapunov functions via piecewise affine approximation. *IFAC-PapersOnLine* **2019**, *52*, 370–375. [CrossRef]
5. Bhattacharyya, J.; Roelke, D.L.; Pal, S.; Banerjee, S. Sliding mode dynamics on a prey-predator system with intermittent harvesting policy. *Nonlinear Dyn.* **2019**, *98*, 1299–1314. [CrossRef]
6. Popov, M.; Friction under large-amplitude normal oscillations. *Facta Univ.-Ser. Mech. Eng.* **2021**, *19*, 105–113. [CrossRef]
7. Antali, M.; Stepan, G. Sliding and crossing dynamics in extended Filippov systemsm. *SIAM J. Appl. Dyn. Syst.* **2018**, *17*, 823–858. [CrossRef]
8. Walsh, J.; Widiasih, E. A discontinuous ODE model of the glacial cycles with diffusive heat transport. *Mathematics* **2021**, *8*, 316. [CrossRef]
9. Althubiti, S.; Aldawish, I.; Awrejcewicz, J.; Bazighifan, O. New oscillation results of even-order emden-fowler neutral differential equations. *Symmetry* **2021**, *13*, 2177. [CrossRef]
10. Santra, S.S.; Alotaibi, H.; Noeiaghdam, S.; Sidorov, D. On nonlinear forced impulsive differential equations under canonical and non-canonical conditions. *Symmetry* **2021**, *13*, 2066. [CrossRef]
11. Freire, E.; Ponce, E.; Torres, F. On the critical crossing cycle bifurcation in planar Filippov systems. *J. Differ. Equ.* **2015**, *259*, 7086–7107. [CrossRef]
12. Cristiano, R.; Pagano, D.J. Two-parameter boundary equilibrium bifurcations in 3D-Filippov systems. *J. Nonlinear Sci.* **2019**, *29*, 2845–2875. [CrossRef]
13. Han, X.J.; Zhang, Y.; Bi, Q.S.; Kurths, J. Two novel bursting patterns in the Duffing system with multiple-frequency slow parametric excitations. *Chaos* **2018**, *28*, 043111. [CrossRef] [PubMed]
14. Yu, Y.; Zhang, Z.D.; Han, X.J. Periodic or chaotic bursting dynamics via delayed pitchfork bifurcation in a slow-varying controlled system. *Commun. Nonlinear Sci. Numer. Simul.* **2018**, *56* 380–391. [CrossRef]
15. Ma, X.D.; Jiang, W.A.; Zhang, X.F.; Han, X.J.; Bi, Q.S. Complex bursting dynamics of a Mathieu-van der Pol-Duffing energy harvester. *Phys. Scr.* **2021**, *96* 015213. [CrossRef]
16. Duan, L.X.; Liang, T.T.; Zhao, Y.Q.; Xi, H.G. Multi-time scale dynamics of mixed depolarization block bursting. *Nonlinear Dyn.* **2021**, *103*, 1043–1053. [CrossRef]
17. Abdelouahab, M.S.; Lozi, R. Hopf-like bifurcation and mixed mode oscillation inn a fractional-order FitzHugh-Nagumo model. In Proceedings of the Third International Conference of Mathematical Sciences, Istanbul, Turkey, 4–8 September 2019; Volume 2183, p. 100003.
18. Liu, Y.R.; Lu, S.Q.; Lu, B.; Kurths, J. Mixed-mode oscillations for slow-fast perturbed systems. *Physic Scr.* **2021**, *96*, 125258. [CrossRef]
19. Ma, X.D.; Yu, Y.; Wang, L.F. Complex mixed-mode vibration types triggered by the pitchfork bifurcation delay in a driven van der Pol-Duffing oscillator. *Appl. Math. Comput.* **2021**, *411*, 126522. [CrossRef]
20. Yu, Y.; Zhang, C.; Chen, Z.Y.; Zhang, Z.D. *Canard-Induced Mixed Mode Oscillations as a Mechanism for the Bonhoeffer-van der Pol Circuit under Parametric Perturbation*; Emerald Publishing Limited: Bingley, UK, 2021. [CrossRef]
21. Chen, Z.Y.; Chen, F.Q.; Zhou, L.Q. Slow-fast motions induced by multi-stability and strong transient effects in an accelerating viscoelastic beam. *Nonlinear Dyn.* **2021**, *106*, 45–66. [CrossRef]
22. Wojcik, J.; Shilnikov, A. Voltage interval mappings for activity transitions in neuron models for elliptic bursters. *Phys. D Nonlinear Phenom.* **2011**, *240*, 1164–1180. [CrossRef]
23. Zhang, C.; Bi, Q.S. On two-parameter bifurcation analysis of the periodic parameter-switching Lorenz oscillator. *Nonlinear Dyn.* **2015**, *81*, 577–583. [CrossRef]
24. Yue, Y.; Han, X.J.; Zhang, C.; Bi, Q.S. Mixed-mode oscillations in a nonlinear time delay oscillator with time varying parameters. *Commun. Nonlinear Sci. Numer. Simul.* **2017**, *47*, 23–34. [CrossRef]
25. Karamchandani, A.J.; Graham, J.N.; Riecke, H. Pulse-coupled mixed-mode oscillators: Cluster states and extreme noise sensitivity. *Chaos* **2018**, *28*, 043115. [CrossRef] [PubMed]
26. Meng, P.; Wang, Q.Y.; Lu, Q.S. Bursting synchronization dynamics of pancreatic β-cells with electrical and chemical coupling. *Cogn. Neurodyn.* **2013**, *7*, 197–212. [CrossRef]
27. Han, X.J.; Bi, Q.S.; Zhang, C.; Yue, Y. Delayed bifurcations to repetitive spiking and classifcation of delay-induced bursting. *Int. J. Bifurc. Chaos* **2014**, *24*, 1450098. [CrossRef]
28. Simpson, D.J.W.; Kuske, R. Mixed-mode oscillations in a stochastic piecewise-linear system. *Phys. D Nonlinear Phenom.* **2011**, *240*, 1189–1198. [CrossRef]

29. Wang, Z.X.; Zhang, Z.D.; Bi, Q.S. Bursting oscillations with delayed C-bifurcations in a modified Chua's circuit. *Nonlinear Dyn.* **2020**, *100*, 2899–2915. [CrossRef]
30. Ponce, E.; Pagano, D.J. Chaos through sliding bifurcations in a boost converter under a SMC strategy. *IFAC Proc. Vol.* **2009**, *42*, 279–284. [CrossRef]
31. Jeffrey, M.R.; Colombo, A. The two-fold singularity of discontinuous vector fields. *SIAM J. Appl. Dyn. Syst.* **2009**, *8*, 624–640. [CrossRef]
32. de Carvalho, T.; Teixeira, M.A. Basin of attraction of a cusp-fold singularity in 3D piecewise smooth vector fields. *J. Math. Anal. Appl.* **2014**, *418*, 11–30. [CrossRef]

mathematics

MDPI

Article

Chaotic Dynamics of Non-Autonomous Nonlinear System for a Sandwich Plate with Truss Core

Dongmei Zhang and Feng Li *

School of Mathematics and Statistics, Linyi University, Linyi 276005, China; zhangdongmei@lyu.edu.cn
* Correspondence: lifeng@lyu.edu.cn; Tel.: +86-135-1869-5076

Abstract: This paper deals with the multi-pulse chaotic dynamics of a sandwich plate with truss core under transverse and in-plane excitations. In order to analyze the complicated nonlinear behaviors of the sandwich plate model by means of the improved extended Melnikov technique, the two-degrees non-autonomous system is transformed into an appropriate form. Through theoretical analysis, the sufficient conditions for the existence of multi-pulse homoclinic orbits and the criterion for the occurrence of chaotic motion are obtained. The damping coefficients and transverse excitation parameters are considered as the control parameters to discuss chaotic behaviors of the sandwich plate system. Numerical results and the maximal Lyapunov exponents are performed to further test the existence of the multi-pulse jumping orbits. The theoretical predictions and numerical results demonstrate that the chaos phenomena may exist in the parametrical excited sandwich plate.

Keywords: chaos; multi-pulse orbit; extended Melnikov method; Lyapunov exponent

MSC: 37G25

1. Introduction

The truss core sandwich materials belong to a new type of lightweight structure and are widely used in mechanical engineering and other various areas. Different types of sandwich structures have attracted the attention of many researchers. Analytical and numerical techniques can be applied to investigate the resonant response, bifurcation and chaotic dynamics for these sandwich materials.

For instance, Chen et al. [1,2] discussed the stability and nonlinear response of the harmonic-excited plate with tetrahedral core under influence of thermal loads. Boorle and Mallick [3] studied the global response of composite sandwich plates to the effect of some geometric parameters. In 2014, Zhang et al. [4] studied the periodic and chaotic motions of the sandwich plate with truss core. The influence of different excitation parameters on nonlinear dynamic behaviors were investigated by numerical methods. By introducing the nonlinear wave equation, Zhang et al. [5] applied the Menikov method to confirm the chaotic motions for this sandwich plate. Furthermore, based on the model given in [4], Chen et al. [6] discussed the local bifurcations and slow-fast motions for this four-dimensional nonlinear system under slow parametric and fast external excitation. However, the multi-pulse chaotic dynamics of this system have not been studied analytically. Based on the dimensionless governing equation, we conduct further research to obtain the conditions for the occurrence of chaotic motion by theoretical methods.

The bifurcation problems [7,8], single-pulse orbits and multi-pulse orbits [9] have been the top issue in dynamic research. Many researchers have developed analytical methods to study chaotic motions for the high-dimensional nonlinear systems. The Melnikov method is a classical approach to detect chaotic dynamics which was developed by Wiggins, Kovacic and Yagasaki. In 1998, Camassa et al. [10] proposed an extended Melnikov method which may be employed to deal with the multi-pulse jumping orbits for a class of Hamiltonian systems with perturbation. Subsequently, Yagasaki [11,12] developed the Melnikov method to investigate the chaotic dynamics of high-dimensional non-autonomous systems. The paper [13] demonstrates how to employ the extended Melnikov method to analyze the multi-pulse chaotic dynamics for the parametrically excited viscoelastic moving belt. Afterwards, Zhang et al. [14] investigated the chaotic dynamics of the rotating ring truss antenna. The double parameter homoclinic orbits were detected by means of the extended Melnikov function. In [15], Zhang and Chen proved the existence of single-pulse jumping homoclinic orbits of the sandwich plate with truss core on a certain parameter range. Ahmadi et al. [16] investigated a new five-dimensional chaotic system. The phenomenon of extreme multi-stability are considered for the variety of conditions. In [17], many complex dynamic behaviors of another 5D chaotic system with equilibrium were discovered.

These analytical techniques can deal with autonomous systems. In most instances, we need to discuss the dynamical problems of non-autonomous systems. The literature [18] used the improved Melnikov method to detect the chaotic behaviors of the buckled thin plate model. In 2012, Zhang et al. [19] studied the chaotic dynamics of another type of sandwich plate. Based on the non-autonomous nonlinear governing equations, Wu et al. [20] investigated the global bifurcations for the circular mesh antenna model. It is worth mentioning that the Melnikov method is improved to handle six-dimensional nonlinear systems by Zhang and Hao in papers [21].

The paper handles the global bifurcation and chaotic motion of a simply supported sandwich plate with truss core subjected to parametrical excitations. From the explicit formulas of normal form, the improved extended Melnikov method [10,18] is used to study the chaotic dynamics for this non-autonomous system. The damping coefficients and transverse excitation parameters are chosen as the control parameters to discuss the influence on the dynamic behaviors of the sandwich plate system with truss core. The numerical results also show that the chaotic motions may occur for the sandwich plate with truss core subject to parametrical excitations which demonstrates the validation of the theoretical prediction.

The paper is outlined as follows. In Section 2, the main theory of the extended Melnikov method for the non-autonomous system is exhibited. In Section 3, the dynamical model is described for the sandwich plate with truss core under transverse and in-plane excitations. The chaotic motions of the four dimensional non-autonomous systems are analyzed based on the improved extended Melnikov method. In Section 4, based on the phase portraits, waveforms and Lyapunov exponents, numerical simulations are utilized to study the dynamic behaviors of the sandwich plate. Finally, we give the conclusions in Section 5.

2. Formulation

The main theory of the improved Melnikov method [10,18] for the non-automonous nonlinear system will be listed in this section. Consider a general Hamilton system:

$$\begin{aligned} \dot{x} &= JD_xH(x,v_1) + \epsilon g^x(x,v,\phi,\mu,\epsilon), \\ \dot{v}_1 &= \epsilon g^{v_1}(x,v,\phi,\mu,\epsilon), \\ \dot{v}_2 &= \Omega(x,v_1) + \epsilon g^{v_2}(x,v,\phi,\mu,\epsilon), \\ \dot{\phi} &= \omega, \end{aligned} \tag{1}$$

where $x = (x_1, x_2) \in R^2, 0 < \epsilon << 1, \mu \in R^p$ represents the parameters in the perturbed system. D_x indicates the partial derivatives about x, $g = (g^x, g^{v_1}, g^{v_2})$ denotes a periodic function of t. When $\epsilon = 0$, the unperturbed system can be given by

$$\begin{aligned} \dot{x} &= JD_xH(x,v_1), \\ \dot{v}_1 &= 0, \\ \dot{v}_2 &= \Omega(x,v_1), \end{aligned} \tag{2}$$

which is an uncoupled nonlinear dynamical system. The following two assumptions are required according to the results of [10].

Assumption 1. *For every* $v_1 \in [R_1, R_2]$, *there exist a hyperbolic equilibrium* $x = x_0(v_1)$ *and a homoclinic orbit* $x^h(t, v_1)$ *connected to* $x_0(v_1)$.

Assumption 2. *For some* $v_1 = v_{10} \in [R_1, R_2]$, *the function* Ω *satisfies the following conditions*

$$\Omega(x_0(v_{10}), v_{10}) = 0, \frac{d\Omega(x_0(v_1), v_1)}{dv_1}(v_{10}) \neq 0.$$

From Assumption 2, we may find simple zeros about v_1 which can be called the resonance bands. A partial manifold is defined as

$$M = \{(x, v) | x = x_0(v_1), R_1 \leq v_1 \leq R_2, -L < v_2 < L\},$$

which is normally hyperbolic and possesses three-dimensional stable manifolds $W^s(M)$ and unstable manifolds $W^u(M)$. The existence of the homoclinic orbit of system (2) indicates that the stable manifolds $W^s(M)$ and unstable manifolds $W^u(M)$ intersect non-transversally along Γ, which can be given

$$\Gamma = \{(x, v) | x = x_{\pm}^h(t, v_1), R_1 \leq v_1 \leq R_2, v_2 = \int_{-\infty}^{t} D_{v_1} H(x^h, v_1) ds + v_{20}\}.$$

The perturbed system (1) is a five-dimensional system. In order to investigate the dynamics of non-autonomous systems, a cross-section is introduced in the phase space. The expression of cross section is defined as

$$\Sigma^{\phi_0} = \{(x, v_1, v_2, \phi) | \phi = \phi_0\}. \tag{3}$$

The variable ϕ is first fixed on Σ^{ϕ_0} and then vary throughout the circle S^1. In the full five-dimensional phase space $R^4 \times S^1$, the invariant manifold $M(t)$ can be written by

$$M(t) = \{(x, v, \phi) | x = x_0(v_1), R_1 \leq v_1 \leq R_2, -L < v_2 < L, \phi = \omega t + \phi_0\}. \tag{4}$$

Based on the analysis in [10], it can be known that $M(t)$ is a three-dimensional normally hyperbolic invariant manifold and the expression of the manifold $M_\epsilon(t)$ is written as

$$M_\epsilon(t) = \{(x, v, \phi) | x = x_0(v_1) + O(\epsilon), R_1 \leq v_1 \leq R_2, -L < v_2 < L, \phi = \omega t + \phi_0\}. \tag{5}$$

The manifolds $M_\epsilon(t)$, $W_\epsilon^s(M(t))$ and $W_\epsilon^u(M(t))$ are C^r ϵ-close to the manifolds $M(t)$, $W^s(M(t))$ and $W^u(M(t))$, respectively. The 1-pulse Melnikov function and k-pulse Melnikov function [10] in the Cartesian coordinate are shown by

$$\begin{aligned} M(v_0, \phi_0, \mu) &= \int_{-\infty}^{+\infty} \langle n(p^h(t)), g(p^h(t), \omega t + \phi_0, \mu, 0) \rangle dt, \\ M_k(v_0, \phi_0, \mu) &= \sum_{j=0}^{k-1} M(v_{10}, v_{20} + j\Delta v_2(v_{10}), \phi_0, \mu), \end{aligned} \tag{6}$$

where symbol$\langle , \rangle$ denotes the Euclidean inner product of two functions,

$$\begin{aligned} n &= (D_x H(x, v_1), (D_{v_1} H(x, v_1) - (D_{v_1} H(x(v_{10}), v_1), 0), \\ g &= (g^x(x, v, \omega t, \mu, 0), g^{v_1}(x, v, \omega t, \mu, 0), g^{v_2}(x, v, \omega t, \mu, 0)), \\ p^h(t) &= (x^h(t, v_1), v_1, v_2^h(t, v_1) + v_{20}). \end{aligned} \tag{7}$$

and

$$\Delta v_2(v_{10}) = \int_{-\infty}^{+\infty} \Omega(x^h(\tau, v_1), v_{10}) d\tau. \tag{8}$$

The term Δv_2 denotes the distance between two equilibrium points. From Assumption 2, we may find that the vector x is located on a fast manifold. No manifold is on the manifold M. This means the nonfolding condition in [10] is satisfied naturally. Thus, there exist some integer k, $v_{20} = \bar{v}_{20}$, $\phi = \bar{\phi}_0$, and $\mu = \bar{\mu}$, so that the k-pulse Melnikov function $M_k(v_0, \phi_0, \mu)$ has a simple zero point, namely

$$M_k(v_{10}, \bar{v}_{20}, \bar{\phi}_0, \bar{\mu}) = 0, D_{v_2} M_k(v_{10}, \bar{v}_{20}, \bar{\phi}_0, \bar{\mu}) \neq 0. \tag{9}$$

The stable manifold $W^s(M_\epsilon^{\phi_0})$ and unstable manifold $W^u(M_\epsilon^{\phi_0})$ intersect transversely along surface $\Sigma(\bar{v}_{20})$. This means that the perturbed system has multi-pulse homoclinic orbits.

3. Chaotic Analysis of Perturbed System

The model of the sandwich plate with truss core considered in this paper is exhibited in Figure 1 [4]. A Cartesian coordinate oxy system is established in the middle surface of the sandwich plate. It can be supposed that the displacements of a point in the middle surface are represented by u, v and w in the x, y and z directions, respectively. Moreover, a, b and h denote the length, width and thickness of the sandwich plate, respectively. The transverse excitation of the sandwich plate is denoted by $f = F(x, y)\cos\Omega_1 t$ and the in-plane excitation is represented by $p = p_0 - p_1 \cos\Omega_2 t$.

According to [4], the nonlinear partial differential equations of the sandwich plate are given as follows

$$\begin{aligned}
&\frac{\partial^2 u_0}{\partial x^2} + a_1 \frac{\partial w_0}{\partial x}\frac{\partial^2 w_0}{\partial x^2} + a_2 \frac{\partial w_0}{\partial y}\frac{\partial^2 w_0}{\partial x \partial y} + a_3 \frac{\partial^2 v_0}{\partial x \partial y} + a_4 \frac{\partial^2 w_0}{\partial y^2} + a_5 \frac{\partial w_0}{\partial x}\frac{\partial^2 w_0}{\partial y^2} \\
&= a_6 \ddot{u}_0 + a_7 \ddot{\varphi}_x + a_8 \frac{\partial \ddot{w}_0}{\partial x}, \\
&\frac{\partial^2 v_0}{\partial y^2} + b_1 \frac{\partial w_0}{\partial x}\frac{\partial^2 w_0}{\partial x^2} + b_2 \frac{\partial w_0}{\partial x}\frac{\partial^2 w_0}{\partial x \partial y} + b_3 \frac{\partial^2 u_0}{\partial x \partial y} + b_4 \frac{\partial^2 v_0}{\partial y^2} + a_5 \frac{\partial w_0}{\partial x}\frac{\partial^2 w_0}{\partial x^2} \\
&= b_6 \ddot{v}_0 + b_7 \ddot{\varphi}_y + b_8 \frac{\partial \ddot{w}_0}{\partial y}, \\
&\frac{\partial^2 w_0}{\partial x^2} + c_1 \frac{\partial w_0}{\partial x}\frac{\partial^2 u_0}{\partial x^2} + c_2 (\frac{\partial w_0}{\partial x})^2 \frac{\partial^2 w_0}{\partial x^2} + c_3 \frac{\partial w_0}{\partial x}\frac{\partial^2 v_0}{\partial x \partial y} + c_4 \frac{\partial w_0}{\partial x}\frac{\partial w_0}{\partial y}\frac{\partial^2 w_0}{\partial x \partial y} \\
&+ c_5 \frac{\partial u_0}{\partial x}\frac{\partial^2 w_0}{\partial x^2} + c_6 \frac{\partial v_0}{\partial y}\frac{\partial^2 w_0}{\partial x^2} + c_7 (\frac{\partial w_0}{\partial x})^2 \frac{\partial^2 w_0}{\partial y^2} + c_8 (\frac{\partial w_0}{\partial y})^2 \frac{\partial^2 w_0}{\partial x^2} \\
&+ c_9 \frac{\partial w_0}{\partial y}\frac{\partial^2 v_0}{\partial y^2} + c_{10} (\frac{\partial w_0}{\partial y})^2 \frac{\partial^2 w_0}{\partial y^2} + c_{11} \frac{\partial w_0}{\partial y}\frac{\partial^2 u_0}{\partial x \partial y} + c_{12} \frac{\partial u_0}{\partial y}\frac{\partial^2 w_0}{\partial y^2} + c_{13} \frac{\partial w_0}{\partial x}\frac{\partial^2 u_0}{\partial y^2} \\
&+ c_{14} \frac{\partial u_0}{\partial y}\frac{\partial^2 w_0}{\partial x \partial y} + c_{15} \frac{\partial u_0}{\partial x}\frac{\partial^2 w_0}{\partial y^2} + c_{16} \frac{\partial v_0}{\partial x}\frac{\partial^2 w_0}{\partial x \partial y} + c_{17} \frac{\partial w_0}{\partial y}\frac{\partial^2 v_0}{\partial x^2} + c_{18} \frac{\partial^3 \varphi_x}{\partial x^3} \\
&+ c_{19} \frac{\partial^3 \varphi_y}{\partial x^2 \partial y} + c_{20} \frac{\partial^4 w_0}{\partial x^4} + c_{21} \frac{\partial^4 w_0}{\partial y^4} + c_{22} \frac{\partial^3 \varphi_x}{\partial x \partial y^2} + c_{23} \frac{\partial^4 \varphi_x}{\partial x^2 \partial y^2} + c_{24} \frac{\partial^3 \varphi_y}{\partial y^3} + c_{25} \frac{\partial \varphi_y}{\partial y} \\
&+ c_{26} \frac{\partial^2 w_0}{\partial y^2} + c_{27} \frac{\partial \varphi_x}{\partial x} + c_{28} F \cos(\Omega_1 t) + c_{29} \gamma \dot{w}_0 + c_{30} (p_0 - p_1 \cos(\Omega_2 t)) \frac{\partial^2 w_0}{\partial x^2} \\
&= c_{31} \ddot{w}_0 + c_{32} \frac{\partial \ddot{w}_0}{\partial x^2} + c_{33} \frac{\partial \ddot{w}_0}{\partial 9^2} + c_{34} (\frac{\partial \ddot{u}_0}{\partial x} + \frac{\partial \ddot{v}_0}{\partial y}) + c_{35} (\frac{\partial \ddot{\varphi}_x}{\partial x} + \frac{\partial \ddot{\varphi}_y}{\partial y}), \\
&\frac{\partial^2 \varphi_x}{\partial x^2} + d_1 \frac{\partial^2 \varphi_y}{\partial x \partial y} + d_2 \frac{\partial^3 w_0}{\partial x^3} + d_3 \frac{\partial^3 w_0}{\partial x \partial y^2} + d_4 \frac{\partial^2 \varphi_x}{\partial y^2} + d_5 \varphi_x + d_6 \frac{\partial w_0}{\partial x} \\
&= d_7 \ddot{u}_0 + d_8 \ddot{\varphi}_x + d_9 \frac{\partial \ddot{w}_0}{\partial x}, \\
&\frac{\partial^2 \varphi_y}{\partial y^2} + e_1 \frac{\partial^2 \varphi_x}{\partial x \partial y} + e_2 \frac{\partial^3 w_0}{\partial y^3} + e_3 \frac{\partial^3 w_0}{\partial y \partial x^2} + e_4 \frac{\partial^2 \varphi_y}{\partial x^2} + e_5 \varphi_y + e_6 \frac{\partial w_0}{\partial y} \\
&= e_7 \ddot{v}_0 + e_8 \ddot{\varphi}_y + e_9 \frac{\partial \ddot{w}_0}{\partial y},
\end{aligned} \tag{10}$$

where

$$u = u_0 + z\phi_x - z^3\frac{4}{3h^2}(\phi_x + \frac{\partial w_0}{\partial x}),$$
$$v = v_0 + z\phi_y - z^3\frac{4}{3h^2}(\phi_y + \frac{\partial w_0}{\partial y}), \tag{11}$$
$$w = w_0.$$

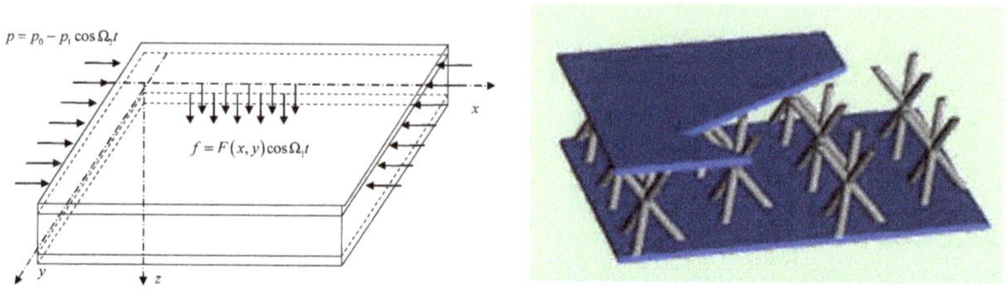

(a) **(b)**

Figure 1. The model of the sandwich plate with truss core: (**a**) schematic with the coordinate system; (**b**) the 3D-Kagome truss core sandwich structure.

Here, we mainly consider the first two modes of the sandwich plate. Applying the Galerkin technique, the two-degrees of freedom nonlinear equations of the sandwich plate with truss core were given as [4]

$$\begin{aligned}\ddot{w}_1 + \mu_1\dot{w}_1 + \beta_{11}w_1 + \beta_{16}(p_0 - p_1\cos(\Omega_2 t))w_1 + \beta_{12}w_1w_2^2 + \beta_{13}w_2w_1^2 + \beta_{14}w_1^3 \\ + \beta_{15}w_2^3 = \beta_{17}F_1\cos\Omega_1 t, \\ \ddot{w}_2 + \mu_2\dot{w}_2 + \beta_{21}w_2 + \beta_{26}(p_0 - p_1\cos(\Omega_2 t))w_2 + \beta_{22}w_2w_1^2 + \beta_{23}w_1w_2^2 + \beta_{24}w_2^3 \\ + \beta_{25}w_1^3 = \beta_{27}F_2\cos\Omega_1 t,\end{aligned} \tag{12}$$

where all the coefficients in (12) can be found in [4], w_1 and w_2 are the amplitudes of two modes, and Ω_1 and Ω_2 denote the frequencies of the transverse and in-plane excitations. Further, F_1 and F_2 represent the amplitudes of the transverse excitation corresponding to w_1 and w_2, respectively, and μ_1 and μ_2 are the damping coefficients.

Introducing the following transformations for Equation (12)

$$x_1 = w_1, x_2 = \dot{w}_1, x_3 = w_2, x_4 = \dot{w}_2,$$

this system can be given by

$$\begin{aligned}\dot{x_1} =& x_2, \\ \dot{x_2} =& -\beta_{11}x_1 - \beta_{12}x_1x_3^2 - \beta_{13}x_3x_1^2 - \beta_{14}x_1^3 - \beta_{15}x_3^3 - \mu_1x_2 + F_1\cos\Omega_1 t \\ & - f_1x_1\cos\Omega_2 t, \\ \dot{x_3} =& x_4, \\ \dot{x_4} =& -\beta_{21}x_3 - \beta_{22}x_1^2x_3 - \beta_{23}x_1x_3^2 - \beta_{24}x_3^3 - \beta_{25}x_1^3 - \mu_2x_4 + F_2\cos\Omega_1 t \\ & - f_2x_3\cos\Omega_2 t,\end{aligned} \tag{13}$$

where $\beta_{11} \to \beta_{11} + \beta_{16}p_0$, $\beta_{12} \to \beta_{21} + \beta_{26}p_0$, $F_1 \to \beta_{17}F_1$, $F_2 \to \beta_{27}F_2$, $f_1 \to \beta_{16}p_1$, $f_2 \to \beta_{26}p_1$. If μ, f_1, f_2, F_1 and F_2 are considered as perturbation parameters, the system (13) can rewritten as

$$\begin{aligned}
\dot{x_1} &= x_2, \\
\dot{x_2} &= -\beta_{11}x_1 - \beta_{12}x_1x_3^2 - \beta_{13}x_3x_1^2 - \beta_{14}x_1^3 - \beta_{15}x_3^3, \\
\dot{x_3} &= x_4, \\
\dot{x_4} &= -\beta_{21}x_3 - \beta_{22}x_1^2x_3 - \beta_{23}x_1x_3^2 - \beta_{24}x_3^3 - \beta_{25}x_1^3.
\end{aligned} \tag{14}$$

The Maple program is applied to obtain the normal form without the perturbation parameters up to 3-order, namely

$$\begin{aligned}
\dot{x_1} &= x_2, \\
\dot{x_2} &= -\frac{1}{2}\beta_{12}x_1(x_3^2 + x_4^2) - \beta_{14}x_1^3, \\
\dot{x_3} &= x_4 + \frac{1}{2}\beta_{22}x_1^2x_4 + \beta_{24}(x_3^2 + x_4^2), \\
\dot{x_4} &= -\beta_{21}x_3 - \beta_{24}(x_3^2 + x_4^2) - \frac{1}{2}\beta_{22}x_1^2x_3.
\end{aligned} \tag{15}$$

It can be seen that the four terms $\beta_{13}x_1^2x_3$, $\beta_{15}x_3^3$, $\beta_{23}x_3^2x_1$, $\beta_{25}x_1^3$ in (14) can only have influence on higher order terms. Thus, the damping coefficients, the forces coefficients and the aforementioned four terms are considered as perturbation terms which can be added small positive parameter ϵ. Then, we have

$$\begin{aligned}
\dot{x_1} =& x_2, \\
\dot{x_2} =& -\beta_{11}x_1 - \beta_{12}x_1x_3^2 - \beta_{14}x_1^3 - \epsilon\beta_{15}x_3^3 - \epsilon\beta_{13}x_3x_1^2 - \epsilon\mu_1x_2 + \epsilon F_1\cos\Omega_1 t \\
& - \epsilon f_1x_1\cos\Omega_2 t, \\
\dot{x_3} =& x_4, \\
\dot{x_4} =& -\beta_{21}x_3 - \beta_{22}x_1^2x_3 - \beta_{24}x_3^3 - \epsilon\beta_{23}x_1x_3^2 - \epsilon\beta_{25}x_1^3 - \epsilon\mu_2x_4 + \epsilon F_2\cos\Omega_1 t \\
& - \epsilon f_2x_3\cos\Omega_2 t.
\end{aligned} \tag{16}$$

The frequencies Ω_1 and Ω_2 satisfy the relations $Z_1\phi = \Omega_1 t$, $Z_2\phi = \Omega_2 t$, where Z_1 and Z_2 are non-negative integers. The transformations are introduced for Equation (16)

$$x_1 = \sqrt{\frac{\beta_{12}}{\bar{\beta}_{22}}}u_1, x_2 = \sqrt{\frac{\beta_{12}}{\bar{\beta}_{22}}}u_2, x_3 = v_1, x_4 = \mu_2 v_2$$

We may obtain the Hamilton form with the perturbation

$$\begin{aligned}
\dot{u_1} =& u_2, \\
\dot{u_2} =& -\beta_{11}u_1 - \beta_{12}u_1v_1^2 - \bar{\beta}_{14}u_1^3 - \epsilon\mu_1u_2 - \epsilon\bar{\beta}_{13}u_1^2v_1 - \epsilon\bar{\beta}_{15}v_1^3 + \epsilon\bar{F}_1\cos Z_1\phi \\
& - \epsilon f_1u_1\cos Z_2\phi, \\
\dot{v_1} =& -\epsilon\mu_2v_2, \\
\dot{v_2} =& -\bar{\beta}_{21}v_1 - \beta_{12}u_1^2v_1 - \bar{\beta}_{24}v_1^3 - \epsilon\mu_2v_2 - \epsilon\bar{\beta}_{23}u_1^2v_1 - \epsilon\bar{\beta}_{25}v_1^3 + \epsilon\bar{F}_2\cos Z_1\phi \\
& - \epsilon\bar{f}_2v_1\cos Z_2\phi, \\
\dot{\phi} =& 1,
\end{aligned} \tag{17}$$

where $\bar{\beta}_{14} = \beta_{14}\frac{\beta_{12}}{\bar{\beta}_{22}}$, $\bar{\beta}_{13} = \beta_{13}\sqrt{\frac{\beta_{12}}{\bar{\beta}_{22}}}$, $\bar{\beta}_{15} = \beta_{15}\sqrt{\frac{\beta_{12}}{\bar{\beta}_{22}}}$, $\bar{\beta}_{21} = \frac{\beta_{21}}{\mu_2}$, $\bar{\beta}_{22} = \frac{\beta_{22}}{\mu_2}$, $\bar{\beta}_{23} = \frac{\beta_{13}}{\mu_2}\sqrt{\frac{\beta_{12}}{\bar{\beta}_{22}}}$, $\bar{\beta}_{24} = \frac{\beta_{24}}{\mu_2}$, $\bar{F}_1 = F_1\sqrt{\frac{\bar{\beta}_{22}}{\beta_{12}}}$, $\bar{f}_2 = \frac{f_2}{\mu_2}$, $\bar{F}_2 = \frac{F_2}{\mu_2}$.

According to the previous theoretical results, a cross-section Σ^{ϕ_0} is introduced in the full five-dimensional phase space. When $\epsilon = 0$, the expression of the unperturbed system is

$$\begin{aligned} \dot{u_1} &= u_2, \\ \dot{u_2} &= -\beta_{11}u_1 - \beta_{12}u_1v_1^2 - \bar{\beta}_{14}u_1^3, \\ \dot{v_1} &= 0, \\ \dot{v_2} &= -\bar{\beta}_{21}v_1 - \beta_{12}u_1^2v_1 - \bar{\beta}_{24}v_1^3. \end{aligned} \tag{18}$$

The Hamiltonian of (18) can be given as

$$H = \frac{1}{2}u_2^2 + \frac{1}{2}\beta_{11}u_1^2 + \frac{1}{4}\beta_{12}u_1^2v_1^2 + \frac{1}{4}\bar{\beta}_{14}u_1^4 + \frac{1}{4}\bar{\beta}_{24}v_1^4 + \frac{1}{2} - \bar{\beta}_{21}v_1^2$$

It can be seen that the system (18) is an uncoupled system. Considering the first two equations of (18)

$$\begin{aligned} \dot{u_1} &= u_2, \\ \dot{u_2} &= -\beta_{11}u_1 - \beta_{12}u_1v_1^2 - \bar{\beta}_{14}u_1^3. \end{aligned} \tag{19}$$

The Hamiltonian is given as

$$H_0(u_1, u_2) = \frac{1}{2}u_2^2 + \frac{1}{2}Ru_1^2 + \frac{1}{4}\bar{\beta}_{14}u_1^4, \tag{20}$$

where $R = \beta_{11} + \beta_{12}v_1^2$.

Here, we consider the stability of the equilibrium solution within a certain range of parameters, that is $\beta_{12} < 0$, $\bar{\beta}_{14} > 0$, $R = \beta_{11} + \beta_{12}v_1^2 < 0$. Let $\bar{R} = -R$. According to the condition $\beta_{11} + \beta_{12}v_1^2 < 0$, the domain of v_1 is that $v_1 > \sqrt{\frac{2\beta_{11}}{-\beta_{12}}}$.

The system (19) has three trivial solutions. The singular point $(u_1, u_2) = (0, 0)$ is a saddle point. The singular points $(u_1, u_2) = (\pm\sqrt{\frac{\bar{R}}{\bar{\beta}_{14}}}, 0)$ are two centers. In this case, system (19) can exhibit the homoclinic bifurcations. We may obtain the expression of the homoclinic orbits

$$\begin{aligned} u_1(t) &= \pm\sqrt{\frac{2\bar{R}}{\bar{\beta}_{14}}}\operatorname{sech}\sqrt{\bar{R}}t, \\ u_2(t) &= \pm\bar{R}\sqrt{\frac{2}{\bar{\beta}_{14}}}\operatorname{sech}\sqrt{\bar{R}}t\tanh\sqrt{\bar{R}}t. \end{aligned} \tag{21}$$

According to system (18), the resonant value can be obtained as $v_{10} = \sqrt{\frac{\bar{\beta}_{21}}{-\bar{\beta}_{24}}}$. At the same time, the condition $\sqrt{\frac{\bar{\beta}_{21}}{-\bar{\beta}_{24}}} > \sqrt{\frac{2\beta_{11}}{-\beta_{12}}}$, namely $\bar{\beta}_{21}\beta_{12} < 2\bar{\beta}_{24}\beta_{11}$ need to be satisfied. Thus, the correlation coefficients of system (18) also need to satisfy $\bar{\beta}_{24} < 0$, $\beta_{12}\bar{\beta}_{21} < 2\beta_{11}\bar{\beta}_{24}$. Then the phase shift can be calculated as

$$\Delta v_2 = \int_{-\infty}^{+\infty}(-\bar{\beta}_{21}v_1 - \beta_{12}u_1^2v_1 - \bar{\beta}_{24}v_1^3)dt = -\frac{4\beta_{12}}{\bar{\beta}_{14}}\sqrt{\frac{\bar{\beta}_{21}}{\bar{\beta}_{24}}}\bar{R}. \tag{22}$$

In light of Equation (18), the 1-pulse Melnikov function can be calculated as

$$
\begin{aligned}
M = & \int_{-\infty}^{+\infty} \mu_2[\bar{\beta}_{13}u_1^2v_1 + \bar{\beta}_{15}v_1^3 - \mu_1 u_2 + F_1\cos(\Omega_1 t + Z_1\phi_0) - \mu_1 f_1 \cos(\Omega_2 t + Z_2\phi_0)]dt \\
& - \int_{-\infty}^{+\infty} \mu_2 v_2[-\bar{\beta}_{21}v_1 - \beta_{12}u_1^2v_1 - \bar{\beta}_{24}v_1^3]dt \\
= & -\frac{4\mu_1\bar{R}^{\frac{3}{2}}}{3\bar{\beta}_{14}} - \frac{\pi f_2\Omega_2^2}{\bar{\beta}_{14}}\sin(Z_2\phi_0)\operatorname{csch}\frac{\pi\omega}{2\sqrt{\bar{R}}} - \pi\Omega_1 F_1\sqrt{\frac{2}{\bar{\beta}_{14}}}\sin(Z_1\phi_0)\operatorname{sech}\frac{\pi\Omega_1}{2\sqrt{\bar{R}}} - \mu_2\Delta v_2 v_{20}.
\end{aligned}
\tag{23}
$$

Further, we can calculate the k-pulse Melnikov function

$$
\begin{aligned}
M_k = & -\frac{4\mu_1\bar{R}^{\frac{3}{2}}}{3\bar{\beta}_{14}}k - k\frac{\pi f_2\Omega_2^2}{\bar{\beta}_{14}}\sin(Z_2\phi_0)\operatorname{csch}\frac{\pi\omega}{2\sqrt{\bar{R}}} \\
& - k\pi\Omega_1 F_1\sqrt{\frac{2}{\bar{\beta}_{14}}}\sin(Z_1\phi_0)\operatorname{sech}\frac{\pi\Omega_1}{2\sqrt{\bar{R}}} - \mu_2\Delta v_2 v_{20}k - \frac{k(k-1)}{2}\mu_2\Delta v_2^2.
\end{aligned}
\tag{24}
$$

For the k-pulse Melnikov function M_k has simple zeros, the relevant parameters should satisfy

$$
\begin{aligned}
& -\frac{4\mu_1\bar{R}^{\frac{3}{2}}}{3\bar{\beta}_{14}} - \frac{\pi f_2\Omega_2^2}{\bar{\beta}_{14}}\sin(Z_2\phi_0)\operatorname{csch}\frac{\pi\omega}{2\sqrt{\bar{R}}} - \pi\Omega_1 F_1\sqrt{\frac{2}{\bar{\beta}_{14}}}\sin(Z_1\phi_0)\operatorname{sech}\frac{\pi\Omega_1}{2\sqrt{\bar{R}}} \\
& - \mu_2\Delta v_2 v_{20} - \frac{(k-1)}{2}\mu_2\Delta v_2^2 = 0.
\end{aligned}
\tag{25}
$$

Equation (25) can be reformulated as

$$
\begin{aligned}
k = & -\frac{8\mu_1\bar{R}^{\frac{3}{2}}}{3\bar{\beta}_{14}\mu_2\Delta v_2^2} - \frac{2\pi f_2\Omega_2^2}{\bar{\beta}_{14}\mu_2\Delta v_2^2}\sin(Z_2\phi_0)\operatorname{csch}\frac{\pi\omega}{2\sqrt{\bar{R}}} \\
& - \frac{2\pi\Omega_1 F_1}{\mu_2\Delta v_2^2}\sqrt{\frac{2}{\bar{\beta}_{14}}}\sin(Z_1\phi_0)\operatorname{sech}\frac{\pi\Omega_1}{2\sqrt{\bar{R}}} - \frac{2v_{20}}{\Delta v_2^2} + 1.
\end{aligned}
\tag{26}
$$

Then, the suitable parameters are chosen to satisfy the following condition

$$
D_{v_{20}}M_k = -\mu_2\Delta v_2 k = \frac{4\beta_{12}\mu_2 k}{\bar{\beta}_{14}}\sqrt{\frac{\bar{\beta}_{21}}{\bar{\beta}_{24}}}\bar{R} \neq 0. \tag{27}
$$

At the same time, the following expression should be a non-negative integer by selecting suitable parameters in Equation (26).

$$
\begin{aligned}
N = & -\frac{8\mu_1\bar{R}^{\frac{3}{2}}}{3\bar{\beta}_{14}\mu_2\Delta v_2^2} - \frac{2\pi f_2\Omega_2^2}{\bar{\beta}_{14}\mu_2\Delta v_2^2}\sin(Z_2\phi_0)\operatorname{csch}\frac{\pi\omega}{2\sqrt{\bar{R}}} \\
& - \frac{2\pi\Omega_1 F_1}{\mu_2\Delta v_2^2}\sqrt{\frac{2}{\bar{\beta}_{14}}}\sin(Z_1\phi_0)\operatorname{sech}\frac{\pi\Omega_1}{2\sqrt{\bar{R}}} - \frac{2v_{20}}{\Delta v_2^2}.
\end{aligned}
\tag{28}
$$

If the stable manifold $W^s(M_\epsilon^{\phi_0})$ and unstable manifold $W^u(M_\epsilon^{\phi_0})$ of system (17) intersect transversely, there exist chaotic motions for the sandwich plate with truss core under parametricaly excitations.

4. Numerical Simulations

In order to test the analytical predictions, we choose the original system (12) to perform numerical simulations. The Runge–Kutta algorithm through the software Matlab is utilized to explore the existence of chaotic motions in the sandwich plate. This part mainly discusses the influence of the damping coefficient and in-plane excitation on chaotic motions of the sandwich plate model. So μ_1 and f are selected as the controlling parameters to discover the law for the complicated behaviors.

Considering the conditions $\beta_{12} < 0$, $\beta_{14} > 0$, $\beta_{21} < 0$ and $\beta_{24} > 0$, the parameters of system (12) are chosen as follows: $\mu_1 = \mu_2 = \mu = 0.4$, $\beta_{11} = 27.8$, $\beta_{16}p_0 = 0.05$, $\beta_{12} = -0.1$, $\beta_{16}p_1 = 0.05$, $\beta_{13} = -1.5$, $\beta_{14} = 32$, $\beta_{15} = -0.51$, $\beta_{17}F_1 = 85.8$, $\beta_{21} = -1.08$, $\beta_{26}p_0 = 0.057$, $\beta_{25} = -5$, $\beta_{22} = -23.2$, $\beta_{26}p_1 = 0.057$, $\beta_{23} = -15.1$, $\beta_{24} = 31.6$, $f = \beta_{27}F_2 = 13.3$. Initial conditions are selected as $(w_1, \dot{w}_1, w_2, \dot{w}_2) = (0.02, 0.01, 0.04, 0.01)$. Figure 2 exhibits the phase portraits and waveforms in plane or space. Moreover, the maximal Lyapunov exponent of system (12) is $0.585523 > 0$. It can be shown that there exist chaotic motions for the nonlinear system. It is demonstrated again the existence of Shilnikov-type multi-pulse orbits in the sense of Smale horseshoes of the truss core sandwich plate.

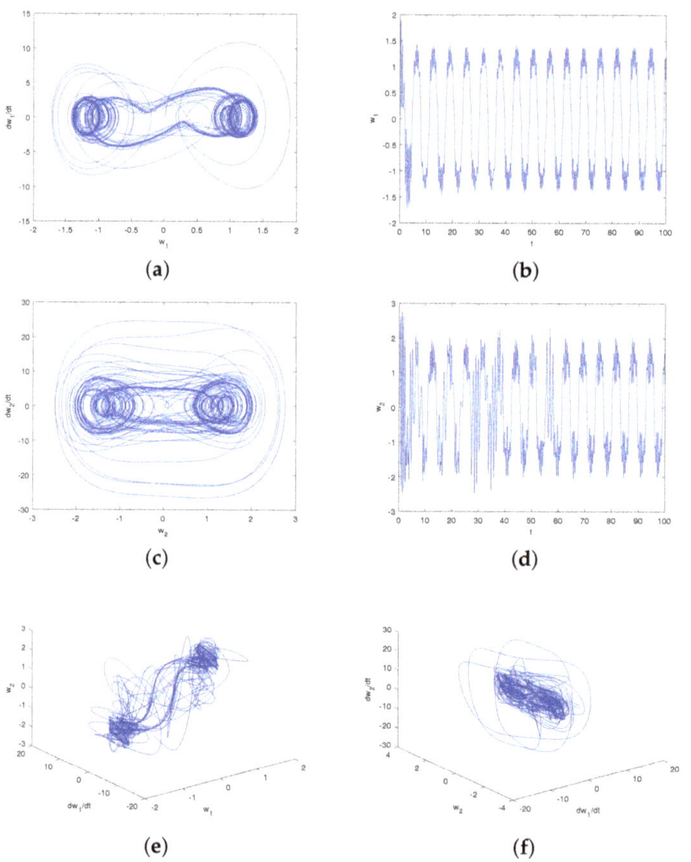

Figure 2. The phase portraits and waveforms of the sandwich plate with truss core when $\mu = 0.4$ and $f = 13.3$: (**a**) the phase portrait on plane $(w_1, \frac{dw_1}{dt})$; (**b**) the waveform on plane (t, w_1); (**c**) the phase portrait on plane $(w_2, \frac{dw_2}{dt})$; (**d**) the waveform on plane (t, w_2); (**e**) the phase portraits in the three-dimensional space $(w_1, \frac{dw_1}{dt}, w_2)$; (**f**) the phase portraits in the three-dimensional space $(\frac{dw_1}{dt}, w_2, \frac{dw_2}{dt})$.

According to the aforementioned analysis, the excitation coefficient and damping coefficient parameters play an important role on chaos of the sandwich plate with truss core. So we select the excitation coefficients f and damping coefficients μ as the controlling parameters to detect the chaotic dynamics for the sandwich plate. Figure 3 demonstrates the existence of the multi-pulse jumping chaotic motion when $\mu = 0.1$, $f = 50$. Do not change other parameters and initial conditions. The maximal Lyapunov exponent of system (12) is also calculated as 0.427282. It is easy to find that parameter conditions are also satisfied, which demonstrates the existence of the multi-pulse chaotic motion in Figure 3. Figure 4 represents the existence of the multi-pulse jumping chaotic motions when $\mu = 0.06$, $f = 100$. The maximal Lyapunov exponent of system (12) in this case is 0.450072. It is found that from Figure 4 that the phase portraits and waveforms are different from those given in Figures 2 and 3.This indicates that different μ and f have important impact on the chaotic motions of the sandwich plate with truss core. Finally, the Lyapunov exponent spectrum of system (12) for $f = 13.3$ and $f = 50$ are also given in Figure 5.

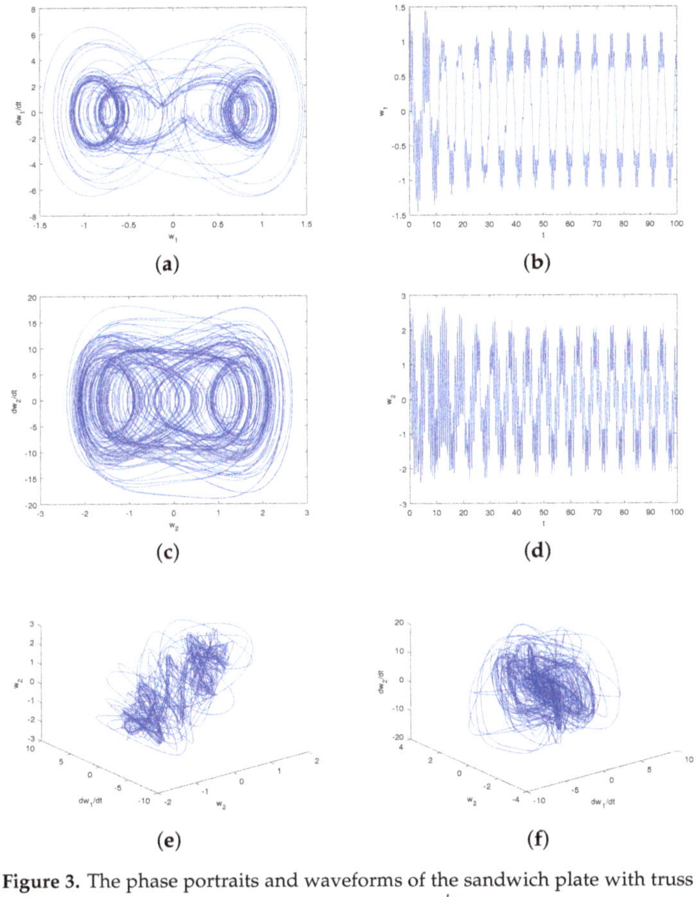

Figure 3. The phase portraits and waveforms of the sandwich plate with truss core when $\mu = 0.1$ and $f = 50$: (**a**) the phase portrait on plane $(w_1, \frac{dw_1}{dt})$; (**b**) the waveform on plane (t, w_1); (**c**) the phase portrait on plane $(w_2, \frac{dw_2}{dt})$; (**d**) the waveform on plane (t, w_2); (**e**) the phase portraits in the three-dimensional space $(w_1, \frac{dw_1}{dt}, w_2)$; (**f**) the phase portraits in the three-dimensional space $(\frac{dw_1}{dt}, w_2, \frac{dw_2}{dt})$.

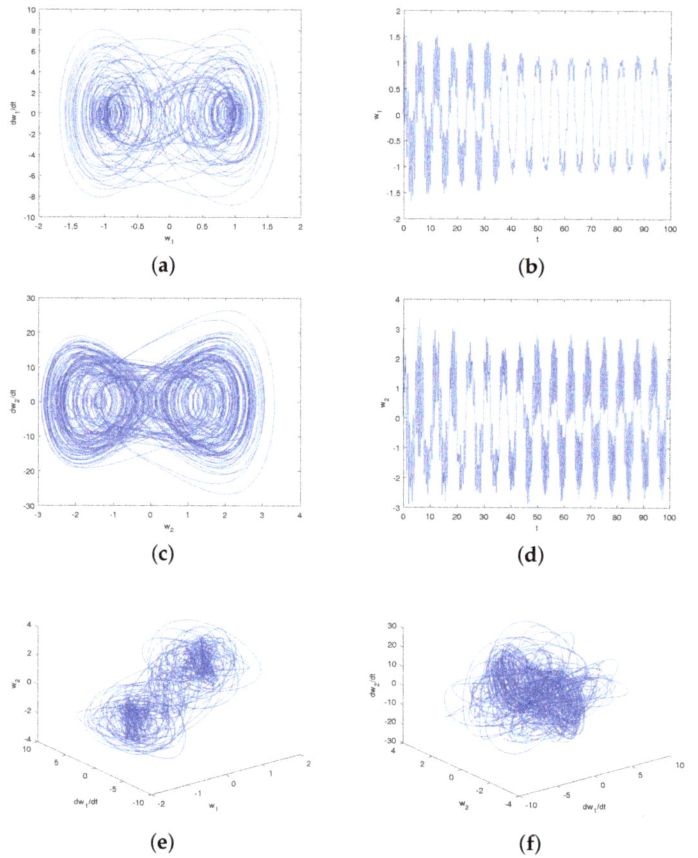

Figure 4. The phase portraits and waveforms of the sandwich plate with truss core when $\mu = 0.06$ and $f = 100$: (**a**) the phase portrait on plane $(w_1, \frac{dw_1}{dt})$; (**b**) the waveform on plane (t, w_1); (**c**) the phase portrait on plane $(w_2, \frac{dw_2}{dt})$; (**d**) the waveform on plane (t, w_2); (**e**) the phase portraits in the three-dimensional space $(w_1, \frac{dw_1}{dt}, w_2)$; (**f**) the phase portraits in the three-dimensional space $(\frac{dw_1}{dt}, w_2, \frac{dw_2}{dt})$.

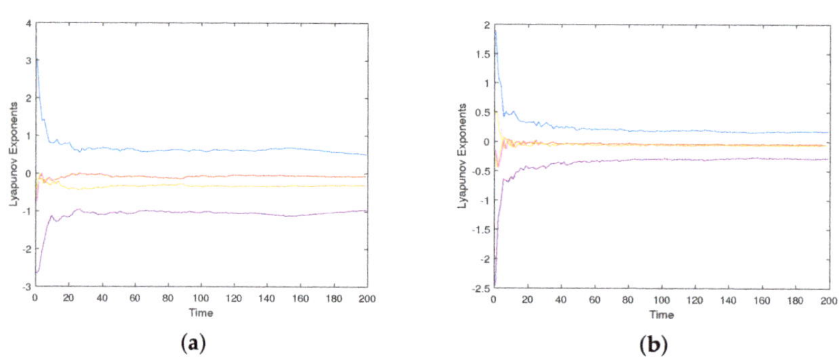

Figure 5. The Lyapunov exponent spectrum system (12): (**a**) when $\mu = 0.4$ and $f = 13.3$; (**b**) when $\mu = 0.1$ and $f = 50$.

5. Conclusions

The chaotic dynamics are investigated for a simply supported sandwich plate by using rigorous analytical approaches. The improved extended Melnikov method in [10,18] is applied to detect chaotic motions of the non-autonomous nonlinear system. By introducing Σ^{ϕ_0}, the four-dimensional non-autonomous system is transformed into a five-dimensional autonomous system, by which the chaotic motions can be investigated by directly employing this analytical method. The k-pulse Melnikov function M_k has simple zeros. Furthermore, we obtain the parameter conditions for the occurrence of chaotic motion.

Numerical simulations are also used to detect the complicated chaotic motions of the truss core sandwich plate model. Moreovecr, the numerical results verify the possibility of chaotic behaviors when the structural parameters satisfy specific conditions given by theoretical analysis. The chaotic motions of the sandwich plate with truss core can be exhibited by the phase portraits, the waveforms and the maximum Lyapunov exponents for different control parameters. Based on the theoretical analysis and numerical results, it is observed that the chaotic motions of the sandwich plate with truss core can be affected by the excitation coefficients and damping coefficients. Thus, the nonlinear dynamical behaviors of the sandwich plate model can be controlled by varying the structural damping and transverse excitations parameters, respectively. The analytic results bear certain guiding significance for the design and control of the system.

The extended Melnikov method is an effective theoretical technique in detecting the chaotic motions of the high-dimensional nonlinear system. However, a limitation of several analytical methods is that we must follow the special form of the high-dimensional system when detecting chaotic motions. Therefore, future work should focus on how to improve the analytical methods to adapt research of more general forms for a high-dimensional nonlinear system.

Author Contributions: D.Z.: Conceptualization, Data curation, Writing—original draft; F.L.: Methodology, Writing—review and editing. All authors have read and agreed to the published version of the manuscript.

Funding: This work is supported by the National Natural Science Foundation of China (Nos. 11902133 and 12071198).

Institutional Review Board Statement: Not applicable.

Informed Consent Statement: Not applicable.

Data Availability Statement: Not applicable.

Conflicts of Interest: The authors declare no conflict of interest.

References

1. Chen, J.E.; Liu, Y.Q.; Liu, W.; Su, X.Y. Themal buckling analysis of truss core sandwich plates. *Appl. Math. Mech.* **2013**, *34*, 1177–1186. [CrossRef]
2. Chen, J.E.; Zhang, W.; Yao, M.H.; Liu, J. Vibration reduction in truss core sandwich plate with internal nonlinear energy sink. *Compos. Struct.* **2018**, *193*, 180–188. [CrossRef]
3. Boorle, R.K.; Mallick, P.K. Global bending response of composite sandwich plates with coorugated core: Part I: Effect of geometric parameters. *Compos. Struct.* **2016**, *141*, 375–388. [CrossRef]
4. Zhang, W.; Chen, J.E.; Cao, D.X.; Chen, L.H. Nonlinear dynamic responses of a truss core sandwich plate. *Compos Struct.* **2014**, *108*, 367–386. [CrossRef]
5. Zhang, W.; Wu, Q.L.; Yao, M.H.; Dowell, E.H. Analysis on global and chaotic dynamics of nonlinear wave equations for truss core sandwich plate. *Compos. Struct.* **2018**, *94*, 21–37. [CrossRef]
6. Chen, Z.Y.; Chen, F.Q.; Zhou, L.Q. Slow-fast dynamics in the truss core sandwich plate under excitations with high and low frequencies. *Appl. Math. Model.* **2020**, *88*, 382–395. [CrossRef]
7. Li, F.; Jin, Y.L., Tian, Y. Integrability and linearizability of cubic Z2 systems with non-resonant singular points. *J. Diff. Equ.* **2020**, *269*, 9026–9049. [CrossRef]
8. Ramakrishnan, B.; Ahmadi, A.; Nazarimehr, F.; Natiq, H.; Jafari, S.; Hussain, I. Oyster oscillator: A novel mega-stable nonlinear chaotic system. *Eur. Phys. J. Spec. Top.* **2021** . [CrossRef]

9. Yao, M.H.; Zhang, W.; Yao, Z.G. Muti-pulse orbits dynamics of composite laminated piezoelectric rectangular plate. *Sci. China Technol. Sci.* **2011**, *154*, 2064–2079. [CrossRef]
10. Camassa, R.; Kovacic G.; Tin, S.K. A Melnikov method for homoclinic orbits with many pulse. *Arch. Ration Mech. Anal.* **1998**, *143*, 105–193. [CrossRef]
11. Yagasaki, K. The method of Melnikov for perturbations of multi-degree of freeedom Hamiltonian systems. *Nonlinearity* **1999**, *12*, 799–822. [CrossRef]
12. Yagasaki, K. Horseshoes in two-degree-of-freedom Hamiltonian systems with saddle-centers. *Arch. Rational Mech. Anal.* **2000**, *154*, 275–296. [CrossRef]
13. Yao, M.H.; Zhang, W.; Zu, J.W. Multi-pulse chaotic dynamics in non-planar motion of parametrically excited viscoelastic moving belt. *J. Sound Vib.* **2012**, *331*, 2624–2653. [CrossRef]
14. Zhang, W.; Zheng, Y.; Liu, T.; Guo, X.Y. Multi-pulse jumping double-parameter chaotic dynamics of eccentric rotating ring truss antenna under combined parametric and external excitations. *Nonlinear Dyn.* **2019**, *98*, 761–800. [CrossRef]
15. Zhang, D.M.; Chen, F.Q. Global bifurcations and single-pulse homoclinic orbits of a plate subjected to the transverse and in-plane excitations. *Math. Methods Appl. Sci.* **2017**, *40*, 4338–4339. [CrossRef]
16. Ahmadi, A.; Wang, X.; Fahimeh Nazarimehr, F.; Alsaadi, F.E.; Alsaadi, F.E.; Pham, V.T. Coexisting infinitely many attractors in a new chaotic system with a curve of equilibria: Its extreme multi-stability and Kolmogorov-Sinai entropy computation. *Adv. Mech. Eng.* **2019**, *2*, 1–8. [CrossRef]
17. Khalaf, A.J.M.; Abdolmohammadi, H.R.; Ahmadi, A.; Moysis, L.; Volos, C.; Hussain, I. Extreme multi-stability analysis of a novel 5D chaotic system with hidden attractors line equilibrium permutation entropy and its secure communication scheme. *Eur. Phys. J. Special Top.* **2020**, *229*, 1175–1188. [CrossRef]
18. Zhang, W.; Zhang, J.H.; Yao, M.H. The extended Melnikov method for non-autonomous nonlinear dynamical systems and application to multi-pulse chaotic dynamics of a buckled thin plate. *Nonlinear Anal. Real World Appl.* **2010**, *11*, 1442–1457. [CrossRef]
19. Zhang, J.H.; Zhang, W. Multi-pulse chaotic dynamics of non-autonomous nonlinear system for a honeycomb sandwich plate. *Acta Mech. Sin.* **2012**, *223*, 1047–1066. [CrossRef]
20. Wu, Q.L.; Zhang, W.; Dowell, E.H. Detecting multi-pulse chaotic dynamics of high-dimensional non-autonomous nonlinear system for circular mesh antenna. *Int. J. Non-Linear Mech.* **2018**, *102*, 25–40. [CrossRef]
21. Hao, W.L.; Zhang, W.; Yao, M.H. Multi-pulse chaotic dynamics of six-dimensional non-autonomous nonlinear system for a honeycomb sandwich plate. *Int. J. Bifurc. Chaos* **2014**, *24*, 1450138. [CrossRef]

mathematics

MDPI

Article

Exact Solutions and Non-Traveling Wave Solutions of the (2+1)-Dimensional Boussinesq Equation

Lihui Gao [1], Chunxiao Guo [1,*], Yanfeng Guo [2,3] and Donglong Li [2]

1 School of Science, China University of Mining and Technology, Beijing 100083, China; sqt2000701003@student.cumtb.edu.cn
2 School of Science, Guangxi University of Science and Technology, Liuzhou 545006, China; guoyanfeng@cug.edu.cn (Y.G.); lidl@21cn.com (D.L.)
3 School of Mathematics and Physics, China University of Geosciences, Wuhan 430074, China
* Correspondence: 109053@cumtb.edu.cn

Abstract: By the extended $(\frac{G'}{G})$ method and the improved tanh function method, the exact solutions of the (2+1) dimensional Boussinesq equation are studied. Firstly, with the help of the solutions of the nonlinear ordinary differential equation, we obtain the new traveling wave exact solutions of the equation by the homogeneous equilibrium principle and the extended $(\frac{G'}{G})$ method. Secondly, by constructing the new ansatz solutions and applying the improved tanh function method, many non-traveling wave exact solutions of the equation are given. The solutions mainly include hyperbolic, trigonometric and rational functions, which reflect different types of solutions for nonlinear waves. Finally, we discuss the effects of these solutions on the formation of rogue waves according to the numerical simulation.

Keywords: (2+1)-dimensional Boussinesq equation; homogeneous equilibrium principle; extended $(\frac{G'}{G})$ method; improved tanh function method

MSC: 35C08; 35C11

1. Introduction

As is well known, many nonlinear phenomena can finally be described by nonlinear partial differential equations. With the wide application of nonlinear partial differential equations in practical problems, the research on solutions of high-dimensional nonlinear partial differential equations has gradually become a hot topic. There are many methods to solve the exact solution, such as Hirota's bilinear form [1], conformable triple Sumudu decomposition method [2], Painlevé analysis [3], Exp-function method, ansatz method [4], etc. Most explicit exact solutions of equations are obtained through transformation and operation, but in fact, there is no unified solution method. Therefore, many scientists are committed to finding a universally applicable method.

A few years ago, Wang et al. in [5] used the $(\frac{G'}{G})$-expansion method to deal with nonlinear evolution equations. The idea of this method is that the traveling wave solutions of nonlinear evolution equations can be expressed by a polynomial of $(\frac{G'}{G})$, where $G = G(\xi)$ satisfies a linear ordinary differential equation. The degree of the polynomial can be determined by the homogeneous balance between the highest derivative term and the nonlinear term in nonlinear evolution equations, and the coefficients of the polynomial can be obtained by solving algebraic equations. Solitary waves can be derived from traveling waves, and traveling wave solutions will be expressed by hyperbolic functions, trigonometric functions and rational functions.

Furthermore, in order to find the non-traveling wave solutions of nonlinear evolution equations, Xie et al. in [6] introduced the generalized Riccati equation and then improved the tanh function method; that is, various ansatz solutions were proposed on the basis of the generalized Riccati equation. In order to show that abundant non-traveling wave solutions can be obtained by this method, they chose the (3+1)-dimensional Kadomtsev–Petviashvili equation, which can describe water waves, and finally obtained abundant soliton-like solutions, periodic solutions and rational solutions.

These two methods are concise and effective, and they can be widely used in many nonlinear evolution equations. The Boussinesq equation is a wave equation introduced by Joseph Boussinesq, which describes the dispersive and nonlinear properties of shallow water. This equation is widely applied in the research on changes in wave-induced set-up and current [7], and it is an important nonlinear partial differential equation. Many scholars have studied the exact solutions of such equations in different ways.

Song et al. in [8] gave the solitary wave number of the generalized (2+1)-dimensional Boussinesq equation, and they obtained the exact solitary wave solutions by using the bifurcation method of dynamic systems under different parameter conditions.

$$u_{tt} - \alpha u_{xx} - \beta u_{yy} - \gamma(u^2)_{xx} - \delta u_{xxxx} = 0, \tag{1}$$

where α, β, γ and δ are arbitrary constants. Zhao et al. in [9] applied the improved $(\frac{G'}{G})$-expansion method with a second-order linear ordinary differential equation, assuming that the form of the solution has positive and negative power terms, and they obtained the exact solutions of this equation expressed by the hyperbolic function, trigonometric function and rational function. Yang et al. in [10] used the Riccati equation to obtain abundant solutions for this equation.

When $\alpha = \beta = \gamma = \delta = 1$, the generalized (2+1)-dimensional Boussinesq equation is simplified as

$$u_{tt} - u_{xx} - u_{yy} - (u^2)_{xx} - u_{xxxx} = 0. \tag{2}$$

Zeng et al. in [11] have obtained the exact solutions of this equation by using Bäcklund transformation and performing mathematical calculations. Wang in [12] employed Hirota's bilinear method and Riemann-theta functions to construct the explicit triple periodic wave solutions for this equation under the Bäcklund transformation. Liu et al. in [13] constructed a general higher-order breather solution by using Hirota's bilinear method combined with perturbation expansion. Taking a long-wave limit for the obtained breather solution, and then making further parameter constraints, general smooth rational solutions would be succinctly constructed.

When $\alpha = \beta = \delta = 1, \gamma = -3$, Wang et al. in [14] used the $(\frac{G'}{G})$-expansion method to construct a new exact solution of the (2+1)-dimensional Boussinesq equation

$$u_{tt} - u_{xx} - u_{yy} + 3(u^2)_{xx} - u_{xxxx} = 0. \tag{3}$$

Li et al. in [15] further improved the $(\frac{G'}{G})$-expansion method and constructed the solutions in the forms of $(\frac{G'}{G+G'})$ and $(\frac{G'}{G^2})$, respectively, and they obtained and discussed the existence of the extended solution of the (2+1)-dimensional Boussinesq equation and its solution process. Jiao in [16] used the step-by-step procedure to obtain Jacobian elliptic function solutions of similarity equations, thus generating truncated series solutions of the original perturbed Boussinesq equation.

Many phenomena in nature can be simulated by functions, such as bell-shaped sech functions and kink-shaped tanh functions, which can model wave phenomena such as plasma, elastic medium, fluids, etc. [6]. In order to obtain more abundant new solutions that can explain the corresponding nonlinear phenomena, we employ the extended $(\frac{G'}{G})$ method in [17,18] and improved the tanh function method in [19,20] to study Equation (3). In Section 2, using the solutions of nonlinear ordinary differential equation, adding the constant d, as well as positive and negative power terms, many exact solutions are constructed by the extended $(\frac{G'}{G})$ method. Moreover, we discuss the structure and properties of the exact solutions under the same and different undetermined coefficients, and we analyze the effects of these solutions on the formation of rogue waves. In Section 3, by using the improved tanh function method, constructing new ansatz solutions of the generalized Riccati equation, and assuming that the solution has a positive power term and negative power term, we obtain three groups of non-traveling wave solutions composed of arbitrary functions $\mu(y,t)$ and $c(y,t)$. Furthermore, we discuss the different trajectories of the image in a certain direction for different differentiable functions. In Section 4, some conclusions are given.

2. Extended ($\frac{G'}{G}$) Method

2.1. Preliminary

The extended ($\frac{G'}{G}$) method is based on the general method, changing the auxiliary nonlinear ordinary differential equations and undetermined functions. For a given nonlinear partial differential equation

$$P(u, u_t, u_x, u_{tt}, u_{xt}, u_{xx}, ...) = 0, \tag{4}$$

the main steps of the extended ($\frac{G'}{G}$) method are as follows.

Step 1 Making the traveling wave transformation on Equation (4), we suppose that $u(\xi) = u(x, y, ..., t), \xi = a_1 x + a_2 y + ... - bt$, in which $a_j (j = 1, 2, ...)$ and b are undetermined real constants. Then, we integrate and simplify it to an ordinary differential equation

$$P(e, u, u', u'', ...) = 0, \tag{5}$$

where e is a integral constant, and $u' = \frac{du}{d\xi}, u'' = \frac{d^2u}{d\xi^2}, ...$

Step 2 Supposing that the solution of Equation (5) has the following form

$$u(\xi) = \sum_{i=-N}^{N} e_i (d + H(\xi))^i, \tag{6}$$

where $e_i (i = 0, \pm 1, \pm 2, ..., \pm N)$ are undetermined constants and $e_i \neq 0$, N is determined by the homogeneous balance principle, and $H(\xi) = \frac{G'(\xi)}{G(\xi)}$ satisfies an auxiliary nonlinear partial differential equation of G.

Step 3 Substituting (6) into Equation (5), we use the auxiliary equation to convert the left-hand side of Equation (5) into a polynomial of $(d + H(\xi))$. Equating each coefficient of the same power term of $(d + H(\xi))$ to zero, then we obtain the algebraic equations about undetermined coefficients.

Step 4 Solving the algebraic equations of $e_i (i = 0, \pm 1, \pm 2, ..., \pm N)$ and e, we finally substitute the solutions of the auxiliary equation to determine the specific form of (6).

The choice of auxiliary equations determines the structure and properties of solutions of nonlinear partial differential equation. Generally speaking, the ($\frac{G'}{G}$)-expansion method in [14] is to use a second-order linear ordinary differential equation $G'' + \lambda G' + \mu G = 0$, which includes three types of solutions.

In Ref. [21], the author mentioned a nonlinear auxiliary ordinary differential equation

$$AGG'' - BGG' - C(G')^2 - EG^2 = 0, \tag{7}$$

where A, B, C and E are undermined coefficients. Taking $M = A - C, \omega = B^2 + 4EM$, and $\Delta = ME$, the solutions of this equation are as follows.

When $B \neq 0$ and $\omega > 0$,

$$H(\xi) = (\frac{G'}{G}) = \frac{B}{2M} + \frac{\sqrt{\omega}}{2M} \frac{C_1 \sinh(\frac{\sqrt{\omega}}{2A}\xi) - C_2 \cosh(\frac{\sqrt{\omega}}{2A}\xi)}{C_2 \sinh(\frac{\sqrt{\omega}}{2A}\xi) + C_1 \cosh(\frac{\sqrt{\omega}}{2A}\xi)}. \tag{8}$$

When $B \neq 0$ and $\omega < 0$,

$$H(\xi) = (\frac{G'}{G}) = \frac{B}{2M} + \frac{\sqrt{-\omega}}{2M} \frac{-C_1 \sin(\frac{\sqrt{-\omega}}{2A}\xi) + C_2 \cos(\frac{\sqrt{-\omega}}{2A}\xi)}{C_2 \sin(\frac{\sqrt{-\omega}}{2A}\xi) + C_1 \cos(\frac{\sqrt{-\omega}}{2A}\xi)}. \quad (9)$$

When $B \neq 0$ and $\omega = 0$,

$$H(\xi) = (\frac{G'}{G}) = \frac{B}{2M} + \frac{C_2}{C_1 + C_2\xi}. \quad (10)$$

When $B = 0$ and $\Delta > 0$,

$$H(\xi) = (\frac{G'}{G}) = \frac{\sqrt{\Delta}}{M} \frac{C_1 \sinh(\frac{\sqrt{\Delta}}{A}\xi) + C_2 \cosh(\frac{\sqrt{\Delta}}{A}\xi)}{C_2 \sinh(\frac{\sqrt{\Delta}}{A}\xi) - C_1 \cosh(\frac{\sqrt{\Delta}}{A}\xi)}. \quad (11)$$

When $B = 0$ and $\Delta < 0$,

$$H(\xi) = (\frac{G'}{G}) = \frac{\sqrt{-\Delta}}{M} \frac{-C_1 \sin(\frac{\sqrt{-\Delta}}{A}\xi) + C_2 \cos(\frac{\sqrt{-\Delta}}{A}\xi)}{C_2 \sin(\frac{\sqrt{-\Delta}}{A}\xi) + C_1 \cos(\frac{\sqrt{-\Delta}}{A}\xi)}. \quad (12)$$

In the subsequent sections, we will use the extended $(\frac{G'}{G})$ method to solve the exact solutions of (2+1)-dimensional Boussinesq equation with $AGG'' - BGG' - C(G')^2 - EG^2 = 0$ as an auxiliary equation.

2.2. Expression Form of Traveling Wave Solution

Considering the following (2+1)-dimensional Boussinesq equation

$$u_{tt} - u_{xx} - u_{yy} + 3(u^2)_{xx} - u_{xxxx} = 0,$$

through traveling wave transformation $u(\xi) = u(x,y,t)$, $\xi = x + ay - bt$, where a, b are two non-zero constants, Equation (3) becomes

$$(b^2 - 1 - a^2)u'' + 3(u^2)'' - u'''' = 0.$$

Integrating it twice, we obtain

$$u'' - 3u^2 + cu + e = 0, \quad (13)$$

where e is a real integral constant, $c = a^2 + 1 - b^2$. We suppose that Equation (13) has the following solution

$$u(\xi) = \sum_{i=-N}^{N} e_i (d + H(\xi))^i. \quad (14)$$

When the power of the highest-order derivative term u'' and the nonlinear term u^2 are equal, then $N = 2$. Furthermore, (14) can be written as

$$u(\xi) = e_{-2}(d + H)^{-2} + e_{-1}(d + H)^{-1} + e_0 + e_1(d + H) + e_2(d + H)^2. \quad (15)$$

Substituting (15) into Equation (13), and taking $\Theta = Md^2 + Bd - E$, then we obtain the following algebraic equations about undetermined coefficients.

$$
\begin{cases}
-3A^2e_2(e_2 - \frac{2M^2}{A^2}) = 0, \\
-6A^2(e_2 - \frac{2M^2}{A^2})((e_1 + \frac{2M(2dM+B)}{A^2})) - 10M^2(e_1 + \frac{2M(2dM+B)}{A^2}) = 0, \\
3A^2(\frac{M(B+2dM)}{A^2} - e_1)(e_1 + \frac{2M(B+2dM)}{A^2}) - 12M^2(e_0 - \frac{12M\Theta + A^2c + \omega}{6A^2}) \\
\quad + 6A^2(e_2 - \frac{2M^2}{A^2})((\frac{12M\Theta + A^2c + \omega}{6A^2} - e_0) + \frac{(B+2dM)^2}{2A^2}) = 0, \\
-6A^2(e_2 - \frac{2M^2}{A^2})(e_{-1} + \frac{\Theta(B+2dM)}{A^2}) - 6M\Theta(e_1 + \frac{2M(B+2dM)}{A^2}) \\
\quad - 12M^2e_{-1} = 0, \\
A^2e_0(c + 3e_0 + e) - 6A^2(e_2e_{-2} + e_1e_{-1}) + 2M^2e_{-2} + 2e_2\Theta^2 - e_1(B+2dM)\Theta \\
\quad - e_{-1}M(B+2dM) = 0, \\
-6A^2(e_{-2} - \frac{2\Theta^2}{A^2})(e_1 + \frac{M(B+2dM)}{A^2}) - 6M\Theta(e_{-1} + \frac{2(B+2dM)\Theta}{A^2}) \\
\quad - 12\Theta^2e_1 = 0, \\
3A^2(e_{-1} + \frac{2(B+2dM)\Theta}{A^2})(\frac{(B+2dM)\Theta}{A^2} - e_{-1})) - 12\Theta(e_0 - \frac{12M\Theta + A^2c + \omega}{6A^2}) \\
\quad + 6A^2(e_{-2} - \frac{2\Theta^2}{A^2})((\frac{12M\Theta + A^2c + \omega}{6A^2} - e_0) + \frac{(B+2dM)^2}{2A^2}) = 0, \\
-6A^2(e_{-2} - \frac{2\Theta^2}{A^2})(e_{-1} + \frac{5(B+2dM)\Theta}{3A^2}) + 10\Theta^2(e_{-1} + \frac{2(B+2dM)\Theta}{A^2}) = 0, \\
-3A^2e_{-2}(e_{-2} - \frac{2\Theta^2}{A^2}) = 0.
\end{cases}
$$

By solving these equations with Maple, we obtain three groups of coefficient relations about $e_{-2}, e_{-1}, e_0, e_1, e_2$ and e.

Group 1

$$e = \frac{\omega^2 - A^4c^2}{12A^4}, e_{-2} = 0, e_{-1} = 0,$$

$$e_0 = \frac{12M(Md^2 + Bd - E) + A^2c + \omega}{6A^2}, e_1 = -\frac{2M(2dM+B)}{A^2}, e_2 = \frac{2M^2}{A^2}.$$

Group 2

$$e = \frac{\omega^2 - A^4c^2}{12A^4}, e_{-2} = \frac{2(Md^2 + Bd - E)^2}{A^2}, e_{-1} = -\frac{2(2dM+B)(Md^2 + Bd - E)}{A^2},$$

$$e_0 = \frac{12M(Md^2 + Bd - E) + A^2c + \omega}{6A^2}, e_1 = 0, e_2 = 0.$$

Group 3

$$e = \frac{256M^2(Md^2 + E)^2 - A^4c^2}{12A^4}, e_{-2} = \frac{2(Md^2 + E)^2}{A^2}, e_{-1} = 0,$$

$$e_0 = \frac{A^2c - 8M(Md^2 + E)}{6A^2}, e_1 = 0, e_2 = \frac{2M^2}{A^2}, B = -2dM.$$

Considering the exact solutions of each group when the conditions (8)–(12) are satisfied, for convenience, in (8) and (11), $C_1^2 - C_2^2 = 1$, $C_3 = \text{arccosh}C_1 = \text{arcsinh}C_2$. In (10), $C_2 \neq 0$, $C_3 = \frac{C_1}{C_2}$. In (9) and (12), $C_1^2 + C_2^2 = 1$, $C_3 = \arccos C_1 = \arcsin C_2$.

The exact solutions of Group 1 are as follows.

$$u_{1,1}(\xi) = \frac{12M(Md^2 + Bd - E) + A^2c + \omega}{6A^2}$$

$$
\begin{aligned}
&-\frac{2M(2dM+B)}{A^2}(d+\frac{B}{2M}+\frac{\sqrt{\omega}}{2M}\tanh(\frac{\sqrt{\omega}}{2A}\xi-C_3))\\
&+\frac{2M^2}{A^2}(d+\frac{B}{2M}+\frac{\sqrt{\omega}}{2M}\tanh(\frac{\sqrt{\omega}}{2A}\xi-C_3))^2,\\
u_{1,2}(\xi)=&\ \frac{12M(Md^2+Bd-E)+A^2c+\omega}{6A^2}\\
&-\frac{2M(2dM+B)}{A^2}(d+\frac{B}{2M}+\frac{\sqrt{-\omega}}{2M}\tan(-\frac{\sqrt{-\omega}}{2A}\xi+C_3))\\
&+\frac{2M^2}{A^2}(d+\frac{B}{2M}+\frac{\sqrt{-\omega}}{2M}\tan(-\frac{\sqrt{-\omega}}{2A}\xi+C_3))^2,\\
u_{1,3}(\xi)=&\ \frac{12M(Md^2+Bd-E)+A^2c+\omega}{6A^2}-\frac{2M(2dM+B)}{A^2}(d+\frac{B}{2M}+\frac{1}{\xi+C_3})\\
&+\frac{2M^2}{A^2}(d+\frac{B}{2M}+\frac{1}{\xi+C_3})^2,\\
u_{1,4}(\xi)=&\ \frac{12M^2d^2-8ME+A^2c}{6A^2}+\frac{2M^2}{A^2}(d+\frac{\sqrt{\Delta}}{M}\tanh(\frac{\sqrt{\Delta}}{A}\xi+C_3))^2\\
&-\frac{4M^2d}{A^2}(d+\frac{\sqrt{\Delta}}{M}\tanh(\frac{\sqrt{\Delta}}{A}\xi+C_3)),\\
u_{1,5}(\xi)=&\ \frac{12M^2d^2-8ME+A^2c}{6A^2}+\frac{2M^2}{A^2}(d+\frac{\sqrt{-\Delta}}{M}\tan(-\frac{\sqrt{-\Delta}}{A}\xi+C_3))^2\\
&-\frac{4M^2d}{A^2}(d+\frac{\sqrt{-\Delta}}{M}\tan(-\frac{\sqrt{-\Delta}}{A}\xi+C_3)).
\end{aligned}
$$

The exact solutions of Group 2 are as follows.

$$
\begin{aligned}
u_{2,1}(\xi)=&\ \frac{12M(Md^2+Bd-E)+A^2c+\omega}{6A^2}\\
&-\frac{2(2dM+B)(Md^2+Bd-E)}{A^2}(d+\frac{B}{2M}+\frac{\sqrt{\omega}}{2M}\tanh(\frac{\sqrt{\omega}}{2A}\xi-C_3))^{-1}\\
&+\frac{2(Md^2+Bd-E)^2}{A^2}(d+\frac{B}{2M}+\frac{\sqrt{\omega}}{2M}\tanh(\frac{\sqrt{\omega}}{2A}\xi-C_3))^{-2},\\
u_{2,2}(\xi)=&\ \frac{12M(Md^2+Bd-E)+A^2c+\omega}{6A^2}\\
&-\frac{2(2dM+B)(Md^2+Bd-E)}{A^2}(d+\frac{B}{2M}+\frac{\sqrt{-\omega}}{2M}\tan(-\frac{\sqrt{-\omega}}{2A}\xi+C_3))^{-1}\\
&+\frac{2(Md^2+Bd-E)^2}{A^2}(d+\frac{B}{2M}+\frac{\sqrt{-\omega}}{2M}\tan(-\frac{\sqrt{-\omega}}{2A}\xi+C_3))^{-2},\\
u_{2,3}(\xi)=&\ \frac{12M(Md^2+Bd-E)+A^2c+\omega}{6A^2}\\
&-\frac{2(2dM+B)(Md^2+Bd-E)}{A^2}(d+\frac{B}{2M}+\frac{1}{\xi+C_3})^{-1}\\
&+\frac{2(Md^2+Bd-E)^2}{A^2}(d+\frac{B}{2M}+\frac{1}{\xi+C_3})^{-2},\\
u_{2,4}(\xi)=&\ \frac{12M^2d^2-8ME+A^2c}{6A^2}+\frac{2(Md^2-E)^2}{A^2}(d+\frac{\sqrt{\Delta}}{M}\tanh(\frac{\sqrt{\Delta}}{A}\xi+C_3))^{-2}\\
&-\frac{4dM(Md^2-E)}{A^2}(d+\frac{\sqrt{\Delta}}{M}\tanh(\frac{\sqrt{\Delta}}{A}\xi+C_3))^{-1},\\
u_{2,5}(\xi)=&\ \frac{12M^2d^2-8ME+A^2c}{6A^2}\\
&-\frac{4dM(Md^2-E)}{A^2}(d+\frac{\sqrt{-\Delta}}{M}\tan(-\frac{\sqrt{-\Delta}}{A}\xi+C_3))^{-1}\\
&+\frac{2(Md^2-E)^2}{A^2}(d+\frac{\sqrt{-\Delta}}{M}\tan(-\frac{\sqrt{-\Delta}}{A}\xi+C_3))^{-2}.
\end{aligned}
$$

The exact solutions of Group 3 are as follows.

$$
\begin{aligned}
u_{3,1}(\xi)=&\ \frac{A^2c-8M(Md^2+E)}{6A^2}+\frac{2M^2}{A^2}(\frac{\sqrt{\omega}}{2M}\tanh(\frac{\sqrt{\omega}}{2A}\xi-C_3))^2\\
&+\frac{2(Md^2+E)^2}{A^2}(\frac{\sqrt{\omega}}{2M}\tanh(\frac{\sqrt{\omega}}{2A}\xi-C_3))^{-2},
\end{aligned}
$$

$$u_{3,2}(\xi) = \frac{A^2c - 8M(Md^2+E)}{6A^2} + \frac{2M^2}{A^2}(\frac{\sqrt{-\omega}}{2M}\tan(-\frac{\sqrt{-\omega}}{2A}\xi + C_3))^2$$
$$+ \frac{2(Md^2+E)^2}{A^2}(\frac{\sqrt{-\omega}}{2M}\tan(-\frac{\sqrt{-\omega}}{2A}\xi + C_3))^{-2},$$
$$u_{3,3}(\xi) = \frac{A^2c - 8M(Md^2+E)}{6A^2} + \frac{2M^2}{A^2}(\frac{1}{\xi + C_3})^2 + \frac{2(Md^2+E)^2}{A^2}(\frac{1}{\xi + C_3})^{-2},$$
$$u_{3,4}(\xi) = \frac{A^2c - 8ME}{6A^2} + \frac{2M^2}{A^2}(\frac{\sqrt{\Delta}}{M}\tanh(\frac{\sqrt{\Delta}}{A}\xi + C_3))^2$$
$$+ \frac{2E^2}{A^2}(\frac{\sqrt{\Delta}}{M}\tanh(\frac{\sqrt{\Delta}}{A}\xi + C_3))^{-2},$$
$$u_{3,5}(\xi) = \frac{A^2c - 8ME}{6A^2} + \frac{2M^2}{A^2}(\frac{\sqrt{-\Delta}}{M}\tan(-\frac{\sqrt{-\Delta}}{A}\xi + C_3))^2$$
$$+ \frac{2E^2}{A^2}(\frac{\sqrt{-\Delta}}{M}\tan(-\frac{\sqrt{-\Delta}}{A}\xi + C_3))^{-2}.$$

Next, we numerically simulate the solutions, and the images are shown in Figures 1–13, where $r = x - \frac{t}{2}$, w $= y - \frac{t}{2}$.

2.3. Numerical Simulation of Solutions under Different Undetermined Coefficient Values

Firstly, we discuss the structure and properties of the exact solutions under different undetermined coefficient values.

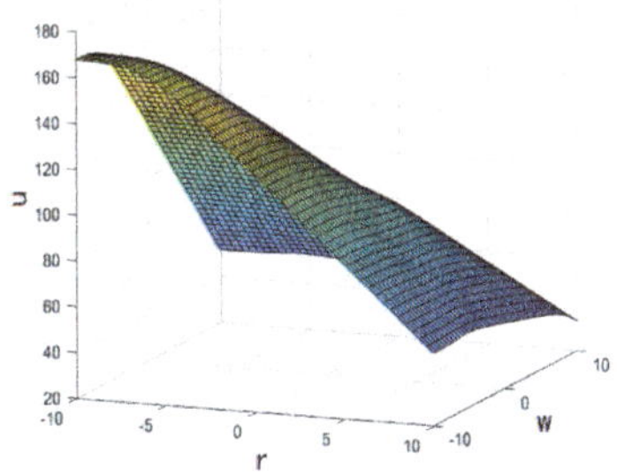

Figure 1. Hyperbolic function $u_{1,1}(\xi)$ as $a = 1, c = 1, e = \frac{3}{64}, A = 2, B = 1, C_3 = \sqrt{5}, E = 1, M = 1, \omega = 5, e_0 = \frac{13}{24}, e_1 = \frac{3}{2}, C = 1, e_2 = \frac{1}{2}, d = -2$.

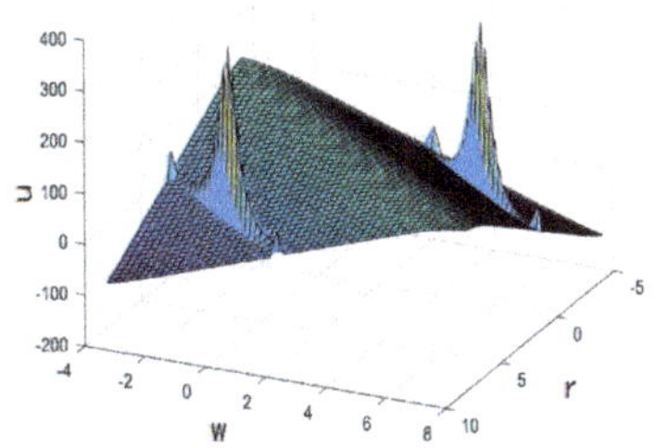

Figure 2. Hyperbolic function $u_{3,1}(\xi)$ as $a = 1, c = 1, e = \frac{133}{4}, A = 2, B = 4, C_3 = \sqrt{20}, E = 1, M = 1, \omega = 20, e_0 = -\frac{11}{6}, e_{-2} = \frac{25}{2}, C = 1, e_2 = \frac{1}{2}, d = -2$.

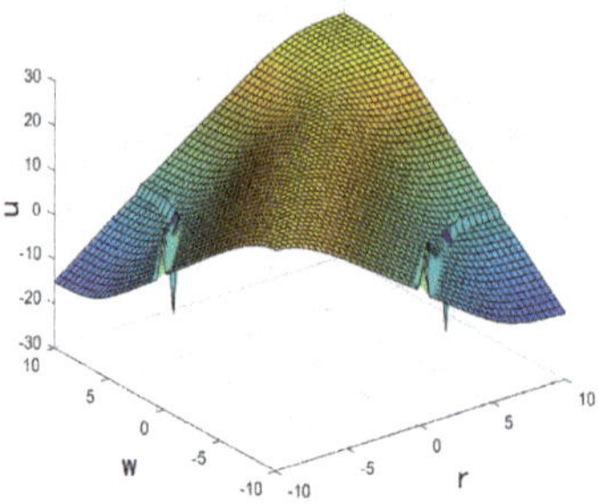

Figure 3. Hyperbolic function $u_{3,4}(\xi)$ as $a = 1, c = 1, e = \frac{5}{4}, A = 2, B = 0, C_3 = 2, E = 1, M = 1, \Delta = 1, e_0 = -\frac{1}{2}, e_{-2} = \frac{1}{2}, C = 1, e_2 = \frac{1}{2}, d = 0$.

When the exact solution has the form of hyperbolic function, such as $u_{1,1}, u_{1,4}, u_{2,1}, u_{2,4}, u_{3,1}$ and $u_{3,4}$. If the solution does not contain the negative power term of $(d + H(\xi))$, such as $u_{1,1}$ and $u_{1,4}$, it can be inferred from the properties of the hyperbolic tangent function that the image of the solution is smooth. If the solution contains negative power terms of $(d + H(\xi))$, when the denominator of the solution gradually approaches zero by ξ, the image of the solution for $u_{2,1}, u_{2,4}, u_{3,1}$ and $u_{3,4}$ may reflect sharp points. However, there must be sharp points in the image of solutions $u_{3,1}$ and $u_{3,4}$. For $u_{3,4}$, due to the condition of the auxiliary equation solution $B = -2dM = 0$, and $\Delta > 0$, but $M \neq 0, d = 0$. In this case, the denominator of the negative power term of $(d + H(\xi))$ is $\frac{\sqrt{\Delta}}{M} \tanh(\frac{\sqrt{\Delta}}{A}\xi + C_3)$, and ξ can always obtain the value $-\frac{AC_3}{\sqrt{\Delta}}$, so the blow-up phenomenon cannot be avoided and rogue waves will appear in actual phenomena.

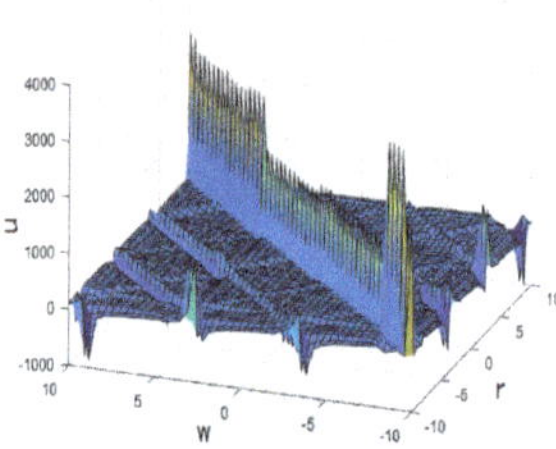

Figure 4. Trigonometric function $u_{1,5}(\xi)$ as $a = 1, c = 1, A = 2, B = 0, E = -1, M = 1, \Delta = -1, C = 1, e_0 = \frac{13}{6}, e_1 = 2, e_2 = \frac{1}{2}, e = 0, C_3 = 2, d = -2$.

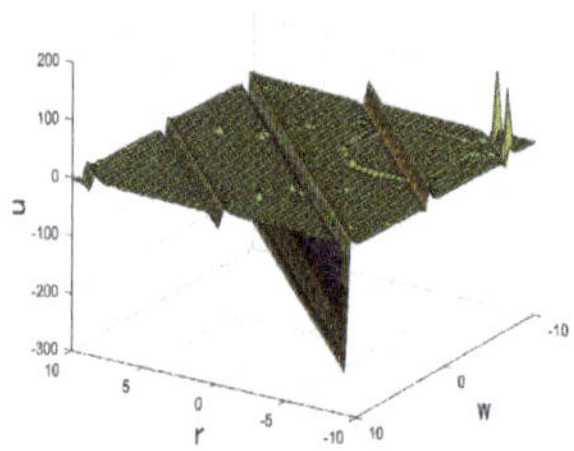

Figure 5. Trigonometric function $u_{2,2}(\xi)$ as $a = 1, c = 1, e = -\frac{1}{16}, B = 1, E = -\frac{3}{4}, M = 1, \omega = -2, C = 1, e_0 = \frac{9}{8}, e_{-1} = \frac{33}{8}, e_{-2} = \frac{121}{32}, A = 2, C_3 = \sqrt{2}, d = -2$.

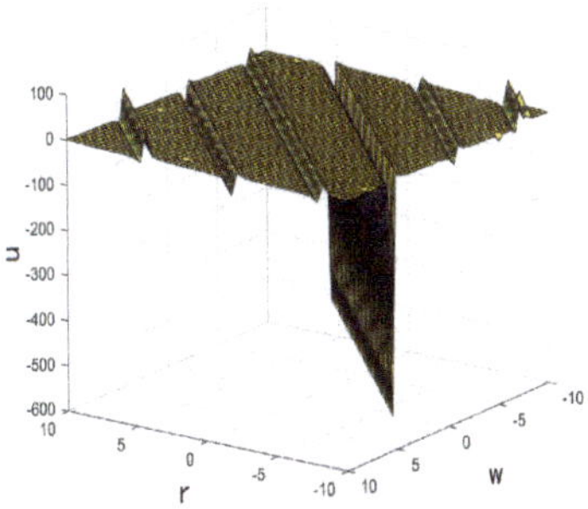

Figure 6. Trigonometric function $u_{2,5}(\xi)$ as $a = 1, c = 1, A = 2, B = 0, E = -1, M = 1, \Delta = -1, C = 1, e_0 = \frac{13}{6}, e_{-2} = \frac{25}{2}, e_{-1} = 10, e = 0, C_3 = 2, d = -2$.

When the exact solution has the form of trigonometric function, such as $u_{1,2}$,$u_{1,5}$,$u_{2,2}$, $u_{2,5}$,$u_{3,2}$ and $u_{3,5}$, from the properties of the tangent function, we deduce that whether the solution contains negative power terms of $(d + H(\xi))$, the image of the solution will have segmented periodic spikes.

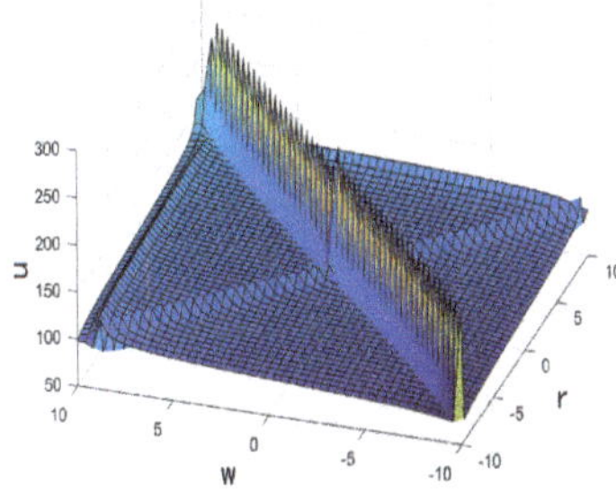

Figure 7. Rational function$u_{1,3}(\xi)$ as $a = 1, c = 1, e = -\frac{1}{12}, B = 2, E = 1, M = -1, \omega = 0, C = 2, e_0 = \frac{11}{6}, e_1 = -4, e_2 = 2, A = 1, C_3 = 1, d = 2$.

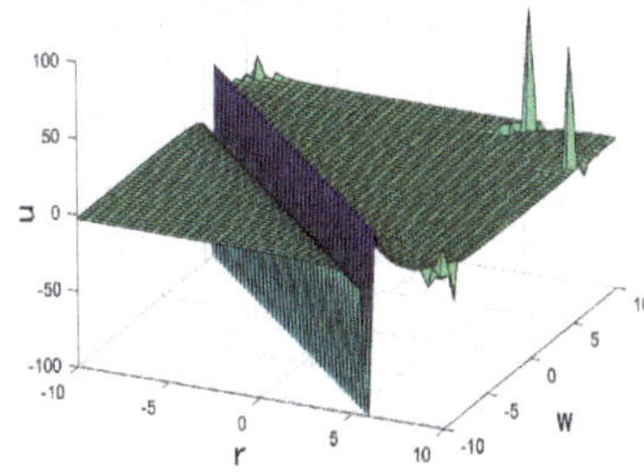

Figure 8. Rational function $u_{2,3}(\xi)$ as $a = 1, c = 1, e = -\frac{1}{12}, B = 2, E = 1, M = -1, \omega = 0, C = 2, e_{-1} = -4, A = 1, e_{-2} = 2, e_0 = \frac{11}{6}, C_3 = 2, d = 2$.

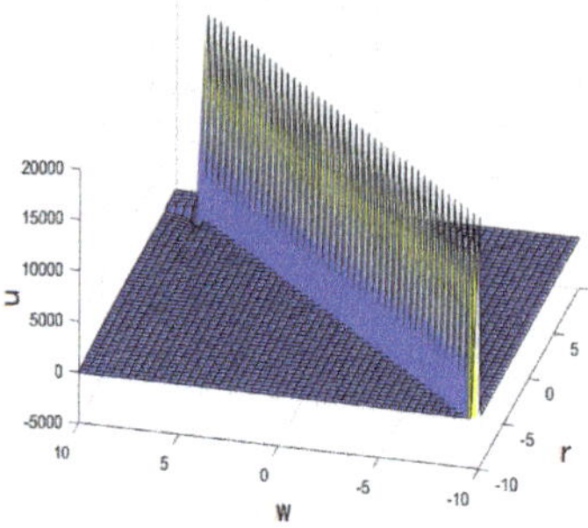

Figure 9. Rational function $u_{3,3}(\xi)$ $a = 1, c = 1, e = -\frac{1}{12}, B = 4, E = 4, M = -1, \omega = 0, C = 2,$ $e_0 = -\frac{1}{6}, A = 1, e_2 = 2, e_{-2} = 0, C_3 = 2, d = 2.$

When the exact solution has the form of rational function, such as $u_{1,3}$, $u_{2,3}$ and $u_{3,3}$, since there is always a rational function of ξ in the denominator, there will be sharp points in the image of the solution.

2.4. Numerical Simulation of Solutions under the Same Situation

Now, we discuss the influence of d on the structure and properties of the solution under the same situation.

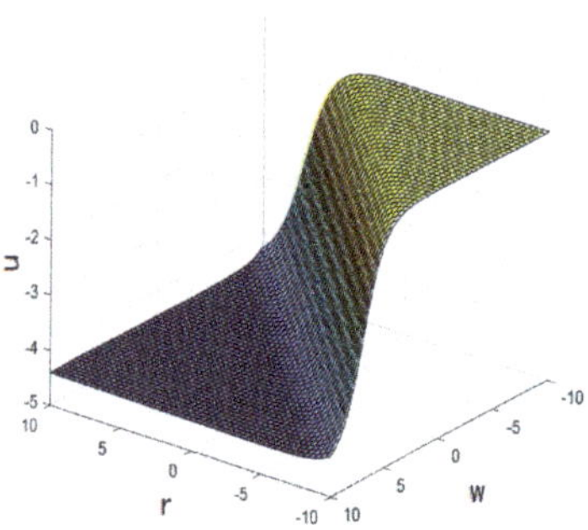

Figure 10. Hyperbolic function $u_{2,4}(\xi)$ as $d = -2, a = 1, c = 1, A = 2, B = 0, C_3 = 2, C = 1,$ $e = 0, E = 1, M = 1, \Delta = 1, e_0 = \frac{3}{2}, e_{-1} = 6, e_{-2} = \frac{9}{2}.$

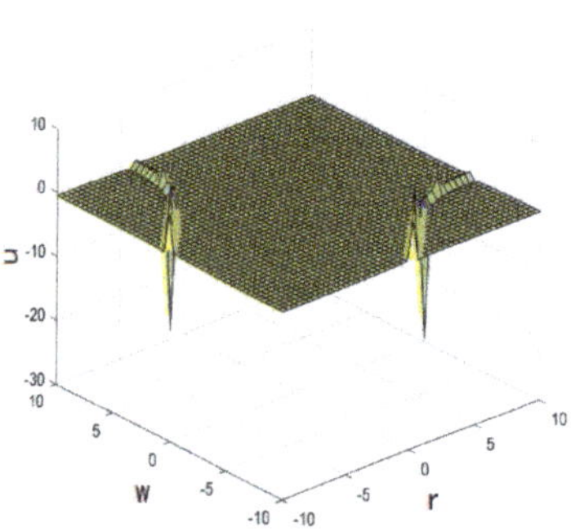

Figure 11. Hyperbolic function $u_{2,4}(\xi)$ as $d = 0, a = 1, c = 1, A = 2, B = 0, C_3 = 2, C = 1, e = 0,$ $E = 1, M = 1, \Delta = 1, e_0 = -\frac{1}{2}, e_{-1} = 0, e_{-2} = \frac{1}{2}.$

Taking the solution $u_{2,4}$ as an example, which denominator will be $\frac{\sqrt{\Delta}}{M}\tanh(\frac{\sqrt{\Delta}}{2A}\xi + C_3)$ when $d = 0$, that is a hyperbolic tangent function, but if ξ infinitely approaches $-\frac{AC_3}{\sqrt{\Delta}}$, the solution value tends to be infinity, and therefore, blow-up occurs. When $|d| > \frac{\sqrt{\Delta}}{|M|}$, the denominator $d+\frac{\sqrt{\Delta}}{M}\tanh(\frac{\sqrt{\Delta}}{A}\xi+C_3)\neq 0$; then, the function image will be smooth at this time.

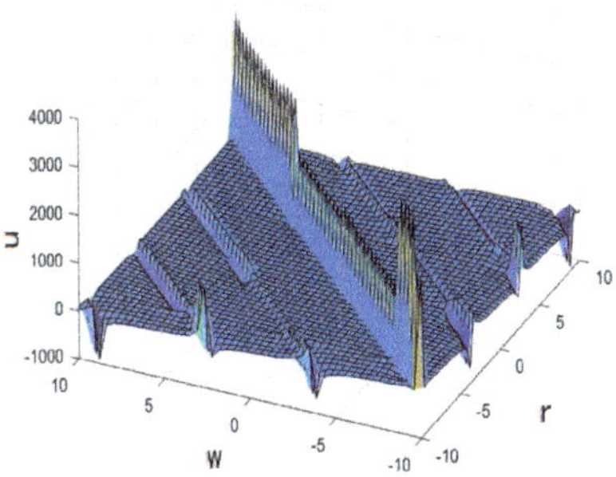

Figure 12. Trigonometric function $u_{3,2}(\xi)$ as $d=-1$, $a=1, c=1, A=2, B=2, E=-2, e=\frac{5}{4}$, $C=1, M=1, \omega=-4$, $C_3=-2, e_0=\frac{1}{6}, e_2=\frac{1}{2}, e_{-2}=\frac{1}{2}$.

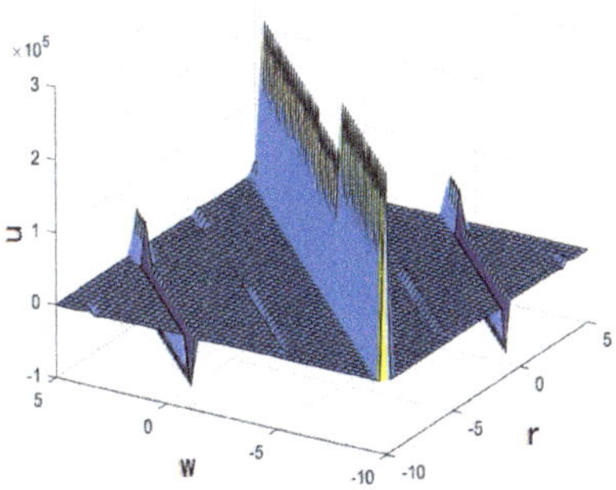

Figure 13. Trigonometric function $u_{3,2}(\xi)$ as $d=0$, $a=1, c=1, A=2, B=0, E=-2, e=\frac{21}{4}$, $C=1, M=1, \omega=-8$, $C_3=-2, e_0=\frac{1}{2}, e_2=\frac{1}{2}, e_{-2}=2$.

For $u_{3,2}$, it is known from the image properties of tangent function that there always exists a ξ so that $\frac{\sqrt{-\omega}}{2M}\tan(-\frac{\sqrt{-\omega}}{2A}\xi+C_3)$ is equal to zero no matter what the value d is; then, the solution value is always infinite. These values are periodic, and periodic blow-up will occur.

Comparing those methods mentioned in Refs. [14,15], we add a constant d and negative power terms. Different properties of solutions are obtained by controlling the variable d. The negative power term affects the solution to blow up.

3. Improved Tanh Function Method

3.1. Preliminary

The improved tanh function method makes full use of the generalized Riccati equation

$$\varphi'=r+p\varphi+q\varphi^2, \tag{16}$$

on the basis of the tanh function method, where r, p and q are real constants. For the nonlinear partial differential Equation (4), the steps of the improved tanh function method are as follows.

Step 1 Supposing that Equation (4) has the following form of solution

$$u(x,y,t) = \sum_{i=-N'}^{N'} \mu_i(y,t)\varphi^i(kx+\eta(y,t)), \tag{17}$$

where $\mu_i(y,t)(i = 0,1,2,...,N')$and $\eta(y,t)$ are differentiable functions, and the value N' here is determined by the homogeneous balance principle.

Step 2 Substitute (17) into Equation (4), and repeatedly use Equation (16) to convert the left-hand side of Equation (4) into a polynomial about $\varphi(kx+\eta(y,t))$. Equate each coefficient of the same power term to zero, and then obtain the algebraic equations about undetermined functions.

Step 3 Solve the algebraic equations to determine $\mu_i(y,t)$ and $\eta(y,t)$, and finally substitute the solution of the generalized Riccati equation into (17).

In the subsequent sections, with the help of the generalized Riccati equation, we will apply the improved tanh function method to solve the non-traveling wave exact solutions of the (2+1)-dimensional Boussinesq equation.

3.2. *Expression of Non-Traveling Wave Exact Solution*

For the (2+1) dimensional Boussinesq equation

$$u_{tt} - u_{xx} - u_{yy} + 3(u^2)_{xx} - u_{xxxx} = 0,$$

in order to balance the highest derivative term u_{xxxx} and nonlinear term $(u^2)_{xx}$, we suppose that Equation (3) has the following form of solution.

$$u(x,y,t) = \frac{a(y,t)}{\varphi^2} + \frac{b(y,t)}{\varphi} + c(y,t) + d(y,t)\varphi + e(y,t)\varphi^2, \tag{18}$$

where $\varphi = \varphi(kx+\eta(y,t))$, k is a real number but $k \neq 0$, $a(y,t)$, $b(y,t)$, $c(y,t)$, $d(y,t)$, $e(y,t)$ and $\eta(y,t)$ are differentiable functions.

Substituting (18) into Equation (3), and taking $c_0 = \frac{k^4p^2+8k^4qr+k^2-(\eta_t{}^2-\eta_y{}^2)}{6k^2}$, then we obtain the coefficients of φ.

$$\begin{cases} 60ek^2q^2(e-2k^2q^2)=0, \\ 12kq(p(e-2k^2q^2)(9e+2k^2q^2)+q(d-2k^2pq)(6e-2k^2q^2))=0, \\ (e-2k^2q^2)(6k^2p^2(c-c_0)+4k^4q^2p^2)+12k^4q^4(c-c_0)+e(8k^2p^2+16k^2qr) \\ \qquad +k^2q(d-2k^2pq)(21ep-3dp-4k^2pq^2)=0, \\ 6k^2(d-2k^2pq)[q(20k^2p^2q+32k^2q^2r+5dp)+9(p^2+2qr)(e-2k^2q^2)] \\ \quad +6k^2[2rp(e-2k^2q^2)(7e+2k^2q^2)+2q(beq-k^2p^3(e-2k^2q^2))] \\ \qquad +2eq(\eta_t t-\eta_y y)+4q(e_t\eta_t-e_y\eta_y)=0, \\ 6k^2[(e-2k^2q^2)(3pq(b-2k^2pr)+15pr(d-2k^2pq)+6er^2)+4k^2p^2qr-2k^2p^4] \\ \quad +2q(d_t\eta_t-d_y\eta_y)+4p(e_t\eta_t-e_y\eta_y)+(e_{tt}-e_{yy})+(2ep+dq)(\eta_t t-\eta_y y) \\ \quad +2(d-2k^2pq)((p^2+2qr)(d-2k^2pq)+k^2pq(3p^2+20qr))+6k^2p^2q^2b=0, \\ 6k^2[r(b-2k^2pr)(4k^2p^2q+6er+3dr)+(e-2k^2q^2)(bp^2-4k^2p^3r+2bqr)] \\ \quad +12bk^4q^2(p^2+2qr)+(2er+dq)(\eta_{tt}-\eta_{yy})+2p(d_t\eta_t-d_y\eta_y) \\ \qquad +4r(e_t\eta_t-e_y\eta_y)+(d_{tt}-d_{yy})=0, \\ 6k^2[(b-2k^2pr)(4k^2p^2r+b+dr^2(d-2k^2pq)+ap(a-2k^2r^2)(d-2k^2pq)] \\ \quad +6prk^2(e-2k^2q^2))+(dr-bq)(\eta_{tt}-\eta_{yy})-2q(b_t\eta_t-b_y\eta_y) \\ \qquad +2r(d_t\eta_t-d_y\eta_y)+(c_{tt}-c_{yy})=0, \\ 6k^2[q(b-2k^2pr)(4k^2p^2r+6aq+3bq)+(a-2k^2r^2)(dr^2-4k^2p^3q+2bqr)] \\ \quad +12dk^4r^2(p^2+2pr)-(2aq+bp)(\eta_{tt}-\eta_{yy})-2p(b_t\eta_t-b_y\eta_y) \\ \qquad -4q(a_t\eta_t-a_y\eta_y)+(b_{tt}-b_{yy})=0, \\ 6k^2[(a-2k^2r^2)(3pr(d-2k^2pq)+15pq(b-2k^2pr)+6aq^2)+4k^2p^2qr-2k^2p^4] \\ \quad -(2ap+br)(\eta_t t-\eta_y y)+2r(b_t\eta_t-b_y\eta_y)-4p(a_t\eta_t-a_y\eta_y)-(a_{tt}-a_{yy}) \\ \quad +2(b-2k^2pr)((p^2+2qr)(b-2k^2pr)+k^2pr(3p^2+20qr))+6k^2p^2r^2d=0, \\ 6k^2(b-2k^2pr)[r(20k^2p^2r+32k^2q^2q+5bp)+9(p^2+2qr)(a-2k^2r^2)] \\ \quad +6k^2[2ap(a-2k^2r^2)(7a+2k^2r^2)+2r(adr-k^2p^3(a-2k^2r^2))] \\ \qquad -2ar(\eta_{tt}-\eta_{yy})-4q(a_t\eta_t-a_y\eta_y)=0, \\ (a-2k^2r^2)(6k^2p^2(c-c_0)+a(8k^2p^2+16k^2qr)+4k^4r^2p^2)+12k^4r^4(c-c_0) \\ \qquad +k^2r(b-2k^2pr)(21ap-3br-4k^2pr^2)=0, \\ 12kr(p(a-2k^2r^2)(9a+2k^2r^2)+r(b-2k^2pr)(6a-2k^2r^2))=0, \\ 60ak^2q^2(a-2k^2r^2)=0. \end{cases}$$

We can obtain the following results by solving those equations with Maple.

Case 1

$$a=0, b=0, d=2k^2pq, e=2k^2q^2, \eta(y,t)=f_1(y)+f_2(y)t+f_3(t),$$

$$c=\frac{1}{6k^2}(k^4p^2+8k^4qr+k^2-((f_2(y)+f_3'(t))^2-(f_1'(y)+f_2'(y)t)^2)),$$

where $f_1(y), f_2(y)$ and $f_3(t)$ are arbitrary differentiable functions, and $\eta_{tt}^2=\eta_{yy}^2=\eta_{yt}^2$, while the other two cases are the same.

Case 2

$$a=2k^2r^2, b=2k^2pr, d=0, e=0, \eta(y,t)=f_1(y)+f_2(y)t+f_3(t),$$

$$c=\frac{1}{6k^2}(k^4p^2+8k^4qr+k^2-((f_2(y)+f_3'(t))^2-(f_1'(y)+f_2'(y)t)^2)).$$

Case 3

$$a=2k^2r^2, b=0, d=0, e=0, e=2k^2q^2, \eta(y,t)=f_1(y)+f_2(y)t+f_3(t),$$

$$p=0, c=\frac{1}{6k^2}(8k^4qr+k^2-((f_2(y)+f_3'(t))^2-(f_1'(y)+f_2'(y)t)^2)).$$

For simplicity, we take $M=\frac{\sqrt{p^2-4qr}}{2}$, $N=\frac{\sqrt{4qr-p^2}}{2}$, $\zeta=kx+\eta(y,t)$. Substituting the solutions of the generalized Riccati equation into three cases, we obtain

Case 1

When $p^2-4qr>0$, $pq\neq 0$(or $qr\neq 0$),

$$u_1=c-\frac{k^2}{2}[p^2-4M^2\tanh^2(M\zeta)],$$
$$u_2=c-\frac{k^2}{2}[p^2-4M^2\coth^2(M\zeta)],$$
$$u_3=c-\frac{k^2}{2}[p^2-4M^2(\tanh(2M\zeta)\pm i\text{sech}(2M\zeta))^2],$$
$$u_4=c-\frac{k^2}{2}[p^2-4M^2(\coth(2M\zeta)\pm\text{csch}(2M\zeta))^2],$$
$$u_5=c-\frac{k^2}{2}[p^2-M^2(\tanh(\frac{M\zeta}{2})+\coth(\frac{M\zeta}{2}))^2],$$
$$u_6=c-\frac{k^2p^2}{2}+2k^2M^2\frac{(\sqrt{A^2+B^2}-A\cosh(2M\zeta))^2}{(A\sinh(2M\zeta)+B)^2},$$
$$u_7=c-\frac{k^2p^2}{2}+2k^2M^2\frac{(\sqrt{B^2-A^2}+A\sinh(2M\zeta))^2}{(A\cosh(2M\zeta)+B)^2},$$
$$u_8=c+4k^2qr\cosh(M\zeta)\frac{2qr\cosh(M\zeta)+p(2M\sinh(M\zeta)-p\cosh(M\zeta))}{(2M\sinh(M\zeta)-p\cosh(M\zeta))^2},$$
$$u_9=c+4k^2qr\sinh(M\zeta)\frac{2qr\sinh(M\zeta)+p(2M\cosh(M\zeta)-p\sinh(M\zeta))}{(2M\cosh(M\zeta)-p\sinh(M\zeta))^2},$$
$$u_{10}=c+4k^2qr\cosh(2M\zeta)\frac{(2qr-p^2)\cosh(2M\zeta)+p(2M\sinh(2M\zeta)\pm i2M)}{(2M\sinh(2M\zeta)-p\cosh(2M\zeta)\pm i2M)^2},$$
$$u_{11}=c+4k^2qr\sinh(2M\zeta)\frac{(2qr-p^2)\sinh(2M\zeta)+p(2M\cosh(2M\zeta)\pm 2M)}{(2M\cosh(2M\zeta)-p\sinh(2M\zeta)\pm 2M)^2},$$
$$u_{12}=c+8k^2qr\Phi_1(\zeta)\frac{2(2qr-p^2)\Phi_1(\zeta)+p(4M\cosh^2(\frac{M\zeta}{2})-2M)}{(4M\cosh^2(\frac{M\zeta}{2})-2p\Phi_1(\zeta)-2M)^2},$$

where $\Phi_1(\zeta)=\sinh(\frac{M\zeta}{2})\cosh(\frac{M\zeta}{2})$, A and B are two non-zero real constants and satisfy $B^2-A^2>0$.

When $p^2-4qr<0$, $pq\neq 0$(or $qr\neq 0$),

$$u_{13}=c-\frac{k^2}{2}[p^2-4N^2\tan^2(N\zeta)],$$
$$u_{14}=c-\frac{k^2}{2}[p^2-4N^2\cot^2(N\zeta)],$$
$$u_{15}=c-\frac{k^2}{2}[p^2-4N^2(\tan(2N\zeta)\pm\sec(2N\zeta))^2],$$
$$u_{16}=c-\frac{k^2}{2}[p^2-4N^2(\cot(2N\zeta)\pm\csc(2N\zeta))^2],$$
$$u_{17}=c-\frac{k^2}{2}[p^2-N^2(\tan(\frac{N\zeta}{2})-\cot(\frac{N\zeta}{2}))^2],$$
$$u_{18}=c-\frac{k^2p^2}{2}+2k^2N^2\frac{(\sqrt{A^2-B^2}\mp A\cos(2N\zeta))^2}{(A\sin(2N\zeta)+B)^2},$$
$$u_{19}=c-\frac{k^2p^2}{2}+2k^2N^2\frac{(\sqrt{A^2-B^2}\mp A\sin(2N\zeta))^2}{(A\cos(2N\zeta)+B)^2},$$
$$u_{20}=c+4k^2qr\cos(N\zeta)\frac{2qr\cos(N\zeta)-p(2N\sin(N\zeta)+p\cos(N\zeta))}{(2N\sin(N\zeta)+p\cos(N\zeta))^2},$$
$$u_{21}=c+4k^2qr\sin(N\zeta)\frac{2qr\sin(N\zeta)+p(2N\cos(N\zeta)-p\sin(N\zeta))}{(2N\cos(N\zeta)-p\sin(N\zeta))^2},$$

$$u_{22} = c + 4k^2 qr\cos(2N\zeta)\frac{2qr\cos(2N\zeta) - p(2N\sin(2N\zeta) + p\cos(2N\zeta) \pm 2N)}{(2N\sin(2N\zeta) + p\cos(2N\zeta) \pm 2N)^2},$$
$$u_{23} = c + 4k^2 qr\sin(2N\zeta)\frac{2qr\sin(2N\zeta) + p(2N\cos(2N\zeta) - p\sin(2N\zeta) \pm 2N)}{(2N\cos(2N\zeta) - p\sin(2N\zeta) \pm 2N)^2},$$
$$u_{24} = c + 8k^2 qr\Phi_2(\zeta)\frac{2(2qr - p^2)\Phi_2(\zeta) + p(4N\cos^2(\frac{N\zeta}{2}) - 2N)}{(4N\cos^2(\frac{N\zeta}{2}) - 2p\Phi_2(\zeta) - 2N)^2},$$

where $\Phi_2(\zeta) = \sin(\frac{N\zeta}{2})\cos(\frac{N\zeta}{2})$, A and B are two non-zero real constants and satisfy $A^2 - B^2 > 0$.

When $r = 0$, $pq \neq 0$,

$$u_{25} = \frac{1}{6k^2}(k^4p^2 + k^2 - ((f_2(y) + f_3'(t))^2 - (f_1'(y) + f_2'(y)t)^2)) - 2k^2p^2c_1\frac{\cosh(p\zeta) - \sinh(p\zeta)}{(c_1 + \cosh(p\zeta) - \sinh(p\zeta))^2},$$
$$u_{26} = \frac{1}{6k^2}(k^4p^2 + k^2 - ((f_2(y) + f_3'(t))^2 - (f_1'(y) + f_2'(y)t)^2)) - 2k^2p^2c_1\frac{\cosh(p\zeta) + \sinh(p\zeta)}{(c_1 + \cosh(p\zeta) + \sinh(p\zeta))^2}.$$

When $q \neq 0$, $r = p = 0$,

$$u_{27} = \frac{1}{6k^2}(k^2 - ((f_2(y) + f_3'(t))^2 - (f_1'(y) + f_2'(y)t)^2)) + \frac{2k^2q^2}{(c_2 + q\zeta)^2}.$$

Case 2

When $p^2 - 4qr > 0$, $pq \neq 0$(or $qr \neq 0$),

$$u_{28} = c - 4k^2 qr\frac{2Mp\tanh(M\zeta) + p^2 - 2qr}{(2M\tanh(M\zeta) + p)^2},$$
$$u_{29} = c - 4k^2 qr\frac{2Mp\coth M\zeta + p^2 - 2qr}{(2M\coth(M\zeta) + p)^2},$$
$$u_{30} = c - 4k^2 qr\frac{p(2M\tanh(2M\zeta) + p \pm iM\text{sech}(2M\zeta)) - 2qr}{(2M\tanh(2M\zeta) + p \pm iM\text{sech}(2M\zeta))^2},$$
$$u_{31} = c - 4k^2 qr\frac{p(2M\coth(2M\zeta) + p \pm M\text{csch}(2M\zeta)) - 2qr}{(2M\coth(2M\zeta) + p \pm M\text{csch}(2M\zeta))^2},$$
$$u_{32} = c - 8k^2 qr\frac{p(2M\tanh(\frac{M\zeta}{2}) + 2M\coth(\frac{M\zeta}{2}) + 2p) - 4qr}{(2M\tanh(\frac{M\zeta}{2}) + 2M\coth(\frac{M\zeta}{2}) + 2p)^2},$$
$$u_{33} = c - 4k^2 qrF_1(\zeta)\frac{p(2AM\cosh(2M\zeta) + pF_1(\zeta) - 2M\sqrt{A^2 + B^2}) - 2qrF_1(\zeta)}{(2AM\cosh(2M\zeta) + pF_1(\zeta) - 2M\sqrt{A^2 + B^2})^2},$$
$$u_{34} = c - 4k^2 qrF_2(\zeta)\frac{p(2AM\sinh(2M\zeta) + pF_2(\zeta) + 2M\sqrt{B^2 - A^2}) - 2qrF_2(\zeta)}{(2AM\sinh(2M\zeta) + pF_2(\zeta) + 2M\sqrt{B^2 - A^2})^2},$$
$$u_{35} = c - \frac{k^2}{2}[p^2 - M^2\text{csch}^2(\frac{M\zeta}{2})(2\cosh(\frac{M\zeta}{2}) - \text{sech}(\frac{M\zeta}{2}))^2],$$

where $F_1(\zeta) = A\sinh(2M\zeta) + B$, $F_2(\zeta) = (A\cosh(2M\zeta) + B)$,

A and B are two non-zero real constants and satisfy $B^2 - A^2 > 0$.

When $p^2 - 4qr < 0$, $pq \neq 0$(or $qr \neq 0$),

$$u_{36} = c + 4k^2 qr\frac{2Np\tan(N\zeta) - p^2 + 2qr}{(2N\tan(N\zeta) - p)^2},$$
$$u_{37} = c - 4k^2 qr\frac{2Np\cot(N\zeta) + p^2 - 2qr}{(2N\cot(N\zeta) + p)^2},$$
$$u_{38} = c + 4k^2 qr\frac{p(2N\tan(2N\zeta) - p \pm N\sec(2N\zeta)) + 2qr}{(2N\tan(2N\zeta) - p \pm N\sec(2N\zeta))^2},$$
$$u_{39} = c - 4k^2 qr\frac{p(2N\cot(2N\zeta) + p \pm N\csc(2N\zeta)) - 2qr}{(2N\cot(2N\zeta) + p \pm N\csc(2N\zeta))^2},$$

$$u_{40} = c + 8k^2qr\frac{p(2N\tan(\frac{N\zeta}{2}) - 2N\cot(\frac{N\zeta}{2}) - 2p) + 4qr}{(2N\tan(\frac{N\zeta}{2}) - 2N\cot(\frac{N\zeta}{2}) - 2p)^2},$$

$$u_{41} = c - 4k^2qrG_1(\zeta)\frac{p(2AN\cos(2N\zeta) + pG_1(\zeta) \mp 2N\sqrt{A^2 - B^2}) - 2qrG_1(\zeta)}{(2AN\cos(2N\zeta) + pG_1(\zeta) \pm 2N\sqrt{A^2 - B^2})^2},$$

$$u_{42} = c + 4k^2qrG_2(\zeta)\frac{p(2AN\sin(2N\zeta) - pG_2(\zeta) \mp 2N\sqrt{A^2 - B^2}) + 2qrG_2(\zeta)}{(2AN\sin(2N\zeta) - pG_2(\zeta) \pm 2N\sqrt{A^2 - B^2})^2},$$

$$u_{43} = c - \frac{k^2}{2}[p^2 - N^2\csc(\frac{N\zeta}{2})(2\cos(\frac{N\zeta}{2}) - \sec(\frac{N\zeta}{2}))^2],$$

where $G_1(\zeta) = A\sin(2N\zeta) + B$, $G_2(\zeta) = A\cos(2N\zeta) + B$, A and B are two non-zero real constants and satisfy $A^2 - B^2 > 0$.

When $r = 0, pq \neq 0$, the solution is independent of x.

When $q \neq 0, r = p = 0$, the solution is independent of x.

Case 3 ($p = 0$)

When $p^2 - 4qr > 0$, $pq \neq 0$(or $qr \neq 0$),

$$u_{44} = c + 2k^2\frac{M^4\tanh^4(M\zeta) + q^2r^2}{M^2\tanh^2(M\zeta)},$$

$$u_{45} = c + 2k^2\frac{M^4\coth^4(M\zeta) + q^2r^2}{M^2\coth^2(M\zeta)},$$

$$u_{46} = c + 2k^2\frac{M^4(\tanh(2M\zeta) \pm i\,\mathrm{sech}(2M\zeta))^4 + q^2r^2}{M^2(\tanh(2M\zeta) \pm i\,\mathrm{sech}(2M\zeta))^2},$$

$$u_{47} = c + 2k^2\frac{M^4(\coth(2M\zeta) \pm \mathrm{csch}(2M\zeta))^4 + q^2r^2}{M^2(\coth(2M\zeta) \pm \mathrm{csch}(2M\zeta))^2},$$

$$u_{48} = c + k^2\frac{M^4(\tanh(\frac{M\zeta}{2}) + \coth(\frac{M\zeta}{2}))^4 + 16q^2r^2}{2M^2(\tanh(\frac{M\zeta}{2}) + \coth(\frac{M\zeta}{2}))^2},$$

$$u_{49} = c + \frac{k^2(2M\sqrt{A^2 + B^2} - 2AM\cosh(2M\zeta))^2}{2(A\sinh(2M\zeta) + B)^2} + \frac{8k^2r^2q^2(A\sinh(2M\zeta) + B)^2}{(2M\sqrt{A^2 + B^2} - 2AM\cosh(2M\zeta))^2},$$

$$u_{50} = c + \frac{k^2(2M\sqrt{B^2 - A^2} + 2AM\sinh(2M\zeta))^2}{2(A\cosh(2M\zeta) + B)^2} + \frac{8k^2r^2q^2(A\cosh(2M\zeta) + B)^2}{(2M\sqrt{B^2 - A^2} + 2AM\sinh(2M\zeta))^2},$$

$$u_{51} = c + 2k^2\frac{M^4\sinh^4(M\zeta) + \cosh^4(M\zeta)q^2r^2}{M^2\sinh^2(M\zeta)\cosh^2(M\zeta)},$$

$$u_{52} = c + 2k^2\frac{M^4\cosh^4(M\zeta) + \sinh^4(M\zeta)q^2r^2}{M^2\sinh^2(M\zeta)\cosh^2(M\zeta)},$$

$$u_{53} = c + \frac{k^2(2M\sinh(2M\zeta) \pm i2M)^2}{2\cosh^2(2M\zeta)} + \frac{8k^2q^2r^2\cosh^2(2M\zeta)}{(2M\sinh(2M\zeta) \pm i2M)^2},$$

$$u_{54} = c + \frac{k^2(2M\cosh(2M\zeta) \pm 2M)^2}{2\sinh^2(2M\zeta)} + \frac{8k^2q^2r^2\sinh^2(2M\zeta)}{(2M\cosh(2M\zeta) \pm 2M)^2},$$

$$u_{55} = c + \frac{k^2(4M\cosh^2(\frac{M\zeta}{2}) - 2M)^2}{8\sinh^2(\frac{M\zeta}{2})\cosh^2(\frac{M\zeta}{2})} + \frac{32k^2qr\sinh^2(\frac{M\zeta}{2})\cosh^2(\frac{M\zeta}{2})}{(4M\cosh^2(\frac{M\zeta}{2}) - 2M)^2},$$

where A and B are two non-zero real constants and satisfy $B^2 - A^2 > 0$.

When $p^2 - 4qr < 0$, $pq \neq 0$(or $qr \neq 0$),

$$u_{56} = c + 2k^2\frac{N^4\tan^4(N\zeta) + q^2r^2}{N^2\tan(N\zeta)},$$

$$u_{57} = c + 2k^2 \frac{N^4\cot^4(N\zeta) + q^2r^2}{N^2\cot(N\zeta)},$$
$$u_{58} = c + 2k^2 \frac{N^4(\tan(2N\zeta) \pm \sec(2N\zeta))^4 + q^2r^2}{N^2(\tan(2N\zeta) \pm \sec(2N\zeta))^2},$$
$$u_{59} = c + 2k^2 \frac{N^4(\cot(2N\zeta) \pm \csc(2N\zeta))^4 + q^2r^2}{N^2(\cot(2N\zeta) \pm \csc(2N\zeta))^2},$$
$$u_{60} = c + k^2 \frac{N^4(\tan(\frac{N\zeta}{2}) - \cot(\frac{N\zeta}{2}))^4 + 16q^2r^2}{2N^2(\tan(\frac{N\zeta}{2}) - \cot(\frac{N\zeta}{2}))^2},$$
$$u_{61} = c + \frac{2k^2(\pm N\sqrt{A^2 - B^2} - AN\cos(2N\zeta))^2}{(A\sin(2N\zeta) + B)^2} + \frac{2k^2r^2q^2(A\sin(2N\zeta) + B)^2}{(\pm N\sqrt{A^2 - B^2} - AN\cos(2N\zeta))^2},$$
$$u_{62} = c + \frac{2k^2(\pm N\sqrt{A^2 - B^2} + AN\sin(2N\zeta))^2}{(A\cos(2N\zeta) + B)^2} + \frac{2k^2r^2q^2(A\cos(2N\zeta) + B)^2}{(\pm N\sqrt{A^2 - B^2} + AN\sin(2N\zeta))^2},$$
$$u_{63} = c + 2k^2 \frac{N^4\sin^4(N\zeta) + \cos^4(N\zeta)q^2r^2}{N^2\sin^2(N\zeta)\cos^2(N\zeta)},$$
$$u_{64} = c + 2k^2 \frac{N^4\cos^4(N\zeta) + \sin^4(N\zeta)q^2r^2}{N^2\sin^2(N\zeta)\cos^2(N\zeta)},$$
$$u_{65} = c + \frac{k^2(2N\sin(2N\zeta) \pm 2N)^2}{2\cos^2(2N\zeta)} + \frac{8k^2q^2r^2\cos^2(2N\zeta)}{(2N\sin(2N\zeta) \pm 2N)^2},$$
$$u_{66} = c + \frac{k^2(2N\cos(2N\zeta) \pm 2N)^2}{2\sin^2(2N\zeta)} + \frac{8k^2q^2r^2\sin^2(2N\zeta)}{(2N\cos(2N\zeta) \pm 2N)^2},$$
$$u_{67} = c + \frac{k^2(4N\cos^2(\frac{N\zeta}{2}) - 2N)^2}{8\sin^2(\frac{N\zeta}{2})\cos^2(\frac{N\zeta}{2})} + \frac{32k^2qr\sin^2(\frac{N\zeta}{2})\cos^2(\frac{N\zeta}{2})}{(4N\cos^2(\frac{N\zeta}{2}) - 2N)^2},$$

where A and B are two non-zero real constants and satisfy $A^2 - B^2 > 0$.

When $r = 0$, $pq \neq 0$, but $p = 0$, the solution is independent of x.

3.3. Property Analysis of the Solution

The solutions obtained in this section all include arbitrary differentiable functions $f_1(y), f_2(y)$ and $f_3(t)$, which may give the prediction of physical phenomena with given parameters. According to the expressions of solutions in Case 1, these non-traveling wave solutions can be regarded as kink type, periodic type and singular solitary wave type. Below, we take $z = kx$, $v = y + t$ and give the numerical simulation for the solutions of Case 1.

Figures 14 and 15, respectively, show that when $f_1(y) = y, f_2(y) = 0$, $f_3(t) = t$, $\zeta = kx + y + t = z + v$, the image of u_{25} shows a linear trajectory in a certain direction; when $f_1(y) = y^2$, $f_2(y) = 2y$, $f_3(t) = t^2$, $\zeta = kx + (y+t)^2 = z + v^2$, the image of u_{25} shows a parabolic trajectory in a certain direction. If $c_1 = 1, p = 1$, the denominator $(1 + \cosh(\zeta) - \sinh(\zeta))^2$ of u_{25} is always not equal to zero; then, no blow-up occurs, so the images are of all solitary wave. In Figures 16 and 17, u_{20} mainly includes sine functions and cosine functions. If $N = 1$, $p = 2$, the denominator $(2\sin(\zeta) + 2\cos(\zeta))^2$ of u_{20} can be equal to zero, which leads to singularity. However, by comparing $\zeta = z + v$ with $\zeta = z + v^2$ as an independent variable of trigonometric function, we can intuitively find that the sharps in Figure 17 are multiplied more than those in Figure 16. From the properties of trigonometric function, it can be seen that the images are periodic type. Moreover, each trigonometric function solution in Case 1 is a periodic singular solitary wave solution.

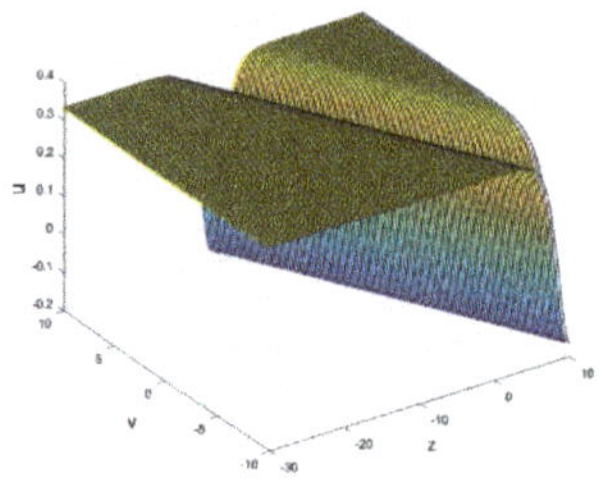

Figure 14. Linear solitary wave solution $u_{25}(\zeta)$ as $k = 1, p = 1, q = 1, r = 0, f_1(y) = y$, $f_2(y) = 0, f_3(t) = t, c_1 = 1, c = \frac{1}{3}$.

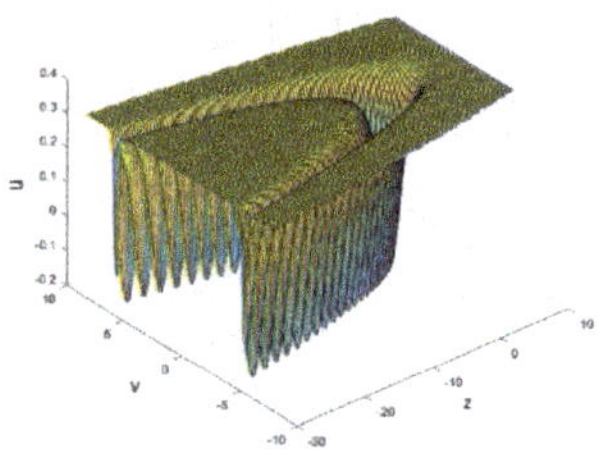

Figure 15. Parabolic solitary wave solution $u_{25}(\zeta)$ as $k = 1, p = 1, q = 1, r = 0, f_1(y) = y^2, f_2(y) = 2y, f_3(t) = t^2, c_1 = 1, c = \frac{1}{3}$.

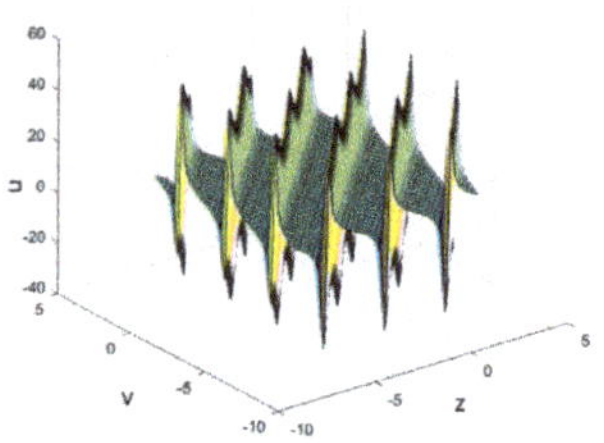

Figure 16. Parabolic and periodic singular wave solution $u_{20}(\zeta)$ as $k = 1, p = 2, q = 2, r = 2$, $N = 1, f_1(y) = y, f_2(y) = 0, f_3(t) = t, c = \frac{7}{2}$.

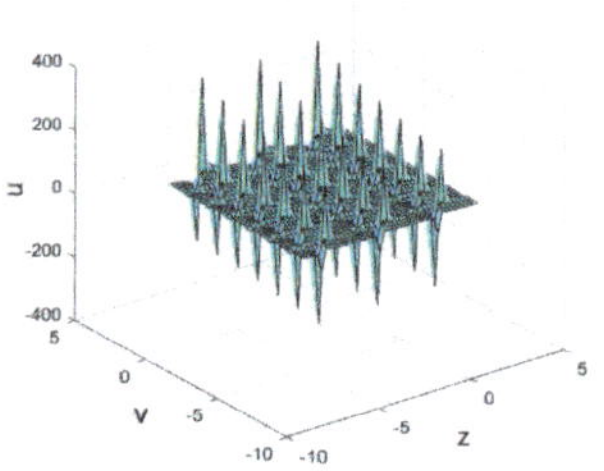

Figure 17. Parabolic and periodic singular wave solution $u_{20}(\zeta)$ as $k = 1, p = 2, q = 2, r = 2$, $N = 1, f_1(y) = y^2, f_2(y) = 2y, f_3(t) = t^2, c = \frac{7}{2}$.

4. Conclusions

In this paper, the exact solutions of the (2+1)-dimension Boussinesq equation are obtained by using the extended $(\frac{G'}{G})$ method. For hyperbolic function solutions, such as $u_{3,4}$, the denominator can always obtain zero if $d = 0$, and the blow-up phenomenon cannot be avoided. For the trigonometric function solutions, periodic blow-up will occur because of the property and periodicity of the tangent function. For rational function solutions, the solution $u_{3,3}$ contains both positive and negative power terms $(d + H(\xi))$, the image of solution $u_{3,3}$ is therefore like a superposition of the image of solution $u_{1,3}$ and $u_{2,3}$. Moreover, the rational function of ξ always appears as the denominator, which will lead to blow-up. The formation of rogue waves is reflected by those solutions.

The extended $(\frac{G'}{G})$ method is to add a coefficient d to each item in the $(\frac{G'}{G})$-expansion, so that the solution becomes the form of $(d + H(\xi))$. In the fourth hyperbolic function solution of Group 2, it is observed that the smoothness of the image can be controlled by d.

The improved tanh function method is also applied to obtain many non-traveling wave solutions, including kink solutions, periodic solitary wave solutions, and singular solitary wave solutions. Numerical simulation and analysis enables us to better explain the rogue wave phenomenon in natural phenomena. The image of the solution changes greatly under the influence of differentiable function $f_1(y)$, $f_2(y)$ and $f_3(t)$. For example, if $f_1(y) = y^2$, $f_2(y) = 2y$, $f_3(t) = t^2$, the image of the solution shows a parabolic trajectory in a certain direction. If we extend these arbitrary differentiable functions, considering trigonometric functions, hyperbolic trigonometric functions, exponential functions, and so on, the equation will have more abundant solutions.

We also find that $u_{1,1}$ and u_1 can be expressed as $k_1 + k_2\tanh^2(k_3\phi + k_4)$ when $B = -2dM$ and $\phi(x,y,t) = \varphi(kx + \eta(y,t))$ is a linear transformation satisfing $\eta_{yy}^2 = \eta_{tt}^2 = \eta_{yt}^2$. Observing the solutions obtained by those two methods, we find that in the extended $(\frac{G'}{G})$ method, the $B = -2dM$ is satisfied. In the improved tanh function method, if $\varphi(kx + \eta(y,t))$ is a linear transformation of x, y and t, that satisfies the condition $\eta_{yy}^2 = \eta_{tt}^2 = \eta_{yt}^2$, which is recorded as $\phi(x,y,t)$. $u_{1,1}$ and u_1 can be simply expressed as $k_1 + k_2\tanh^2(k_3\phi + k_4)$, where $k_i (i = 1,2,3,4)$ are constants. Moreover, $u_{1,2}$ and u_{13} can be simply expressed as $k_5 + k_6\tan^2(k_7\phi + k_8)$, $u_{1,3}$ and u_{27} can be expressed as $k_9 + \frac{k_{10}}{(k_{11}\phi + k_{12})^2}$. Here, we only list the solutions of Group 1 and Case 1 obtained by those two methods. These phenomena suggest that there may be some relationships between solutions obtained by different methods for the same equation.

Author Contributions: Writing—orginal draft preparation, C.G. and L.G.; writing—review and editing, Y.G. and D.L. All authors have read and agreed to the published version of the manuscript.

Funding: This work is supported by the National Natural Science Foundation of China (Nos. 11771444 and 11861013) and the Fundamental Research Funds for the Central Universities 2022YJSLX01.

Institutional Review Board Statement: Not applicable.

Informed Consent Statement: Not applicable.

Data Availability Statement: Not applicable.

Conflicts of Interest: The author declares no conflict of interest.

References

1. Ghanbari, B. Employing Hirota's bilinear form to find novel lump waves solutions to an important nonlinear model in fluid mechanics. *Results Phys.* **2021**, *29*, 104689. [CrossRef]
2. Eltayebh, H.; Mesloub, S. Application of Multi-Dimensional of Conformable Sumudu Decomposition Method for Solving Conformable Singular Fractional Coupled Burger's Equation. *Acta Math. Sci.* **2021**, *41*, 1679–1698. [CrossRef]
3. Wang, Q.; Li, L.Z. Painlevé analysis, Lie symmetry and exact solutions to the generalized time dependent coefficients Gardner equation. *J. Shandong Univ. Sci.* **2019**, *54*, 37–44.
4. Guner, O. New exact solutions for the seventh-order time fractional Sawada-Kotera-Ito equation via various methods. *Waves Random Complex Media* **2020**, *30*, 441–457. [CrossRef]
5. Wang, M.L.; Li, X.Z.; Zhang, J.L. The (G′/G)-expansion method and travelling wave solutions of nonlinear evolution equations in mathematical physics. *Phys. Lett. A* **2008**, *372*, 417–423. [CrossRef]
6. Xie, F.D.; Zhang, Y.; Lü, Z.S. Symbolic computation in non-linear evolution equation: application to (3+1)-dimensional Kabomtsev-Petviashvili equation. *Chaos Solitons Fractals* **2005**, *24*, 257–263. [CrossRef]
7. Du, B.R; Zhu, L.S. The application of Boussinesq Equations in the Research on Changes in Wave Induced Set-up and Current after Completion of Engineering. *Guangdong Shipbuild.* **2012**, *31*, 47–51.

8. Song, M.; Shao, S.G.; Exact solitary wave solutions of the generalized (2+1)dimensional Boussinesq equation. *Appl. Math. Comput.* **2010**, *7*, 3557–3563. [CrossRef]
9. Zhao, Y.M.; Yang, Y.J.; Jiang, Y. Application of the improved (G′/G)-expansion method to exact solutions for generalized (2+1)-dimensional Boussinesq equation. *Pure Appl. Math.* **2012**, *28*, 176–180.
10. Yang, J.; Feng, Q.J. The Solitary Wave Solutions for Generalized (2+1)-dimensional Boussinesq Equation. *Math. Pract. Theory* **2017**, *47*, 230–237.
11. Zeng, X.; Zhang, H.Q. Backlund transformation and exact solutions for (2 +1)-dimensional Boussinesq equation. *Acta Phys. Sin.* **2005**, *54*, 1476–1480. [CrossRef]
12. Wang, J.M. On Triply Periodic Wave Solutions for (2+1)-Dimensional Boussinesq Equation. *Commun. Theor. Phys.* **2012**, *57*, 563–567. [CrossRef]
13. Liu, Y.K.; Li, B.; An, H.L. General high-order breathers, lumps in the (2+1)-dimensional Boussinesq equation. *Nonlinear Dyn.* **2018**, *92*, 2061–2076. [CrossRef]
14. Wang, W.L.; Feng, S.Q.; Guo, L.N. The Exact Solutions of (2+1)-dimensional Boussinesq Equation. *J. Neijiang Norm. Univ.* **2011**, *26*, 21–23.
15. Li, Z.Q.; Liu, H.Z. Generalized Solution of (2+1)-dimensional Boussinesq Equation. *J. Binzhou Univ.* **2018**, *34*, 38–41.
16. Jiao, X.Y. Truncated series solutions to the (2+1)-dimensional perturbed Boussinesq equation by using the approximate symmetry method. *Chin. Phys. B* **2018**, *27*, 127–133. [CrossRef]
17. Yin, J.Y. Extended expansion method for (G′/G) and new exact solutions of Zakharov equations. *Acta Phys. Sin.* **2013**, *62*, 1–5.
18. Liao, G.J.; Huang, L.W.; Chen, X.; Guo, Y.F. Using extended expansion method to obtain exact solutions of (2+1)-dimensional breaking soliton equation. *J. Guangxi Univ. Sci. Technol.* **2019**, *30*, 110–117.
19. Xu,Y.Q.; Zheng, X.X.; Xin, J. Abundant new non-travelling wave solutions for the (3+1)-dimensional Boiti-Leon-Manna-Pempinelli equation. *J. Appl. Anal. Comput.* **2021**, *11*, 2052–2069.
20. Zhang, S.; Xia, T.C. Symbolic Computation and New Families of Exact Non-travelling Wave Solutions of (2+1)-dimensional Broer-Kaup Equation. *Commun. Theor. Phys.* **2006**, *45*, 985–990.
21. Nather, H.; Abdullah, F.A. New generalized and improved (G′/G)-expansion method for nonlinear evolution equations in mathematical physics. *J. Egypt. Math. Soc.* **2014**, *22*, 390-395. [CrossRef]

mathematics

MDPI

Article

On the Fractional-Order Complex Cosine Map: Fractal Analysis, Julia Set Control and Synchronization

A. A. Elsadany [1,2,*], A. Aldurayhim [1], H. N. Agiza [3], Amr Elsonbaty [1,4]

1 Department of Mathematics, Faculty of Science and Humanities in Al-Kharj, Prince Sattam bin Abdulaziz University, Al-Kharj 11942, Saudi Arabia
2 Basic Science Department, Faculty of Computers and Information, Suez Canal University, New Campus, Ismailia 41522, Egypt
3 Department of Mathematics, Faculty of Science, Mansoura University, Mansoura 35516, Egypt
4 Mathematics & Engineering Physics Department, Faculty of Engineering, Mansoura University, Mansoura 35516, Egypt
* Correspondence: aelsadany1@yahoo.com

Abstract: In this paper, we introduce a generalized complex discrete fractional-order cosine map. Dynamical analysis of the proposed complex fractional order map is examined. The existence and stability characteristics of the map's fixed points are explored. The existence of fractal Mandelbrot sets and Julia sets, as well as their fractal properties, are examined in detail. Several detailed simulations illustrate the effects of the fractional-order parameter, as well as the values of the map constant and exponent. In addition, complex domain controllers are constructed to control Julia sets produced by the proposed map or to achieve synchronization of two Julia sets in master/slave configurations. We identify the more realistic synchronization scenario in which the master map's parameter values are unknown. Finally, numerical simulations are employed to confirm theoretical results obtained throughout the work.

Keywords: complex cosine map; discrete fractional; fractal sets; Julia set control; Julia sets synchronization

MSC: 39A30; 40A05; 92D25; 92C50

1. Introduction

Explaining the behavior of complex fractional-order maps is a huge challenge [1–3]. The complex maps that have been discovered to have fascinating and insightful constructs in geometry are familiar as Julia and Mandelbrot fractal sets [4–10]. Dimensions of these sets are known to be fractal and have a variety of intriguing applications, including electric fields, electromagnetic fields, and secure communication [11–15]. The fractional generalized Hénon map's chaotic behavior was looked at in [16], whereas the presence of chaotic behaviour in the fractional discrete memristor system was shown in [17].

In order to understand the dynamics of spatiotemporal systems in the presence of memory, coupled fractional maps can be explored. Power-law memory systems can be found in a variety of branches of physics, from electromagnetic waves in dielectric media to adaptation through biological systems [18,19]. Discrete-time systems exhibiting unusual complexity characteristics, such as hidden attractors [20], coexisting multiple attractors [21], and hyperchaotic behavior, are also of great interest. In [22], the chaos, 0–1 test, C_0 complexity, entropy, and control of discrete fractional Duffing systems are examined. In [23], it is addressed how fractional-order discrete-time chaotic systems can be synchronized and used for secure communication. In [24], a strategy for utilizing chaotic behavior in fractional maps to be applied for image encryption was demonstrated as a recent example of fractional systems being applied to encryption. Researchers used fractional-order maps to investigate image encryption in [25,26]. Scholars used a pseudo-random number generator [27] to help them investigate the links between multiple fractional chaotic systems.

A fractal is a geometric pattern that is self-similar at all scales and has a non-integer constant Hausdorff dimension [28]. Since porous media, aquifers, turbulence, and other media commonly display fractal properties, fractal theory, a compact part of nonlinear physics, has considerable applicability in these areas [29,30]. In contrast, a fractional operator is an expression of a fractional differentiation, since it describes the memory and hereditary aspects of the phenomenon [31]. Complex systems are better modeled by fractional-order equations than by integer order equations. Fractional-order systems are used in various fields of engineering and science, including electromagnetics, viscoelasticity, fluid mechanics, electrochemistry, biological population models, optics, and signal processing [32–35]. Memory is a key characteristic of fractional-order differential and discrete equations. Fractional-order differentiation of fractal geometry sets has limited results [36]. Fractional-order Mandelbrot sets and Julia sets have rarely been discussed [37,38]. There are several complicated iterative equations that are related to the complex maps and the related Julia set phenomena. Julia set control is one method for controlling and synchronizing the fractal properties of a complicated system. Thus, applying fractional calculus to deterministic non-linear fractals such as Julia and Mandelbrot sets formed by fractional maps yields an appealing and novel theory with applications in image and data compression, computer graphics, and encrypted communication. Consequently, the purpose of this paper is to investigate this challenging task involving fractals and fractional calculus, including theoretical and numerical features, as well as control and synchronization based on the complex dynamics of a proposed fractional complex cosine map.

The purpose of this research is to investigate nonlinear dynamics and fractal features of discrete fractional complex cosine maps that have not yet been examined in the literature. According to the knowledge of the authors, this is the first attempt to introduce this complex discrete fractional cosine map. The control and synchronization of fractal sets in integer order complex maps is a very recent topic of research in the science of nonlinear dynamics. In this paper, we investigate the problem of controlling and synchronizing discrete-time fractional complex maps-based fractal sets. This paper's primary purpose is an extensive study into the complexity and dynamics of the discrete fractional complex cosine map. The existence of several periodic and chaotic attractors is highlighted by means of bifurcation diagrams, maximal Lyapunov exponents, and the 0–1 test.

The structure of this paper is as follows: in Section 2, mathematical basics are explained; in Section 3, the proposed discrete fractional complex cosine map's mathematical model is shown; Section 4 looks at how the proposed map controls and synchronizes Julia sets; and Section 5 contains the conclusion and final discussion.

2. Mathematical Basics

In this section, we introduce some preliminaries about fractional-order difference calculus, as follows.

Definition 1 (See [28]). *Let the order $\alpha > 0$, $\alpha \notin \mathbb{N}$, the start point $k \in \mathbb{R}$, $t \in \mathbb{N}_{k+m-\alpha}$, and $m = [\alpha] + 1$. Then the following α-order Caputo-like left delta difference of $F(t)$ is written as follows:*

$$^{C}\Delta_{k}^{\alpha}F(t) := \frac{1}{\Gamma(m-\alpha)} \sum_{s=k}^{t-(m-\alpha)} (t-\sigma(s))^{(m-\alpha-1)} \Delta_{s}^{m}F(s), \tag{1}$$

where $\sigma(s) = s+1$ and $t^{(\alpha)} = \frac{\Gamma(t+1)}{\Gamma(t+1-\alpha)}$.

From Refs. [39–41], we can directly obtain the following Theorem 1.

Theorem 1. *For the following nonlinear system with the α-order Caputo-like left delta difference calculus:*

$$\begin{cases} {}^{C}\Delta_k^{\alpha} X(t) = F(t+\alpha-1, X(t+\alpha-1)), \\ \Delta^j X(k) = X_j, \quad j = 0, \ldots, n-1, \quad n = [\alpha]+1. \end{cases} \tag{2}$$

The equivalent system of system (2) is:

$$X(t) = X_0(t) + \frac{1}{\Gamma(\alpha)} \sum_{s=k+n-\alpha}^{t-\alpha} (t-\sigma(s))^{(\alpha-1)} F(s+\alpha-1, X(s+\alpha-1)), \quad t \in \mathbb{N}_{k+n}, \tag{3}$$

where

$$X_0(t) = \sum_{j=0}^{n-1} \frac{(t-k)^{(j)}}{\Gamma(j+1)} \Delta^j X(k).$$

From Theorem 1, we can directly obtain the following theorem.

Theorem 2. *If the start point $k = 0$, we can simplify system (2) as*

$$X(n) = X(0) + \frac{1}{\Gamma(\alpha)} \sum_{j=1}^{n} \frac{\Gamma(n-j+\alpha)}{\Gamma(n-j+1)} F(X(j-1)), \quad n \in \mathbb{N}. \tag{4}$$

For an N dimensional nonlinear system (2) with fractional-order $\alpha \in (0,1)$ and fixed point $\overline{X}$, if $X(t) = (X_1(t), X_2(t), \cdots, X_N(t))^T$ and $F(t) = (F_1(t), F_2(t), \cdots, F_N(t))^T$ are continuously differentiable at $\overline{X}$, and its Jacobian matrix has the following form:

$$J(\overline{X}) = \frac{\partial f(X)}{\partial X}\bigg|_{X=\overline{X}} = \begin{pmatrix} \frac{\partial F_1(\overline{X})}{\partial X_1} & \frac{\partial F_1(\overline{X})}{\partial X_2} & \cdots & \frac{\partial F_1(\overline{X})}{\partial X_n} \\ \frac{\partial F_2(\overline{X})}{\partial X_1} & \frac{\partial F_2(\overline{X})}{\partial X_2} & \cdots & \frac{\partial F_2(\overline{X})}{\partial X_n} \\ \vdots & \vdots & \ddots & \vdots \\ \frac{\partial F_n(\overline{X})}{\partial X_1} & \frac{\partial F_n(\overline{X})}{\partial X_2} & \cdots & \frac{\partial F_n(\overline{X})}{\partial X_n} \end{pmatrix},$$

then we can obtain the following theorem by using the linearization theorem.

Theorem 3 (See [39,40]). *The N-dimensional system (2) is locally asymptotically stable if all eigenvalues $\lambda_i, i = 1, 2, \cdots N$ of $J(\overline{X})$ satisfy*

$$\lambda_i \in \left\{ z \in \mathbb{C} : |z| < \left(2\cos\frac{|Argz| - \pi}{2-\alpha}\right)^{\alpha} \text{ and } |Argz| > \frac{\alpha\pi}{2} \right\}, \tag{5}$$

where the symbol Argz means the argument of the complex value z.

3. The Discrete Fractional-Order Complex Cosine Map

We propose a new discrete fractional cosine map which appears as this:

$${}^{C}\Delta_a^{\alpha} z(t) = \cos[z(t+\alpha-1)^p + q], \tag{6}$$

where z and $q \in \mathbb{C}$, whereas q takes positive real values greater than or equal to one. The fixed points of the discrete fractional map (6) can be obtained by solving

$$\cos[z^{*^p} + q] = 0,$$

which results in different scenarios for fixed points depending on the value of p as follows:

(1) For $p = 1$, the fixed point is $z^* = (2m+1)\frac{\pi}{2} - q$, where $m \in \mathbb{Z}$.

(2) For $p = 2$, the fixed point is $z^* = [((2m+1)\frac{\pi}{2} - q_r)^2 + q_i{}^2]^{\frac{1}{4}}[\cos(\frac{\theta^*}{2}) + i\sin(\frac{\theta^*}{2})]$, $[((2m+1)\frac{\pi}{2} - q_r)^2 + q_i{}^2]^{\frac{1}{4}}[\cos(\frac{\theta^*+2\pi}{2}) + i\sin(\frac{\theta^*+2\pi}{2})]$, where q is assumed in the form $q = q_r + iq_i$ and θ^* is the principal argument of $(2m+1)\frac{\pi}{2} - q_r - iq_i$.

(3) For $p = 3$, the fixed point is $z^* = [((2m+1)\frac{\pi}{2} - q_r)^2 + q_i{}^2]^{\frac{1}{6}}[\cos(\frac{\theta^*}{3}) + i\sin(\frac{\theta^*}{3})]$, $[((2m+1)\frac{\pi}{2} - q_r)^2 + q_i{}^2]^{\frac{1}{6}}[\cos(\frac{\theta^*+2\pi}{3}) + i\sin(\frac{\theta^*+2\pi}{3})]$ and $[((2m+1)\frac{\pi}{2} - q_r)^2 + q_i{}^2]^{\frac{1}{4}}$ $[\cos(\frac{\theta^*+4\pi}{3}) + i\sin(\frac{\theta^*+4\pi}{3})]$.

(4) In a general case for any value of p, the fixed point is $z^* = \eta^{\frac{1}{p}}[\cos(\frac{\theta^*+2k\pi}{p}) + i\sin(\frac{\theta^*+2k\pi}{p})]$, $\eta = [((2m+1)\frac{\pi}{2} - q_r)^2 + q_i{}^2]^{\frac{1}{2}}, k \in \mathbb{Z}$.

Next, certain analytical results on the asymptotic stability of complex fractional map fixed points (6) are provided.

3.1. Stability Analysis of Fixed Points

Theorem 4. *The fractional complex cosine map (6) has a locally asymptotically stable fixed point z^* if and only if:*

$$\left|(-1)^{m+1}pz^{*^{p-1}}\right| < (2\cos\frac{Arg((-1)^{m+1}pz^{*^{p-1}}) - \pi}{2-\alpha})^{\alpha}, \ \left|Arg((-1)^{m+1}pz^{*^{p-1}})\right| > \frac{\alpha\pi}{2}. \tag{7}$$

Proof. Let $\delta(t) = z(t) - z^*$ and consider the following linearized map derived from Equation (6):

$$\begin{aligned} {}^C\Delta_a^\alpha\delta(t) &= -pz^{*^{p-1}}\sin[z^{*^p} + q]\delta(t+\alpha-1), \\ &= (-1)^{m+1}pz^{*^{p-1}}\delta(t+\alpha-1), \\ &= \lambda\delta(t+\alpha-1). \end{aligned} \tag{8}$$

The real and imaginary parts of (8) are separated as follows

$${}^C\Delta_a^\alpha\delta_r(t) + i{}^C\Delta_a^\alpha\delta_i(t) = (\lambda_r + i\lambda_i)(\delta_r(t+\alpha-1) + i\delta_i(t+\alpha-1)),$$

and hence the following two dimensional discrete fractional system is obtained

$$\begin{aligned} {}^C\Delta_a^\alpha\delta_r(t) &= \lambda_r\delta_r(t+\alpha-1) - \lambda_i\delta_i(t+\alpha-1), \\ {}^C\Delta_a^\alpha\delta_i(t) &= \lambda_i\delta_r(t+\alpha-1) + \lambda_r\delta_i(t+\alpha-1). \end{aligned}$$

The above system can be expressed in the form

$$\begin{pmatrix} {}^C\Delta_a^\alpha\delta_r(t) \\ {}^C\Delta_a^\alpha\delta_i(t) \end{pmatrix} = \begin{pmatrix} \lambda_r & -\lambda_i \\ \lambda_i & \lambda_r \end{pmatrix}\begin{pmatrix} \delta_r(t+\alpha-1) \\ \delta_i(t+\alpha-1) \end{pmatrix}, \tag{9}$$

where the eigenvalues of the 2×2 coefficients matrix is found to be $\Lambda = \lambda_r \pm \mathrm{i}\lambda_i = \lambda, \bar{\lambda}$.

Let

$$B = \begin{pmatrix} \lambda_r & -\lambda_i \\ \lambda_i & \lambda_r \end{pmatrix},$$

with $tr(B) = 2\lambda_r$ and $\det(B) = \lambda_r^2 + \lambda_i^2 > 0$, then the origin of (9) satisfies the following conditions for asymptotic stability:

$$\sqrt{\lambda_r^2 + \lambda_i^2} < (2\cos\frac{\left|\cot^{-1}(\frac{\lambda_r}{\lambda_i})\right| - \pi}{2-\alpha})^{\alpha}, \ \left|\cot^{-1}(\frac{\lambda_r}{\lambda_i})\right| > \frac{\alpha\pi}{2}.$$

Equivalently,

$$\left|(-1)^{m+1}pz^{*^{p-1}}\right| < (2\cos\frac{\left|Arg((-1)^{m+1}pz^{*^{p-1}})\right|-\pi}{2-\alpha})^{\alpha},\ \left|Arg((-1)^{m+1}pz^{*^{p-1}})\right| > \frac{\alpha\pi}{2}.$$

In particular, satisfying the above conditions implies that $\|\delta(t)\| = O(t^{-\alpha})$ as $t \to \infty$, i.e., the solutions δ_r and δ_i algebraically decay to zero in the way that z^* is locally asymptotically stable for the fractional complex map (6). □

Corollary 1. *For $p = 1$ and $m = 0$, the fixed point $z^* = \frac{\pi}{2} - q$ is locally asymptotically stable when $0 < \alpha \leq 1$.*

Proof. For $p = 1$ and $m = 0$, we obtain $(-1)^{m+1}pz^{*^{p-1}} = -1$, and so $\left|Arg((-1)^{m+1}pz^{*^{p-1}})\right| = \pi$. Thus the conditions (7) reduce to

$$1 < 2^{\alpha},\ \pi > \frac{\alpha\pi}{2},$$

which are satisfied at $0 < \alpha \leq 1$. □

Corollary 2. *For $p = 2$ and $m = 0$, the fixed points $z^* = \left|\frac{\pi}{2} - q\right|^{\frac{1}{2}}e^{i\frac{\theta^*}{2}}$ and $\left|\frac{\pi}{2} - q\right|^{\frac{1}{2}}e^{i\frac{\theta^*+2\pi}{2}}$ are locally asymptotically stable when*

$$\left|\frac{\pi}{2} - q\right|^{\frac{1}{2}} < 2^{\alpha-1}(\cos\frac{\left|\frac{\theta^*}{2}+\pi\right|-\pi}{2-\alpha})^{\alpha},\ \left|\frac{\theta^*}{2}+\pi\right| > \frac{\alpha\pi}{2},$$

and

$$\left|\frac{\pi}{2} - q\right|^{\frac{1}{2}} < 2^{\alpha-1}(\cos\frac{\left|\frac{\theta^*}{2}+2\pi\right|-\pi}{2-\alpha})^{\alpha},\ \left|\frac{\theta^*}{2}+2\pi\right| > \frac{\alpha\pi}{2}.$$

Proof. For $p = 2$ and $m = 0$, we obtain $(-1)^{m+1}pz^{*^{p-1}} = 2\left|\frac{\pi}{2} - q\right|^{\frac{1}{2}}e^{i(\frac{\theta^*}{2}+\pi)}, 2\left|\frac{\pi}{2} - q\right|^{\frac{1}{2}}e^{i(\frac{\theta^*}{2}+2\pi)}$ and hence $\left|Arg((-1)^{m+1}pz^{*^{p-1}})\right| = \left|\frac{\theta^*}{2}+\pi\right|, \left|\frac{\theta^*}{2}+2\pi\right|$, for the two fixed points, respectively. Thus the conditions (7) reduce to

$$2\left|\frac{\pi}{2} - q\right|^{\frac{1}{2}} < (2\cos\frac{\left|\frac{\theta^*}{2}+\pi\right|-\pi}{2-\alpha})^{\alpha},\ \left|\frac{\theta^*}{2}+\pi\right| > \frac{\alpha\pi}{2},$$

for the first fixed point and for the second fixed point it follows that

$$2\left|\frac{\pi}{2} - q\right|^{\frac{1}{2}} < (2\cos\frac{\left|\frac{\theta^*}{2}+2\pi\right|-\pi}{2-\alpha})^{\alpha},\ \left|\frac{\theta^*}{2}+2\pi\right| > \frac{\alpha\pi}{2}.$$

□

The previous theoretical results are validated using numerical simulations. In the first case, let $p = 1, \alpha = 0.95, q = 2 - 1.5i$ and $m = 0$. Then the fixed point $z^* = -0.429204 + 1.5i$ is locally asymptotically stable according to Corollary 2, see Figure 1a,b. Now, consider the second case where $p = 2, \alpha = 0.85, q = 1.2 - 0.2i$ and $m = 0$, and the fixed points are $0.629322 + 0.158901i$ and $-0.629322 - 0.158901i$. The conditions for asymptotic stability indicate that the first fixed point $0.629322 + 0.158901i$ is asymptotically stable whereas the second one is unstable, as shown in Figure 1c,d. In the third case, taking $p = 2, \alpha = 0.7,$

$q = 1 + 0.3i$ and $m = 0$, the fixed points are found to be $0.7796 - 0.1924i$ and $-0.779624 + 0.1924i$. Stability conditions reveal that the first fixed point is asymptotically stable while the second one is unstable. Numerical simulations in Figure 1e,f verify these predictions.

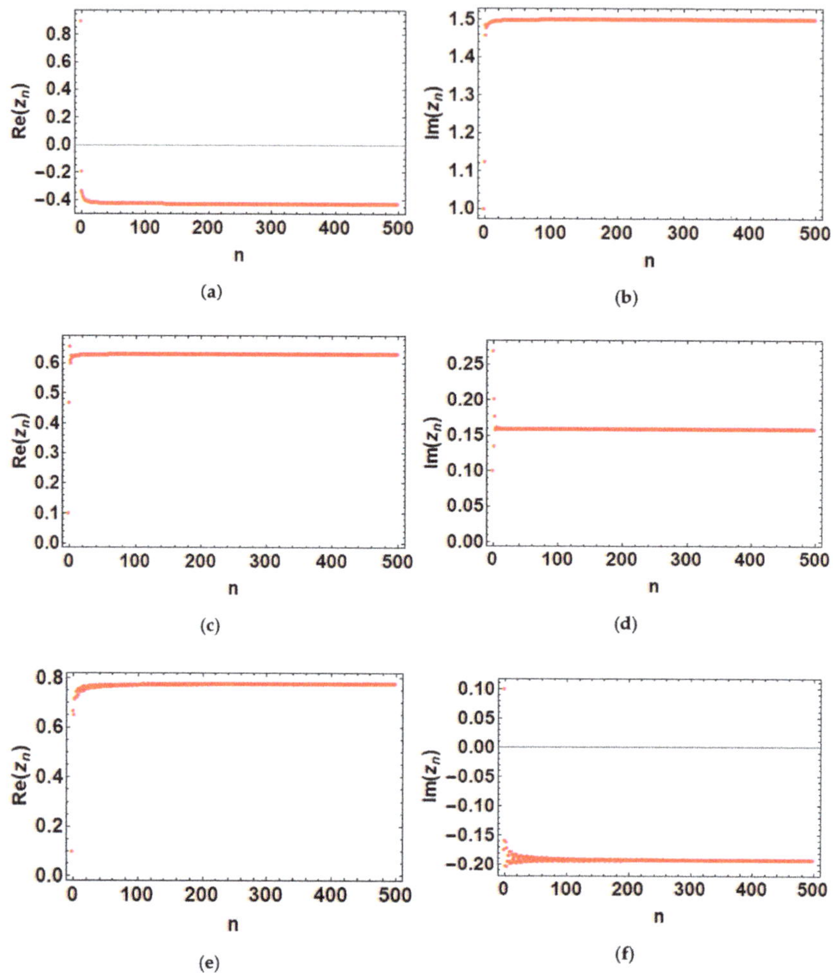

Figure 1. The time series solutions of the generalized fractional complex cosine map at (**a**,**b**) $p = 1$, $\alpha = 0.95$, $q = 2 - 1.5i$, (**c**,**d**) $p = 2$, $\alpha = 0.85$, $q = 1.2 - 0.2i$, and (**e**,**f**) $p = 2$, $\alpha = 0.7$, $q = 1 + 0.3i$.

3.2. The Fractional Cosine Map Generates Fractal Sets

We extend the ideas of Julia and Mandelbrot fractal sets to the more general case of discrete fractional-order complex-valued maps. Consider the following fractional-order map

$$^{C}\Delta_a^{\alpha} z(t) = f(z(t + \alpha - 1), q), \tag{10}$$

where $f : \mathbb{C} \to \mathbb{C}$ and $q \in \mathbb{C}$, then the Julia set induced by (10) is defined as follows [9–11]:

Definition 2. *The filled-in Julia set of discrete fractional map (10) is the set Ψ of initial points $z \in \mathbb{C}$ whose evolutions under (10) are limited. The boundary of Ψ, i.e., $\partial\Psi$, is referred to as the Julia set of discrete fractional map (10) and it is denoted by J_f^{α}.*

The key properties of Julia set J_f^α are listed below [9–11]:

(1) $J_f^\alpha \neq \varnothing$, i.e., it is a non-empty set.

(2) J_f^α is fully invariant with respect to (10) in both forward and backward directions of iterations.

(3) Assume that the fractional map (10) has an attractive fixed point of period p at some specific values of α, then J_f^α contains the basin of attraction for this fixed point, namely, $\partial\beta_p^\alpha$. The same is true for infinity fixed point.

The Mandelbrot set, introduced by Benoit Mandelbrot in 1979 [9,10], is generalized to our fractional case in the way that the Mandelbrot set Φ_f^α is composed of the set of points in the plane of complex-valued parameter q at which the evolution from initial point $z(0) = 0$ is bounded at the specified fixed value of α.

The quantification of fractal properties of Julia and Mandelbrot sets can be carried out by calculating the associated space filling capacity or dimension. The well-known box-counting dimension is the most accessible among scientists and it can be defined as follows:

Definition 3. *For non-empty bounded subset Ω of $\mathbb{R}^n$, consider the collections of boxes with side lengths ϵ required to cover Ω. The Minkowski–Bouligand dimension or the box-counting dimension is defined as*

$$\dim_\Omega = \lim_{\epsilon\to 0} \frac{\log(N_\epsilon)}{\log(1/\epsilon)},$$

where N_ϵ is the number of boxes to cover Ω. In addition, the lower box dimension (lower Minkowski dimension) and the upper box dimension (Kolmogorov dimension) of Ω are also defined by

$$\underline{\dim}_\Omega = \underline{\lim}_{\epsilon\to 0} \frac{\log(N_\epsilon)}{\log(1/\epsilon)}, \quad \overline{\dim}_\Omega = \overline{\lim}_{\epsilon\to 0} \frac{\log(N_\epsilon)}{\log(1/\epsilon)},$$

respectively.

Numerical simulations are carried out to explore the generation of Mandelbrot and Julia sets from the dynamics of the proposed generalized fractional cosine map. The results for different values of the fractional order α, the constant q, and the exponent p are shown in the next table. In addition, Table 1 provides the box-counting dimensions for the various simulation scenarios investigated.

Table 1. Summary of cases considered in numerical simulations and the associated fractal dimensions.

Figure	Fractal Set	Parameters	Fractal Dimension
Figure 2	Mandelbrot sets	$\alpha = 1$, different values of p.	1.5244, 1.582, 1.6148, 1.6594, 1.5615, 1.5442
Figure 3	Mandelbrot sets	$\alpha = 0.9$, different values of p.	1.8838, 1.8836, 1.8994, 1.8893
Figure 4	Mandelbrot sets	$\alpha = 0.75$, different values of p.	1.8643, 1.8828, 1.8748, 1.909, 1.8762, 1.8967
Figure 5	Mandelbrot sets	$\alpha = 0.5$, different values of p.	1.633, 1.6722, 1.6782, 1.6838, 1.6857, 1.6337, 1.5536
Figure 6	Mandelbrot sets	$\alpha = 0.3$, different values of p.	1.8572, 1.8908, 1.8904, 1.5768
Figure 7	Julia sets	$\alpha = 1$, different values of p and q.	1.8426, 1.8665, 1.4931, 1.5469
Figure 8	Julia sets	$\alpha = 0.8$, different values of p and q.	1.8765, 1.489, 1.8525, 1.8503
Figure 9	Julia sets	$\alpha = 0.5$, different values of p and q.	1.5016, 1.8864, 1.5078, 1.4836, 1.8021, 1.8034

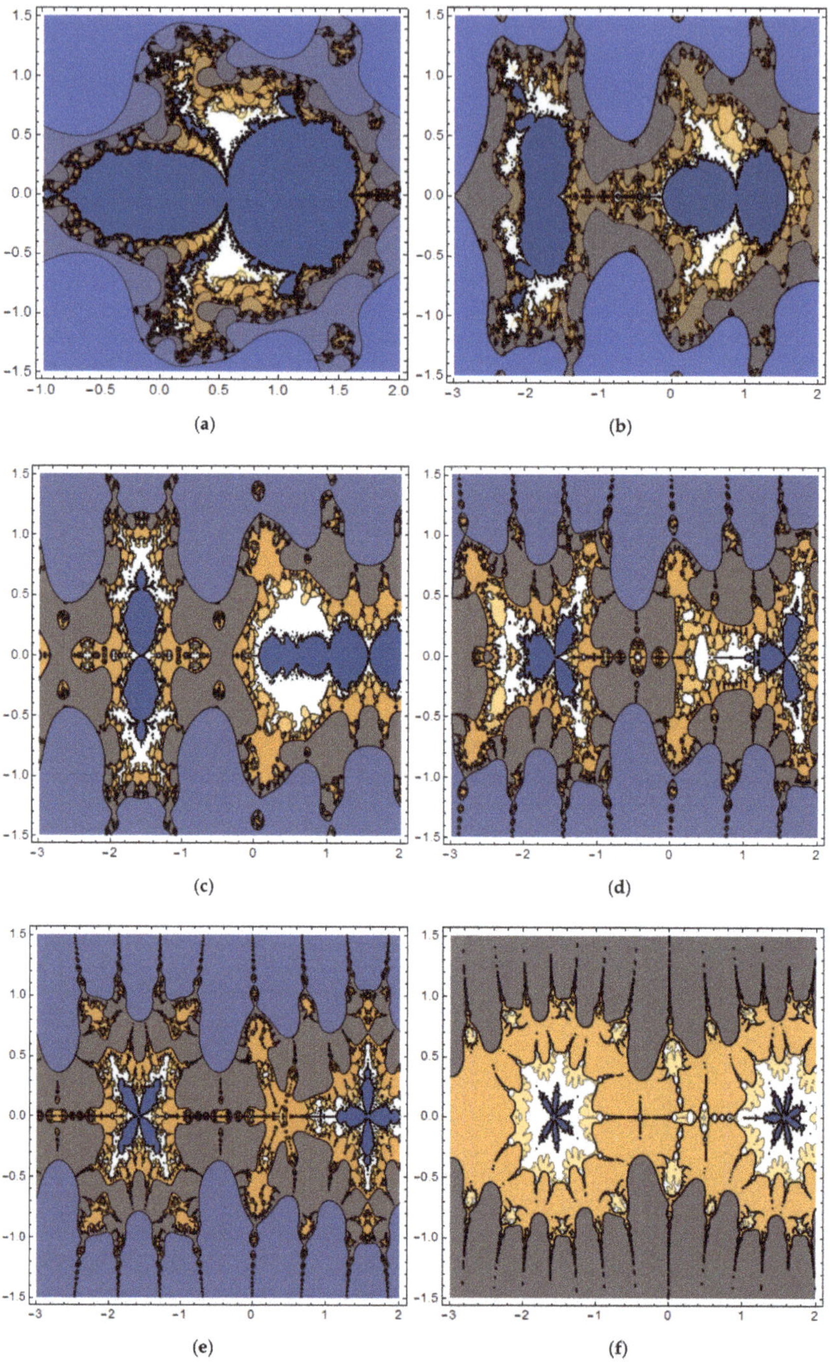

Figure 2. The Mandelbrot sets generated by the generalized fractional cosine map at $\alpha = 1$, where (**a**) $p = 2$, (**b**) $p = 2.5$, (**c**) $p = 3$, (**d**) $p = 4.3$, (**e**) $p = 5$, and (**f**) $p = 7.7$.

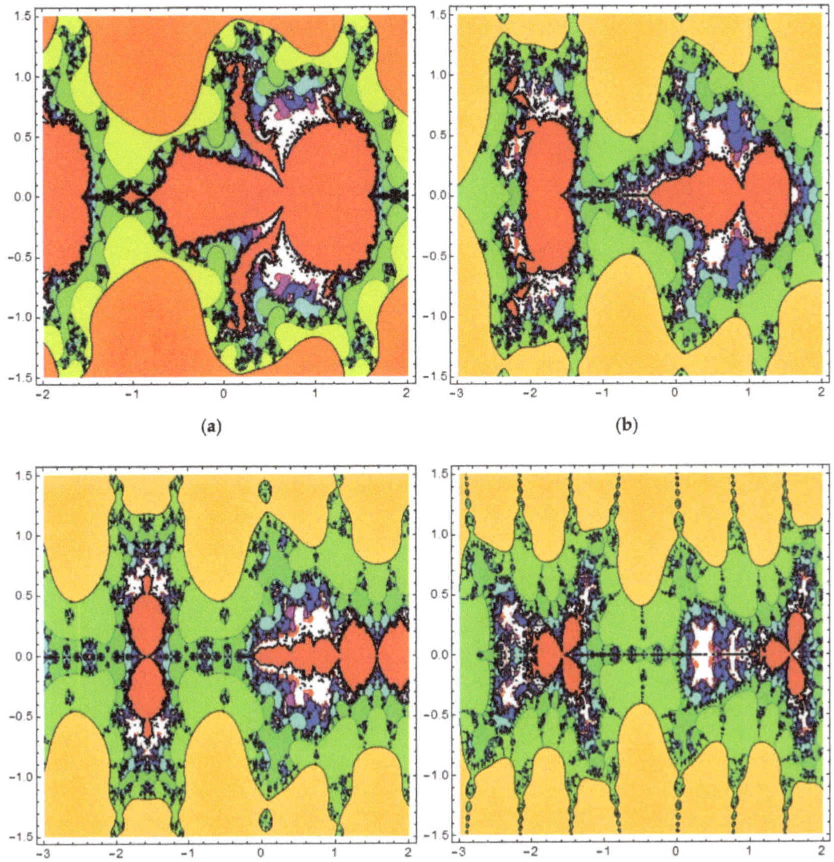

(a) (b) (c) (d)

Figure 3. The Mandelbrot sets generated by the generalized fractional cosine map at $\alpha = 0.9$, where (**a**) $p = 2$, (**b**) $p = 2.5$, (**c**) $p = 3$, and (**d**) $p = 4.3$.

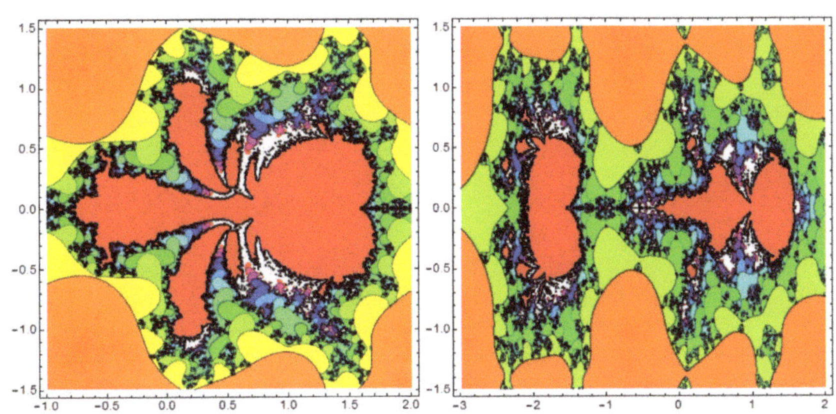

(a) (b)

Figure 4. *Cont.*

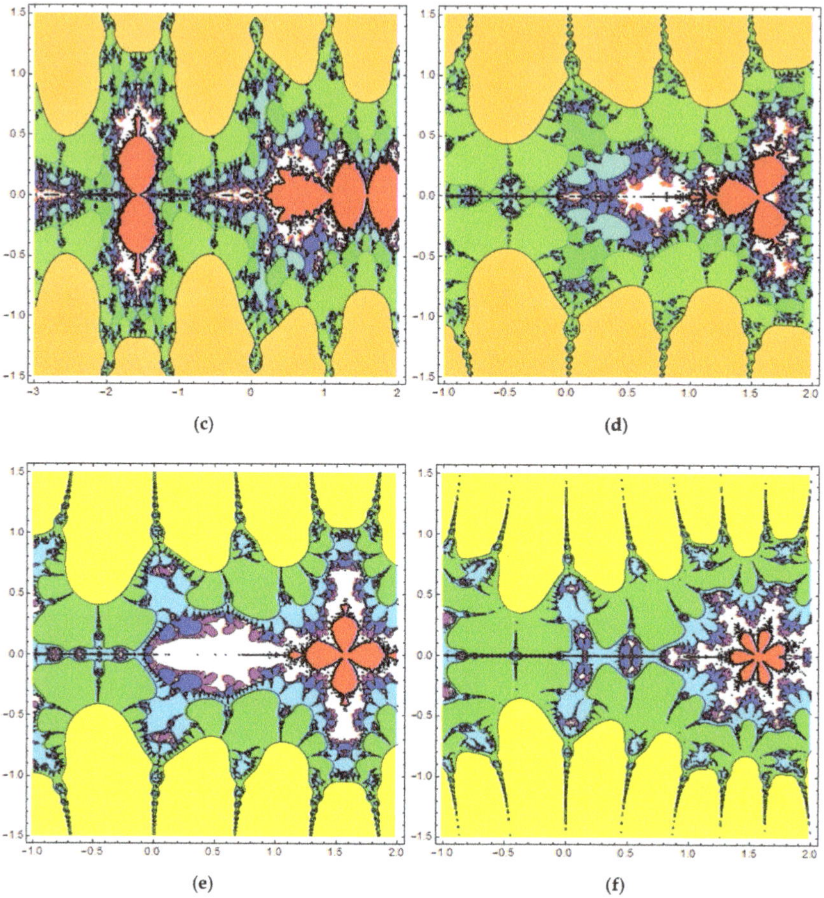

Figure 4. The Mandelbrot sets generated by the generalized fractional cosine map at $\alpha = 0.75$, where (**a**) $p = 2$, (**b**) $p = 2.5$, (**c**) $p = 3$, (**d**) $p = 4.3$, (**e**) $p = 5$, and (**f**) $p = 7.7$.

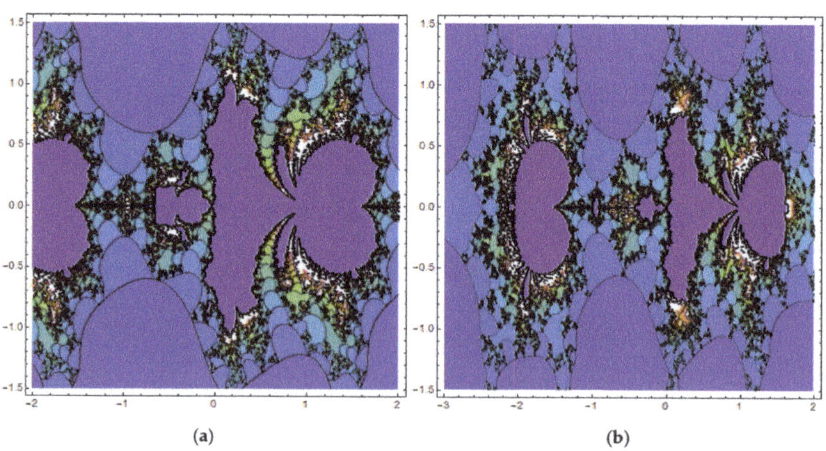

Figure 5. *Cont.*

Figure 5. The Mandelbrot sets generated by the generalized fractional cosine map at $\alpha = 0.5$, where (**a**) $p = 2$, (**b**) $p = 2.5$, (**c**) $p = 3$, (**d**) $p = 4.3$, (**e**) $p = 5$ and (**f**) $p = 7.7$.

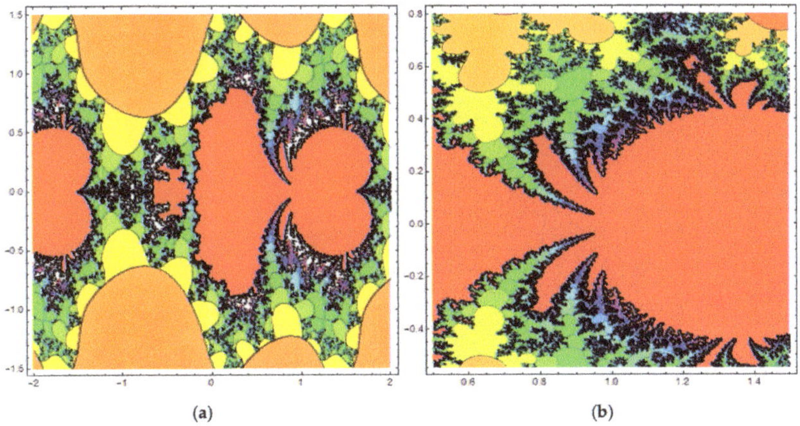

Figure 6. *Cont.*

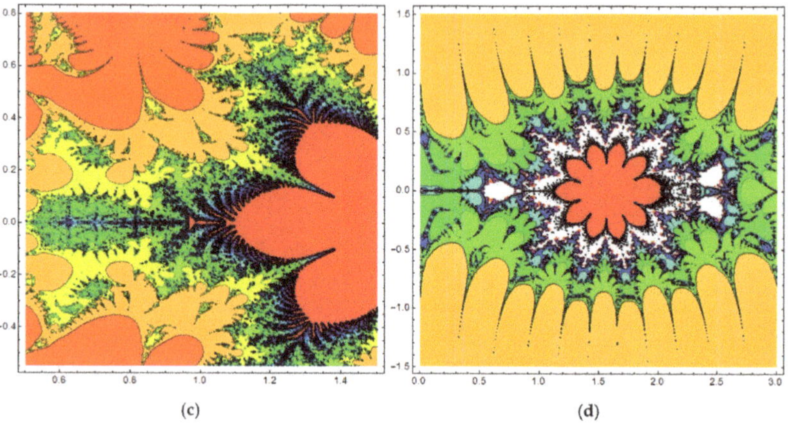

Figure 6. The Mandelbrot sets generated by the generalized fractional cosine map at $\alpha = 0.3$, where (**a**) $p = 2$, (**b**) $p = 2.5$, (**c**) $p = 7.7$, and (**d**) $p = 11.3$.

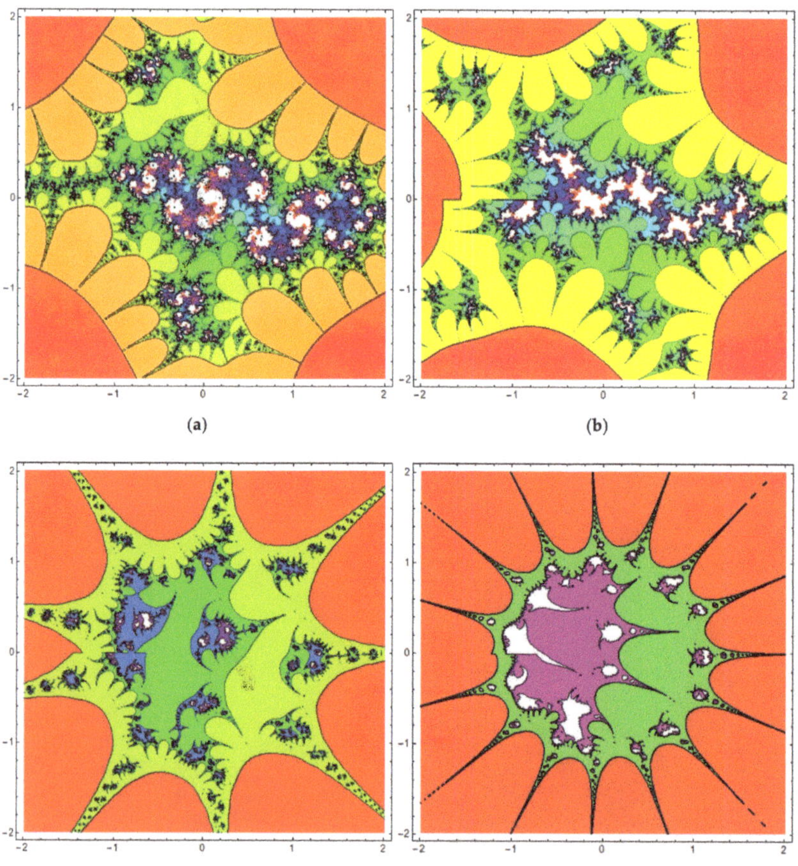

Figure 7. The Julia sets generated by the generalized fractional cosine map at $\alpha = 1$ and $q = 0.5 + 0.52i$, where (**a**) $p = 2$, (**b**) $p = 2.5$, (**c**) $p = 4.3$, and (**d**) $p = 7.7$.

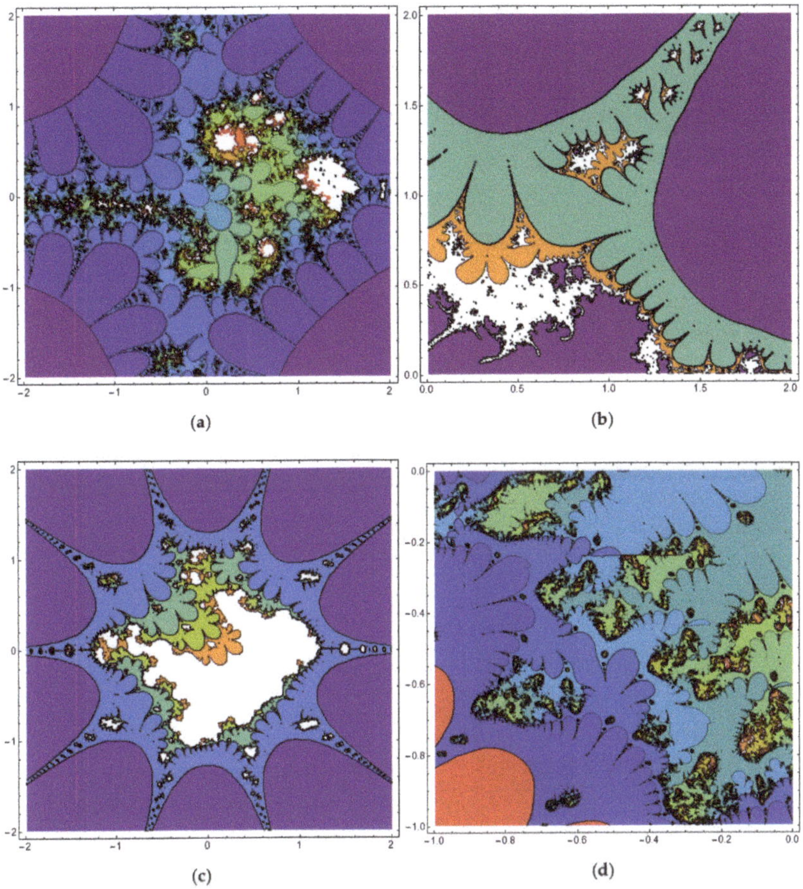

Figure 8. The Julia sets generated by the generalized fractional cosine map at $\alpha = 0.8$ and $q = 1.9 - 0.25i$, where (**a**) $p = 2$, (**b**) $p = 3.5$, (**c**) $p = 5$, and (**d**) $p = 11.5$.

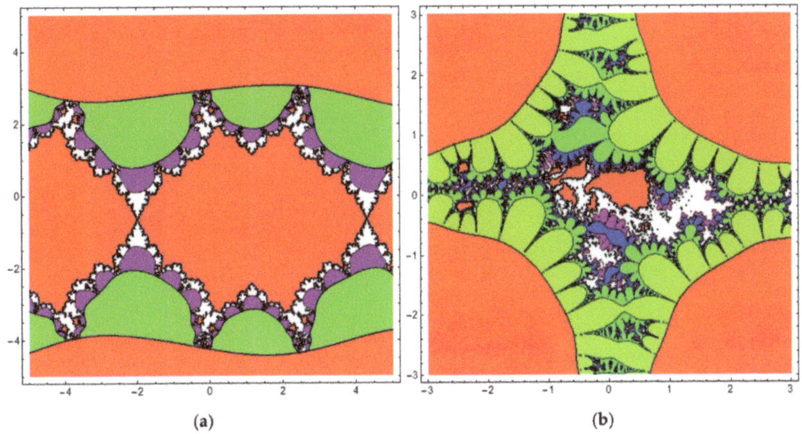

Figure 9. *Cont.*

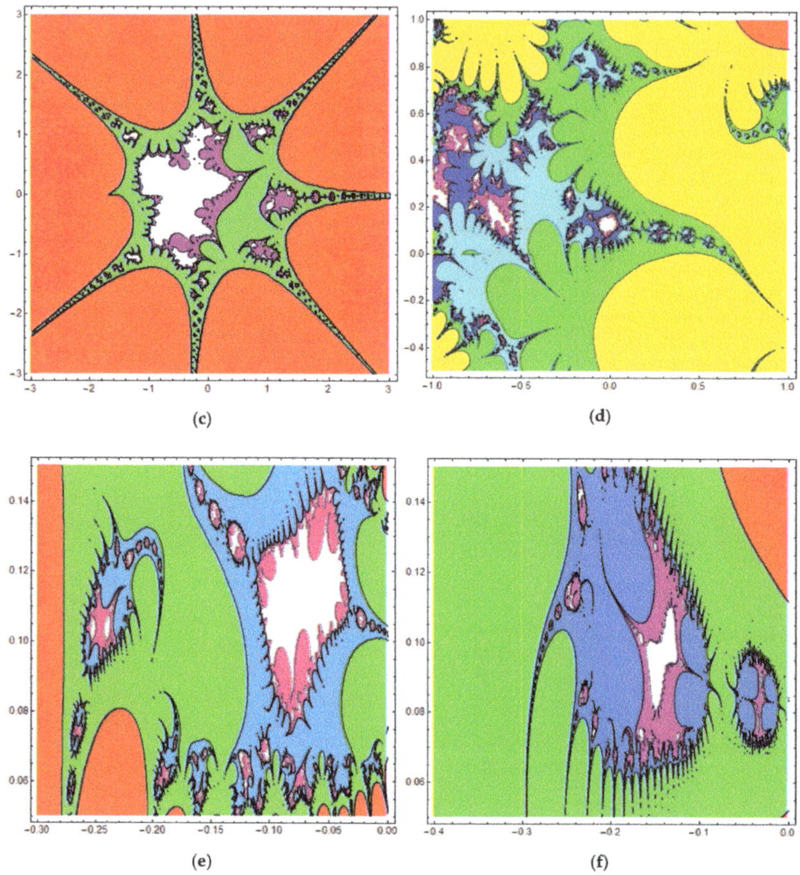

Figure 9. (**a–c**) The Julia sets generated by the generalized fractional cosine map at $\alpha = 0.5$ and $q = 0.41 + 0.65i$, where (**a**) $p = 1$, (**b**) $p = 2$, (**c**) $p = 3.8$. (**d–f**) The values of the parameters are $\alpha = 0.5$ and $q = -0.1 - 0.7i$, where (**d**) $p = 5.3$, (**e**) $p = 7$, (**f**) $p = 11.5$.

4. The Control and Synchronization of Julia Sets

This section examines the regulation and synchronization of Julia sets generated by the fractional-order cosine map. This section begins with a brief mathematical overall view.

Consider two different fractional-order cosine maps The first is called the master (driving) map and has the output $z_1(t)$ whereas the second map is referred to as the slave (response) map and it gives the output $z_2(t)$.

Definition 4. *The synchronization is said to be achieved between $z_1(t)$ and $z_2(t)$ if $z_2 \to z_1$ as $t \to \infty$. Equivalently, it can be written as [11–13]*

$$\lim_{t\to\infty} |z_2(t) - z_1(t)| = 0.$$

The synchronization of two solution trajectories indicates that their convergence and divergence characteristics are identical. Let $J^{\alpha}_{f_1}$ and $J^{\alpha}_{f_2}$ denote the Julia sets of fractional master and fractional slave maps, respectively, where they have fractional order α. The definition of synchronization between two Julia sets is as follows [11–14].

Definition 5. *The asymptotic synchronization of two Julia sets $J^{\alpha}_{f_1}$ and $J^{\alpha}_{f_2}$ is achieved if*

$$\lim_{t\to\infty}(J^{\alpha}_{f_1} \cup J^{\alpha}_{f_2} - J^{\alpha}_{f_1} \cap J^{\alpha}_{f_2}) = \varnothing.$$

4.1. Control of Julia Sets Generated by the Fractional Cosine Map

The Julia sets created by the fractional cosine map are controlled by varying the type of stability of a particular fixed point on the map. The proposed form of the feedback controller is

$$v(t) = -\kappa(z(t) - \bar{z}) - \cos[z(t+\alpha-1)^p + q], \tag{11}$$

where $\bar{z}$ is the target fixed point and the complex-valued controller gain $\kappa = \kappa_r + i\kappa_i$ is calculated as follows:

Theorem 5. *Suppose that the feedback controller (11) satisfies the following conditions*

$$\kappa_r > 0, \ \sqrt{\kappa_r^2 + \kappa_i^2} < 2^{\alpha},$$

subsequently, the unstable fixed point $\bar{z}$ of controlled fractional-order cosine map

$$^{C}\Delta_a^{\alpha} z(t) = \cos[z(t+\alpha-1)^p + q] + v(t+\alpha-1),$$

is stabilized by changing the Julia set in its neighborhood.

Proof. Using control signal (11), the controlled fractional cosine map can be written as:

$$^{C}\Delta_a^{\alpha} z(t) = -\kappa(z(t+\alpha-1) - \bar{z}). \tag{12}$$

Let $u(t) = z(t) - \bar{z}$, then (12) represents a structure

$$^{C}\Delta_a^{\alpha} u(t) = -\kappa u(t+\alpha-1),$$

and the associated real-valued two dimensional fractional map is obtained as

$$\begin{aligned}
^{C}\Delta_a^{\alpha} u_r(t) &= -\kappa_r u_r(t+\alpha-1) + \kappa_i u_i(t+\alpha-1), \\
^{C}\Delta_a^{\alpha} u_i(t) &= -\kappa_i u_r(t+\alpha-1) - \kappa_r u_i(t+\alpha-1).
\end{aligned}$$

Define matrix J by

$$J = \begin{pmatrix} -\kappa_r & \kappa_i \\ -\kappa_i & -\kappa_r \end{pmatrix},$$

and hence the eigenvalues of J are given by $-\kappa_r \pm i\kappa_i$. The sufficient conditions for local asymptotic stability of $\kappa_r > 0$ and $\sqrt{\kappa_r^2 + \kappa_i^2} < 2^{\alpha}$. □

4.2. Synchronization of Julia Sets

Assume the driving system has the following configuration:

$$^{C}\Delta_a^{\alpha} z_1(t) = \cos[z_1(t+\alpha-1)^p + q_1], \tag{13}$$

and take into account the following response system

$$^{C}\Delta_a^{\alpha} z_2(t) = \cos[z_2(t+\alpha-1)^p + q_2] + \rho(z_1, z_2, t+\alpha-1), \tag{14}$$

where $\rho(z_1, z_2, t+\alpha-1)$ is an appropriate controller to be designed.

Now, two different scenarios will be investigated in the following two theorems. The first one involves the case where the values of the constants q_1 and q_2 are known a priori.

Theorem 6. *Suppose that the values of constants q_1 and q_2 in the two fractional maps (13) and (14), respectively, are known. Then, the following controller*

$$\rho(z_1, z_2, t+\alpha-1) = \cos[z_1(t+\alpha-1)^p + q_1] - \cos[z_2(t+\alpha-1)^p + q_2] - \gamma(z_2(t+\alpha-1) - z_1(t+\alpha-1)), \quad (15)$$

with gain $\gamma = \gamma_r + i\gamma_i$ satisfying $|\gamma| < 2^\alpha$ and $\gamma_r > 0$, can realize Julia set synchronization between the driving system (13) and the response system (14) for any initial condition.

Proof. One can obtain the fractional error map by subtracting (13) from (14) which can be written as

$$\begin{aligned} {}^C\Delta_a^\alpha e(t) &= \cos[z_2(t+\alpha-1)^p + q_2] - \cos[z_1(t+\alpha-1)^p + q_1] + \rho(z_1, z_2, t+\alpha-1), \\ e(t) &= z_2(t) - z_1(t). \end{aligned}$$

By substituting from (15) into the above error map, we get

$${}^C\Delta_a^\alpha e(t) = -\gamma e(t+\alpha-1),$$

or

$${}^C\Delta_a^\alpha (e_r(t) + e_i(t)) = (-\gamma_r - i\gamma_i)(e_r(t+\alpha-1) + ie_i(t+\alpha-1)),$$

which can be changed into the 2D system

$$\begin{aligned} {}^C\Delta_a^\alpha e_r(t) &= -\gamma_r e_r(t+\alpha-1) + \gamma_i e_i(t+\alpha-1), \\ {}^C\Delta_a^\alpha e_i(t) &= -\gamma_i e_r(t+\alpha-1) - \gamma_r e_i(t+\alpha-1). \end{aligned}$$

The eigenvalues of the above system are found as $-\gamma_r \pm i\gamma_i$ which imply that the asymptotic stability conditions are achieved if $|\gamma| < 2^\alpha$ and $\gamma_r > 0$. □

The second scenario involves the case where the value of constant q_1 is unknown and, therefore, an adaptive controller is to be designed along with complex-valued update laws to realize the synchronization.

Theorem 7. *Suppose that the value of constants q_1 in the fractional map (13) is unknown. Then, the following controller*

$$\begin{aligned} \rho(z_1, z_2, t+\alpha-1) = {} & \hat{\beta}_1(t+\alpha-1)\cos(z_1(t+\alpha-1)^p) + \hat{\beta}_2(t+\alpha-1)\sin(z_1(t+\alpha-1)^p) \\ & - \cos[z_2(t+\alpha-1)^p + q_2] - \gamma e(t+\alpha-1), \end{aligned} \quad (16)$$

along with the following update laws

$$\Delta\hat{\beta}_1(n) = -\frac{\eta_1(e(n+1)\cos(z_1(n)^p) - e(n)\cos(z_1(n+1)^p))}{\cos(z_1(n+1)^p)\cos(z_1(n)^p)}, \quad (17)$$

$$\Delta\hat{\beta}_2(n) = -\frac{\eta_2(e(n+1)\sin(z_1(n)^p) - e(n)\sin(z_1(n+1)^p))}{\sin(z_1(n+1)^p)\sin(z_1(n)^p)} \quad (18)$$

where $\hat{\beta}_1$, $\hat{\beta}_2$ are the estimates of $\cos(q_1)$ and $-\sin(q_1)$, respectively, and the complex-valued gains γ, η_1 and η_2 satisfying $|\gamma + \eta_1 + \eta_2| < 2^\alpha$ and $\gamma_r + \eta_{1r} + \eta_{2r} > 0$ can achieve Julia set synchronization between the driving system (13) and the response system (14) for any initial condition.

Proof. The proof is arranged in the following steps. First, the drive map is simplified to the following form:

$$\begin{aligned} {}^C\Delta_a^\alpha z_1(t) &= \cos(q_1)\cos(z_1(t+\alpha-1)^p) - \sin(q_1)\sin(z_1(t+\alpha-1)^p) \\ &= \beta_1\cos(z_1(t+\alpha-1)^p) + \beta_2\sin(z_1(t+\alpha-1)^p), \\ \beta_1 &= \cos(q_1),\ \ \beta_2 = -\sin(q_1). \end{aligned}$$

The fractional error map is then expressed as

$${}^C\Delta_a^\alpha e(t) = \cos[z_2(t+\alpha-1)^p + q_2] - \beta_1\cos(z_1(t+\alpha-1)^p) - \beta_2\sin(z_1(t+\alpha-1)^p) + \rho(z_1, z_2, t+\alpha-1).$$

Second, by substituting (16) into the fractional error map, we obtain

$$\begin{aligned} {}^C\Delta_a^\alpha e(t) &= (\hat{\beta}_1(t+\alpha-1) - \beta_1)\cos(z_1(t+\alpha-1)^p) + (\hat{\beta}_2(t+\alpha-1) - \beta_2)\sin(z_1(t+\alpha-1)^p) - \gamma e(t+\alpha-1), \\ &= \tilde{\beta}_1(t+\alpha-1)\cos(z_1(t+\alpha-1)^p) + \tilde{\beta}_2(t+\alpha-1)\sin(z_1(t+\alpha-1)^p) - \gamma e(t+\alpha-1). \end{aligned}$$

In addition, note that

$$\Delta\hat{\beta}_1(n) = \Delta\tilde{\beta}_1(n),\ \Delta\hat{\beta}_2(n) = \Delta\tilde{\beta}_2(n),$$

and hence the update laws (17)–(18) can be solve to give

$$\tilde{\beta}_1(n) = -\frac{\eta_1 e(n)}{\cos(z_1(n)^p)},\ \ \tilde{\beta}_2(n) = -\frac{\eta_2 e(n)}{\sin(z_1(n)^p)}.$$

Third, the error map is, therefore, reduced to

$${}^C\Delta_a^\alpha e(t) = -(\gamma + \eta_1 + \eta_2)e(t+\alpha-1),$$

which implies that the corresponding 2D fractional error map in $\mathbb{R}^2$ has the eigenvalues $-(\gamma_r + \eta_{1r} + \eta_{2r}) \pm i(\gamma_i + \eta_{1i} + \eta_{2i})$ at the zero fixed point. Therefore, the following conditions are sufficient to confirm the fixed point stability

$$|\gamma + \eta_1 + \eta_2| < 2^\alpha,\ \gamma_r + \eta_{1r} + \eta_{2r} > 0.$$

□

To validate the theoretical results obtained in this section, numerical simulations are now used. For $p = 2$, $q = 1.2 - 0.2i$ and $\alpha = 0.8$, it can be found that the fixed point $-0.62932 - 0.1589012i$ is an unstable fixed point for the fractional cosine map (6). Applying the controller (11) with $\bar{z} = -0.62932 - 0.1589i$ and $\kappa = 1$, the fixed point is stabilized, as shown in Figure 10a,b. In a second example, consider a master system with $p = 2$, $q_1 = 1.2 - 0.2i$ and $\alpha = 0.9$ while the slave system is supposed to have $p = 2$, $q_2 = 0.433 - 0.55i$ and $\alpha = 0.9$. Using the adaptive controller (15) with $\gamma = 1 + 0.3i$, the synchronization conditions are satisfied and the synchronization between the two systems are achieved. The evolution of the synchronization error with time is illustrated in Figure 10c,d for its real and imaginary parts. The third example involves the more realistic case where the value of q_1 is unknown in the master system. The value of q_2 in the slave system is set to $0.433 - 0.55i$ and the other shared values of parameters are $p = 2$ and $\alpha = 0.85$. The adaptive controller (16) along with update laws (17)–(18) are employed to achieve the synchronization between the two systems and estimate the unknown values of $\cos(q_1)$ and $-\sin(q_1)$. In the simulations shown in Figure 11, the assigned values to $\cos(q_1)$ and $\sin(q_1)$ are $0.369629 + 0.18765i$ and $0.950742 - 0.072956i$, respectively. Figure 11a–f shows the real and imaginary parts of the synchronization error, $\hat{\beta}_1$ and $\hat{\beta}_2$. The Julia set generated by the controlled map is affected by the stabilization of specific fixed points in the fractional cosine map or the induced synchronization between master/slave systems. For example, Figure 12 depicts the Julia sets generated by the slave fractional cosine map before and after attaining the synchronization state where it is clear that significant changes in its structure are introduced.

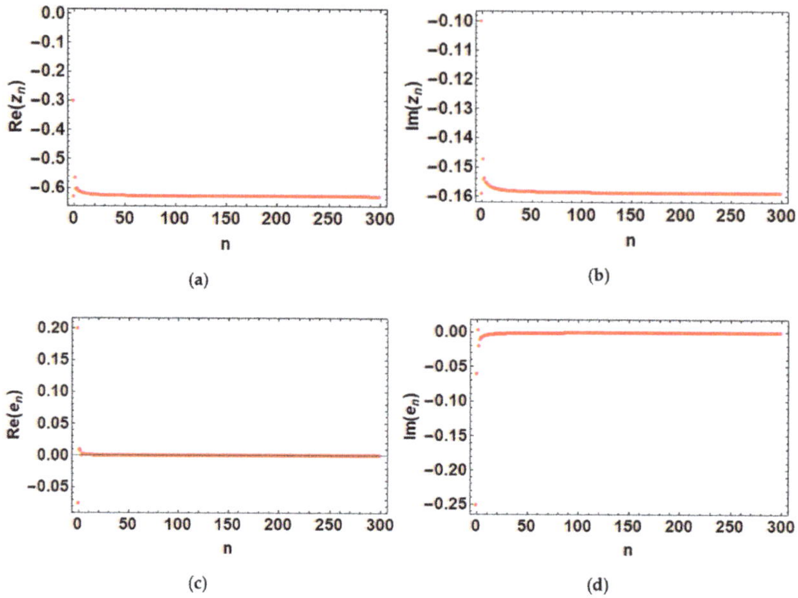

Figure 10. (**a**,**b**) Stabilization of fixed point $\bar{z} = -0.62932 - 0.1589i$ of the generalized fractional cosine map under the influence of the proposed controller (11) with $\kappa = 1$. (**c**,**d**) The real and imaginary parts of the synchronization error between a master system with $p = 2$, $q_1 = 1.2 - 0.2i$, $\alpha = 0.9$ and a slave system with $p = 2$, $q_2 = 0.433 - 0.55i$ and $\alpha = 0.9$ when the adaptive controller (15) is employed and $\gamma = 1 + 0.3i$.

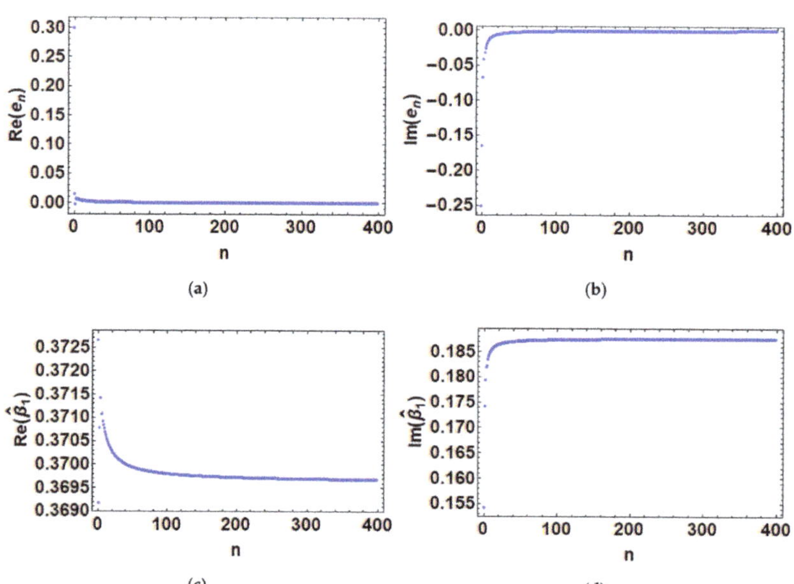

Figure 11. *Cont.*

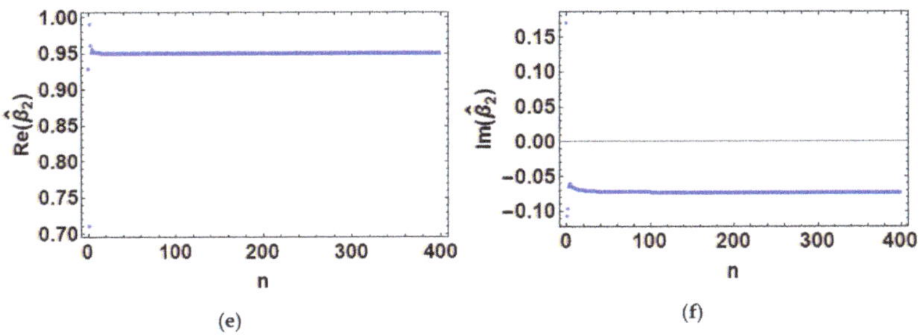

Figure 11. The real and imaginary parts of the synchronization error, $\hat{\beta}_1$ and $\hat{\beta}_2$ where the value of q_1 is unknown in the master system, the value of q_2 in the slave system is set to $0.433 - 0.55i$ and the other values of parameters are $p = 2$, $\alpha = 0.85$, $\gamma = 0.3 + 0.3i$, $\eta_1 = 0.2$ and $\eta_2 = 0.2$ (**a**,**b**). The assigned values to $\cos(q_1)$ and $\sin(q_1)$ are $0.369629 + 0.18765i$ (**c**,**d**) and $0.950742 - 0.072956i$ (**e**,**f**).

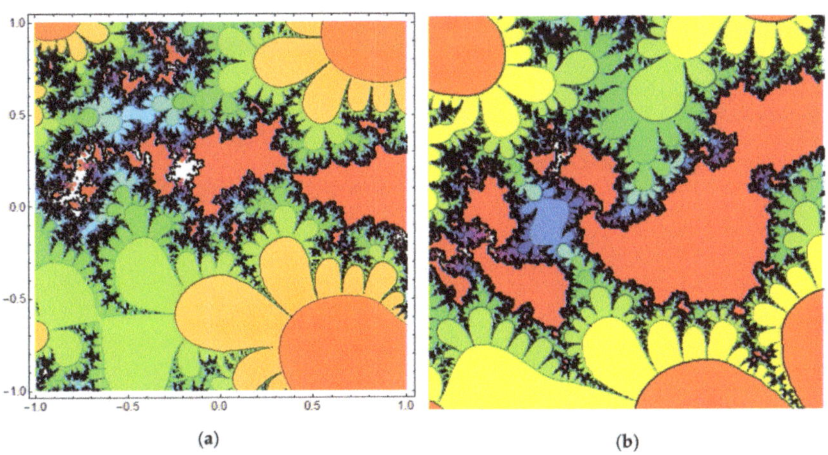

Figure 12. The effects of synchronization on the Julia sets generated by the slave fractional cosine map described in Figure 11 (**a**) before and (**b**) after attaining synchronization state.

5. Conclusions

This research introduces a framework for investigating the fractal and dynamic properties of an extended discrete fractional cosine map with complex values. The Mandelbrot and Julia sets of the proposed map are investigated for a variety of parameters. Julia sets in complex domains: control and synchronization issues discussed. In particular, an efficient adaptive controller is constructed to achieve synchronization when there is an unknown value of the parameter in driving (master system). The proposed map has promising applications in the field of image encryption which can be conducted in future work. Our findings can be used to create a reliable and efficient chaotic color/grayscale image encrypting system. The next step in our future work is to apply the present discrete fractional complex cosine map and examine/compare the performance of the corresponding encryption schemes.

Author Contributions: All authors jointly worked on the results, and they read and approved the final manuscript. All authors have read and agreed to the published version of the manuscript.

Funding: This study is supported via funding from Prince Sattam bin Abdulaziz University project number (PSAU/2023/R1444).

Data Availability Statement: All data and material used and/or analyzed during the current study are available from the corresponding author on reasonable request.

Acknowledgments: This study is supported via funding from Prince Sattam bin Abdulaziz University project number (PSAU/2023/R/1444).

Conflicts of Interest: The authors declare that there are no conflict of interest regarding the publication of this paper.

References

1. Tu, P.N.V. *Dynamical Systems—An Introduction with Applications in Economics and Biology*; Springer: Berlin/Heidelberg, Germany, 1995.
2. Strogatz, S.H. *Nonlinear Dynamics and Chaos with Applications to Physics, Biology, Chemistry, and Engineering*; CRC Press: Boca Raton, FL, USA, 2018.
3. Kuznetsov, Y.A. *Elements of Applied Bifurcation Theory*; Springer Science and Business Media: Berlin/Heidelberg, Germany, 2013.
4. Kocarev, L.; Lian, S. *Chaos-Based Cryptography*; Springer: Berlin/Heidelberg, Germany, 2011.
5. Izhikevich, E.M. *Dynamical Systems in Neuroscience: The Geometry of Excitability and Bursting*; MIT Press: Cambridge, MA, USA, 2007.
6. Stavroulakis, P. *Chaos Applications in Telecommunications*; CRC Press: Boca Raton, FL, USA, 2006.
7. Chen, G.; Yu, X. *Chaos Control- Theory and Applications*; Springer: Berlin/Heidelberg, Germany, 2003.
8. Guckenheimer, J.; Holmes, P.; *Nonlinear Oscillations, Dynamical Systems, and Bifurcations of Vector Fields*; Springer Science and Business Media: Berlin/Heidelberg, Germany, 2013.
9. Mandelbrot, B.B.; Evertsz, C.J.; Gutzwiller, M.C. *Fractals and Chaos: The Mandelbrot Set and Beyond*; Springer: Berlin/Heidelberg, Germany, 2004.
10. Peitgen, H.; Jurgens, H.; Saupe, D. *Chaos and Fractals: New Frontiers in Science*; Springer: Berlin/Heidelberg, Germany, 1992.
11. Wang, Y.; Shutang, L.; Li, H. Adaptive synchronization of Julia sets generated by Mittag-Leffler function. *Commun. Nonlinear Sci. Numer. Simul.* **2020**, *83*, 105115. [CrossRef]
12. Wang, Y.; Liu, S.; Li, H. On fractional difference logistic maps: Dynamic analysis and synchronous control. *Nonlinear Dyn.* **2020**, *102*, 579–588. [CrossRef]
13. Wang, Y.; Liu, S.; Wang, W. Fractal dimension analysis and control of Julia set generated by fractional Lotka–Volterra models. *Commun. Nonlinear Sci. Numer. Simul.* **2019**, *72*, 417–431. [CrossRef]
14. Falconer, K. *Fractal Geometry: Mathematical Foundations and Applications*; John Wiley and Sons Ltd.: Chichester, UK, 2014.
15. Liu, S.T.; Zhang, Y.P.; Liu, C.A. *Fractal Control and Its Applications*; Springer Nature: Berlin/Heidelberg, Germany, 2020.
16. Jouini, L.; Ouannas, A.; Khennaoui, A.-A.; Wang, X.; Grassi, G.; Pham, V.-T. The fractional form of a new three-dimensional generalized Hénon map. *Adv. Differ. Equ.* **2019**, *2019*, 122. [CrossRef]
17. Peng, Y.; He, S.; Sun, K. Chaos in the discrete memristor-based system with fractional-order difference. *Results Phys.* **2021**, *24*, 104106. [CrossRef]
18. Edelman, M. Fractional Maps as Maps with Power-Law Memory. In *Nonlinear Dynamics and Complexity*; Springer: Berlin/Heidelberg, Germany, 2014; pp. 79–120.
19. Edelman, M. Universality in systems with power-law memory and fractional dynamics. In *Chaotic, Fractional, and Complex Dynamics: New Insights and Perspectives*; Springer: Berlin/Heidelberg, Germany, 2018; pp. 147–171.
20. Wang, C.; Ding, Q. A new two-dimensional map with hidden attractors. *Entropy* **2018**, *20*, 322. [CrossRef] [PubMed]
21. Almatroud, A.O.; Khennaoui, A.-A.; Ouannas, A.; Pham, V.-T. Infinite line of equilibriums in a novel fractional map with coexisting infinitely many attractors and initial offset boosting. *Int. J. Nonlinear Sci. Numer. Simul.* **2021**.. [CrossRef]
22. Ouannas, A.; Khennaoui, A.A.; Momani, S.; Pham, V.T. The discrete fractional duffing system: Chaos, 0–1 test, C0 complexity, entropy, and control. *Chaos Interdiscip. J. Nonlinear Sci.* **2020**, *30*, 083131. [CrossRef] [PubMed]
23. Padron, J.P.; Perez, J.P.; Díaz, J.J.P.; Huerta, A.M. Time-Delay Synchronization and Anti-Synchronization of Variable-Order Fractional Discrete-Time Chen–Rossler Chaotic Systems Using Variable-Order Fractional Discrete-Time PID Control. *Mathematics* **2021**, *9*, 2149. [CrossRef]
24. Talhaoui, M.Z.; Wang, X. A new fractional one dimensional chaotic map and its application in high-speed image encryption. *Inf. Sci.* **2020**, *550*, 13–26. [CrossRef]
25. Elsonbaty, A.; Elsadany, A.; Kamal, F. On Discrete Fractional Complex Gaussian Map: Fractal Analysis, Julia Sets Control, and Encryption Application. *Math. Probl. Eng.* **2022**, *2022*, 8148831. [CrossRef]
26. Askar, S.; Al-Khedhairi, A.; Elsonbaty, A.; Elsadany, A. Chaotic Discrete Fractional-Order Food Chain Model and Hybrid Image Encryption Scheme Application. *Symmetry* **2021**, *13*, 161. [CrossRef]
27. Al-Khedhairi, A.; Elsonbaty, A.; Elsadany, A.A.; Hagras, E.A.A. Hybrid Cryptosystem Based on Pseudo Chaos of Novel Fractional Order Map and Elliptic Curves. *IEEE Access* **2020**, *8*, 57733–57748. [CrossRef]
28. Pesin, Y.B.; Climenhaga, V. *Lectures on Fractal Geometry and Dynamical Systems*; American Mathematical Society: Providence, RI, USA, 2009.
29. Brambila, F. Fractal Analysis—Applications in Physics, Engineering and Technology. Available online: https://www.intechopen.com/books/fractal-analysis-applications-in-physics-engineering-andtechnology (accessed on 28 October 2018).
30. Stauffer, D.; Aharony, A. *Introduction to Percolation Theory*; Taylor and Francis: Abingdon, UK, 2018.

31. Daftardar-Gejji, V. (Ed.) *Fractional Calculus and Fractional Differential Equations*; Springer: Singapore, 2019.
32. Sun, H.; Zhang, Y.; Baleanu, D.; Chen, W.; Chen, Y. A new collection of real world applications of fractional calculus in science and engineering. *Commun. Nonlinear Sci. Numer. Simul.* **2018**, *64*, 213–231. [CrossRef]
33. Radwan, A.G.; Khanday, F.A.; Said, L.A. (Eds) *Fractional-Order Design: Devices, Circuits, and Systems*; Academic Press: Cambridge, MA, USA, 2021.
34. Ray, S.S.; Sahoo, S. *Generalized Fractional Order Differential Equations Arising in Physical Models*; Chapman and Hall/CRC: Boca Raton, FL, USA, 2018.
35. Das, S.; Pan, I. *Fractional Order Signal Processing: Introductory Concepts and Applications*; Springer Science and Business Media: Berlin/Heidelberg, Germany, 2011.
36. Butera, S.; Di Paola, M. A physically based connection between fractional calculus and fractal geometry. *Ann. Phys.* **2014**, *350*, 146–158. [CrossRef]
37. Wang, Y.; Li, X.; Wang, D.; Liu, S. A brief note on fractal dynamics of fractional Mandelbrot sets. *Appl. Math. Comput.* **2022**, *432*, 127353. [CrossRef]
38. Danca, M.F.; Feckan, M. Mandelbrot set and Julia sets of fractional order. *arXiv* **2022**, arXiv:2210.02037.
39. Abdeljawad, T. On Riemann and Caputo fractional differences. *Comput. Math. Appl.* **2011**, *62*, 1602–1611. [CrossRef]
40. Čermák, J.; Győri, I.; Nechvátal, L. On explicit stability conditions for a linear fractional difference system. *Fract. Calc. Appl. Anal.* **2015**, *18*, 651. [CrossRef]
41. Abu-Saris, R.; Al-Mdallal, Q. On the asymptotic stability of linear system of fractional-order difference equations. *Fract. Calc. Appl. Anal.* **2013**, *16*, 613–629. [CrossRef]

mathematics

MDPI

Article

Bursting Dynamics in a Singular Vector Field with Codimension Three Triple Zero Bifurcation

Weipeng Lyu [1,2], Shaolong Li [2], Zhenyang Chen [2] and Qinsheng Bi [1,*]

[1] Faculty of Civil Engineering and Mechanics, Jiangsu University, Zhenjiang 212013, China; lvwp@yctu.edu.cn
[2] Faculty of Mathematics and Statistics, Yancheng Teachers University, Yancheng 224002, China; lisl01@yctu.edu.cn (S.L.); chenzy01@yctu.edu.cn (Z.C.)
[*] Correspondence: qbi@ujs.edu.cn

Abstract: As a kind of dynamical system with a particular nonlinear structure, a multi-time scale nonlinear system is one of the essential directions of the current development of nonlinear dynamics theory. Multi-time scale nonlinear systems in practical applications are often complex forms of coupling of high-dimensional and high codimension characteristics, leading to various complex bursting oscillation behaviors and bifurcation characteristics in the system. For exploring the complex bursting dynamics caused by high codimension bifurcation, this paper considers the normal form of the vector field with triple zero bifurcation. Two kinds of codimension-2 bifurcation that may lead to complex bursting oscillations are discussed in the two-parameter plane. Based on the fast–slow analysis method, by introducing the slow variable $W = A\sin(\omega t)$, the evolution process of the motion trajectory of the system changing with W was investigated, and the dynamical mechanism of several types of bursting oscillations was revealed. Finally, by varying the frequency of the slow variable, a class of chaotic bursting phenomena caused by the period-doubling cascade is deduced. Developing related work has played a positive role in deeply understanding the nature of various complex bursting phenomena and strengthening the application of basic disciplines such as mechanics and mathematics in engineering practice.

Keywords: bifurcation and chaos; multiple time scales; triple zero bifurcation; bursting oscillation

MSC: 34C15; 34C23; 34C05; 34D45; 37G10; 37G18

1. Introduction

Multi-time scale nonlinear systems have a broad engineering background. The coupling of different scales involving the interaction of dynamic behavior at multiple scales will lead to many extraordinary nonlinear phenomena. Their complexity and mechanism research has become one of the essential directions for the development of current nonlinear dynamics theory [1]. Most nonlinear systems encountered in natural science and practical engineering applications are coupled by several subsystems [2]. The evolution process from the dynamic behavior at the subsystem level to the dynamic behavior at the fundamental system level will involve different time and space scales, resulting in scale differences between the dynamical characteristics of these subsystems in different environments so that the whole system presents various multi-scale effects [3]. For example, large-scale rotating machinery must consider the large-scale motion of components and the deformation of the members themselves [4], electronic circuit systems with high nonlinear electronic coupling [5–7], and the transition metal-catalyzed gas-phase chemical reaction, where adsorption, desorption, and the response between adsorbents are much faster than the oxidation process under the metal surface [8,9]. Such systems cannot be superimposed but exhibit more complex dynamic properties. The process behaves as a typical nonlinear feature, with complex motions such as harmonic oscillations, periodic jumps, quasi-periodic motions, and period-doubling cascades to chaos [10,11]. These nonlinear phenomena can lead to the instability of the entire system in the actual engineering problem, which may be detrimental to industrial applications [12,13]. Therefore, it is urgent to study the dynamic mechanism of such phenomena.

So far, although specific results have been achieved in the complexity of multi-time scale nonlinear systems, due to the particularity of such systems, their related research is still preliminary, and many problems need to be further studied. High codimension bifurcation not only has a variety of bifurcation characteristics but also has a high sensitivity to parameter perturbation, which will not only lead to the diversity of quiescent states and spiking states but, in some circumstances, under the influence of appropriate slow subsystems, it will even lead to the simultaneous existence of different bifurcation characteristics in the same burster. Consequently, in the case of high codimension bifurcation, the fast–slow system has various complex bifurcation characteristics, which leads to the diversification of the motion trajectory of the system. It is necessary to explore the bursting oscillations under high codimension bifurcation and their mechanism.

The qualitative geometry of the flow in each bifurcation form can be obtained by analyzing the dynamic characteristics of the normal form, thereby simplifying the process of analyzing the existing system. Therefore, studying the bursting oscillation behavior of normal form in a singular vector field with high codimension bifurcation has become one of the hot topics [14,15]. The normal form is derived from a simple set of differential equations that study the stability and bifurcation properties of a dynamic system near the equilibria. In addition to the apparent reduction of high-dimensional systems, normal form theory can also classify nonlinear dynamic systems based on the singularity in the unfolding. In recent years, scholars have conducted in-depth research on the complex dynamic behavior of vector fields under high codimension bifurcation. In studying the dynamics of the double pendulum model, Mandadi and Huseyin proposed possible double zero bifurcation, zero-Hopf bifurcation, and double Hopf bifurcation in the system [16]. Yu and Huseyin [17,18] then derived the explicit expression of a singularity normal form with triple zero and zero-zero-Hopf eigenvalues. They explored static and dynamic bifurcation properties of singularity systems near the equilibria, but these results were limited to first-order approximations. Yu and Bi [19] constructed a homogeneous polynomial for calculating the coefficient of normal form using the Lie derivative as an operator for the singular vector field with a Jordan block form in the linear part. They developed the MAPLE program of the corresponding recursive algorithm and studied the dynamic characteristics of a triple zero eigenvalue singularity perturbation model of the double pendulum system on its central manifold. Then, the evolution of the limit cycle near the equilibria of a normal form under the singularity condition is analyzed, and based on that, the complex dynamic behavior, such as chaos induced by the period-doubling cascade, is discussed. Algaba et al. [20,21] discovered similar movements while studying double-zero and triple-zero eigenvalue singularity systems and found a class of global dynamic behavior between homoclinic and heteroclinic orbits. Next, based on the NTT (nonlinear time transformation) method, they derived a recursive algorithm for calculating the analytic formula of the global connection curve of the high-order approximation symmetric Bogdanov–Takens normal form. The theoretically derived phase trajectories can be well matched with the results of numerical simulations [22].

The complex bifurcation characteristics under high codimension bifurcation will lead to the more sophisticated dynamic behavior of fast–slow systems, so scholars at home and abroad have carried out a lot of work studying the mechanism of high codimension bifurcation in the occurrence of complex dynamics of singular systems. Duan et al. [23] classified the burster pattern of the Chay neuron model and divided the bifurcation region within the parametric plane to reveal the dynamical mechanism of bursting oscillations. Next, based on a two-parameter bifurcation analysis, they also found that the codimension-1 and codimension-2 bifurcations of the fast subsystem are essential for the transition mechanisms between different firing activities. The bifurcation curves of the fast subsystem can provide crucial information about the possible types of bursting in the neuronal model under given parameter conditions [24]. Braun and Mereu [25] analyze the zero-Hopf bifurcation occurring in a 3D jerk system after persuading a quadratic perturbation of the coefficients. The second-order averaging theory proves that up to three periodic orbits are born as the perturbation parameter tends to zero. Bao et al. [26] presented a new 5D two-memristor-based jerk (TMJ) system and emphatically studied complex dynamical effects induced by the initial conditions of memristors and non-memristors therein. Consequently, the dynamical effects of the initial conditions on the 5D TMJ system are disclosed comprehensively. Golubitsky et al. [1] proposed a classification method of bursting oscillation, which defined the codimension as the smallest codimension of the first occurrence of singularity in the unfolding by changing the slow-varying unfolding parameter and systematically classifying the currently known busting oscillators induced by the bifurcation of codimension-1 and codimension-2. Saggio [27] conducted a similar study, and they comprehensively classified the burster mode of the fast two-dimensional subsystem on the spherical surface of the unfolding parameter.

This paper studies the bursting oscillation near the codimension-3 triple-zero bifurcation point in the normal form of a singular vector with low-frequency excitation. The rest of this paper is organized as follows: In Section 2, the specific version of the second-order truncated normal form with triple zero eigenvalues singularity in the case of universal folding is introduced. In Section 3, we consider the stabilities and bifurcations of the system by regarding $W = Asin(\omega t)$ as the bifurcation parameter. In Section 4, the evolution of system dynamics with the change of $W = Asin(\omega t)$ is analyzed by regarding W as a slow-varying parameter, and the dynamical mechanism of bursting oscillations is investigated by overlapping the transformed phase portrait and the equilibrium branch. Section 5 discusses the chaos evolution caused by the period-doubling cascade. Finally, Section 6 concludes the paper.

2. Mathematical Model

The normal form theory of vector fields provides an effective analytical method for the in-depth study of the stability and bifurcation of high-dimensional nonlinear systems. In addition to the apparent reduction of high-dimensional systems, normal form theory can classify nonlinear dynamic systems according to the singularity in the unfolding. To reveal the complex dynamics of high codimension systems under the effects of fast–slow coupling, this paper analyzes the normal form of a singular vector field with triple zero eigenvalues, the basic idea of which follows.

Consider the following general ODE (ordinary differential equation) system

$$\dot{\mathbf{x}} = \mathbf{L}\mathbf{x} + \mathbf{f}(\mathbf{x}), \mathbf{f} \in C^k(R^n), \tag{1}$$

where $\mathbf{x} \in R^n$ and k is a large number. Without losing the generality, let $\mathbf{x} = 0$ be the equilibrium point of the system, namely $\mathbf{f}(\mathbf{0}) = \mathbf{0}$.

Suppose that the Jordan form of the Jacobian matrix of the system (1) at the equilibrium point is non-semisimple, i.e., it can be expressed as the following block matrix

$$\mathbf{L} = \begin{bmatrix} \mathbf{L}_0 & 0 \\ 0 & \mathbf{L}_1 \end{bmatrix} = \begin{bmatrix} 0 & 1 & 0 & 0 \\ 0 & 0 & 1 & 0 \\ 0 & 0 & 0 & 0 \\ 0 & 0 & 0 & \mathbf{L}_1 \end{bmatrix}, \tag{2}$$

where $\mathbf{L}_1$ has eigenvalues with nonzero real parts, which are given in Jordan canonical form.

Considering the normal form of the singular vector field under high codimension bifurcation, the calculation of the normal form is complicated because the basis of the corresponding nonlinear transformation is coupled during the calculation process. For a system with the singularity of non-semisimple double zero eigenvalues, Kuznetsov YA [28] analyzed the bifurcation characteristics of its critical normal form in detail. The results have been extended to the study of global bifurcation and chaos [29–32]. Based on that, Baider and Sanders [33] give a complete formal classification of such systems. For the normal form with the singularity of non-semisimple triple zero eigenvalues, this paper refers to the calculation process proposed by Bi QS and Yu P [19] and introduces a nonlinear transformation

$$\mathbf{w} = \mathbf{u} + \sum_{k\geq 2} P^k(\mathbf{u}) = \mathbf{u} + \mathbf{P(u)}, \tag{3}$$

where w is a variable on the central manifold, and the form of a homogeneous polynomial constructed by a set of near-identity transformations is

$$\mathbf{D_u\bar{H}(u)L_0u - L\bar{H}(u) = f(u) - D_u\bar{H}(u)C(u) - \bar{C}(u)}, \tag{4}$$

calculating Equation (4) can explicitly express the singularity vector field and its corresponding nonlinear transformation.

When the Jacobian matrix of system (1) has a zero real part of a non-semisimple, i.e., L_0 is a non-semisimple form, then L_0 can be decomposed into

$$\mathbf{L}_0 = \mathbf{S} + \mathbf{N}, \tag{5}$$

where $\mathbf{S} = diag(\lambda_1, \lambda_2, \ldots, \lambda n_0)$, and $\mathbf{N}$ has the form

$$\mathbf{N}_{ij} = \begin{cases} 1 \text{ or } 0, & \text{if } i+1=j; \\ 0, & otherwise. \end{cases} \tag{6}$$

By sorting out the coefficients of the nonlinear term $u_1{}^{m_1}u_2{}^{m_2}\ldots u_{n_0}{}^{m_{n_0}}$, Equation (6) can be rewritten as

$$(\lambda_0\mathbf{I} - \mathbf{L})\mathbf{H}_{\bar{m}} + \sum_{j=1}^{n_0-1}(\mathbf{L}_0)_{j(j+1)}(m_j+1)\mathbf{H}_{m_1m_2\ldots(m_{j+1}-1)\ldots(m_{n_0})} = \tilde{\mathbf{f}}_{\bar{m}} - \bar{\mathbf{C}}_{\bar{m}}, \tag{7}$$

Equation (7) can be used to construct algebraic equations which decide the coefficients of normal form with the singularity of triple zero eigenvalues. Then, by performing a series of recursive operations, the explicit expression of the normal form will finally be obtained as

$$\begin{aligned} \dot{u}_1 &= u_2, \\ \dot{u}_2 &= u_3, \\ \dot{u}_3 &= \sum_{j\geq 2}^{\infty} \begin{pmatrix} (C_{3,00(j-1)}u_3{}^{j-1} + (\sum_{l<j}^{j} C_{3,(j-i)0i}u_1{}^{(j-l)}u_3{}^l \\ + \sum_{l<(j-1)}^{j} (C_{3,(j-l-1)1i}u_1{}^{j-l-1}u_2u_3{}^l + C_{3,(j-l-2)2i}u_1{}^{j-l-2}u_2{}^2u_3{}^l))) \end{pmatrix}, \end{aligned} \tag{8}$$

where $j = 0, 1, 2, \ldots$.

Executing the recursive procedure with MAPLE yields the normal form of a singular vector field truncated to the second order as

$$\begin{aligned} \dot{u}_1 &= u_2, \\ \dot{u}_2 &= u_3, \\ \dot{u}_3 &= C_{3200}u_1{}^2 + C_{3020}u_2{}^2 + C_{3101}u_1u_3, \end{aligned} \tag{9}$$

where $C_{i,\,jkl}$ are the coefficients of normal form.

Inspired by Murdock's classical unfolding theory [34], the parameter perturbations on constant and linear terms are introduced. Then, the first-order perturbation form of a singular vector field with triple zero eigenvalues is obtained as

$$\dot{\mathbf{w}} = \mathbf{Jw} + \mathbf{F(w)} + \mathbf{Q}_0\varepsilon + \varepsilon^{\mathrm{T}}\mathbf{Q}_1\mathbf{w}, \tag{10}$$

where $\varepsilon = (\varepsilon_1, \varepsilon_2, \varepsilon_3)^T$. **F(w)** is the vector of nonlinear terms in the canonical form and

$$\mathbf{Q}_0 = \begin{bmatrix} 0 & 0 & 0 \\ 0 & 0 & 0 \\ 1 & 0 & 0 \end{bmatrix}, \mathbf{Q}_1 = \begin{bmatrix} 0 & 0 & 0 \\ 0 & 1 & 0 \\ 0 & 0 & 1 \end{bmatrix}, \tag{11}$$

then Equation (9) can be rewritten as

$$\begin{aligned} \dot{x} &= y, \\ \dot{y} &= z, \\ \dot{z} &= \varepsilon_1 + \varepsilon_2 y + \varepsilon_3 z + C_{3200}x^2 + C_{3020}y^2 + C_{3101}xz. \end{aligned} \tag{12}$$

Introducing a parametric excitation to the system (12), the following non-autonomous singular vector field is established as

$$\begin{aligned} \dot{x} &= y, \\ \dot{y} &= z, \\ \dot{z} &= \mu_0 + (\mu_1 + W)x + \mu_2 y + \mu_3 z + \alpha x^2 + \beta y^2 + \gamma xz, \\ W &= A\sin(\omega t), \end{aligned} \tag{13}$$

where $\omega \ll 1$, and the parametric excitation W can be expressed as

$$\begin{cases} \dot{W} = \omega W_1, \\ \dot{W}_1 = -\omega W, \end{cases} \tag{14}$$

where $W(0) = 0$, $W_1(0) = A$.

The system (13) can be treated as a fast–slow system, and W represents the slow variable. Thus, according to the fast–slow analysis method [35], regarding W as a control parameter, the bursting dynamics, especially the transition mechanisms, can be explored.

3. Bifurcation Analyses

Based on the fast–slow analysis method, the system (13) includes fast subsystems that regard W as a control parameter. It can be seen that the equilibrium point of the fast subsystem is in the form $x_E = (\pm x_0, 0, 0)$, and its solution equation is

$$\mu_0 + (\mu_1 + W)x_E + \alpha x_E{}^2 = 0, \tag{15}$$

and the characteristic equation at the equilibrium point is

$$P = \lambda^3 + D_1\lambda^2 + D_2\lambda + D_3, \tag{16}$$

where $D_1 = -\gamma x_E - \mu_1$, $D_2 = -\mu_1$, and $D_3 = -2\alpha x_E - W - \mu_1$.

Selecting the system parameter at $\mu_1 = -0.1, \mu_2 = -0.16, \mu_3 = -0.16, \alpha = -0.3$, $\gamma = -15$. According to the Hurwitz stability criterion, the stability condition of system (14) is $D_3 > 0$ and $D_1 D_2 - D_3 > 0$. At this point, the characteristics of the equilibrium point of the system may change through two types of codimension-1 bifurcation. When $D_3 = 0$, the fold bifurcation may occur, and it will cause the transition between equilibria. The nonhyperbolic condition is

$$\text{fold}: -2\alpha x_{\text{fold}} - W_{\text{fold}} - \mu_1 = 0. \tag{17}$$

Combining Equations (15) and (17) can obtain bifurcation sets

$$\begin{aligned} W_{\text{fold}+} &= 0.1 + 2\sqrt{-0.3\mu_0}, \\ W_{\text{fold}-} &= 0.1 - 2\sqrt{-0.3\mu_0}, \end{aligned} \tag{18}$$

$W_{fold\pm}$ represents the critical values of W corresponding to the fold bifurcation of the positive and negative half-axis equilibrium point $E_{\pm}$, respectively.

It should be noted that by substituting W_{fold-} and x_{fold-} into Equation (15), the equilibrium of the negative half-axis of x is always unstable, so only the stability of the equilibrium point E_+ is analyzed below.

When $D_1D_2 - D_3 = 0$, the Hopf bifurcation may occur at the equilibrium point. The nonhyperbolic condition is

$$\text{Hopf}: (\gamma\mu_2+2\alpha)x_{\text{Hopf}} + \mu_2\mu_3 + \mu_1 + W_{\text{Hopf}} = 0. \tag{19}$$

The Hopf bifurcation set can be obtained by solving Equations (15) and (19) simultaneously

$$\mu_0 - 0.004645866667 + 0.1106666667W_{\text{Hopf}} - 0.6481481482{W_{\text{Hopf}}}^2 = 0, \tag{20}$$

and bursting oscillation occurs when the trajectory on the bifurcation parameters plane crosses it.

When the parameter trajectories meet at the intersection of two codimension-1 bifurcations, fold-Hopf bifurcation may occur, and Hopf bifurcation conditions may also degenerate, resulting in Bautin bifurcation. Here, we use the numerical simulation tool MATCONT to perform codimension-2 bifurcation analysis.

Figure 1 shows a two-parameter bifurcation diagram of the system (13) in the $(W,\ \beta)$ plane. Due to the previous analysis, only the bifurcation behavior of equilibrium point E_+ is analyzed here. According to the numerical simulation, it can be obtained that at the point $(-0.13005, 7.6881)-(W, \beta)$, the first Lyapunov coefficient l_1 shrinks to zero, which means the Hopf bifurcation of E_+ degenerates, and Bautin bifurcation occurs. Regarding the formula for calculating the second Lyapunov coefficient proposed by Kuznetsov, $l_2 = -63.89666 < 0$ is obtained by numerical simulation. That is, the Bautin bifurcation point $GH_+ = (-0.13005, 7.6881)$ in the $(W,\ \beta)$ plane divides the Hopf bifurcation set H_+ into two parts: supercritical Hopf bifurcation $(\beta > 7.6881)$ and subcritical Hopf bifurcation $(\beta < 7.6881)$. To further reveal the mechanism of complex bursting oscillations caused by the codimension-2 Bautin bifurcation, we consider the other dynamics of the system with respect to parameter $W = A\sin(\omega t)$ when $\beta = 12$ and $\beta = 7.5$, respectively.

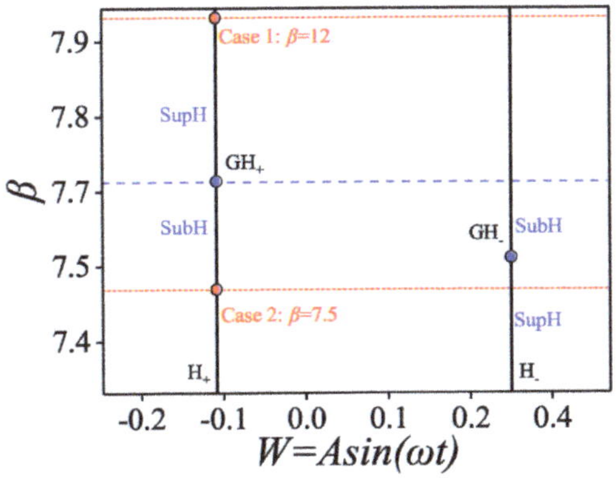

Figure 1. Two-parameter bifurcation diagram in the (W, β) plane.

3.1. *Bifurcation Analysis on* $(W,\ \mu_0)$ *Plane for* $\beta = 12$

Figure 2 divides the unfolding parameter plane into three regions by the Hopf and fold bifurcation sets. The system dynamics will change accordingly when the unfolding parameter trajectory crosses different areas.

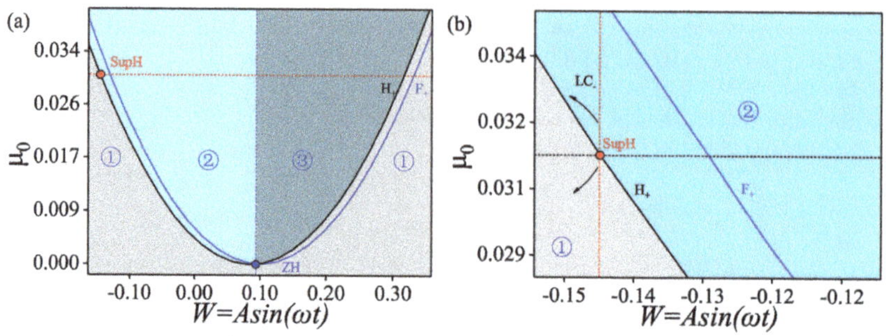

Figure 2. Two-parameter bifurcation diagram in the (W, μ_0) plane for $\beta = 12$. (**a**) The framework of the bifurcation diagram. (**b**) Local enlargement of the bifurcation diagram.

As shown in Figure 2, the system dynamics appear as a stable equilibrium point in region ②. When the unfolding parameter crosses through the Hopf bifurcation set into region ①, the supercritical Hopf bifurcation occurs, and the motion trajectory behaves as a stable limit cycle. It should be pointed out that when the parameter changes to $(0.0936, \tilde{\mu}_0)-(W, \mu_0)$, the bifurcation sets H_+ and F_+ intersect at the point ZH where the fold-Hopf bifurcation occurs. Regarding the numerical simulation results, the corresponding fold-Hopf bifurcation coefficients of critical normal form are $s = -1, \sigma = 1.5$. In area ③ of Figure 2, the motion trajectory appears as a stable limit cycle LC_{ZH} in the (x, y) plane. Further numerical simulation shows that LC_{ZH} will have the period-doubling bifurcation of the limit cycle with the change of slow-varying parameters. Referring to the bifurcation diagram on fold-Hopf bifurcation in the unfolding parametric plane introduced by Kuznetsov, the system will exhibit more rich dynamics when slow-varying parameter W crosses through different regions leading to more complex structures of bursting oscillations.

Figure 3 shows the bifurcation diagram of the system (13) with the variation of slow-varying parameters. The simultaneous Equations (15) and (20) obtain the coordinates $HB_+ = (-0.130049, 0.113583)$ of the Hopf bifurcation point of equilibrium point E_+ in the $(W,\ x)$ plane. The trajectory behaves as a stable limit cycle LC_+ when the equilibrium branch passes the bifurcation point HB_+. It is worth noting that the numerical simulation results show that LC_+ will bifurcate at $LC_{PD}(W = -1.784)$, which will cause the motion trajectory to evolve toward chaos through the period-doubling cascade.

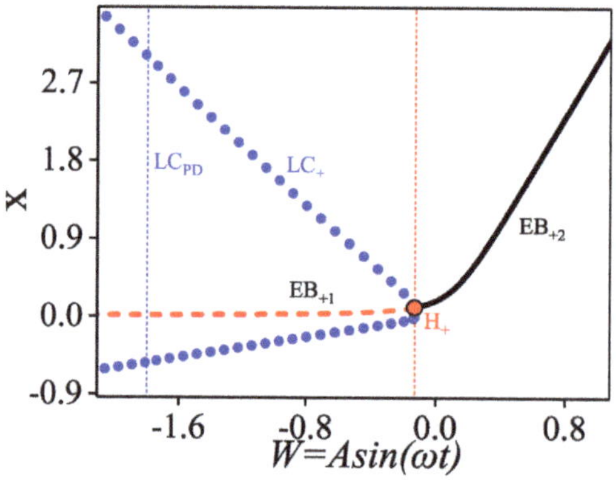

Figure 3. Single-parameter bifurcation diagram on the (W, x) plane for $\beta = 12$.

3.2. Bifurcation Analysis on $(W,\ \mu_0)$ Plane for $\beta = 7.5$

At $\beta = 7.5$, Figure 4 is almost close to Figure 2, but subtle differences remain. Figure 4b shows that a subcritical Hopf bifurcation occurs when the trajectory of W crosses through the Hopf bifurcation set from region ② to region ①. The system behaves as an unstable limit cycle LC_1. According to the previous analysis, due to the first Lyapunov coefficient failure, the Bautin bifurcation will occur at point GH_+, resulting in a stable limit cycle LC_2, at which time the second Lyapunov coefficient is $l_2 < 0$. During the movement of trajectory, LC_1 and LC_2 disappear after colliding at LPC_+ $(W = -0.1295)$, creating a new stable limit cycle LC_3. This process is called FLC (fold bifurcation of the limit cycle).

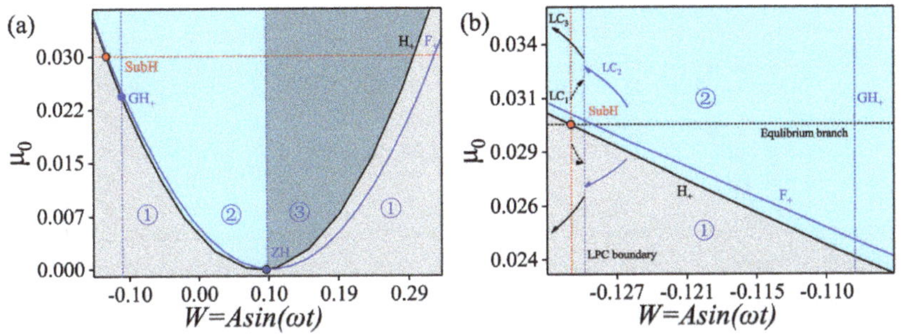

Figure 4. Two-parameter bifurcation diagram on the (W, μ_0) plane for $\beta = 7.5$. (**a**) The framework of the bifurcation diagram. (**b**) Local enlargement of the bifurcation diagram.

Figure 5 also shows the bifurcation diagram of the system (13) when $\mu_0 = 0.03$. The coordinates of the Hopf bifurcation point are $HB_+ = (-0.130049, 0.113583)$. It can be seen that the fold bifurcation of the limit cycle will cause the structure of the spiking state of the burster to be utterly different from that in the case of $\beta = 12$.

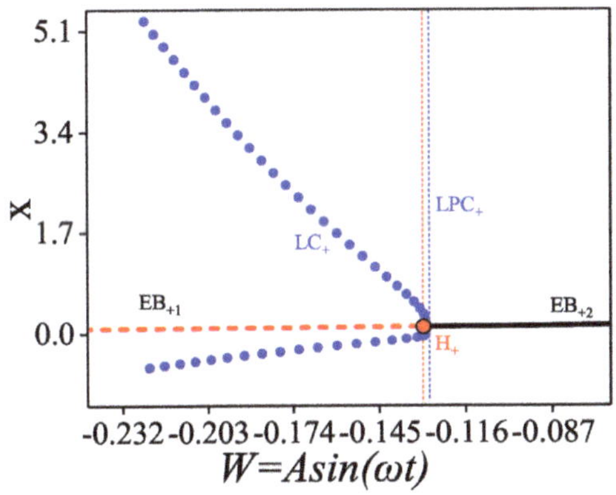

Figure 5. Single-parameter bifurcation diagram on the (W, x) plane for $\beta = 7.5$.

4. Evolution of Bursting Oscillations as Well as Their Mechanism

Based on the results of the above analysis, this section will further explore the influence of bifurcation behavior in different regions on the fast–slow effect of the system (13). Here, we also consider the evolution of dynamics in the case of $\beta = 12$ and $\beta = 7.5$ with the change of the amplitude of the slow-varying parameter W, respectively.

In Figure 6, as the control parameters $W = Asin(\omega t)$ change, the vertical axis is divided into three areas: red, green, and blue, corresponding to different access modes. Considering the excitation frequency $\omega \ll 1$, the equilibrium branch will slowly cross the corresponding region differently with the excitation amplitude A change, showing various dynamic characteristics.

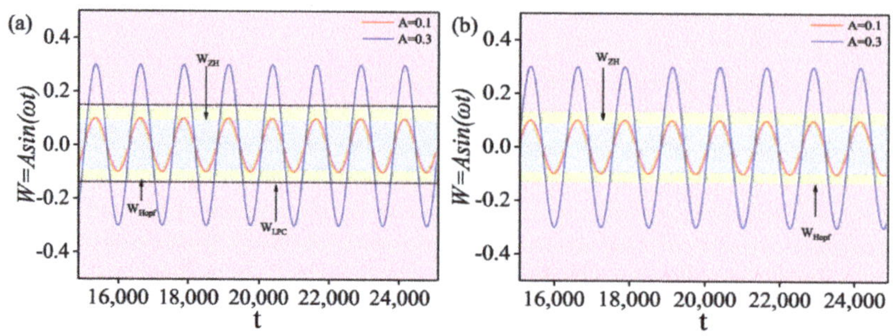

Figure 6. The trace path of the equilibrium branch as it changes with W. (**a**) The case for $\beta = 7.5$. (**b**) The case for $\beta = 12$.

When $A < |W_{ZH}|$, the slow-varying excitation $W = Asin(\omega t)$ will periodically visit the blue area in Figure 6, where the motion trajectory is presented as a stable focus, and no bursting oscillation occurs.

When $A > |W_{ZH}|$, the red line in Figure 6 represents the curve of W for $A = 0.1$, and it can be seen that the control parameter W will visit the blue and green regions over time. Since the bifurcation sets H_+ and F_+ intersect at a point in the green area, the codimension-2 fold-Hopf bifurcation will occur. With the perturbance of the high-order term of the system, the trajectory near the equilibria will periodically cross the fold-Hopf bifurcation point, resulting in the motion trajectory near the equilibria appearing as a limit cycle in the (x, y) plane and a stable focus in the (y, z) plane, respectively. The phase portraits of the motion trajectory in different planes and the corresponding time history are performed in Figure 7. In this case, no bursting oscillation occurs.

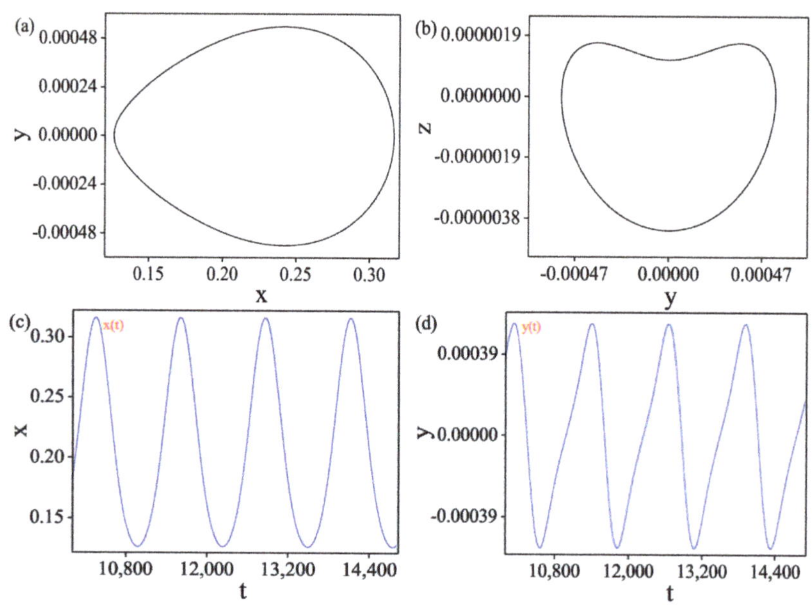

Figure 7. The phase portrait of system trajectory and its time history for $A = 0.1$. (**a**) The phase portrait on the (x, y) plane. (**b**) The phase portrait on the (y, z) plane. (**c**) The time history of $x(t)$. (**d**) The time history of $y(t)$.

When $A > \left|W_{Hopf}\right|$, the blue line in Figure 6 represents the curve of slow-varying excitation for $A = 0.3$, at which time the control parameters will visit the blue, green, and red regions periodically so that the system dynamics behavior is affected by three areas and bursting oscillations will occur at the single equilibrium point E_+.

Here, the TPP (transformed phase portrait) is used to reveal the dynamical mechanism of the bursting oscillation behavior of the system. TPP can be defined as

$$\prod_G = [\mathbf{X(t)}, W] = [x(t), y(t), z(t), A\sin(\omega t)], \forall t = R \tag{21}$$

Equation (21) yields the trajectory of the slow-changing parameters associated with each variable of the system (13) in each subplane projection, such as $(W, x)-plane$, $(W, y)-plane$, and $(W, z)-plane$. Therefore, the TPP is believed to present the evolution process of bursting oscillation and reveals the corresponding induction mechanism. Furthermore, here, we overlap the TPP and the equilibrium branch on the $(W, x)-plane$ to demonstrate the characteristics of the equilibrium point and its bifurcation mechanism when bursting oscillation occurs.

4.1. *Bursting Oscillation for $\beta = 7.5$ as Well as the Mechanism*

Let $A = 0.3$, and as the slow-variable parameter W changes, the movement trajectory will periodically visit the blue, green, and red regions in Figure 6a. Combined with the bifurcation diagram shown in Figure 4 in the previous section, we can find that in the region ①, the equilibrium branch of the system will cross the Hopf bifurcation point with the change of W, at which point the trajectory behaves as an unstable limit cycle LC_1. As the parameters change, the Hopf bifurcation will degenerate, and a stable limit cycle LC_2 will be generated at the degenerate Hopf bifurcation point GH_+. In Figure 6a, when $W > |W_{LPC}|$, as W changes further, the two limit cycles will collide, and the limit cycle will bifurcate at position LPC, resulting in a stable limit cycle LC_3.

As can be seen from Figure 8, the fast–slow effect occurs between the limit cycle generated by the bifurcation of Hopf and the fold-Hopf bifurcation, resulting in bursting oscillations, and each oscillation period can be divided into the spiking state and the quiescent state. To reveal the essential characteristics of the spiking state, here, the Stroboscopic method is used to obtain the trajectory of the Poincaré mapping

$$\sum = [(x, y, z) | t = t_0 + 2N\pi/\omega, N = 1, 2, \ldots]. \tag{22}$$

Figure 9 shows the cross-section of the motion trajectory for one period, and it can be found that the spiking state behaves as a quasi-periodic characteristic. Further numerical calculations show that the corresponding two oscillation frequencies approximate the frequency of the stable limit cycle generated by the subcritical Hopf in the red region and the frequency of the limit cycle caused by the fold-Hopf bifurcation in the green area. Therefore, from the structural point of view of bursting oscillation, the burster can be classified as a quasi-periodic Point–Cycle–Cycle type.

As performed in Figure 10, overlapping the TPP and the equilibrium branch in the (W, x) plane, the dynamical mechanism of bursting oscillation can be revealed. Suppose that the motion of the system (13) starts from region ②, and the trajectory moves to the left along the stable equilibrium branch EB_{+2}, which appears as a quiescent state. When the trajectory moves to the subcritical Hopf bifurcation point at HB_+, the trajectory will cross this bifurcation point and move along EB_{+1} for a while, which is due to the fact that the slow passage effect affects the bifurcation. Some studies in the literature believe that this is in terms of the action of motion inertia, which is affected by factors such as initial value, excitation frequency, and amplitude, which are not discussed here. The effect of Hopf bifurcation occurs after the trajectory passes through the bifurcation delay region in Figure 10, causing the trajectory to jump to the unstable limit cycle LC_1 and move to the right. When W changes to $W = W_{LPC}$, FLC will occur, causing the unstable limit cycle LC_1 to disappear after colliding with the stable limit cycle LC_2 and, at the same time, generating a stable limit cycle LC_3 in the direction of the left, and the motion trajectory will oscillate according to the stable limit cycle LC_3, showing a spiking state. When the slow-varying parameter W changes to the minimum value at $W = -0.3$, the trajectory turns, and the slow passage effect of the Hopf bifurcation at point HB_+ makes the amplitude of the trajectory oscillation gradually decreases with the change of W. As W changes, the trajectory will pass through region ②, enter region ③, transition to the limit cycle generated by the codimension-2 fold-Hopf bifurcation, and continue oscillating according to the limit cycle, at which point the motion of system still behaves as a spiking state. When the slow-varying parameter W changes to the maximum value $W = 0.3$, the trajectory will gradually settle down to the stable equilibrium branch EB_{+2} after turning. The trajectory of the system completes a period of bursting oscillations.

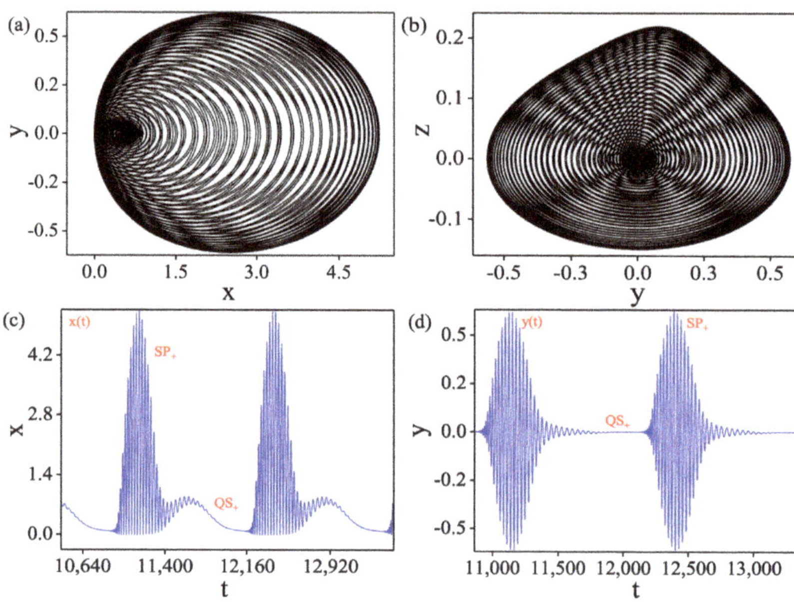

Figure 8. The bursting oscillation for $A = 0.3$. (**a**) The phase portrait on the (x, y) plane. (**b**) The phase portrait on the (y, z) plane. (**c**) The time history of $x(t)$. (**d**) The time history of $y(t)$.

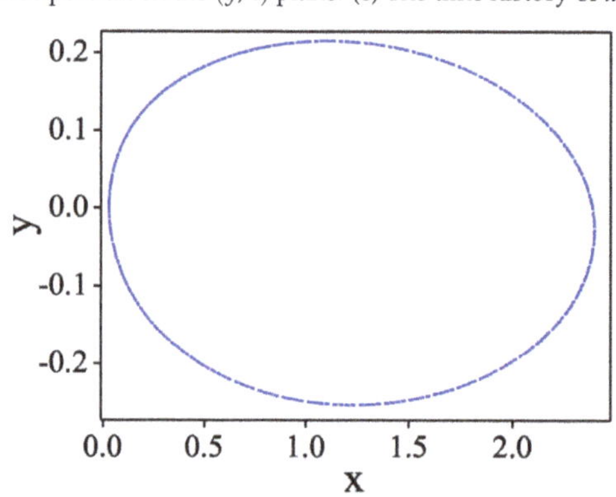

Figure 9. The trajectory of Poincaré mapping corresponding to the bursting oscillations for $A = 0.3$.

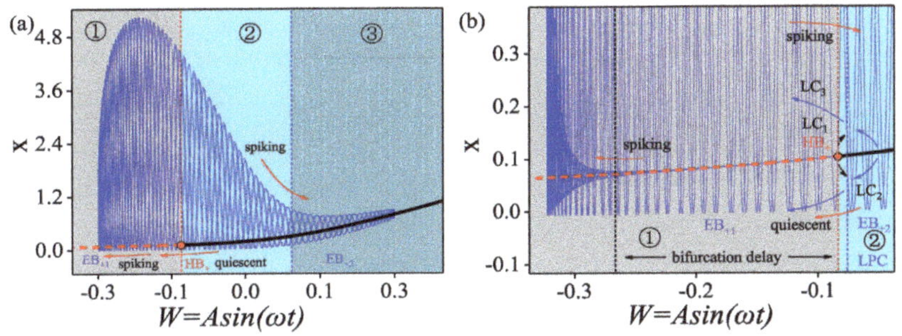

Figure 10. TPP on the (W, x) plane for $A = 0.3$. (**a**) The framework of the TPP. (**b**) Local enlargement of the TPP.

In general, the trajectory of bursting oscillation is divided into three parts. Firstly, the trajectory moves along the stable equilibrium branch EB_{+2} in region ②. Secondly, the trajectory oscillates according to the stable limit cycle after passing through the subcritical Hopf bifurcation and FLC in the region ①. Finally, the trajectory oscillates in the region ③ by the limit cycle generated by the codimension-2 fold-Hopf bifurcation.

According to the classification method on bursting oscillation proposed by Izhikevich, the oscillation can be called subHopf/FLC/fold-Hopf bursting from the bifurcation mechanism. Meanwhile, from the geometric structure, it can be called a quasi-periodic Point–Cycle–Cycle burster.

The TPP will expand to the left and right as the excitation amplitude increases. Likewise, the trajectory near the equilibria will periodically visit the blue, green, and red regions in Figure 6a. Figure 11 shows the trajectory structure of the system in the (x, y) plane when $A = 2.0$ and the corresponding time history. As the slow-varying parameter W changed, the trajectory behaved as a spiking state at all times in the oscillation period. The burster on the spiking state SP_{-} presents a period-doubling characteristic. This is caused by the interaction between the limit cycle induced by the fold-Hopf bifurcation of the codimension-2 and the limit cycle generated by the Hopf bifurcation.

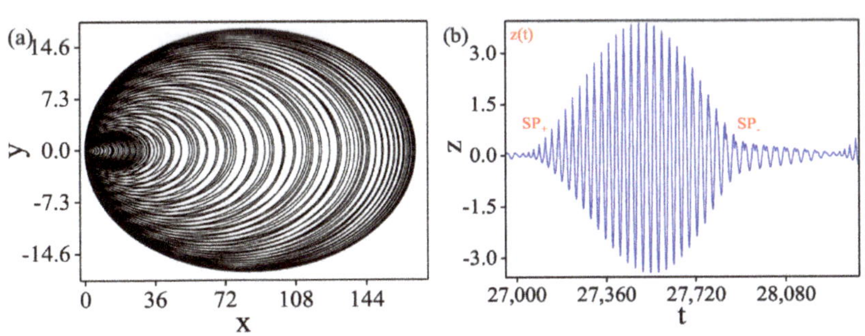

Figure 11. The bursting oscillation for $A = 2.0$. (**a**) The phase portrait on the (x, y) plane. (**b**) The time history of $z(t)$.

Similarly, Figure 12 shows the superposition of the TPP and equilibrium branch in the (W, x) plane when the amplitude of the slow-varying excitation changes to $A = 2.0$. It can be seen in the figure that the trajectory of the system motion is almost the same as when $A = 0.3$. When the trajectory moves to region ③ with the change of W, it oscillates according to the limit cycle generated by the fold-Hopf bifurcation, and the system behaves as a spiking state. The trajectory turns and begins to converge toward the stable equilibrium branch EB_{+2} when W increases to the maximum value. Before converging to EB_{+2}, the trajectory moves to a stable limit cycle LC_3 after it crosses through the Hopf bifurcation point HB_{+} and bifurcation delay region, and it oscillates according to the limit cycle LC_3, at which point the system continues to exhibit a spiking state. This buster can be called a subHopf/FLC/fold-Hopf burster of Cycle–Cycle type.

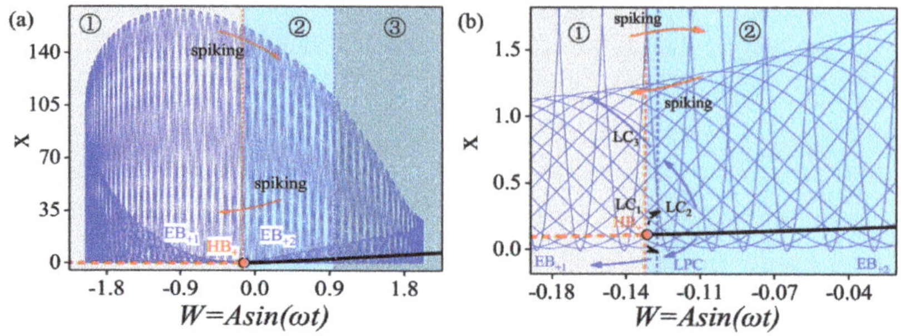

Figure 12. TPP on the (W, x) plane for $A = 2.0$. (**a**) Framework of the TPP. (**b**) Local enlargement of the TPP.

4.2. Bursting Oscillation for $\beta = 12$ as Well as the Mechanism

In this case, set $A = 0.3$. As shown in Figure 6b, with the changing of the $W = Asin(\omega t)$, the equilibrium branch of the system will periodically visit regions blue, green, and red sequentially. Figure 13 shows the structure of the trajectory of the system motion in the $(x,\ y)$ plane and the $(y,\ z)$ plane, respectively, and the corresponding time history has also been given. It can be seen from Figure 13c,d that when $A = 0.3$, with the change of β, the mode of the spiking state of bursting oscillation due to codimension-2 Bautin bifurcation will change qualitatively, where the red curve represents $\beta = 7.5$, and the blue curve represents $\beta = 12$.

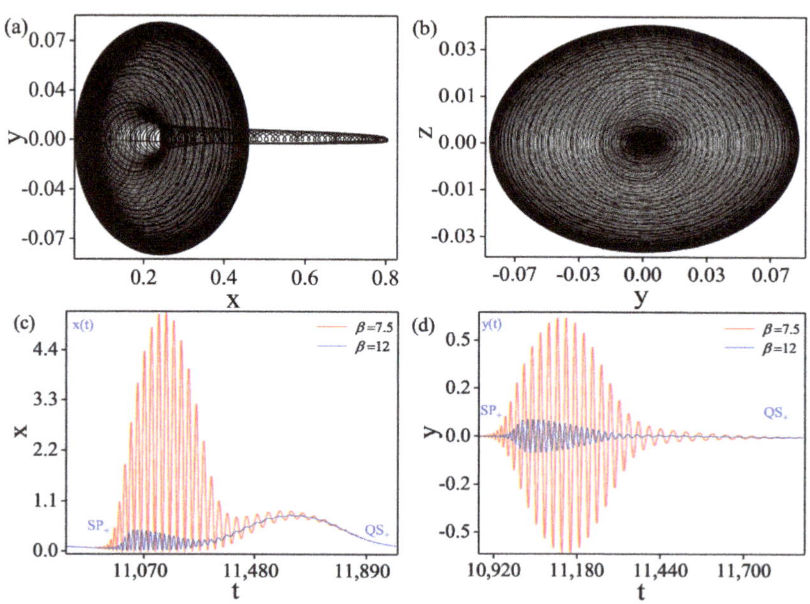

Figure 13. The bursting oscillation for $A = 0.3$. (**a**) The phase portrait on the (x, y) plane. (**b**) The phase portrait on the (y, z) plane. (**c**) Overlap of the time history of $x(t)$. (**d**) Overlap of the time history of $y(t)$.

Figure 14 shows Poincaré mapping (22) of the oscillation trajectory of one period, in which it can be found that the spiking state behaves as a quasi-periodic characteristic. Therefore, the structure of the bursting oscillation is the Point–Cycle–Cycle type in this case.

Figure 15 shows the superposition of the TPP and the equilibrium branch on the $(W,\ x)$ plane. At $A = 0.3$, as W changes, the motion trajectory will periodically traverse regions ②, ①, and ③ in Figure 15. Assuming that the starting point of the movement of the system (13) is in region ②, the trajectory will move to the left along the stable equilibrium branch EB_{+2}. The system will be quiescent, which can also be confirmed by the $x(t)$ time history in Figure 13c. By changing W, the supercritical Hopf bifurcation occurs at the bifurcation point HB_{+}. Due to the delayed effect of the bifurcation, the trajectory will continue to move in the region ① along the unstable equilibrium branch EB_{+1}. When the trajectory crosses the bifurcation delay region in Figure 15b, it will jump to the limit cycle LC_{+}, causing the trajectory to transition between the spiking state and the quiescent state, and the trajectory will oscillate along LC_{+}. At the minimum value of W, the trajectory turns the right and oscillates along LC_{+}. As the slow-varying parameter W changes in the region ③, the codimension-2 fold-Hopf bifurcation will cause the trajectory to jump toward a stable limit cycle, behaving as a spiking state. When W arrives at the maximum, the trajectory shifts to the left and gradually converges to a stable equilibrium branch, completing one period of bursting oscillation.

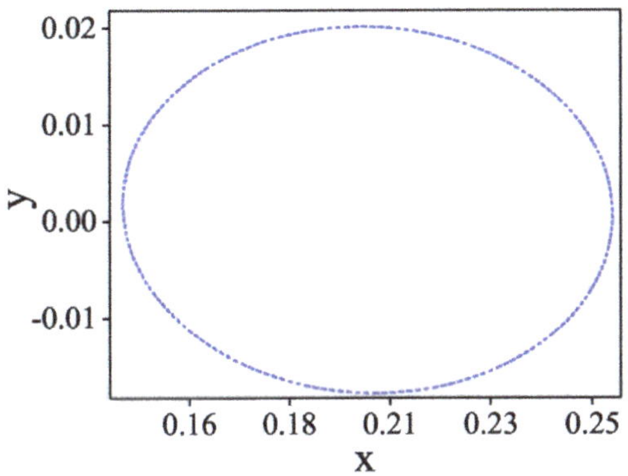

Figure 14. Poincaré mapping (22) for $A = 0.3$.

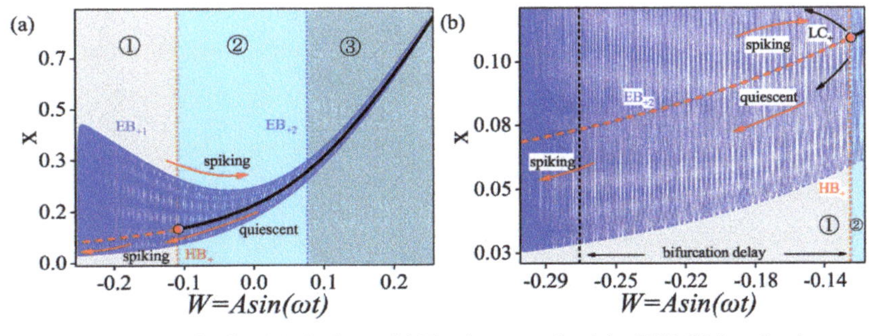

Figure 15. TPP on the for (W, x) plane. (**a**) The framework of the TPP. (**b**) Local enlargement of the TPP.

The trajectory of bursting oscillation is generally divided into three parts. Firstly, the trajectory moves along the stable equilibrium branch EB_{+1} in region ②. Secondly, it oscillates according to the stable limit cycle after passing through the supercritical Hopf bifurcation in region ① and finally oscillates in region ③ around the limit cycle generated by the codimension-2 fold-Hopf bifurcation.

Due to the interaction between the limit cycle induced by the fold-Hopf bifurcation and the limit cycle generated by the Hopf bifurcation, the spiking state presents a quasi-period characteristic. In this case, the burster can be classified as supHopf/fold-Hopf bursting of Point–Cycle–Cycle type.

As the excitation amplitude A increases, the region the trajectory visits no longer changes. Still, its motion pattern changes, and Figure 16 shows the bursting oscillation when $A = 2.0$. From the time history of $x(t)$ in Figure 16, unlike the case of $A = 0.3$, it can be seen that the motion trajectory of the system has been excited at all times. Meanwhile, the trajectory exhibits period-doubling characteristics due to the interaction between the limit cycle generated by the Hopf bifurcation and the limit cycle caused by the fold-Hopf bifurcation. This can also be verified from the time history of the spiking state of bursting oscillation in Figure 16b. The period-doubling characteristic can also be verified by the Poincaré mapping of the oscillation trajectory of the burster, which is shown in Figure 17. Consequently, it can be considered that the motion of the system at this time is quasi-period bursting with period-doubling characteristics.

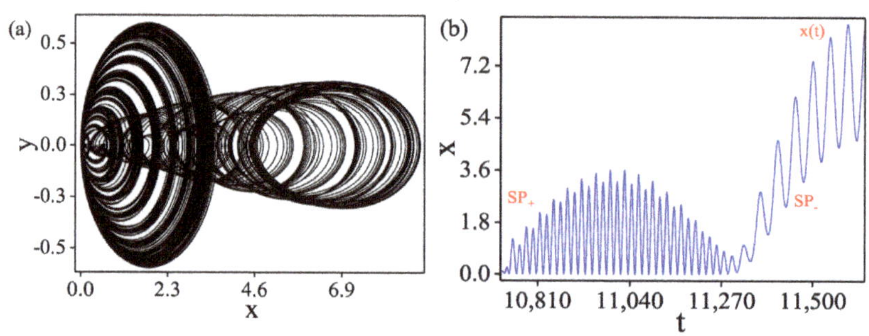

Figure 16. The bursting oscillation for $A = 2.0$. (**a**) The phase portrait on the (x, y) plane. (**b**) The time history of $x(t)$.

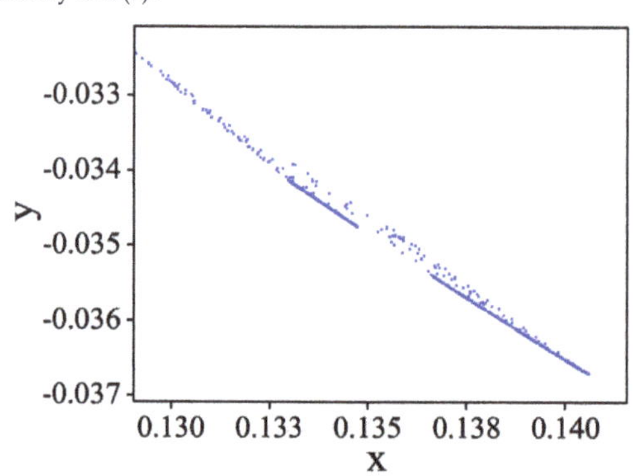

Figure 17. Poincaré mapping (22) for $A = 2.0$.

To reveal the mechanism of bursting behavior, as performed in Figure 18, we overlap the TPP and the equilibrium branch. It can be seen that the trajectory of the system motion is almost the same as when $A = 0.3$. We assume that the starting point of the trajectory is in region ②. When the slow-varying parameter W changes to $W = -1.784$, the period-doubling bifurcation of the limit cycle will occur, causing the trajectory to present as Torus. It should be noted that since the inertia of the movement of the system increases with the increase of the excitation amplitude, the trajectory jumps to a stable limit cycle LC_+ before converging to the equilibrium branch and oscillates according to the limit cycle LC_+. At that time, the system continues to exhibit a spiking state. As W changes, the trajectory returns to region ②, completing one period of bursting oscillation.

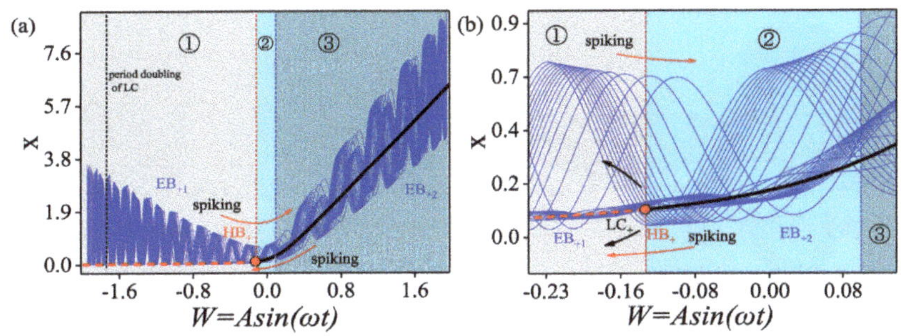

Figure 18. TPP for the (W, x) plane for $A = 2.0$. (**a**) The framework of the TPP. (**b**) Local enlargement of the TPP.

5. Evolution of Chaos

This section discusses the evolution of the dynamical behavior when the fast–slow effects change. According to geometric singular perturbation theory, slow manifolds determine the trajectory of the entire fast–slow system, while fast manifolds can be seen as minor perturbations of slow systems. Therefore, in this section, the evolution of the dynamics of the whole system is analyzed by increasing the frequency ω of the slow variable W. A set of chaotic bursting phenomena induced by the period-doubling cascade of the limit cycle is also deduced.

Let $\beta = 12$ and set the excitation amplitude at $A = 1.0$. Figure 19 shows the trajectory of bursting oscillation with different ω values in the (x, y) plane. The corresponding Poincaré cross-section is given in Figure 20.

When $\omega = 0.005$, from Figure 19a,b, it can be found that the trajectory of the system (13) behaves as a bursting oscillation of a quasi-periodic Cycle–Cycle type. As shown in Figure 19c, when ω increases to $\omega = 0.006$, the trajectory of the bursting presented in the (x, y) plane appears as a doubling period, which is verified by the Poincaré mapping of the trajectory corresponding to the bursting oscillation in Figure 19d. Combined with the analysis of Section 3, with the change of unfolding parameters, the limit cycle generated by the codimension-2 fold-Hopf bifurcation evolves to the Torus, resulting in the bursting oscillation present as Torus–Torus type.

As W increases, the trajectory of motion of the system (13) will evolve toward periodic oscillation. Figure 20 shows that the scale difference between the frequency of the spiking state SP_+ and SP_- of the burster is gradually disappearing. From the time history of $x(t)$ in Figure 20b,d, the difference in time scale between the two spiking states still exists, so it can be considered that the motion trajectory of the system at this time is a bursting oscillation. Figure 20a,c show that the trajectory of the burster is period-4 for $\omega = 0.024$ and period-8 for $\omega = 0.026$, respectively. When ω increases to $\omega = 0.037$, the trajectory of bursting in the (x, y) plane appears irregular, which can be verified in Figure 20f. At this point, it can be considered that the motion of the system evolved from the period-doubling cascade to chaotic bursting.

As ω increases further, the scale differences between the fast and slow subsystems will disappear completely, and Figure 21 also deduces a set of chaotic motions induced by the period-doubling cascade. The corresponding ω are $\omega = 0.109$ (period-2), $\omega = 0.111$ (period-4), $\omega = 0.112$ (period-8) and $\omega = 0.113$ (chaos), respectively.

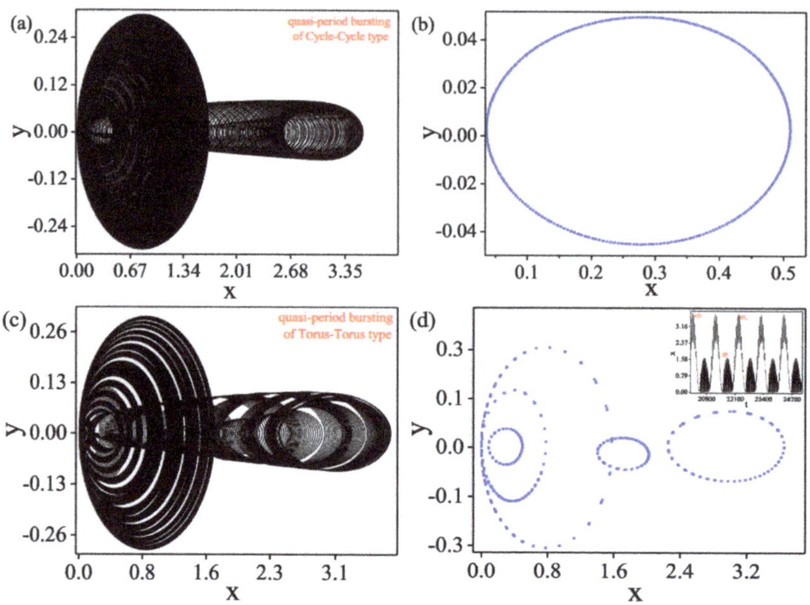

Figure 19. Evolution of bursting oscillations with period-doubling. (**a**) Quasi-period bursting for $\omega = 0.005$. (**b**) Poincaré mapping (22) for $\omega = 0.005$. (**c**) Quasi-period bursting for $\omega = 0.006$. (**d**) Poincaré mapping (22) for $\omega = 0.006$ as well as the time history of $x(t)$.

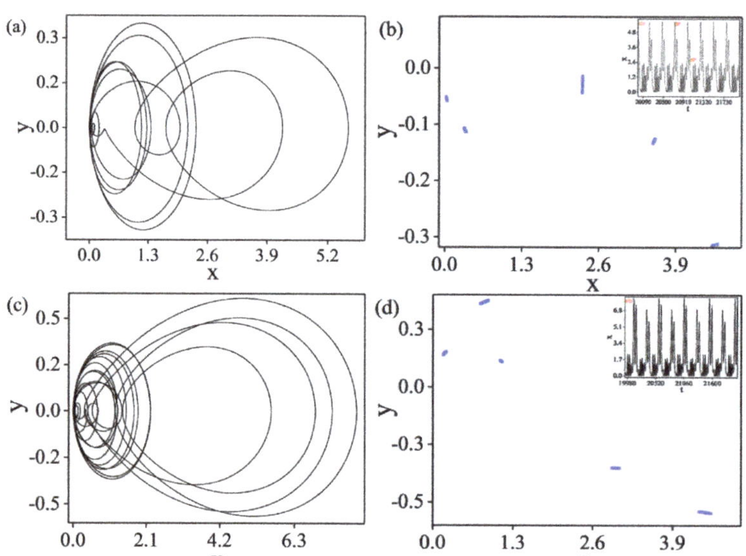

Figure 20. *Cont.*

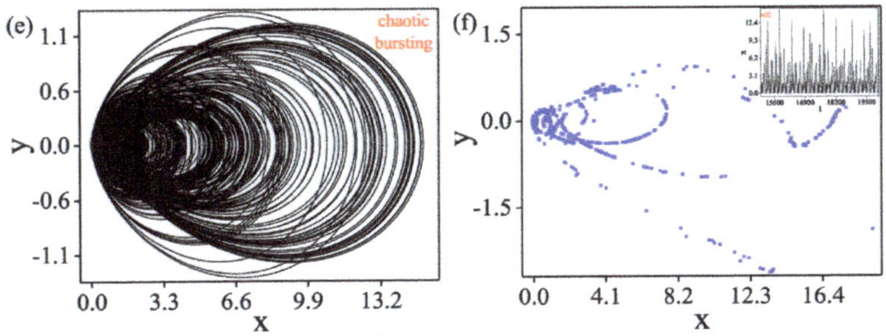

Figure 20. The evolution of a period-doubling cascade to chaotic bursting. (**a**) Bursting with period doubling for $\omega = 0.024$. (**b**) Poincaré mapping (22) for $\omega = 0.024$ as well as the time history of $x(t)$. (**c**) Bursting with period doubling for $\omega = 0.026$; (**d**) Poincaré mapping (22) for $\omega = 0.026$ as well as the time history of $x(t)$. (**e**) Chaotic bursting; (**f**) Poincaré mapping (22) for $\omega = 0.037$ as well as the time history of $x(t)$.

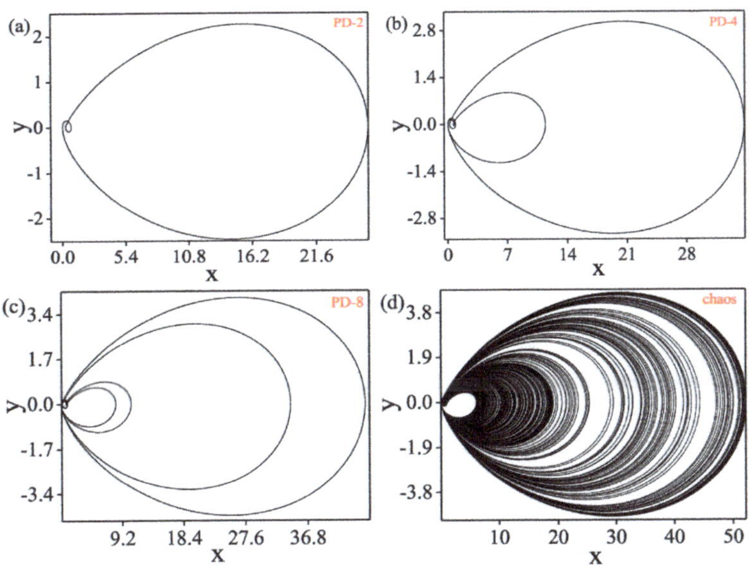

Figure 21. The evolution of a period-doubling cascade to chaos. (**a**) PD-2 for $\omega = 0.109$. (**b**) PD-4 for $\omega = 0.111$. (**c**) PD-8 for $\omega = 0.112$. (**d**) Chaos for $\omega = 0.113$.

6. Conculusions

This paper mainly studies the bursting oscillations and their dynamical mechanism of the second-order truncated triple zero eigenvalues singularity normal form under the unfolding form. Based on the fast–slow analysis method, considering the order gap between excitation and natural frequency, the singular system with parametric excitation can be viewed as a generalized autonomous system. The evolution of system dynamics and the mechanism are analyzed regarding periodic parameter excitation $W = Asin(\omega t)$ as a slow-varying bifurcation parameter. The system exhibits various bursting oscillation patterns when the slow-varying parameters visit different dynamical regions in the two-parameter plane. In particular, due to the singularity of the triple zero eigenvalues, two types of degeneration will occur in the Hopf bifurcation at the equilibrium point of the system, namely the codimension-2 fold-Hopf bifurcation and the Bautin bifurcation, which makes the dynamic behavior change from simple to complex. More diverse structures of the spiking state of bursting oscillation will occur at the single equilibria due to the complexity of the singularity of high codimension bifurcation, such as Cycle–Cycle burster, Torus–Torus burster, and chaotic bursting. With the increase of the approximate order of normal form, the number of equilibrium points of the system will increase, and the difficulty of bifurcation analysis will also increase, so the dynamical mechanism corresponding to bursting oscillations will also become complex, and related research needs to be further carried out.

Author Contributions: Conceptualization, W.L. and Q.B.; methodology, W.L. and Q.B.; validation, Z.C. and W.L.; formal analysis, W.L.; investigation, W.L. and S.L.; writing—original draft preparation, W.L. and S.L.; writing—review and editing, W.L. and Z.C.; funding acquisition, Q.B. and W.L. All authors have read and agreed to the published version of the manuscript.

Funding: This work was supported by the National Natural Science Foundation of China (Grant Nos. 12002299) and by the Natural Science Foundation for Colleges and Universities in Jiangsu Province (Grant Nos. 20KJB110010).

Institutional Review Board Statement: Not applicable.

Informed Consent Statement: Not applicable.

Data Availability Statement: Not applicable.

Acknowledgments: We will like to express our deep thanks to the anonymous referees for their valuable comments.

Conflicts of Interest: The authors declare that there is no conflict of interest regarding the publication of this manuscript.

References

1. Golubitsky, M.; Josic, K.; Kaper, T.J. An unfolding theory approach to bursting in fast-slow systems. In *Global Analysis of Dynamical Systems, A Festschrift/Liber Amicorum Dedicated to Floris Takens for His 60th Birthday*; Broer, H., Krauskopf, B., Vegter, G., Eds.; IOP Publishing: Bristol, UK, 2001; pp. 277–308. [CrossRef]
2. Leimkuhler, B. An efficient multiple time-scale reversible integrator for the gravitational N-body problem. *Appl. Numer. Math.* **2002**, *43*, 175–190. [CrossRef]
3. Fujimoto, K.; Kaneko, K. How fast elements can affect slow dynamics. *Phys. D Nonlinear Phenom.* **2003**, *180*, 1–16. [CrossRef]
4. Hou, L.; Chen, H.; Chen, Y.; Lu, K.; Liu, Z. Bifurcation and stability analysis of a nonlinear rotor system subjected to constant excitation and rub-impact. *Mech. Syst. Signal Process.* **2019**, *125*, 65–78. [CrossRef]
5. Bonet, C.; Jeffrey, M.R.; Martín, P.; Olm, J.M. Novel slow–fast behaviour in an oscillator driven by a frequency-switching force. *Commun. Nonlinear Sci. Numer. Simul.* **2023**, *118*, 107032. [CrossRef]
6. Bao, H.; Wang, N.; Bao, B.; Chen, M.; Jin, P.; Wang, G. Initial condition-dependent dynamics and transient period in memristor-based hypogenetic jerk system with four line equilibria. *Commun. Nonlinear Sci. Numer. Simul.* **2018**, *57*, 264–275. [CrossRef]
7. Bi, Q.; Li, S.; Kurths, J.; Zhang, Z. The mechanism of bursting oscillations with different codimensional bifurcations and nonlinear structures. *Nonlinear Dyn.* **2016**, *85*, 993–1005. [CrossRef]
8. Györgyi, L.; Field, R.J. A three-variable model of deterministic chaos in the Belousov–Zhabotinsky reaction. *Nature* **1992**, *355*, 808–810. [CrossRef]
9. Vanag, V.K.; Zhabotinsky, A.M.; Epstein, I.R. Oscillatory clusters in the periodically illuminated, spatially extended Belousov-Zhabotinsky reaction. *Phys. Rev. Lett.* **2001**, *86*, 552. [CrossRef]
10. Huang, L.; Wu, G.; Zhang, Z.; Bi, Q. Fast–slow dynamics and bifurcation mechanism in a novel chaotic system. *Int. J. Bifurc. Chaos* **2019**, *29*, 1930028. [CrossRef]
11. Wang, J. Active vibration control: Design towards performance limit. *Mech. Syst. Signal Process.* **2022**, *171*, 108926. [CrossRef]
12. Dragan, V.; Stoica, A. Robust stabilization of two-time scale systems with respect to the normalized coprime factorization. *Int. J. Control* **2002**, *75*, 1–10. [CrossRef]
13. Boussaada, I.; Morărescu, I.-C.; Niculescu, S. Inverted pendulum stabilization: Characterization of codimension-three triple zero bifurcation via multiple delayed proportional gains. *Syst. Control Lett.* **2015**, *82*, 1–9. [CrossRef]
14. Xue, M.; Gou, J.; Xia, Y.; Bi, Q. Computation of the normal form as well as the unfolding of the vector field with zero-zero-Hopf bifurcation at the origin. *Math. Comput. Simul.* **2021**, *190*, 377–397. [CrossRef]
15. Zhang, M.; Zhang, X.; Bi, Q. Slow–Fast Behaviors and Their Mechanism in a Periodically Excited Dynamical System with Double Hopf Bifurcations. *Int. J. Bifurc. Chaos* **2021**, *31*, 2130022. [CrossRef]
16. Mandadi, V.; Huseyin, K. Non-linear bifurcation analysis of non-gradient systems. *Int. J. Non-Linear Mech.* **1980**, *15*, 159–172. [CrossRef]
17. Yu, P.; Huseyin, K. Bifurcations associated with a three-fold zero eigenvalue. *Q. Appl. Math.* **1988**, *46*, 193–216. [CrossRef]

18. Yu, P.; Huseyin, K. Bifurcations associated with a double zero of index two and a pair of purely imaginary eigenvalues. *Int. J. Syst. Sci.* **1988**, *19*, 1–21. [CrossRef]
19. Bi, Q.; Yu, P. Computation of normal forms of differential equations associated with non-semisimple zero eigenvalues. *Int. J. Bifurc. Chaos* **1998**, *8*, 2279–2319. [CrossRef]
20. Freire, E.; Gamero, E.; Rodríguez-Luis, A.J.; Algaba, A. A note on the triple-zero linear degeneracy: Normal forms, dynamical and bifurcation behaviors of an unfolding. *Int. J. Bifurc. Chaos* **2002**, *12*, 2799–2820. [CrossRef]
21. Algaba, A.; Domínguez-Moreno, M.C.; Merino, M.; Rodríguez-Luis, A.J. Takens–Bogdanov bifurcations of equilibria and periodic orbits in the Lorenz system. *Commun. Nonlinear Sci. Numer. Simul.* **2016**, *30*, 328–343. [CrossRef]
22. Algaba, A.; Chung, K.-W.; Qin, B.-W.; Rodríguez-Luis, A.J. Computation of all the coefficients for the global connections in the Z2-symmetric Takens-Bogdanov normal forms. *Commun. Nonlinear Sci. Numer. Simul.* **2020**, *81*, 105012. [CrossRef]
23. Duan, L.; Lu, Q.; Wang, Q. Two-parameter bifurcation analysis of firing activities in the Chay neuronal model. *Neurocomputing* **2008**, *72*, 341–351. [CrossRef]
24. Duan, L.; Lu, Q.; Cheng, D. Bursting of Morris-Lecar neuronal model with current-feedback control. *Sci. China Ser. E Technol. Sci.* **2009**, *52*, 771–781. [CrossRef]
25. Braun, F.; Mereu, A.C. Zero-Hopf bifurcation in a 3D jerk system. *Nonlinear Anal. Real World Appl.* **2021**, *59*, 103245. [CrossRef]
26. Bao, H.; Ding, R.; Hua, M.; Wu, H.; Chen, B. Initial-condition effects on a two-memristor-based Jerk system. *Mathematics* **2022**, *10*, 411. [CrossRef]
27. Saggio, M.L.; Spiegler, A.; Bernard, C.; Jirsa, V.K. Fast–slow bursters in the unfolding of a high codimension singularity and the ultra-slow transitions of classes. *J. Math. Neurosci.* **2017**, *7*, 7. [CrossRef]
28. Kuznetsov, Y.A. *Elements of Applied Bifurcation Theory*, 2nd ed.; Springer: New York, NY, USA, 2011.
29. Sen, D.; Ghorai, S.; Banerjee, M.; Morozov, A. Bifurcation analysis of the predator–prey model with the Allee effect in the predator. *J. Math. Biol.* **2022**, *84*, 7. [CrossRef]
30. Yang, R. Turing–Hopf bifurcation co-induced by cross-diffusion and delay in Schnakenberg system. *Chaos Solitons Fractals* **2022**, *164*, 112659. [CrossRef]
31. Maleki, F.; Beheshti, B.; Hajihosseini, A.; Lamooki, G.R.R. The Bogdanov–Takens bifurcation analysis on a three dimensional recurrent neural network. *Neurocomputing* **2010**, *73*, 3066–3078. [CrossRef]
32. Perko, L.M. A global analysis of the Bogdanov–Takens system. *SIAM J. Appl. Math.* **1992**, *52*, 1172–1192. [CrossRef]
33. Baider, A.; Sanders, J.A. Further reduction of the Takens-Bogdanov normal form. *J. Differ. Equ.* **1992**, *99*, 205–244. [CrossRef]
34. Murdock, J. Asymptotic unfoldings of dynamical systems by normalizing beyond the normal form. *J. Differ. Equ.* **1998**, *143*, 151–190. [CrossRef]
35. Rinzel, J. Formal classification of bursting mechanisms in excitable systems. In *Lecture Notes in Biomathematics*; Teramoto, E., Yamaguti, M., Eds.; Springer: Berlin, Germany, 1987; pp. 267–281.

mathematics

MDPI

Article

Investigating Symmetric Soliton Solutions for the Fractional Coupled Konno–Onno System Using Improved Versions of a Novel Analytical Technique

Humaira Yasmin [1,*], Noufe H. Aljahdaly [2], Abdulkafi Mohammed Saeed [3] and Rasool Shah [4]

[1] Department of Basic Sciences, Preparatory Year Deanship, King Faisal University, Al-Ahsa 31982, Saudi Arabia
[2] Department of Mathematics, Faculty of Sciences and Arts, King Abdulaziz University, Rabigh 21911, Saudi Arabia; nhaljahdaly@kau.edu.sa
[3] Department of Mathematics, College of Science, Qassim University, Buraydah 51452, Saudi Arabia; abdulkafi.ahmed@qu.edu.sa
[4] Department of Mathematics, Abdul Wali Khan University, Mardan 23200, Pakistan; rasoolshah@awkum.edu.pk
* Correspondence: hhassain@kfu.edu.sa

Abstract: The present research investigates symmetric soliton solutions for the Fractional Coupled Konno–Onno System (FCKOS) by using two improved versions of an Extended Direct Algebraic Method (EDAM) i.e., modified EDAM (mEDAM) and r+mEDAM. By obtaining precise analytical solutions, this research explores the characteristics and behaviours of symmetric solitons in FCKOS. Further, the amplitude, shape and propagation behaviour of some solitons are visualized by means of a 3D graph. This investigation fosters a more thorough comprehension of non-linear wave phenomena in considered systems and offers helpful insights towards soliton behavior in it. The outcomes reveal that the recommended techniques are successful in constructing symmetric soliton solutions for complex models like the FCKOS.

Keywords: Fractional Coupled Konno–Onno System; extended direct algebraic method; solitons solutions

MSC: 26A33; 34K37; 74S40; 90C32

1. Introduction

Fractional Partial Differential Equations (FPDEs) have attracted a great deal of interest due to their capacity to explain different complicated phenomena that display memory effects, long-range interactions, and anomalous diffusion [1–6]. The importance of FPDEs lies in their capacity to offer more precise and realistic models for a variety of natural and artificial systems [7–12]. In view of such applications, researchers have taken an active interest to address FPDEs with the help of two different approaches called numerical and analytical methods [13–19]. Researchers are more interested in examining analytic solutions to FPDEs than numerical ones as analytical solutions provide more thorough understandings of the characteristics and behaviour of the system, enabling a better comprehension of the underlying mechanisms [20–22]. Secondly, analytical solutions offer computational efficiency, making it possible to do calculations and computations more quickly than with numerical approaches, particularly for FPDEs that are more straightforward or idealised. Therefore, many analytical methodologies like the (G′/G)-expansion method [23], method of homotopy perturbation [24], variational iteration method [25], exp-function method [26], He's semi-inverse method [27], tan-expansion method [28], EDAM [29] etc. were developed to solve FPDEs analytically [30–35].

The coupled integrable dispersion-less system known as the Coupled Konno–Oono System (CKOS) was developed by Konno and Oono [36]. The behaviour of a current-fed string interacting with an external magnetic field and the parallel transport of a curve's points along the direction of time with a magnetic-valued connection are two examples where it has been researched. The importance of the CKOS may be attributed to both its integrability characteristics and its applicability to certain physical phenomena. Integrability's property of the system means that the system has conserved quantities and symmetries. This knowledge may find applications in electromagnetism, materials science, or solid-state physics depending on the particular system being modelled. The CKOS is presented as [37]:

$$\begin{aligned} u_{xt}(x,t) - 2u(x,t)v(x,t) &= 0, \\ v_t(x,t) + 2u(x,t)u_x(x,t) &= 0. \end{aligned} \tag{1}$$

Due to its benefits in mathematical modelling, memory effects, generalisation and flexibility, accuracy and precision, as well as control and optimisation, the fractional form of the CKOS, i.e., FCKOS is favoured in this study. Fractional derivatives offer a more precise illustration of intricate physical processes and more truly portray the behaviour of the system. Memory effects, which are common in real-world systems, are also taken into account by fractional derivatives, allowing the system to preserve knowledge from the past. In comparison to integer-order models, fractional models are more accurate and precise and better fit experimental data. Additionally, using a fractional form allows for the use of cutting-edge control and optimisation methods for improved system performance and stability. The mathematical form of FCKOS is presented as below [38]:

$$\begin{aligned} u_{xt}^{\alpha\beta}(x,t) - 2u(x,t)v(x,t) &= 0, \\ v_t^{\beta}(x,t) + 2u(x,t)u_x^{\alpha}(x,t) &= 0, \end{aligned} \tag{2}$$

where $0 < \alpha, \beta \leq 1$. The functions u(x,t) and v(x,t) present the displacements of two particles that interact in a medium with fractional derivatives. Before this research work, many researchers have tackled both CKOS and FCKOS with the help of different analytical methods; in [39] Kocak et al. have utilized modified exp-function method to obtain travelling wave solution for the CKOS. The exact solutions to the CKOS have been developed via the tanh-function and extended tanh-function approaches in [40]. By employing He's variational technique, Elbrolosy and Elmandouh have studied dynamical behaviour of conformable time-fractional coupled Konno–Oono equation in magnetic field in [38]. Alizamini et al. in [37] have utilized simple EDAM to address CKOS in integer order and have obtained only one set of solution for CKOS by supposing $U(\varphi) = \sum_{l=0}^{n} a_l (G(\varphi))^l$ series form solution. It was found by comparison that their all obtained closed form solutions can be obtained from our employed mEDAM version second case's solution for letting $\alpha = \beta = 1$ thus, their study is the special subcase of our work.

The aim of this study is to construct symmetric soliton solutions for FCKOS via two improved variants of EDAM called mEDAM and r + mEDAM. EDAM is a novel analytical method for solving FPDEs. It applies variable transformations to turn FPDEs into nonlinear Ordinary Differential Equations (NODEs) and then assumes a series form solution to turn these NODEs into a system of algebraic equations. The obtained system of algebraic equations is then solved to obtain families of soliton (also called solitary waves) solutions for FPDEs.A soliton represents a self-sustaining wave that does not dissipate or spread out and keeps its shape and speed. It engages in interaction with other solitons while maintaining its uniqueness and displaying stability. Solitons have special features because of the precise balance between nonlinearity and dispersion. They are investigated in several domains to improve our knowledge of wave behaviour, nonlinear dynamics, and integrable systems. They have practical uses in communication networks, water channels, and biological modelling. Solutions from soliton offer perceptions into the underlying physical operations and system operation.

The derivative operator proposed by Caputo is used to define the fractional derivatives found in (2). This derivative operator is shown as below [41]:

$$D_s^{\sigma} z(s,t) = \begin{cases} \frac{1}{\Gamma(1-\sigma)} \int_0^s \frac{\frac{\partial}{\partial \rho} z(t,\rho)}{(s-\rho)^{\sigma}} d\rho, & \sigma \in (0,1) \\ \frac{\partial z(s,t)}{\partial s}, & \sigma = 1 \end{cases} \tag{3}$$

where the function $z(x,t)$ is suitably smooth. To transform FPDEs present in (2) into NODEs, we use the following two properties of this operator:

$$D_{\varphi}^{\sigma} \varphi^k = \frac{\Gamma(1+k)}{\Gamma(1+k-\sigma)} \varphi^{k-\sigma}, \tag{4}$$

$$D_{\varphi}^{\sigma} y[x(\varphi)] = y_x'(x(\varphi)) D_{\varphi}^{\sigma} x(\varphi) = D_x^{\sigma} y(x(\varphi))[x'(\varphi)]^{\sigma}, \tag{5}$$

where $k \in \mathbb{R}$ and $y(\varphi)$ and $x(\varphi)$ are differentiable functions.

2. Method and Materials

In this section, the working methodology of EDAM is outlined. Consider the following general FPDE [42]:

$$Q(\Phi, \partial_t^{\alpha} \Phi, \partial_{x_1}^{\beta} \Phi, \partial_{x_2}^{\gamma} \Phi, \Phi \partial_{x_1}^{\beta} \Phi, \ldots) = 0, \;\; 0 < \alpha, \beta, \gamma \leq 1, \tag{6}$$

where Φ is a function of t and $x_1, x_2, x_3, \ldots, x_m$.

To solve (6), we take the following steps:

1. Firstly, a variable transformation of the form $\Phi(t, x_1, x_2, x_3, \ldots, x_m) = U(\varphi)$, $\varphi = \varphi(t, x_1, x_2, x_3, \ldots, x_m)$, (where φ can be described in different ways) is carried out to transform (6) into a NODE of the form:

$$T(U, U', U'U, \ldots) = 0, \tag{7}$$

   where derivatives of U in (7) are with regard to φ. Equation (7) can be integrated one or more times occasionally to acquire integration's constant.
2. According to the version of EDAM, we assume one of the following solution for (7):
   1. mEDAM suggests the following series form solution:

$$U(\varphi) = \sum_{l=-n}^{n} a_l (G(\varphi))^l, \tag{8}$$

   2. r + mEDAM suggests the following series form solution:

$$U(\varphi) = \sum_{l=-n}^{n} a_l (r + G(\varphi))^l, \tag{9}$$

   where $a_l (l = n, \ldots, -1, 0, 1, \ldots, n)$ are unknown constants to be determined later, and $G(\varphi)$ is the general solution of the following ODE:

$$G'(\varphi) = Ln(\mu)(A + BG(\varphi) + C(G(\varphi))^2), \tag{10}$$

   where $\mu \neq 0, 1$ and A, B and C are in variables.
3. Taking the homogeneous balance between the highest order derivative and the greatest nonlinear term in (7) gives the positive integer n presented in (8) and (9).
4. After that, we put (8) or (9) into (7) or in equation generated by integrating (7) and then we collect all the terms of $(G(\varphi))$ of the same order which turn out an

expression in $(G(\varphi))$. By the principle of comparing the coefficient, we equate all the coefficients in the expression to zero, which yields a system of algebraic equations in $a_l(l = -n, \ldots -1, 0, 1, \ldots, n)$ and other parameters.

5. We employ Maple software to solve this system of algebraic equations.
6. The symmetric soliton solutions to (6) are then investigated by calculating the unknown coefficients and other parameters and putting them in (8) or (9) along with the $U(\varphi)$(general solution of (10)). By this general solution of (10), the following families of soliton solutions can be generated:

Family. 1: When $R < 0 \quad C \neq 0$ then we obtain the subsequent family of soliton solutions:

$$U_1(\varphi) = -\frac{B}{2C} + \frac{\sqrt{-R}\tan_\mu(1/2\sqrt{-R}\varphi)}{2C},$$

$$U_2(\varphi) = -\frac{B}{2C} - \frac{\sqrt{-R}\cot_\mu(1/2\sqrt{-R}\varphi)}{2C},$$

$$U_3(\varphi) = -\frac{B}{2C} + \frac{\sqrt{-R}(\tan_\mu(\sqrt{-R}\varphi) \pm (\sqrt{pq}\sec_\mu(\sqrt{-R}\varphi)))}{2C},$$

$$U_4(\varphi) = -\frac{B}{2C} - \frac{\sqrt{-R}(\cot_\mu(\sqrt{-R}\varphi) \pm (\sqrt{pq}\csc_\mu(\sqrt{-R}\varphi)))}{2C},$$

and

$$U_5(\varphi) = -\frac{B}{2C} + \frac{\sqrt{-R}(\tan_\mu(1/4\sqrt{-R}\varphi) - \cot_\mu(1/4\sqrt{-R}\varphi))}{4C}.$$

Family. 2: When $R > 0 \quad C \neq 0$ then we obtain the subsequent family of soliton solutions:

$$U_6(\varphi) = -\frac{B}{2C} - \frac{\sqrt{R}\tanh_\mu\left(1/2\sqrt{R}\varphi\right)}{2C},$$

$$U_7(\varphi) = -\frac{B}{2C} - \frac{\sqrt{R}\coth_\mu\left(1/2\sqrt{R}\varphi\right)}{2C},$$

$$U_8(\varphi) = -\frac{B}{2C} - \frac{\sqrt{R}\left(\tanh_\mu\left(\sqrt{R}\varphi\right) \pm \left(\sqrt{pq}sech_\mu\left(\sqrt{R}\varphi\right)\right)\right)}{2C},$$

$$U_9(\varphi) = -\frac{B}{2C} - \frac{\sqrt{R}\left(\coth_\mu\left(\sqrt{R}\varphi\right) \pm \left(\sqrt{pq}csch_\mu\left(\sqrt{R}\varphi\right)\right)\right)}{2C},$$

and

$$U_{10}(\varphi) = -\frac{B}{2C} - \frac{\sqrt{R}\left(\tanh_\mu\left(1/4\sqrt{R}\varphi\right) - \coth_\mu\left(1/4\sqrt{R}\varphi\right)\right)}{4C}.$$

Family. 3: When $AC > 0$ and $B = 0$ then we obtain the subsequent family of soliton solutions:

$$U_{11}(\varphi) = \sqrt{\frac{A}{C}}\tan_\mu\left(\sqrt{AC}\varphi\right),$$

$$U_{12}(\varphi) = -\sqrt{\frac{A}{C}}\cot_\mu\left(\sqrt{AC}\varphi\right),$$

$$U_{13}(\varphi) = \sqrt{\frac{A}{C}}\left(\tan_\mu\left(2\sqrt{AC}\varphi\right) \pm \left(\sqrt{pq}\sec_\mu\left(2\sqrt{AC}\varphi\right)\right)\right),$$

$$U_{14}(\varphi) = -\sqrt{\frac{A}{C}}\left(\cot_\mu\left(2\sqrt{AC}\varphi\right) \pm \left(\sqrt{pq}\csc_\mu\left(2\sqrt{AC}\varphi\right)\right)\right),$$

and

$$U_{15}(\varphi) = \frac{1}{2}\sqrt{\frac{A}{C}}\left(\tan_{\mu}\left(1/2\sqrt{AC}\varphi\right) - \cot_{\mu}\left(1/2\sqrt{AC}\varphi\right)\right).$$

Family. 4: When $AC > 0$ and $B = 0$ then we obtain the subsequent family of soliton solutions:

$$U_{16}(\varphi) = -\sqrt{-\frac{A}{C}}\tanh_{\mu}\left(\sqrt{-AC}\varphi\right),$$

$$U_{17}(\varphi) = -\sqrt{-\frac{A}{C}}\coth_{\mu}\left(\sqrt{-AC}\varphi\right),$$

$$U_{18}(\Phi) = -\sqrt{-\frac{A}{C}}\left(\tanh_{\mu}\left(2\sqrt{-AC}\varphi\right) \pm \left(i\sqrt{pq}sech_{A}\left(2\sqrt{-AC}\varphi\right)\right)\right),$$

$$U_{19}(\varphi) = -\sqrt{-\frac{A}{C}}\left(\coth_{\mu}\left(2\sqrt{-AC}\varphi\right) \pm \left(\sqrt{pq}csch_{\mu}\left(2\sqrt{-AC}\varphi\right)\right)\right),$$

and

$$U_{20}(\varphi) = -\frac{1}{2}\sqrt{-\frac{A}{C}}\left(\tanh_{\mu}\left(1/2\sqrt{-AC}\varphi\right) + \coth_{\mu}\left(1/2\sqrt{-AC}\varphi\right)\right).$$

Family. 5: When $C = A$ and $B = 0$ then we obtain the subsequent family of soliton solutions:

$$U_{21}(\varphi) = \tan_{\mu}(A\varphi),$$

$$U_{22}(\varphi) = -\cot_{\mu}(A\varphi),$$

$$U_{23}(\varphi) = \tan_{\mu}(2A\varphi) \pm \left(\sqrt{pq}\sec_{\mu}(2A\varphi)\right),$$

$$U_{24}(\varphi) = -\cot_{\mu}(2A\varphi) \pm \left(\sqrt{pq}\csc_{\mu}(2A\varphi)\right),$$

and

$$U_{25}(\varphi) = \frac{1}{2}\tan_{\mu}(1/2A\varphi) - 1/2\cot_{\mu}(1/2A\varphi).$$

Family. 6: When $C = -A$ and $B = 0$ then we obtain the subsequent family of soliton solutions:

$$U_{26}(\varphi) = -\tanh_{\mu}(A\varphi),$$

$$U_{27}(\varphi) = -\coth_{\mu}(A\varphi),$$

$$U_{28}(\varphi) = -\tanh_{\mu}(2A\varphi) \pm \left(i\sqrt{pq}sech_{\mu}(2A\varphi)\right),$$

$$U_{29}(\varphi) = -\coth_{\mu}(2A\varphi) \pm \left(\sqrt{pq}csch_{\mu}(2A\varphi)\right),$$

and

$$U_{30}(\varphi) = -\frac{1}{2}\tanh_{\mu}(1/2A\varphi) - 1/2\coth_{\mu}(1/2A\varphi).$$

Family. 7: When $R = 0$ then we obtain the subsequent family of soliton solutions:

$$U_{31}(\varphi) = -2\frac{A(B\Phi\,Ln\mu + 2)}{B^2\varphi\,Ln\mu}.$$

Family. 8: When $B = \nu$, $A = N\lambda(N \neq 0)$ and $C = 0$ then we obtain the subsequent family of soliton solutions:

$$U_{32}(\varphi) = \mu^{\nu\varphi} - N.$$

Family. 9: When $B = C = 0$ then we obtain the subsequent family of soliton solutions:

$$U_{33}(\varphi) = A\varphi\,Ln\mu.$$

Family. 10: When $B = A = 0$ then we obtain the subsequent family of soliton solutions:

$$U_{34}(\varphi) = -\frac{1}{C\varphi Ln\mu}.$$

Family. 11: When $A = 0$, $B \neq 0$ and $C \neq 0$ then we obtain the subsequent family of soliton solutions:

$$U_{35}(\varphi) = -\frac{pb}{C(\cosh_\mu(B\varphi) - \sinh_\mu(B\varphi) + p)},$$

and

$$U_{36}(\varphi) = -\frac{B(\cosh_\mu(B\varphi) + \sinh_\mu(B\varphi))}{C(\cosh_\mu(B\varphi) + \sinh_\mu(B\varphi) + q)},$$

Family. 12: When $B = \nu, C = N\nu(N \neq 0)$ and $A = 0$ we obtain the subsequent family of soliton solutions:

$$U_{37}(\varphi) = \frac{p\mu^{\nu\varphi}}{p - Nq\mu^{\nu\varphi}}.$$

When $R = B^2 - 4AC, p, q > 0$ and are referred to as deformation parameters. The generalised trigonometric and hyperbolic functions are expressed as below:

$$\begin{aligned}
\sin_\mu(\varphi) &= \frac{p\mu^{i\varphi} - q\mu^{-i\varphi}}{2i}, \quad \cos_\mu(\varphi) = \frac{p\mu^{i\varphi} + q\mu^{-i\varphi}}{2}, \\
\sec_\mu(\varphi) &= \frac{1}{\cos_\mu(\varphi)}, \quad \csc_\mu(\varphi) = \frac{1}{\sin_\mu(\varphi)}, \\
\tan_\mu(\varphi) &= \frac{\sin_\mu(\varphi)}{\cos_\mu(\varphi)}, \quad \cot_\mu(\varphi) = \frac{\cos_\mu(\varphi)}{\sin_\mu(\varphi)}.
\end{aligned}$$

Similarly,

$$\begin{aligned}
\sinh_\mu(\varphi) &= \frac{p\mu^{\varphi} - q\mu^{-\varphi}}{2}, \quad \cosh_\mu(\varphi) = \frac{p\mu^{\varphi} + q\mu^{-\varphi}}{2}, \\
sech_\mu(\varphi) &= \frac{1}{\cosh_\mu(\varphi)}, \quad csch_\mu(\varphi) = \frac{1}{\sinh_\mu(\varphi)}, \\
\tanh_\mu(\varphi) &= \frac{\sinh_\mu(\varphi)}{\cosh_\mu(\varphi)}, \quad \coth_\mu(\varphi) = \frac{\cosh_\mu(\varphi)}{\sinh_\mu(\varphi)}.
\end{aligned}$$

3. Results

In this section we implement two proposed versions of EDAM to the targeted model. We start with the following variable transformation:

$$\begin{aligned}
u(t,x) &= U(\varphi), \quad \varphi = k_1\left(\frac{x^\beta}{\Gamma(\beta+1)} - \frac{k_2 t^\alpha}{\Gamma(\alpha+1)}\right), \\
v(t,x) &= V(\varphi), \quad \varphi = k_1\left(\frac{x^\beta}{\Gamma(\beta+1)} - \frac{k_2 t^\alpha}{\Gamma(\alpha+1)}\right),
\end{aligned} \tag{11}$$

which transform (2) to the following set of NODEs:

$$\begin{aligned}
&-k_2 k_1^2 U'' - 2VU = 0, \\
&-k_2 k_1 V' + 2k_1 U' U = 0.
\end{aligned} \tag{12}$$

By integrating second part in (12) with respect to φ yields:

$$V = \frac{H + U^2}{k_2}, \tag{13}$$

where H is constant of integration. Putting (13) in first part of (12) implies:

$$(k_1k_2)^2U'' + 2HU + 2U^3 = 0. \tag{14}$$

To estimate balance number n in (8), we consider homogenous balance between highest order derivative U'' and nonlinear term U^3 in (14) which results that $n = 1$.

3.1. Implementation of mEDAM

First we solve NODE in (14) with the help of mEDAM. Putting $n = 1$ in (8) implies the following series form solution for (14):

$$U(\varphi) = \sum_{l=-1}^{1} a_l(G(\varphi))^l = a_{-1}(G(\varphi))^{-1} + a_0 + a_1(G(\varphi))^1, \tag{15}$$

where a_{-1}, a_0 and a_1 are constants to be calculated, and $G(\varphi)$ is the general solution of ODE in (10). By putting (15) in (14) and collecting all terms with the same powers of $G(\varphi)$, we get an expression in $G(\varphi)$. By equating the coefficients to zero yields a system of algebraic equations in $a_{-1}, a_0, a_1, k_1, k_2, H, \mu, A, B$ and C. Upon solving this system for a_{-1}, a_0, a_1, k_1 and k_2 using Maple, we reach at the following two cases of solutions:
Case. 1

$$\begin{aligned} a_1 &= 0, a_{-1} = 2\frac{HA}{\sqrt{H(-B^2+4CA)}}, a_0 = \sqrt{\frac{H}{-B^2+4CA}}B, \\ k_1 &= \frac{2}{\ln(\mu)k_2}\sqrt{-\frac{H}{-B^2+4CA}}, k_2 = k_2. \end{aligned} \tag{16}$$

Case. 2

$$\begin{aligned} a_1 &= 2\frac{HC}{\sqrt{H(-B^2+4CA)}}, a_{-1} = 0, a_0 = \sqrt{\frac{H}{-B^2+4CA}}B, \\ k_1 &= \frac{2}{\ln(\mu)k_2}\sqrt{-\frac{H}{-B^2+4CA}}, k_2 = k_2. \end{aligned} \tag{17}$$

Assuming case. 1, we get the following families of symmetric soliton solutions for (2):
Family. 1: When $R < 0 \quad A, B, C \neq 0$ then (11), (13) and corresponding general solutions of (10) imply the following family of symmetric soliton solutions:

$$\begin{aligned} u_1(x,t) &= \frac{\frac{2HA}{\sqrt{H(-B^2+4AC)}}}{\left(-\frac{B}{2C} + \frac{\sqrt{-R}\tan_\mu(1/2\sqrt{-R}\varphi)}{2C}\right)} + \sqrt{\frac{H}{-R}}B, \\ v_1(x,t) &= \frac{1}{k_2}((\frac{\frac{2HA}{\sqrt{H(-B^2+4AC)}}}{\left(-\frac{B}{2C} + \frac{\sqrt{-R}\tan_\mu(1/2\sqrt{-R}\varphi)}{2C}\right)} + \sqrt{\frac{H}{-R}}B)^2 + H), \end{aligned} \tag{18}$$

$$\begin{aligned} u_2(x,t) &= \frac{\frac{2HA}{\sqrt{H(-B^2+4AC)}}}{\left(-\frac{B}{2C} - \frac{\sqrt{-R}\cot_\mu(1/2\sqrt{-R}\varphi)}{2C}\right)} + \sqrt{\frac{H}{-R}}B, \\ v_2(x,t) &= \frac{1}{k_2}((\frac{\frac{2HA}{\sqrt{H(-B^2+4AC)}}}{\left(-\frac{B}{2C} - \frac{\sqrt{-R}\cot_\mu(1/2\sqrt{-R}\varphi)}{2C}\right)} + \sqrt{\frac{H}{-R}}B)^2 + H), \end{aligned} \tag{19}$$

$$u_3(x,t) = \frac{\frac{2HA}{\sqrt{H(-B^2+4AC)}}}{\left(-\frac{B}{2C} + \frac{\sqrt{-R}\left(\tan_\mu\left(\sqrt{-R}\varphi\right) \pm \left(\sqrt{pq}\sec_\mu\left(\sqrt{-R}\varphi\right)\right)\right)}{2C}\right)} + \sqrt{\frac{H}{-R}}B,$$
$$v_3(x,t) = \frac{1}{k_2}((\frac{\frac{2HA}{\sqrt{H(-B^2+4AC)}}}{\left(-\frac{B}{2C} + \frac{\sqrt{-R}\left(\tan_\mu\left(\sqrt{-R}\varphi\right) \pm \left(\sqrt{pq}\sec_\mu\left(\sqrt{-R}\varphi\right)\right)\right)}{2C}\right)} + \sqrt{\frac{H}{-R}}B)^2 + H), \tag{20}$$

$$u_4(x,t) = \frac{\frac{2HA}{\sqrt{H(-B^2+4AC)}}}{\left(-\frac{B}{2C} - \frac{\sqrt{-R}\left(\cot_\mu\left(\sqrt{-R}\varphi\right) \pm \left(\sqrt{pq}\csc_\mu\left(\sqrt{-R}\varphi\right)\right)\right)}{2C}\right)} + \sqrt{\frac{H}{-R}}B,$$
$$v_4(x,t) = \frac{1}{k_2}((\frac{\frac{2HA}{\sqrt{H(-B^2+4AC)}}}{\left(-\frac{B}{2C} - \frac{\sqrt{-R}\left(\cot_\mu\left(\sqrt{-R}\varphi\right) \pm \left(\sqrt{pq}\csc_\mu\left(\sqrt{-R}\varphi\right)\right)\right)}{2C}\right)} + \sqrt{\frac{H}{-R}}B)^2 + H), \tag{21}$$

and

$$u_5(x,t) = \frac{\frac{2HA}{\sqrt{H(-B^2+4AC)}}}{\left(-\frac{B}{2C} + \frac{\sqrt{-R}\left(\tan_\mu\left(1/4\sqrt{-R}\varphi\right) - \cot_\mu\left(1/4\sqrt{-R}\varphi\right)\right)}{4C}\right)} + \sqrt{\frac{H}{-R}}B,$$
$$v_5(x,t) = \frac{1}{k_2}((\frac{\frac{2HA}{\sqrt{H(-B^2+4AC)}}}{\left(-\frac{B}{2C} + \frac{\sqrt{-R}\left(\tan_\mu\left(1/4\sqrt{-R}\varphi\right) - \cot_\mu\left(1/4\sqrt{-R}\varphi\right)\right)}{4C}\right)} + \sqrt{\frac{H}{-R}}B)^2 + H). \tag{22}$$

Family. 2: When $R > 0 \quad A, B, C \neq 0$ then (11), (13) and corresponding general solutions of (10) imply the following family of symmetric soliton solutions:

$$u_6(x,t) = \frac{\frac{2HA}{\sqrt{H(-B^2+4AC)}}}{\left(-\frac{B}{2C} - \frac{\sqrt{R}\tanh_\mu\left(1/2\sqrt{R}\varphi\right)}{2C}\right)} + \sqrt{\frac{H}{-R}}B,$$
$$v_6(x,t) = \frac{1}{k_2}((\frac{\frac{2HA}{\sqrt{H(-B^2+4AC)}}}{\left(-\frac{B}{2C} - \frac{\sqrt{R}\tanh_\mu\left(1/2\sqrt{R}\varphi\right)}{2C}\right)} + \sqrt{\frac{H}{-R}}B)^2 + H), \tag{23}$$

$$u_7(x,t) = \frac{\frac{2HA}{\sqrt{H(-B^2+4AC)}}}{\left(-\frac{B}{2C} - \frac{\sqrt{R}\coth_\mu\left(1/2\sqrt{R}\varphi\right)}{2C}\right)} + \sqrt{\frac{H}{-R}}B,$$
$$v_7(x,t) = \frac{1}{k_2}((\frac{\frac{2HA}{\sqrt{H(-B^2+4AC)}}}{\left(-\frac{B}{2C} - \frac{\sqrt{R}\coth_\mu\left(1/2\sqrt{R}\varphi\right)}{2C}\right)} + \sqrt{\frac{H}{-R}}B)^2 + H), \tag{24}$$

$$u_8(x,t) = \frac{\frac{2HA}{\sqrt{H(-B^2+4AC)}}}{\left(-\frac{B}{2C} - \frac{\sqrt{R}\left(\tanh_\mu\left(\sqrt{R}\varphi\right) \pm \left(\sqrt{pq}sech_\mu\left(\sqrt{R}\varphi\right)\right)\right)}{2C}\right)} + \sqrt{\frac{H}{-R}}B,$$
$$v_8(x,t) = \frac{1}{k_2}((\frac{\frac{2HA}{\sqrt{H(-B^2+4AC)}}}{\left(-\frac{B}{2C} - \frac{\sqrt{R}\left(\tanh_\mu\left(\sqrt{R}\varphi\right) \pm \left(\sqrt{pq}sech_\mu\left(\sqrt{R}\varphi\right)\right)\right)}{2C}\right)} + \sqrt{\frac{H}{-R}}B)^2 + H), \tag{25}$$

$$
\begin{aligned}
u_9(x,t) &= \frac{\frac{2HA}{\sqrt{H(-B^2+4AC)}}}{\left(-\frac{B}{2C} - \frac{\sqrt{R}\left(\coth_\mu\left(\sqrt{R}\varphi\right)\pm\left(\sqrt{pq}csch_\mu\left(\sqrt{R}\varphi\right)\right)\right)}{2C}\right)} + \sqrt{\frac{H}{-R}}B, \\
v_9(x,t) &= \frac{1}{k_2}((\frac{\frac{2HA}{\sqrt{H(-B^2+4AC)}}}{\left(-\frac{B}{2C} - \frac{\sqrt{R}\left(\coth_\mu\left(\sqrt{R}\varphi\right)\pm\left(\sqrt{pq}csch_\mu\left(\sqrt{R}\varphi\right)\right)\right)}{2C}\right)} + \sqrt{\frac{H}{-R}}B)^2 + H),
\end{aligned} \tag{26}
$$

and

$$
\begin{aligned}
u_{10}(x,t) &= \frac{\frac{2HA}{\sqrt{H(-B^2+4AC)}}}{\left(-\frac{B}{2C} - \frac{\sqrt{R}\left(\tanh_\mu\left(1/4\sqrt{R}\varphi\right)-\coth_\mu\left(1/4\sqrt{R}\varphi\right)\right)}{4C}\right)} + \sqrt{\frac{H}{-R}}B, \\
v_{10}(x,t) &= \frac{1}{k_2}((\frac{\frac{2HA}{\sqrt{H(-B^2+4AC)}}}{\left(-\frac{B}{2C} - \frac{\sqrt{R}\left(\tanh_\mu\left(1/4\sqrt{R}\varphi\right)-\coth_\mu\left(1/4\sqrt{R}\varphi\right)\right)}{4C}\right)} + \sqrt{\frac{H}{-R}}B)^2 + H).
\end{aligned} \tag{27}
$$

Family. 3: When $AC > 0$ and $B = 0$ then (11), (13) and corresponding general solutions of (10) imply the following family of symmetric soliton solutions:

$$
\begin{aligned}
u_{11}(x,t) &= \sqrt{H}\left(\tan_\mu\left(\sqrt{AC}\varphi\right)\right)^{-1} \\
v_{11}(x,t) &= \frac{1}{k_2}((\sqrt{H}\left(\tan_\mu\left(\sqrt{AC}\varphi\right)\right)^{-1})^2 + H),
\end{aligned} \tag{28}
$$

$$
\begin{aligned}
u_{12}(x,t) &= -\sqrt{H}\left(\cot_\mu\left(\sqrt{AC}\varphi\right)\right)^{-1} \\
v_{12}(x,t) &= \frac{1}{k_2}((-\sqrt{H}\left(\cot_\mu\left(\sqrt{AC}\varphi\right)\right)^{-1})^2 + H),
\end{aligned} \tag{29}
$$

$$
\begin{aligned}
u_{13}(x,t) &= \sqrt{H}\left(\tan_\mu\left(2\sqrt{AC}\varphi\right) \pm \left(\sqrt{pq}\sec_\mu\left(2\sqrt{AC}\varphi\right)\right)\right)^{-1}, \\
v_{13}(x,t) &= \frac{((\sqrt{H}\left(\tan_\mu\left(2\sqrt{AC}\varphi\right) \pm \left(\sqrt{pq}\sec_\mu\left(2\sqrt{AC}\varphi\right)\right)\right)^{-1})^2 + H)}{k_2},
\end{aligned} \tag{30}
$$

$$
\begin{aligned}
u_{14}(x,t) &= -\sqrt{H}\left(\cot_\mu\left(2\sqrt{AC}\varphi\right) \pm \left(\sqrt{pq}\csc_\mu\left(2\sqrt{AC}\varphi\right)\right)\right)^{-1}, \\
v_{14}(x,t) &= \frac{((\sqrt{H}\left(\cot_\mu\left(2\sqrt{AC}\varphi\right) \pm \left(\sqrt{pq}\csc_\mu\left(2\sqrt{AC}\varphi\right)\right)\right)^{-1})^2 + H)}{k_2},
\end{aligned} \tag{31}
$$

and

$$
\begin{aligned}
u_{15}(x,t) &= 2\sqrt{H}\left(\tan_\mu\left(1/2\sqrt{AC}\varphi\right) - \cot_\mu\left(1/2\sqrt{AC}\varphi\right)\right)^{-1}, \\
v_{15}(x,t) &= \frac{1}{k_2}((2\sqrt{H}\left(\tan_\mu\left(1/2\sqrt{AC}\varphi\right) - \cot_\mu\left(1/2\sqrt{AC}\varphi\right)\right)^{-1})^2 + H).
\end{aligned} \tag{32}
$$

Family. 4: When $AC > 0$ and $B = 0$ then (11), (13) and corresponding general solutions of (10) imply the following family of symmetric soliton solutions:

$$
\begin{aligned}
u_{16}(x,t) &= -\sqrt{-H}\left(\tanh_\mu\left(\sqrt{-AC}\varphi\right)\right)^{-1}, \\
v_{16}(x,t) &= \frac{1}{k_2}((-\sqrt{-H}\left(\tanh_\mu\left(\sqrt{-AC}\varphi\right)\right)^{-1})^2 + H),
\end{aligned} \tag{33}
$$

$$u_{17}(x,t) = -\sqrt{-H}\left(\coth_\mu\left(\sqrt{-AC}\varphi\right)\right)^{-1},$$
$$v_{17}(x,t) = \frac{1}{k_2}((-\sqrt{-H}\left(\coth_\mu\left(\sqrt{-AC}\varphi\right)\right)^{-1})^2 + H), \tag{34}$$

$$u_{18}(x,t) = -\sqrt{-H}\left(\tanh_\mu\left(2\sqrt{-AC}\varphi\right) \pm \left(i\sqrt{pq}sech_\mu\left(2\sqrt{-AC}\varphi\right)\right)\right)^{-1},$$
$$v_{18}(x,t) = \frac{1}{k_2}((\sqrt{-H}(\tanh_\mu\left(2\sqrt{-AC}\varphi\right) \pm \left(i\sqrt{pq}sech_\mu\left(2\sqrt{-AC}\varphi\right)\right))^{-1})^2 + H), \tag{35}$$

$$u_{19}(x,t) = -\sqrt{-H}\left(\coth_\mu\left(2\sqrt{-AC}\varphi\right) \pm \left(\sqrt{pq}csch_\mu\left(2\sqrt{-AC}\varphi\right)\right)\right)^{-1},$$
$$v_{19}(x,t) = \frac{1}{k_2}((-\sqrt{-H}(\coth_\mu\left(2\sqrt{-AC}\varphi\right) \pm \left(\sqrt{pq}csch_\mu\left(2\sqrt{-AC}\varphi\right)\right))^{-1})^2 + H), \tag{36}$$

and

$$u_{20}(x,t) = -2\sqrt{-H}\left(\tanh_\mu\left(1/2\sqrt{-AC}\varphi\right) + \coth_\mu\left(1/2\sqrt{-AC}\varphi\right)\right)^{-1}$$
$$v_{20}(x,t) = \frac{1}{k_2}((-2\sqrt{-H}(\tanh_\mu\left(1/2\sqrt{-AC}\varphi\right), + \coth_\mu\left(1/2\sqrt{-AC}\varphi\right))^{-1})^2 + H). \tag{37}$$

Family. 5: When $C = A$ and $B = 0$ then (11), (13) and corresponding general solutions of (10) imply the following family of symmetric soliton solutions:

$$u_{21}(x,t) = -\frac{\sqrt{H}}{\cot_\mu(A\varphi)},$$
$$v_{21}(x,t) = \frac{1}{k_2}((-\frac{\sqrt{H}}{\cot_\mu(A\varphi)})^2 + H), \tag{38}$$

$$u_{22}(x,t) = \frac{\sqrt{H}}{(\tan_\mu(2A\varphi) \pm (\sqrt{pq}\sec_\mu(2A\varphi)))},$$
$$v_{22}(x,t) = \frac{1}{k_2}((\frac{\sqrt{H}}{(\tan_\mu(2A\varphi) \pm (\sqrt{pq}\sec_\mu(2A\varphi)))})^2 + H), \tag{39}$$

$$u_{23}(x,t) = \frac{\sqrt{H}}{(-\cot_\mu(2A\varphi) \mp (\sqrt{pq}\csc_\mu(2A\varphi)))},$$
$$v_{23}(x,t) = \frac{1}{k_2}((\frac{\sqrt{H}}{(-\cot_\mu(2A\varphi) \mp (\sqrt{pq}\csc_\mu(2A\varphi)))})^2 + H), \tag{40}$$

$$u_{24}(x,t) = \frac{\sqrt{H}}{(1/2\tan_\mu(1/2A\varphi) - 1/2\cot_\mu(1/2A\varphi))},$$
$$v_{24}(x,t) = \frac{1}{k_2}((\frac{\sqrt{H}}{(1/2\tan_\mu(1/2A\varphi) - 1/2\cot_\mu(1/2A\varphi))})^2 + H), \tag{41}$$

and

$$u_{25}(x,t) = -\frac{\sqrt{H}}{\tanh_\mu(A\varphi)},$$
$$v_{25}(x,t) = \frac{1}{k_2}((-\frac{\sqrt{H}}{\tanh_\mu(A\varphi)})^2 + H). \tag{42}$$

Family. 6: When $C = -A$ and $B = 0$ then (11), (13) and corresponding general solutions of (10) imply the following family of symmetric soliton solutions:

$$\begin{aligned} u_{26}(x,t) &= -\frac{\sqrt{-H}}{\tanh_{\mu}(A\varphi)}, \\ v_{26}(x,t) &= \frac{1}{k_2}((-\frac{\sqrt{-H}}{\tanh_{\mu}(A\varphi)})^2 + H), \end{aligned} \tag{43}$$

$$\begin{aligned} u_{27}(x,t) &= -\frac{\sqrt{-H}}{\coth_{\mu}(A\varphi)}, \\ v_{27}(x,t) &= \frac{1}{k_2}((-\frac{\sqrt{-H}}{\coth_{\mu}(A\varphi)})^2 + H), \end{aligned} \tag{44}$$

$$\begin{aligned} u_{28}(x,t) &= \frac{\sqrt{-H}}{(-\tanh_{\mu}(2\,A\varphi) \mp (i\sqrt{pq}sech_{\mu}(2\,A\varphi)))}, \\ v_{28}(x,t) &= \frac{1}{k_2}((\frac{\sqrt{-H}}{(-\tanh_{\mu}(2\,A\varphi) \mp (i\sqrt{pq}sech_{\mu}(2\,A\varphi)))})^2 + H), \end{aligned} \tag{45}$$

$$\begin{aligned} u_{29}(x,t) &= \frac{\sqrt{-H}}{(-\coth_{\mu}(2\,A\varphi) \mp (\sqrt{pq}csch_{\mu}(2\,A\varphi)))}, \\ v_{29}(x,t) &= \frac{1}{k_2}((\frac{\sqrt{-H}}{(-\coth_{\mu}(2\,A\varphi) \mp (\sqrt{pq}csch_{\mu}(2\,A\varphi)))})^2 + H), \end{aligned} \tag{46}$$

and

$$\begin{aligned} u_{30}(x,t) &= \frac{\sqrt{-H}}{(-1/2\,\tanh_{\mu}(1/2\,A\varphi) - 1/2\,\coth_{\mu}(1/2\,A\varphi))}, \\ v_{30}(x,t) &= \frac{1}{k_2}((\frac{\sqrt{-H}}{(-1/2\,\tanh_{\mu}(1/2\,A\varphi) - 1/2\,\coth_{\mu}(1/2\,A\varphi))})^2 + H). \end{aligned} \tag{47}$$

Family. 7: When $B = \nu$, $A = N\nu(N \neq 0)$ and $C = 0$ then (11), (13) and corresponding general solutions of (10) imply the following family of symmetric soliton solutions:

$$\begin{aligned} u_{31}(x,t) &= \frac{2\sqrt{-H}N}{(\mu^{\nu\,\varphi} - N)} + \sqrt{H} \\ v_{31}(x,t) &= \frac{1}{k_2}((\frac{2\sqrt{-H}N}{(\mu^{\nu\,\varphi} - N)} + \sqrt{H})^2 + H). \end{aligned} \tag{48}$$

where $\varphi = \frac{2}{\ln(\mu)k_2}\sqrt{-\frac{H}{-B^2+4CA}}(\frac{x^{\beta}}{\Gamma(\beta+1)} - \frac{k_2 t^{\alpha}}{\Gamma(\alpha+1)})$.

Now, assuming case. 2, we get the following families of symmetric soliton solutions for (2):

Family. 8: When $R < 0 \quad A, B, C \neq 0$ then (11), (13) and corresponding general solutions of (10) imply the following family of symmetric soliton solutions:

$$\begin{aligned} u_{32}(x,t) &= \sqrt{\frac{H}{-R}}(B + 2C\left(-\frac{B}{2C} + \frac{\sqrt{-R}\tan_{\mu}(1/2\sqrt{-R}\varphi)}{2C}\right)), \\ v_{32}(x,t) &= \frac{1}{k_2}((\sqrt{\frac{H}{-R}}(B + 2C\left(-\frac{B}{2C} + \frac{\sqrt{-R}\tan_{\mu}(1/2\sqrt{-R}\varphi)}{2C}\right)))^2 + H), \end{aligned} \tag{49}$$

$$u_{33}(x,t) = \sqrt{\frac{H}{-R}}(B + 2C\left(-\frac{B}{2C} - \frac{\sqrt{-R}\cot_\mu(1/2\sqrt{-R}\varphi)}{2C}\right)),$$
$$v_{33}(x,t) = \frac{1}{k_2}((\sqrt{\frac{H}{-R}}(B + 2C\left(-\frac{B}{2C} - \frac{\sqrt{-R}\cot_\mu(1/2\sqrt{-R}\varphi)}{2C}\right)))^2 + H), \quad (50)$$

$$u_{34}(x,t) = \sqrt{\frac{H}{-R}}(B + 2C\left(-\frac{B}{2C} + \frac{\sqrt{-R}(\tan_\mu(\sqrt{-R}\varphi) \pm (\sqrt{pq}\sec_\mu(\sqrt{-R}\varphi)))}{2C}\right)),$$
$$v_{34}(x,t) = \frac{1}{k_2}((\sqrt{\frac{H}{-R}}(B + 2C\left(-\frac{B}{2C} + \frac{\sqrt{-R}(\tan_\mu(\sqrt{-R}\varphi) \pm (\sqrt{pq}\sec_\mu(\sqrt{-R}\varphi)))}{2C}\right)))^2 + H), \quad (51)$$

$$u_{35}(x,t) = \sqrt{\frac{H}{-R}}(B + 2C\left(-\frac{B}{2C} - \frac{\sqrt{-R}(\cot_\mu(\sqrt{-R}\varphi) \pm (\sqrt{pq}\csc_\mu(\sqrt{-R}\varphi)))}{2C}\right)),$$
$$v_{35}(x,t) = \frac{1}{k_2}((\sqrt{\frac{H}{-R}}(B + 2C\left(-\frac{B}{2C} - \frac{\sqrt{-R}(\cot_\mu(\sqrt{-R}\varphi) \pm (\sqrt{pq}\csc_\mu(\sqrt{-R}\varphi)))}{2C}\right)))^2 + H), \quad (52)$$

and

$$u_{36}(x,t) = \sqrt{\frac{H}{-R}}(B + 2C\left(-\frac{B}{2C} + \frac{\sqrt{-R}(\tan_\mu(1/4\sqrt{-R}\varphi) - \cot_\mu(1/4\sqrt{-R}\varphi))}{4C}\right),$$
$$v_{36}(x,t) = \frac{1}{k_2}((\sqrt{\frac{H}{-R}}(B + 2C\left(-\frac{B}{2C} + \frac{\sqrt{-R}(\tan_\mu(1/4\sqrt{-R}\varphi) - \cot_\mu(1/4\sqrt{-R}\varphi))}{4C}\right))^2 + H). \quad (53)$$

Family. 9: When $R > 0 \quad A, B, C \neq 0$ then (11), (13) and corresponding general solutions of (10) imply the following family of symmetric soliton solutions:

$$u_{37}(x,t) = \sqrt{\frac{H}{-R}}(B + 2C\left(-\frac{B}{2C} - \frac{\sqrt{R}\tanh_\mu\left(1/2\sqrt{R}\varphi\right)}{2C}\right)),$$
$$v_{37}(x,t) = \frac{1}{k_2}((\sqrt{\frac{H}{-R}}(B + 2C\left(-\frac{B}{2C} - \frac{\sqrt{R}\tanh_\mu\left(1/2\sqrt{R}\varphi\right)}{2C}\right)))^2 + H), \quad (54)$$

$$u_{38}(x,t) = \sqrt{\frac{H}{-R}}(B + 2C\left(-\frac{B}{2C} - \frac{\sqrt{R}\coth_\mu\left(1/2\sqrt{R}\varphi\right)}{2C}\right)),$$
$$v_{38}(x,t) = \frac{1}{k_2}((\sqrt{\frac{H}{-R}}(B + 2C\left(-\frac{B}{2C} - \frac{\sqrt{R}\coth_\mu\left(1/2\sqrt{R}\varphi\right)}{2C}\right)))^2 + H), \quad (55)$$

$$u_{39}(x,t) = \sqrt{\frac{H}{-R}}(B + 2C\left(-\frac{B}{2C} - \frac{\sqrt{R}\left(\tanh_\mu\left(\sqrt{R}\varphi\right) \pm \left(\sqrt{pq}sech_\mu\left(\sqrt{R}\varphi\right)\right)\right)}{2C}\right)),$$
$$v_{39}(x,t) = \frac{1}{k_2}((\sqrt{\frac{H}{-R}}(B + 2C\left(-\frac{B}{2C} - \frac{\sqrt{R}\left(\tanh_\mu\left(\sqrt{R}\varphi\right) \pm \left(\sqrt{pq}sech_\mu\left(\sqrt{R}\varphi\right)\right)\right)}{2C}\right)))^2 + H), \quad (56)$$

$$u_{40}(x,t) = \sqrt{\frac{H}{-R}}(B+2C\left(-\frac{B}{2C} - \frac{\sqrt{R}\left(\coth_\mu\left(\sqrt{R}\varphi\right) \pm \left(\sqrt{pq}csch_\mu\left(\sqrt{R}\varphi\right)\right)\right)}{2C}\right)),$$
$$v_{40}(x,t) = \frac{1}{k_2}((\sqrt{\frac{H}{-B^2+4\,AC}}(B+2C\times\left(-\frac{B}{2C} - \frac{\sqrt{R}\left(\coth_\mu\left(\sqrt{R}\varphi\right) \pm \left(\sqrt{pq}csch_\mu\left(\sqrt{R}\varphi\right)\right)\right)}{2C}\right)))^2 \tag{57}$$
$$+H),$$

and

$$u_{41}(x,t) = \sqrt{\frac{H}{-R}}(B+2C\left(-\frac{B}{2C} - \frac{\sqrt{R}\left(\tanh_\mu\left(1/4\sqrt{R}\varphi\right) - \coth_\mu\left(1/4\sqrt{R}\varphi\right)\right)}{4C}\right)),$$
$$v_{41}(x,t) = \frac{1}{k_2}((\sqrt{\frac{H}{-R}}(B+2C\left(-\frac{B}{2C} - \frac{\sqrt{R}\left(\tanh_\mu\left(1/4\sqrt{R}\varphi\right) - \coth_\mu\left(1/4\sqrt{R}\varphi\right)\right)}{4C}\right)))^2+H). \tag{58}$$

Family. 10: When $AC > 0$ and $B = 0$ then (11), (13) and corresponding general solutions of (10) imply the following family of symmetric soliton solutions:

$$u_{42}(x,t) = \sqrt{H}\tan_\mu\left(\sqrt{AC}\varphi\right),$$
$$v_{42}(x,t) = \frac{1}{k_2}((\sqrt{H}\tan_\mu\left(\sqrt{AC}\varphi\right))^2+H), \tag{59}$$

$$u_{43}(x,t) = -\cot_\mu\left(\sqrt{AC}\varphi\right),$$
$$v_{43}(x,t) = \frac{1}{k_2}((-\cot_\mu\left(\sqrt{AC}\varphi\right))^2+H), \tag{60}$$

$$u_{44}(x,t) = \sqrt{H}\left(\tan_\mu\left(2\sqrt{AC}\varphi\right) \pm \left(\sqrt{pq}\sec_\mu\left(2\sqrt{AC}\varphi\right)\right)\right),$$
$$v_{44}(x,t) = \frac{1}{k_2}((\sqrt{H}\left(\tan_\mu\left(2\sqrt{AC}\varphi\right) \pm \left(\sqrt{pq}\sec_\mu\left(2\sqrt{AC}\varphi\right)\right)\right))^2+H), \tag{61}$$

$$u_{45}(x,t) = -\sqrt{H}\left(\cot_\mu\left(2\sqrt{AC}\varphi\right) \pm \left(\sqrt{pq}\csc_\mu\left(2\sqrt{AC}\varphi\right)\right)\right),$$
$$v_{45}(x,t) = \frac{1}{k_2}((-\sqrt{H}\left(\cot_\mu\left(2\sqrt{AC}\varphi\right) \pm \left(\sqrt{pq}\csc_\mu\left(2\sqrt{AC}\varphi\right)\right)\right))^2+H), \tag{62}$$

and

$$u_{46}(x,t) = \sqrt{H}\left(\tan_\mu\left(1/2\sqrt{AC}\varphi\right) - \cot_\mu\left(1/2\sqrt{AC}\varphi\right)\right),$$
$$v_{46}(x,t) = \frac{1}{k_2}((\sqrt{H}\left(\tan_\mu\left(1/2\sqrt{AC}\varphi\right) - \cot_\mu\left(1/2\sqrt{AC}\varphi\right)\right))^2+H). \tag{63}$$

Family. 11: When $AC > 0$ and $B = 0$ then (11), (13) and corresponding general solutions of (10) imply the following family of symmetric soliton solutions:

$$u_{47}(x,t) = -\sqrt{-H}\tanh_\mu\left(\sqrt{-AC}\varphi\right),$$
$$v_{47}(x,t) = \frac{1}{k_2}((-\sqrt{-H}\tanh_\mu\left(\sqrt{-AC}\varphi\right))^2+H), \tag{64}$$

$$u_{48}(x,t) = -\sqrt{-H}\coth_\mu\left(\sqrt{-AC}\varphi\right)\frac{1}{\sqrt{H(-B^2+4\,AC)}},$$
$$v_{48}(x,t) = \frac{1}{k_2}((-\sqrt{-H}\coth_\mu\left(\sqrt{-AC}\varphi\right)\frac{1}{\sqrt{H(-B^2+4\,AC)}})^2+H), \tag{65}$$

$$u_{49}(x,t) = -\sqrt{-H}\Big(\tanh_\mu\Big(2\sqrt{-AC}\varphi\Big) \pm \Big(i\sqrt{pq}sech_\mu\Big(2\sqrt{-AC}\varphi\Big)\Big)\Big),$$
$$v_{49}(x,t) = \frac{1}{k_2}((-\sqrt{-H}(\tanh_\mu\Big(2\sqrt{-AC}\varphi\Big) \pm \Big(i\sqrt{pq}sech_\mu\Big(2\sqrt{-AC}\varphi\Big)\Big)))^2 + H), \quad (66)$$

$$u_{50}(x,t) = -\sqrt{-H}\Big(\coth_\mu\Big(2\sqrt{-AC}\varphi\Big) \pm \Big(\sqrt{pq}csch_\mu\Big(2\sqrt{-AC}\varphi\Big)\Big)\Big),$$
$$v_{50}(x,t) = \frac{1}{k_2}((-\sqrt{-H}(\coth_\mu\Big(2\sqrt{-AC}\varphi\Big) \pm \Big(\sqrt{pq}csch_\mu\Big(2\sqrt{-AC}\varphi\Big)\Big)))^2 + H), \quad (67)$$

and

$$u_{51}(x,t) = -\sqrt{-H}\Big(\tanh_\mu\Big(1/2\sqrt{-AC}\varphi\Big) + \coth_\mu\Big(1/2\sqrt{-AC}\varphi\Big)\Big),$$
$$v_{51}(x,t) = \frac{1}{k_2}((-\sqrt{-H}(\tanh_\mu\Big(1/2\sqrt{-AC}\varphi\Big) + \coth_\mu\Big(1/2\sqrt{-AC}\varphi\Big)))^2 + H). \quad (68)$$

Family. 12: When $C = A$ and $B = 0$ then (11), (13) and corresponding general solutions of (10) imply the following family of symmetric soliton solutions:

$$u_{52}(x,t) = \sqrt{H}\tan_\mu(A\varphi),$$
$$v_{52}(x,t) = \frac{1}{k_2}((\sqrt{H}\tan_\mu(A\varphi))^2 + H), \quad (69)$$

$$u_{53}(x,t) = -\sqrt{H}\cot_\mu(A\varphi),$$
$$v_{53}(x,t) = \frac{1}{k_2}((-\sqrt{H}\cot_\mu(A\varphi))^2 + H), \quad (70)$$

$$u_{54}(x,t) = \sqrt{H}(\tan_\mu(2A\varphi) \pm (\sqrt{pq}\sec_\mu(2A\varphi))),$$
$$v_{54}(x,t) = \frac{1}{k_2}((\sqrt{H}(\tan_\mu(2A\varphi) \pm (\sqrt{pq}\sec_\mu(2A\varphi))))^2 + H), \quad (71)$$

$$u_{55}(x,t) = \sqrt{H}(-\cot_\mu(2A\varphi) \mp (\sqrt{pq}\csc_\mu(2A\varphi))),$$
$$v_{55}(x,t) = \frac{1}{k_2}((\sqrt{H}(-\cot_\mu(2A\varphi) \mp (\sqrt{pq}\csc_\mu(2A\varphi))))^2 + H), \quad (72)$$

and

$$u_{56}(x,t) = \sqrt{H}(1/2\tan_\mu(1/2A\varphi) - 1/2\cot_\mu(1/2A\varphi)),$$
$$v_{56}(x,t) = \frac{1}{k_2}((\sqrt{H}(1/2\tan_\mu(1/2A\varphi) - 1/2\cot_\mu(1/2A\varphi)))^2 + H). \quad (73)$$

Family. 13: When $C = -A$ and $B = 0$ then (11), (13) and corresponding general solutions of (10) imply the following family of symmetric soliton solutions:

$$u_{57}(x,t) = -\sqrt{-H}\tanh_\mu(A\varphi),$$
$$v_{57}(x,t) = \frac{1}{k_2}((-\sqrt{-H}\tanh_\mu(A\varphi))^2 + H), \quad (74)$$

$$u_{58}(x,t) = -\sqrt{-H}\coth_\mu(A\varphi),$$
$$v_{58}(x,t) = \frac{1}{k_2}((-\sqrt{-H}\coth_\mu(A\varphi))^2 + H), \quad (75)$$

$$u_{59}(x,t) = \sqrt{-H}(-\tanh_\mu(2A\varphi) \mp (i\sqrt{pq}sech_\mu(2A\varphi))),$$
$$v_{59}(x,t) = \frac{1}{k_2}((\sqrt{-H}(-\tanh_\mu(2A\varphi) \mp (i\sqrt{pq}sech_\mu(2A\varphi))))^2 + H), \quad (76)$$

$$u_{60}(x,t) = \sqrt{-H}(-\coth_\mu(2A\varphi) \mp (\sqrt{pq}csch_\mu(2A\varphi))),$$
$$v_{60}(x,t) = \frac{1}{k_2}((\sqrt{-H}(-\coth_\mu(2A\varphi) \mp (\sqrt{pq}csch_\mu(2A\varphi))))^2 + H), \quad (77)$$

and

$$u_{61}(x,t) = \sqrt{-H}(-1/2\tanh_\mu(1/2\,A\varphi) - 1/2\coth_\mu(1/2\,A\varphi)),$$
$$v_{61}(x,t) = \frac{1}{k_2}((\sqrt{-H}\left(-\frac{1}{2}\tanh_\mu(1/2\,A\varphi) - \frac{1}{2}\coth_\mu(1/2\,A\varphi)\right))^2 + H). \tag{78}$$

Family. 14: When $A = 0$, $B \neq 0$ and $C \neq 0$ then (11), (13) and corresponding general solutions of (10) imply the following family of symmetric soliton solutions:

$$u_{62}(x,t) = \sqrt{-H} - 2\frac{\sqrt{-H}p}{(\cosh_\mu(B\varphi) - \sinh_\mu(B\varphi) + p)},$$
$$v_{62}(x,t) = \frac{1}{k_2}((\sqrt{-H} - 2\frac{\sqrt{-H}p}{(\cosh_\mu(B\varphi) - \sinh_\mu(B\varphi) + p)})^2 + H), \tag{79}$$

and

$$u_{63}(x,t) = \sqrt{-H} - 2\frac{\sqrt{-H}(\cosh_\mu(B\varphi) + \sinh_\mu(B\varphi))}{(\cosh(B\varphi) + \sinh(B\varphi) + q)}$$
$$v_{63}(x,t) = \frac{1}{k_2}((\sqrt{-H} - 2\frac{\sqrt{-H}(\cosh_\mu(B\varphi) + \sinh_\mu(B\varphi))}{(\cosh(B\varphi) + \sinh(B\varphi) + q)})^2 + H). \tag{80}$$

Family. 15: When $B = \nu$, $C = N\nu(N \neq 0)$ and $A = 0$ then (11), (13) and corresponding general solutions of (10) imply the following family of symmetric soliton solutions:

$$u_{64}(x,t) = \sqrt{-H} + 2\frac{\sqrt{-H}Np\mu^{\nu\varphi}}{(p - Nq\mu^{\nu\varphi})},$$
$$v_{64}(x,t) = \frac{1}{k_2}((\sqrt{-H} + 2\frac{\sqrt{-H}Np\mu^{\nu\varphi}}{(p - Nq\mu^{\nu\varphi})})^2 + H). \tag{81}$$

where $\varphi = \frac{2}{\ln(\mu)k_2}\sqrt{-\frac{H}{-B^2+4CA}}(\frac{x^\beta}{\Gamma(\beta+1)} - \frac{k_2t^\alpha}{\Gamma(\alpha+1)})$.

3.2. Implementation of r + mEDAM

To construct more symmetric soliton solutions for (2), we now solve NODE in () with the help of r + mEDAM. Putting $n = 1$ in (9) implies the following series form solution for (14):

$$U(\varphi) = \sum_{l=-1}^{1} a_l(r + G(\varphi))^l = a_{-1}(r + G(\varphi))^{-1} + a_0 + a_1(r + G(\varphi))^1, \tag{82}$$

where a_{-1}, a_0 and a_1 are constants to be calculated, and $G(\varphi)$ is the general solution of ODE in (10). By putting (82) in (14) and collecting all terms with the same powers of $G(\varphi)$, we get an expression in $G(\varphi)$. By equating the coefficients to zero yields a system of algebraic equations in a_{-1}, a_0, a_1, k_1, k_2, H, r ,μ, A, B and C. Upon solving this system for a_{-1}, a_0, a_1, k_1 and k_2 using Maple, we reach at the following two cases of solutions:
Case. 1

$$a_1 = 0, a_{-1} = 2\frac{(A - rB + Cr^2)\sqrt{H}}{\sqrt{4\,AC - B^2}}, a_0 = \frac{\sqrt{H}(-2\,Cr + B)}{\sqrt{4\,AC - B^2}},$$
$$k_1 = \frac{2}{\ln(\mu)k_2}\sqrt{-\frac{H}{4\,AC - B^2}}, k_2 = k_2. \tag{83}$$

Case. 2

$$a_1 = 2\sqrt{\frac{H}{4AC - B^2}}C, a_{-1} = 0, a_0 = \frac{H(-2Cr + B)}{\sqrt{H(4AC - B^2)}},$$
$$k_1 = \frac{2}{\ln(\mu)k_2}\sqrt{-\frac{H}{4AC - B^2}}, k_2 = k_2. \tag{84}$$

Assuming case. 1, we get the following families of symmetric soliton solutions for (2):
Family. 16: When $R < 0 \quad A, B, C \neq 0$ then (11), (13) and corresponding general solutions of (10) imply the following family of symmetric soliton solutions:

$$u_{65}(x,t) = \frac{\frac{2(A-rB+Cr^2)\sqrt{H}}{\sqrt{-R}}}{\left(-\frac{B}{2C} + \frac{\sqrt{-R}\tan_\mu(1/2\sqrt{-R}\varphi)}{2C}\right)} + \frac{\sqrt{H}(-2Cr+B)}{\sqrt{R}},$$
$$v_{65}(x,t) = \frac{1}{k_2}((\frac{\frac{2(A-rB+Cr^2)\sqrt{H}}{\sqrt{-R}}}{\left(-\frac{B}{2C} + \frac{\sqrt{-R}\tan_\mu(1/2\sqrt{-R}\varphi)}{2C}\right)} + \frac{\sqrt{H}(-2Cr+B)}{\sqrt{R}})^2 + H), \tag{85}$$

$$u_{66}(x,t) = \frac{\frac{2(A-rB+Cr^2)\sqrt{H}}{\sqrt{-R}}}{\left(-\frac{B}{2C} - \frac{\sqrt{-R}\cot_\mu(1/2\sqrt{-R}\varphi)}{2C}\right)} + \frac{\sqrt{H}(-2Cr+B)}{\sqrt{-R}},$$
$$v_{66}(x,t) = \frac{1}{k_2}((\frac{\frac{2(A-rB+Cr^2)\sqrt{H}}{\sqrt{-R}}}{\left(-\frac{B}{2C} - \frac{\sqrt{-R}\cot_\mu(1/2\sqrt{-R}\varphi)}{2C}\right)} + \frac{\sqrt{H}(-2Cr+B)}{\sqrt{-R}})^2 + H), \tag{86}$$

$$u_{67}(x,t) = \frac{\frac{2(A-rB+Cr^2)\sqrt{H}}{\sqrt{-R}}}{\left(-\frac{B}{2C} + \frac{\sqrt{-R}\left(\tan_\mu(\sqrt{-R}\varphi)\pm(\sqrt{pq}\sec_\mu(\sqrt{-R}\varphi))\right)}{2C}\right)} + \frac{\sqrt{H}(-2Cr+B)}{\sqrt{-R}},$$
$$v_{67}(x,t) = \frac{1}{k_2}((\frac{\frac{2(A-rB+Cr^2)\sqrt{H}}{\sqrt{-R}}}{\left(-\frac{B}{2C} + \frac{\sqrt{-R}\left(\tan_\mu(\sqrt{-R}\varphi)\pm(\sqrt{pq}\sec_\mu(\sqrt{-R}\varphi))\right)}{2C}\right)} + \frac{\sqrt{H}(-2Cr+B)}{\sqrt{-R}})^2 + H), \tag{87}$$

$$u_{68}(x,t) = \frac{\frac{2(A-rB+Cr^2)\sqrt{H}}{\sqrt{-R}}}{\left(-\frac{B}{2C} - \frac{\sqrt{-R}\left(\cot_\mu(\sqrt{-R}\varphi)\pm(\sqrt{pq}\csc_\mu(\sqrt{-R}\varphi))\right)}{2C}\right)} + \frac{\sqrt{H}(-2Cr+B)}{\sqrt{-R}},$$
$$v_{68}(x,t) = \frac{1}{k_2}((\frac{\frac{2(A-rB+Cr^2)\sqrt{H}}{\sqrt{-R}}}{\left(-\frac{B}{2C} - \frac{\sqrt{-R}\left(\cot_\mu(\sqrt{-R}\varphi)\pm(\sqrt{pq}\csc_\mu(\sqrt{-R}\varphi))\right)}{2C}\right)} + \frac{\sqrt{H}(-2Cr+B)}{\sqrt{-R}})^2 + H), \tag{88}$$

and

$$\begin{aligned} u_{69}(x,t) &= \frac{\frac{2\left(A-rB+Cr^2\right)\sqrt{H}}{\sqrt{-R}}}{\left(-\frac{B}{2C}+\frac{\sqrt{-R}\left(\tan_\mu\left(1/4\sqrt{-R}\varphi\right)-\cot_\mu\left(1/4\sqrt{-R}\varphi\right)\right)}{4C}\right)}+\frac{\sqrt{H}(-2Cr+B)}{\sqrt{-R}}, \\ v_{69}(x,t) &= \frac{1}{k_2}((\frac{\frac{2\left(A-rB+Cr^2\right)\sqrt{H}}{\sqrt{-R}}}{\left(-\frac{B}{2C}+\frac{\sqrt{-R}\left(\tan_\mu\left(1/4\sqrt{-R}\varphi\right)-\cot_\mu\left(1/4\sqrt{-R}\varphi\right)\right)}{4C}\right)}+\frac{\sqrt{H}(-2Cr+B)}{\sqrt{-R}})^2+H). \end{aligned} \tag{89}$$

Family. 17: When $R > 0 \quad C \neq 0$ then (11), (13) and corresponding general solutions of (10) imply the following family of symmetric soliton solutions:

$$\begin{aligned} u_{70}(x,t) &= \frac{\frac{2\left(A-rB+Cr^2\right)\sqrt{H}}{\sqrt{-R}}}{\left(-\frac{B}{2C}-\frac{\sqrt{R}\tanh_\mu\left(1/2\sqrt{R}\varphi\right)}{2C}\right)}+\frac{\sqrt{H}(-2Cr+B)}{\sqrt{-R}}, \\ v_{70}(x,t) &= \frac{1}{k_2}((\frac{\frac{2\left(A-rB+Cr^2\right)\sqrt{H}}{\sqrt{-R}}}{\left(-\frac{B}{2C}-\frac{\sqrt{R}\tanh_\mu\left(1/2\sqrt{R}\varphi\right)}{2C}\right)}+\frac{\sqrt{H}(-2Cr+B)}{\sqrt{-R}})^2+H), \end{aligned} \tag{90}$$

$$\begin{aligned} u_{71}(x,t) &= \frac{\frac{2\left(A-rB+Cr^2\right)\sqrt{H}}{\sqrt{-R}}}{\left(-\frac{B}{2C}-\frac{\sqrt{R}\coth_\mu\left(1/2\sqrt{R}\varphi\right)}{2C}\right)}+\frac{\sqrt{H}(-2Cr+B)}{\sqrt{4AC-B^2}}, \\ v_{71}(x,t) &= \frac{1}{k_2}((\frac{\frac{2\left(A-rB+Cr^2\right)\sqrt{H}}{\sqrt{-R}}}{\left(-\frac{B}{2C}-\frac{\sqrt{R}\coth_\mu\left(1/2\sqrt{R}\varphi\right)}{2C}\right)}+\frac{\sqrt{H}(-2Cr+B)}{\sqrt{4AC-B^2}})^2+H), \end{aligned} \tag{91}$$

$$\begin{aligned} u_{72}(x,t) &= \frac{\frac{2\left(A-rB+Cr^2\right)\sqrt{H}}{\sqrt{-R}}}{\left(-\frac{B}{2C}-\frac{\sqrt{R}\left(\tanh_\mu\left(\sqrt{R}\varphi\right)\pm\left(\sqrt{pq}sech_\mu\left(\sqrt{R}\varphi\right)\right)\right)}{2C}\right)}+\frac{\sqrt{H}(-2Cr+B)}{\sqrt{-R}}, \\ v_{72}(x,t) &= \frac{1}{k_2}((\frac{\frac{2\left(A-rB+Cr^2\right)\sqrt{H}}{\sqrt{-R}}}{\left(-\frac{B}{2C}-\frac{\sqrt{R}\left(\tanh_\mu\left(\sqrt{R}\varphi\right)\pm\left(\sqrt{pq}sech_\mu\left(\sqrt{R}\varphi\right)\right)\right)}{2C}\right)}+\frac{\sqrt{H}(-2Cr+B)}{\sqrt{-R}})^2+H), \end{aligned} \tag{92}$$

$$\begin{aligned} u_{73}(x,t) &= \frac{\frac{2\left(A-rB+Cr^2\right)\sqrt{H}}{\sqrt{-R}}}{\left(-\frac{B}{2C}-\frac{\sqrt{R}\left(\coth_\mu\left(\sqrt{R}\varphi\right)\pm\left(\sqrt{pq}csch_\mu\left(\sqrt{R}\varphi\right)\right)\right)}{2C}\right)}+\frac{\sqrt{H}(-2Cr+B)}{\sqrt{-R}}, \\ v_{73}(x,t) &= \frac{1}{k_2}((\frac{\frac{2\left(A-rB+Cr^2\right)\sqrt{H}}{\sqrt{-R}}}{\left(-\frac{B}{2C}-\frac{\sqrt{R}\left(\coth_\mu\left(\sqrt{R}\varphi\right)\pm\left(\sqrt{pq}csch_\mu\left(\sqrt{R}\varphi\right)\right)\right)}{2C}\right)}+\frac{\sqrt{H}(-2Cr+B)}{\sqrt{-R}})^2+H), \end{aligned} \tag{93}$$

and

$$u_{74}(x,t) = \frac{\frac{2\left(A-rB+Cr^2\right)\sqrt{H}}{\sqrt{-R}}}{\left(-\frac{B}{2C} - \frac{\sqrt{R}\left(\tanh_\mu\left(1/4\sqrt{R}\varphi\right)-\coth_\mu\left(1/4\sqrt{R}\varphi\right)\right)}{4C}\right)} + \frac{\sqrt{H}(-2Cr+B)}{\sqrt{-R}},$$
$$v_{74}(x,t) = \frac{1}{k_2}((\frac{\frac{2\left(A-rB+Cr^2\right)\sqrt{H}}{\sqrt{-R}}}{\left(-\frac{B}{2C} - \frac{\sqrt{R}\left(\tanh_\mu\left(1/4\sqrt{R}\varphi\right)-\coth_\mu\left(1/4\sqrt{R}\varphi\right)\right)}{4C}\right)} + \frac{\sqrt{H}(-2Cr+B)}{\sqrt{-R}})^2 + H). \tag{94}$$

Family. 18: When $AC > 0$ and $B = 0$ then (11), (13) and corresponding general solutions of (10) imply the following family of symmetric soliton solutions:

$$u_{75}(x,t) = (1+\frac{r^2C}{A})\sqrt{H}\left(\tan_\mu\left(\sqrt{AC}\varphi\right)\right)^{-1} - \sqrt{\frac{HC}{A}}r,$$
$$v_{75}(x,t) = \frac{1}{k_2}(((1+\frac{r^2C}{A})\sqrt{H}\left(\tan_\mu\left(\sqrt{AC}\varphi\right)\right)^{-1} - \sqrt{\frac{HC}{A}}r)^2 + H), \tag{95}$$

$$u_{76}(x,t) = -(1+\frac{r^2C}{A})\sqrt{H}\left(\cot_\mu\left(\sqrt{AC}\varphi\right)\right)^{-1} - \sqrt{\frac{HC}{A}}r,$$
$$v_{76}(x,t) = \frac{1}{k_2}((-(1+\frac{r^2C}{A})\sqrt{H}\left(\cot_\mu\left(\sqrt{AC}\varphi\right)\right)^{-1} - \sqrt{\frac{HC}{A}}r)^2 + H), \tag{96}$$

$$u_{77}(x,t) = (1+\frac{r^2C}{A})\sqrt{H}(\tan_\mu\left(2\sqrt{AC}\varphi\right) \pm \left(\sqrt{pq}\sec_\mu\left(2\sqrt{AC}\varphi\right)\right))^{-1} - \sqrt{\frac{HC}{A}}r,$$
$$v_{77}(x,t) = \frac{1}{k_2}(((1+\frac{r^2C}{A})\sqrt{H}(\tan_\mu\left(2\sqrt{AC}\varphi\right) \pm \left(\sqrt{pq}\sec_\mu\left(2\sqrt{AC}\varphi\right)\right))^{-1} - \sqrt{\frac{HC}{A}}r)^2 + H), \tag{97}$$

$$u_{78}(x,t) = -(1+\frac{r^2C}{A})\sqrt{H}(\cot_\mu\left(2\sqrt{AC}\varphi\right) \pm \left(\sqrt{pq}\csc_\mu\left(2\sqrt{AC}\varphi\right)\right))^{-1} - \sqrt{\frac{HC}{A}}r,$$
$$v_{78}(x,t) = \frac{1}{k_2}((-(1+\frac{r^2C}{A})\sqrt{H}(\cot_\mu\left(2\sqrt{AC}\varphi\right) \pm \left(\sqrt{pq}\csc_\mu\left(2\sqrt{AC}\varphi\right)\right))^{-1} - \sqrt{\frac{HC}{A}}r \tag{98}$$

and

$$u_{79}(x,t) = 2(1+\frac{r^2C}{A})\sqrt{H}(\tan_\mu\left(1/2\sqrt{AC}\varphi\right) - \cot_\mu\left(1/2\sqrt{AC}\varphi\right))^{-1} - \sqrt{\frac{HC}{A}}r,$$
$$v_{79}(x,t) = \frac{1}{k_2}((2(1+\frac{r^2C}{A})\sqrt{H}(\tan_\mu\left(1/2\sqrt{AC}\varphi\right) - \cot_\mu\left(1/2\sqrt{AC}\varphi\right))^{-1} - \sqrt{\frac{HC}{A}}r)^2 + H). \tag{99}$$

Family. 19: When $AC > 0$ and $B = 0$ then (11), (13) and corresponding general solutions of (10) imply the following family of symmetric soliton solutions:

$$u_{80}(x,t) = -(1+\frac{r^2C}{A})\sqrt{-H}\left(\tanh_\mu\left(\sqrt{-AC}\varphi\right)\right)^{-1} - \sqrt{\frac{HC}{A}}r,$$
$$v_{80}(x,t) = \frac{1}{k_2}((-(1+\frac{r^2C}{A})\sqrt{-H}\left(\tanh_\mu\left(\sqrt{-AC}\varphi\right)\right)^{-1} - \sqrt{\frac{HC}{A}}r)^2 + H), \tag{100}$$

$$u_{81}(x,t) = -(1+\frac{r^2C}{A})\sqrt{-H}\left(\coth_\mu\left(\sqrt{-AC}\varphi\right)\right)^{-1} - \sqrt{\frac{HC}{A}}r,$$
$$v_{81}(x,t) = \frac{1}{k_2}((-(1+\frac{r^2C}{A})\sqrt{-H}\left(\coth_\mu\left(\sqrt{-AC}\varphi\right)\right)^{-1} - \sqrt{\frac{HC}{A}}r)^2 + H))^2 + H), \tag{101}$$

$$u_{82}(x,t) = -(1+\frac{r^2C}{A})\sqrt{-H}(\tanh_\mu\left(2\sqrt{-AC}\varphi\right) \pm \left(i\sqrt{pq}sech_\mu\left(2\sqrt{-AC}\varphi\right)\right))^{-1} - \sqrt{\frac{HC}{A}}r,$$
$$v_{82}(x,t) = \frac{1}{k_2}((\frac{-(1+\frac{r^2C}{A})\sqrt{-H}}{(\tanh_\mu\left(2\sqrt{-AC}\varphi\right) \pm \left(i\sqrt{pq}sech_\mu\left(2\sqrt{-AC}\varphi\right)\right))} - \sqrt{\frac{HC}{A}}r)^2 + H), \quad (102)$$

$$u_{83}(x,t) = -(1+\frac{r^2C}{A})\sqrt{-H}(\coth_\mu\left(2\sqrt{-AC}\varphi\right) \pm \left(\sqrt{pq}csch_\mu\left(2\sqrt{-AC}\varphi\right)\right))^{-1} - \sqrt{\frac{HC}{A}}r,$$
$$v_{83}(x,t) = \frac{1}{k_2}((\frac{-(1+\frac{r^2C}{A})\sqrt{-H}}{(\coth_\mu\left(2\sqrt{-AC}\varphi\right) \pm \left(\sqrt{pq}csch_\mu\left(2\sqrt{-AC}\varphi\right)\right))} - \sqrt{\frac{HC}{A}}r)^2 + H), \quad (103)$$

and

$$u_{84}(x,t) = -2(1+\frac{r^2C}{A})\sqrt{-H}(\tanh_\mu\left(1/2\sqrt{-AC}\varphi\right) + \coth_\mu\left(1/2\sqrt{-AC}\varphi\right))^{-1} - \sqrt{\frac{HC}{A}}r,$$
$$v_{84}(x,t) = \frac{1}{k_2}((\frac{-2(1+\frac{r^2C}{A})\sqrt{-H}}{(\tanh_\mu\left(1/2\sqrt{-AC}\varphi\right) + \coth_\mu\left(1/2\sqrt{-AC}\varphi\right))} - \sqrt{\frac{HC}{A}}r)^2 + H). \quad (104)$$

Family. 20: When $C = A$ and $B = 0$ then (11), (13) and corresponding general solutions of (10) imply the following family of symmetric soliton solutions:

$$u_{85}(x,t) = (1+r^2)\sqrt{H}\frac{1}{\tan_\mu(A\varphi)} - \sqrt{H}r,$$
$$v_{85}(x,t) = \frac{1}{k_2}(((1+r^2)\sqrt{H}\frac{1}{\tan_\mu(A\varphi)} - \sqrt{H}r)^2 + H), \quad (105)$$

$$u_{86}(x,t) = -(1+r^2)\sqrt{H}\frac{1}{\cot_\mu(A\varphi)} - \sqrt{H}r,$$
$$v_{86}(x,t) = \frac{1}{k_2}((-(1+r^2)\sqrt{H}\frac{1}{\cot_\mu(A\varphi)} - \sqrt{H}r)^2 + H), \quad (106)$$

$$u_{87}(x,t) = \frac{(1+r^2)\sqrt{H}}{(\tan_\mu(2A\varphi) \pm (\sqrt{pq}\sec_\mu(2A\varphi)))} - \sqrt{H}r,$$
$$v_{87}(x,t) = \frac{1}{k_2}((\frac{(1+r^2)\sqrt{H}}{(\tan_\mu(2A\varphi) \pm (\sqrt{pq}\sec_\mu(2A\varphi)))} - \sqrt{H}r)^2 + H), \quad (107)$$

$$u_{88}(x,t) = \frac{(1+r^2)\sqrt{H}}{(-\cot_\mu(2A\varphi) \mp (\sqrt{pq}\csc_\mu(2A\varphi)))} - \sqrt{H}r,$$
$$v_{88}(x,t) = \frac{1}{k_2}((\frac{(1+r^2)\sqrt{H}}{(-\cot_\mu(2A\varphi) \mp (\sqrt{pq}\csc_\mu(2A\varphi)))} - \sqrt{H}r)^2 + H), \quad (108)$$

and

$$u_{89}(x,t) = \frac{(1+r^2)\sqrt{H}}{(1/2\tan_\mu(1/2A\varphi) - 1/2\cot_\mu(1/2A\varphi))} - \sqrt{H}r,$$
$$v_{89}(x,t) = \frac{1}{k_2}((\frac{(1+r^2)\sqrt{H}}{(1/2\tan_\mu(1/2A\varphi) - 1/2\cot_\mu(1/2A\varphi))} - \sqrt{H}r)^2 + H). \quad (109)$$

Family. 21: When $C = -A$ and $B = 0$ then Equations (19) and (10) imply the following solitary wave solutions:

$$\begin{aligned} u_{90}(x,t) &= -(1-r^2)\sqrt{-H}\frac{1}{\tanh_\mu(A\varphi)} + \sqrt{-H}r, \\ v_{90}(x,t) &= \frac{1}{k_2}((-(1-r^2)\sqrt{-H}\frac{1}{\tanh_\mu(A\varphi)} + \sqrt{-H}r)^2 + H), \end{aligned} \tag{110}$$

$$\begin{aligned} u_{91}(x,t) &= -(1-r^2)\sqrt{-H}\frac{1}{\coth_\mu(A\varphi)} + \sqrt{-H}r, \\ v_{91}(x,t) &= \frac{1}{k_2}((-(1-r^2)\sqrt{-H}\frac{1}{\coth_\mu(A\varphi)} + \sqrt{-H}r)^2 + H), \end{aligned} \tag{111}$$

$$\begin{aligned} u_{92}(x,t) &= \frac{(1-r^2)\sqrt{-H}}{(-\tanh_\mu(2A\varphi) \mp (i\sqrt{pq}sech_\mu(2A\varphi)))} + \sqrt{-H}r, \\ v_{92}(x,t) &= \frac{1}{k_2}((\frac{(1-r^2)\sqrt{-H}}{(-\tanh_\mu(2A\varphi) \mp (i\sqrt{pq}sech_\mu(2A\varphi)))} + \sqrt{-H}r)^2 + H), \end{aligned} \tag{112}$$

$$\begin{aligned} u_{93}(x,t) &= \frac{(1-r^2)\sqrt{-H}}{(-\coth_\mu(2A\varphi) \mp (\sqrt{pq}csch_\mu(2A\varphi)))} + \sqrt{-H}r, \\ v_{93}(x,t) &= \frac{1}{k_2}((\frac{(1-r^2)\sqrt{-H}}{(-\coth_\mu(2A\varphi) \mp (\sqrt{pq}csch_\mu(2A\varphi)))} + \sqrt{-H}r)^2 + H), \end{aligned} \tag{113}$$

and

$$\begin{aligned} u_{94}(x,t) &= \frac{(1-r^2)\sqrt{-H}}{(-1/2\tanh_\mu(1/2A\varphi) - 1/2\coth_\mu(1/2A\varphi))} + \sqrt{-H}r, \\ v_{94}(x,t) &= \frac{((\frac{(1-r^2)\sqrt{-H}}{(-1/2\tanh_\mu(1/2A\varphi)-1/2\coth_\mu(1/2A\varphi))} + \sqrt{-H}r)^2 + H)}{k_2}. \end{aligned} \tag{114}$$

Family. 22: When $B = \nu$, $a = N\nu (N \neq 0)$ and $C = 0$ then (11), (13) and corresponding general solutions of (10) imply the following family of symmetric soliton solutions:

$$\begin{aligned} u_{95}(x,t) &= 2\frac{(N-r)\sqrt{-H}}{(\mu^{\nu\varphi} - N)} + \frac{\sqrt{H}(-2Cr+B)}{\sqrt{4AC-B^2}}, \\ v_{95}(x,t) &= \frac{1}{k_2}((2\frac{(N-r)\sqrt{-H}}{(\mu^{\nu\varphi} - N)} + \frac{\sqrt{H}(-2Cr+B)}{\sqrt{4AC-B^2}})^2 + H). \end{aligned} \tag{115}$$

Family. 23: When $A = 0$, $B \neq 0$ and $C \neq 0$ then (11), (13) and corresponding general solutions of (10) imply the following family of symmetric soliton solutions:

$$\begin{aligned} u_{96}(x,t) &= -2\frac{(-rB+Cr^2)\sqrt{H}C(\cosh_\mu(B\varphi) - \sinh_\mu(B\varphi) + p)}{pB^2 i} + \frac{\sqrt{H}(-2Cr+B)}{Bi}, \\ v_{96}(x,t) &= \frac{1}{k_2}((-2\frac{(-rB+Cr^2)\sqrt{H}C(\cosh_\mu(B\varphi) - \sinh_\mu(B\varphi) + p)}{pB^2 i} + \frac{\sqrt{H}(-2Cr+B)}{Bi})^2 + H), \end{aligned} \tag{116}$$

and

$$u_{97}(x,t) = -2\,\frac{(-rB+Cr^2)\sqrt{H}C(\cosh_\mu(B\varphi)+\sinh_\mu(B\varphi)+q)}{B^i(\cosh_\mu(B\varphi)+\sinh_\mu(B\varphi))} + \frac{\sqrt{H}(-2\,Cr+B)}{Bi},$$
$$v_{97}(x,t) = \frac{1}{k_2}((-2\,\frac{(-rB+Cr^2)\sqrt{H}C(\cosh_\mu(B\varphi)+\sinh_\mu(B\varphi)+q)}{B^i(\cosh_\mu(B\varphi)+\sinh_\mu(B\varphi))} + \frac{\sqrt{H}(-2\,Cr+B)}{Bi})^2 + H). \tag{117}$$

Family. 24: When $B=\nu$, $C=N\nu(N\neq 0)$ and $A=0$ then (11), (13) and corresponding general solutions of (10) imply the following family of symmetric soliton solutions:

$$u_{98}(x,t) = 2\,\frac{(Nr^2-r)\sqrt{H}(p-Nq\mu^{\nu\,\varphi})}{pi\mu^{\nu\,\varphi}} + \frac{\sqrt{H}(-2Nr+1)}{i},$$
$$v_{98}(x,t) = \frac{1}{k_2}((2\,\frac{(Nr^2-r)\sqrt{H}(p-Nq\mu^{\nu\,\varphi})}{pi\mu^{\nu\,\varphi}} + \frac{\sqrt{H}(-2Nr+1)}{i})^2 + H), \tag{118}$$

where $\varphi = \frac{2}{\ln(\mu)k_2}\sqrt{-\frac{H}{-B^2+4\,CA}}(\frac{x^\beta}{\Gamma(\beta+1)} - \frac{k_2 t^\alpha}{\Gamma(\alpha+1)})$.

Now assuming case. 2, we get the following families of symmetric soliton solutions for (2):

Family. 25: When $R<0\quad A,B,C\neq 0$ then (11), (13) and corresponding general solutions of (10) imply the following family of symmetric soliton solutions:

$$u_{99}(x,t) = \frac{H(-2\,Cr+B)}{\sqrt{-RH}} + \sqrt{\frac{H}{-R}}\Big(-B+\sqrt{-R}\tan_\mu\Big(1/2\,\sqrt{-R}\varphi\Big)\Big),$$
$$v_{99}(x,t) = \frac{1}{k_2}((\frac{H(-2\,Cr+B)}{\sqrt{-RH}} + \sqrt{\frac{H}{-R}}\Big(-B+\sqrt{-R}\tan_\mu\Big(1/2\,\sqrt{-R}\varphi\Big)\Big))^2 + H), \tag{119}$$

$$u_{100}(x,t) = \frac{H(-2\,Cr+B)}{\sqrt{-RH}} + \sqrt{\frac{H}{-R}}\Big(-B-\sqrt{-R}\cot_\mu\Big(1/2\,\sqrt{-R}\varphi\Big)\Big),$$
$$v_{100}(x,t) = \frac{1}{k_2}((\frac{H(-2\,Cr+B)}{\sqrt{-RH}} + \sqrt{\frac{H}{-R}}\Big(-B-\sqrt{-R}\cot_\mu\Big(1/2\,\sqrt{-R}\varphi\Big)\Big))^2 + H), \tag{120}$$

$$u_{101}(x,t) = \frac{H(-2\,Cr+B)}{\sqrt{-RH}} + \sqrt{\frac{H}{-R}}\Big(-B+\sqrt{-R}\Big(\tan_\mu\Big(\sqrt{-R}\varphi\Big) \pm \Big(\sqrt{pq}\sec_\mu\Big(\sqrt{-R}\varphi\Big)\Big)\Big)\Big),$$
$$v_{101}(x,t) = \frac{1}{k_2}((\frac{H(-2\,Cr+B)}{\sqrt{-RH}} + \sqrt{\frac{H}{-R}}\Big(-B+\sqrt{-R}\Big(\tan_\mu\Big(\sqrt{-R}\varphi\Big) \pm \Big(\sqrt{pq}\sec_\mu\Big(\sqrt{-R}\varphi\Big)\Big)\Big)\Big))^2 + H), \tag{121}$$

$$u_{102}(x,t) = \frac{H(-2\,Cr+B)}{\sqrt{-RH}} + \sqrt{\frac{H}{-R}}\Big(-B-\sqrt{-R}\Big(\cot_\mu\Big(\sqrt{-R}\varphi\Big)\Big(\sqrt{pq}\csc_\mu\Big(\sqrt{-R}\varphi\Big)\Big)\Big)\Big),$$
$$v_{102}(x,t) = \frac{1}{k_2}((\frac{H(-2\,Cr+B)}{\sqrt{-RH}} + \sqrt{\frac{H}{-R}}\Big(-B-\sqrt{-R}\Big(\cot_\mu\Big(\sqrt{-R}\varphi\Big)\Big(\sqrt{pq}\csc_\mu\Big(\sqrt{-R}\varphi\Big)\Big)\Big)\Big))^2 + H), \tag{122}$$

and

$$u_{103}(x,t) = \frac{H(-2\,Cr+B)}{\sqrt{-RH}} + \sqrt{\frac{H}{-R}}\left(-B+\frac{\sqrt{-R}(\tan_\mu(1/4\,\sqrt{-R}\varphi)-\cot_\mu(1/4\,\sqrt{-R}\varphi))}{2}\right),$$
$$v_{103}(x,t) = \frac{1}{k_2}((\frac{H(-2\,Cr+B)}{\sqrt{-RH}} + \sqrt{\frac{H}{-R}}\left(-B+\frac{\sqrt{-R}(\tan_\mu(1/4\,\sqrt{-R}\varphi)-\cot_\mu(1/4\,\sqrt{-R}\varphi))}{2}\right))^2 + H). \tag{123}$$

Family. 26: When $R > 0 \quad A, B, C \neq 0$ then (11), (13) and corresponding general solutions of (10) imply the following family of symmetric soliton solutions:

$$\begin{aligned} u_{104}(x,t) &= \frac{H(-2Cr+B)}{\sqrt{-RH}} + \sqrt{\frac{H}{-R}}\Big(-B - \sqrt{R}\tanh_{\mu}\Big(1/2\sqrt{R}\varphi\Big)\Big), \\ v_{104}(x,t) &= \frac{1}{k_2}((\frac{H(-2Cr+B)}{\sqrt{-RH}} + \sqrt{\frac{H}{-R}}\Big(-B - \sqrt{R}\tanh_{\mu}\Big(1/2\sqrt{R}\varphi\Big)\Big))^2 + H), \end{aligned} \tag{124}$$

$$\begin{aligned} u_{105}(x,t) &= \frac{H(-2Cr+B)}{\sqrt{-RH}} + \sqrt{\frac{H}{-R}}\Big(-B - \sqrt{R}\coth_{\mu}\Big(1/2\sqrt{R}\varphi\Big)\Big), \\ v_{105}(x,t) &= \frac{1}{k_2}((\frac{H(-2Cr+B)}{\sqrt{-RH}} + \sqrt{\frac{H}{-R}}\Big(-B - \sqrt{R}\coth_{\mu}\Big(1/2\sqrt{R}\varphi\Big)\Big))^2 + H), \end{aligned} \tag{125}$$

$$\begin{aligned} u_{106}(x,t) &= \frac{H(-2Cr+B)}{\sqrt{-RH}} + \sqrt{\frac{H}{-R}}\Big(-B - \sqrt{R}\Big(\tanh_{\mu}\Big(\sqrt{R}\varphi\Big) \pm \Big(\sqrt{pq}sech_{\mu}\Big(\sqrt{R}\varphi\Big)\Big)\Big)\Big), \\ v_{106}(x,t) &= \frac{1}{k_2}((\frac{H(-2Cr+B)}{\sqrt{-RH}} + \sqrt{\frac{H}{-R}}\Big(-B - \sqrt{R}\Big(\tanh_{\mu}\Big(\sqrt{R}\varphi\Big) \pm \Big(\sqrt{pq}sech_{\mu}\Big(\sqrt{R}\varphi\Big)\Big)\Big)\Big))^2 + H), \end{aligned} \tag{126}$$

$$\begin{aligned} u_{107}(x,t) &= \frac{H(-2Cr+B)}{\sqrt{-RH}} + \sqrt{\frac{H}{-R}}\Big(-B - \sqrt{R}\Big(\coth_{\mu}\Big(\sqrt{R}\varphi\Big) \pm \Big(\sqrt{pq}csch_{\mu}\Big(\sqrt{R}\varphi\Big)\Big)\Big)\Big), \\ v_{107}(x,t) &= \frac{1}{k_2}((\frac{H(-2Cr+B)}{\sqrt{-RH}} + \sqrt{\frac{H}{-R}}\Big(-B - \sqrt{R}\Big(\coth_{\mu}\Big(\sqrt{R}\varphi\Big) \pm \Big(\sqrt{pq}csch_{\mu}\Big(\sqrt{R}\varphi\Big)\Big)\Big)\Big))^2 + H), \end{aligned} \tag{127}$$

and

$$\begin{aligned} u_{108}(x,t) &= \frac{H(-2Cr+B)}{\sqrt{-RH}} + \sqrt{\frac{H}{-R}}\left(-B - \frac{\sqrt{R}\Big(\tanh_{\mu}\Big(1/4\sqrt{R}\varphi\Big) - \coth_{\mu}\Big(1/4\sqrt{R}\varphi\Big)\Big)}{2}\right), \\ v_{108}(x,t) &= \frac{1}{k_2}((\frac{H(-2Cr+B)}{\sqrt{-RH}} + \sqrt{\frac{H}{-R}}\left(-B - \frac{\sqrt{R}\Big(\tanh_{\mu}\Big(1/4\sqrt{R}\varphi\Big) - \coth_{\mu}\Big(1/4\sqrt{R}\varphi\Big)\Big)}{2}\right))^2 + H). \end{aligned} \tag{128}$$

Family. 27: When $AC > 0$ and $B = 0$ then (11), (13) and corresponding general solutions of (10) imply the following family of symmetric soliton solutions:

$$\begin{aligned} u_{109}(x,t) &= -r\sqrt{\frac{HC}{A}} + \sqrt{H}\tan_{\mu}\Big(\sqrt{AC}\varphi\Big), \\ v_{109}(x,t) &= \frac{1}{k_2}((-r\sqrt{\frac{HC}{A}} + \sqrt{H}\tan_{\mu}\Big(\sqrt{AC}\varphi\Big))^2 + H), \end{aligned} \tag{129}$$

$$\begin{aligned} u_{110}(x,t) &= -r\sqrt{\frac{HC}{A}} - \sqrt{H}\cot_{\mu}\Big(\sqrt{AC}\varphi\Big), \\ v_{110}(x,t) &= \frac{1}{k_2}((-r\sqrt{\frac{HC}{A}} - \sqrt{H}\cot_{\mu}\Big(\sqrt{AC}\varphi\Big))^2 + H), \end{aligned} \tag{130}$$

$$\begin{aligned} u_{111}(x,t) &= -r\sqrt{\frac{HC}{A}} + \sqrt{H}(\tan_{\mu}\Big(2\sqrt{AC}\varphi\Big) \pm \Big(\sqrt{pq}\sec_{\mu}\Big(2\sqrt{AC}\varphi\Big)\Big)), \\ v_{111}(x,t) &= \frac{1}{k_2}((-r\sqrt{\frac{HC}{A}} + \sqrt{H}(\tan_{\mu}\Big(2\sqrt{AC}\varphi\Big) \pm \Big(\sqrt{pq}\sec_{\mu}\Big(2\sqrt{AC}\varphi\Big)\Big)))^2 + H), \end{aligned} \tag{131}$$

$$\begin{aligned} u_{112}(x,t) &= -r\sqrt{\frac{HC}{A}} - 2\sqrt{H}(\cot_\mu\left(2\sqrt{AC}\varphi\right) \pm \left(\sqrt{pq}\csc_\mu\left(2\sqrt{AC}\varphi\right)\right)), \\ v_{112}(x,t) &= \frac{1}{k_2}((-r\sqrt{\frac{HC}{A}} - 2\sqrt{H}(\cot_\mu\left(2\sqrt{AC}\varphi\right) \pm \left(\sqrt{pq}\csc_\mu\left(2\sqrt{AC}\varphi\right)\right)))^2 + H), \end{aligned} \tag{132}$$

and

$$\begin{aligned} u_{113}(x,t) &= -r\sqrt{\frac{HC}{A}} + \sqrt{H}(\tan_\mu\left(1/2\sqrt{AC}\varphi\right) - \cot_\mu\left(1/2\sqrt{AC}\varphi\right)), \\ v_{113}(x,t) &= \frac{1}{k_2}((-r\sqrt{\frac{HC}{A}} + \sqrt{H}(\tan_\mu\left(1/2\sqrt{AC}\varphi\right) - \cot_\mu\left(1/2\sqrt{AC}\varphi\right)))^2 + H). \end{aligned} \tag{133}$$

Family. 28: When $AC < 0$ and $B = 0$ then (11), (13) and corresponding general solutions of (10) imply the following family of symmetric soliton solutions:

$$\begin{aligned} u_{114}(x,t) &= -r\sqrt{\frac{-HC}{A}} - \sqrt{-H}\tanh_\mu\left(\sqrt{-AC}\varphi\right), \\ v_{114}(x,t) &= \frac{1}{k_2}((-r\sqrt{\frac{-HC}{A}} - \sqrt{-H}\tanh_\mu\left(\sqrt{-AC}\varphi\right))^2 + H), \end{aligned} \tag{134}$$

$$\begin{aligned} u_{115}(x,t) &= -r\sqrt{\frac{-HC}{A}} - \sqrt{-H}\coth_\mu\left(\sqrt{-AC}\varphi\right), \\ v_{115}(x,t) &= \frac{1}{k_2}((-r\sqrt{\frac{-HC}{A}} - \sqrt{-H}\coth_\mu\left(\sqrt{-AC}\varphi\right))^2 + H), \end{aligned} \tag{135}$$

$$\begin{aligned} u_{116}(x,t) &= -r\sqrt{\frac{-HC}{A}} - \sqrt{-H}(\tanh_\mu\left(2\sqrt{-AC}\varphi\right) \pm \left(i\sqrt{pq}sech_\mu\left(2\sqrt{-AC}\varphi\right)\right)), \\ v_{116}(x,t) &= \frac{1}{k_2}((-r\sqrt{\frac{-HC}{A}} - \sqrt{-H}(\tanh_\mu\left(2\sqrt{-AC}\varphi\right) \pm \left(i\sqrt{pq}sech_\mu\left(2\sqrt{-AC}\varphi\right)\right)))^2 + H), \end{aligned} \tag{136}$$

$$\begin{aligned} u_{117}(x,t) &= -r\sqrt{\frac{-HC}{A}} - \sqrt{-H}(\coth_\mu\left(2\sqrt{-AC}\varphi\right) \pm \left(\sqrt{pq}csch_\mu\left(2\sqrt{-AC}\varphi\right)\right)), \\ v_{117}(x,t) &= \frac{1}{k_2}((-r\sqrt{\frac{-HC}{A}} - \sqrt{-H}(\coth_\mu\left(2\sqrt{-AC}\varphi\right) \pm \left(\sqrt{pq}csch_\mu\left(2\sqrt{-AC}\varphi\right)\right)))^2 + H), \end{aligned} \tag{137}$$

and

$$\begin{aligned} u_{118}(x,t) &= -r\sqrt{\frac{-HC}{A}} - \sqrt{-H}(\tanh_\mu\left(1/2\sqrt{-AC}\varphi\right) + \coth_\mu\left(1/2\sqrt{-AC}\varphi\right)), \\ v_{118}(x,t) &= \frac{1}{k_2}((-r\sqrt{\frac{-HC}{A}} - \sqrt{-H}(\tanh_\mu\left(1/2\sqrt{-AC}\varphi\right) + \coth_\mu\left(1/2\sqrt{-AC}\varphi\right)))^2 + H). \end{aligned} \tag{138}$$

Family. 29: When $C = A$ and $B = 0$ then (11), (13) and corresponding general solutions of (10) imply the following family of symmetric soliton solutions:

$$\begin{aligned} u_{119}(x,t) &= \sqrt{H}(1-r)\tan_\mu(A\varphi), \\ v_{119}(x,t) &= \frac{1}{k_2}((\sqrt{H}(1-r)\tan_\mu(A\varphi))^2 + H), \end{aligned} \tag{139}$$

$$\begin{aligned} u_{120}(x,t) &= -\sqrt{H}(1+r)\cot_\mu(A\varphi), \\ v_{120}(x,t) &= \frac{1}{k_2}((-\sqrt{H}(1+r)\cot_\mu(A\varphi))^2 + H), \end{aligned} \tag{140}$$

$$\begin{aligned} u_{121}(x,t) &= \sqrt{H}(1-r)(\tan_\mu(2\,A\varphi) \pm (\sqrt{pq}\sec_\mu(2\,A\varphi))), \\ v_{121}(x,t) &= \frac{1}{k_2}((\sqrt{H}(1-r)(\tan_\mu(2\,A\varphi) \pm (\sqrt{pq}\sec_\mu(2\,A\varphi))))^2 + H), \end{aligned} \tag{141}$$

$$\begin{aligned} u_{122}(x,t) &= -\sqrt{H}(1+r)(-\cot_\mu(2\,A\varphi) \mp (\sqrt{pq}\csc_\mu(2\,A\varphi))), \\ v_{122}(x,t) &= \frac{1}{k_2}((-\sqrt{H}(1+r)(-\cot_\mu(2\,A\varphi) \mp (\sqrt{pq}\csc_\mu(2\,A\varphi))))^2 + H), \end{aligned} \tag{142}$$

and

$$\begin{aligned} u_{123}(x,t) &= \sqrt{H}(1-r)(1/2\,\tan_\mu(1/2\,A\varphi) - 1/2\,\cot_\mu(1/2\,A\varphi)), \\ v_{123}(x,t) &= \frac{((\sqrt{H}(1-r)(1/2\,\tan_\mu(1/2\,A\varphi) - 1/2\,\cot_\mu(1/2\,A\varphi)))^2 + H)}{k_2}. \end{aligned} \tag{143}$$

Family. 30: When $C = -A$ and $B = 0$ then (11), (13) and corresponding general solutions of (10) imply the following family of symmetric soliton solutions:

$$\begin{aligned} u_{124}(x,t) &= \sqrt{-H}(r-1)\tanh_\mu(A\varphi), \\ v_{124}(x,t) &= \frac{1}{k_2}((\sqrt{-H}(r-1)\tanh_\mu(A\varphi))^2 + H), \end{aligned} \tag{144}$$

$$\begin{aligned} u_{125}(x,t) &= \sqrt{-H}(r-1)\coth_\mu(A\varphi), \\ v_{125}(x,t) &= \frac{1}{k_2}((\sqrt{-H}(r-1)\coth_\mu(A\varphi))^2 + H), \end{aligned} \tag{145}$$

$$\begin{aligned} u_{126}(x,t) &= \sqrt{-H}(r+1)(-\tanh_\mu(2\,A\varphi) \mp (i\sqrt{pq}sech_\mu(2\,A\varphi))), \\ v_{126}(x,t) &= \frac{((\sqrt{-H}(r+1)(-\tanh_\mu(2\,A\varphi) \mp (i\sqrt{pq}sech_\mu(2\,A\varphi))))^2 + H)}{k_2}, \end{aligned} \tag{146}$$

$$\begin{aligned} u_{127}(x,t) &= \sqrt{-H}(r+1)(-\coth_\mu(2\,A\varphi) \mp (\sqrt{pq}csch_\mu(2\,A\varphi))), \\ v_{127}(x,t) &= \frac{((\sqrt{-H}(r+1)(-\coth_\mu(2\,A\varphi) \mp (\sqrt{pq}csch_\mu(2\,A\varphi))))^2 + H)}{k_2}, \end{aligned} \tag{147}$$

and

$$\begin{aligned} u_{128}(x,t) &= \sqrt{-H}(r+1)\left(\frac{1}{2}\tanh_\mu\left(\frac{1}{2}A\varphi\right) - \frac{1}{2}\coth_\mu\left(\frac{1}{2}A\varphi\right)\right), \\ v_{128}(x,t) &= \frac{((\sqrt{-H}(r+1)\left(-\frac{1}{2}\tanh_\mu\left(\frac{1}{2}A\varphi\right) - \frac{1}{2}\coth_\mu\left(\frac{1}{2}A\varphi\right)\right))^2 + H)}{k_2}. \end{aligned} \tag{148}$$

Family. 31: When $A = 0$, $B \neq 0$ and $C \neq 0$ then (11), (13) and corresponding general solutions of (10) imply the following family of symmetric soliton solutions:

$$\begin{aligned} u_{129}(x,t) &= \frac{H(-2\,Cr + B)}{\sqrt{-HB^2}} - 2\sqrt{-H}p(\cosh_\mu(B\varphi) - \sinh_\mu(B\varphi) + p)^{-1}, \\ v_{129}(x,t) &= \frac{1}{k_2}((\frac{H(-2\,Cr + B)}{\sqrt{-HB^2}} - 2\sqrt{-H}p(\cosh_\mu(B\varphi) - \sinh_\mu(B\varphi) + p)^{-1})^2 + H), \end{aligned} \tag{149}$$

and

$$\begin{aligned} u_{130}(x,t) &= \frac{H(-2\,Cr + B)}{\sqrt{-HB^2}} - 2\sqrt{-H}\frac{\cosh_\mu(B\varphi) + \sinh_\mu(B\varphi)}{\cosh_\mu(B\varphi) + \sinh_\mu(B\varphi) + q}, \\ v_{130}(x,t) &= \frac{((\frac{H(-2\,Cr+B)}{\sqrt{-HB^2}} - 2\sqrt{-H}\frac{\cosh_\mu(B\varphi)+\sinh_\mu(B\varphi)}{\cosh_\mu(B\varphi)+\sinh_\mu(B\varphi)+q})^2 + H)}{k_2}. \end{aligned} \tag{150}$$

Family. 32: When $B = \nu, C = N\nu(N \neq 0)$ and $A = 0$ then (11), (13) and corresponding general solutions of (10) imply the following family of symmetric soliton solutions:

$$\begin{aligned} u_{131}(x,t) &= \sqrt{-H}(-2Nr+1) + 2\sqrt{-H}Np\mu^{\nu\varphi}(p - Nq\mu^{\nu\varphi})^{-1}, \\ v_{131}(x,t) &= \frac{((\sqrt{-H}(-2Nr+1) + 2\sqrt{-H}Np\mu^{\nu\varphi}(p - Nq\mu^{\nu\varphi})^{-1})^2 + H)}{k_2}. \end{aligned} \tag{151}$$

where $\varphi = \frac{2}{\ln(\mu)k_2}\sqrt{-\frac{H}{-B^2+4CA}}(\frac{x^\beta}{\Gamma(\beta+1)} - \frac{k_2 t^\alpha}{\Gamma(\alpha+1)})$.

4. Discussion and Graphs

We successfully constructed families of symmetric soliton solutions for FCKOS by employing two adapted versions of EDAM i.e., mEDAM and r+EDAM in this study. By supposing series form solutions, we were capable to apply these approaches to translate the given system of NODEs formed from the model into a system of algebraic equations. We were capable to obtain the model's symmetric soliton solutions by solving this algebraic system.

In Figure 1, the 3D graph of the first equation in (28) is depicted in Figure 1 for $A = 3, B = 0, C = 1, \mu = e, H = 3,\ k_2 = 2,\ \alpha = \beta = 1$. This profile shows a symmetric lump wave which is significant wave that can come into view in a range of physical systems. Figure 2, the 3D graph of the second equation in (80) is plotted in Figure 2 for $A = 0, B = 2, C = 1, \mu = e, H = 2 = k_2,\ \alpha = 0.5,\ \beta = 0.9$. This profile shows a symmetric kink wave which descends or ascends from one asymptotic state to another and at infinity it attains a constant velocity profile. Figure 3, the 3D graph of first equation in (95) is illustrated in Figure 3 for $A = 2, B = 0, C = 4,\ \mu = 3, H = -5, k_2 = 2,\ r = p = q = 1, \alpha = \beta = 1$. This profile shows a symmetric solitary wave which has a fixed shape and constant speed which is asymptotically zero at large distance. The 3D graph of the real part of the second equation in (107) is illustrated in Figure 4 for $A = 1, B = 0, C = 1, \mu = e, H = -2,\ k_2 = 109, r = 5,\ p = 2,\ q = 10,\ \alpha = 0.9,\ \beta = 0.5$. This profile shows a symmetric periodic wave which are travelling waves that show periodicity while propagating. The constructed symmetric soliton solutions include solitary waves, lump waves, periodic waves, kink waves, etc. all of which show symmetries in their profiles. The existence of symmetries improve the stability and robustness of solitons and it offer insight into conservation laws and essential physical properties. The study of these symmetric solitons contributes to a healthier understanding of the complicated dynamics concerning dispersion, nonlinearity and supplementary influencing factors in targeted FCKOS. This investigation present precious insights into intricate wave phenomena and their applications in various fields of nonlinear physics (Figures 1–4).

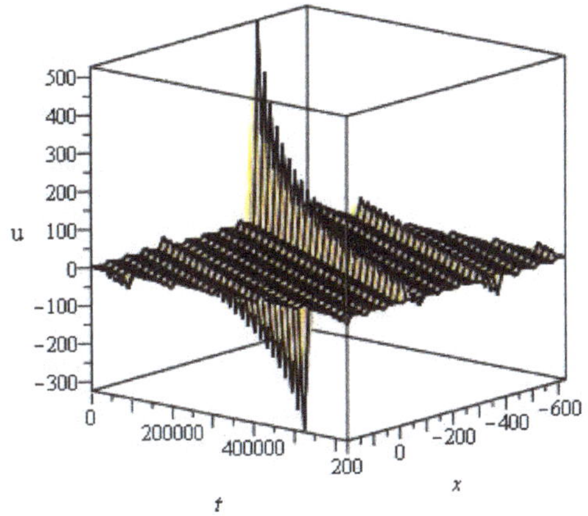

Figure 1. The 3D graph of the first equation in (28) is depicted in Figure 1 for $A = 3, B = 0, C = 1$, $\mu = e, H = 3,\ k_2 = 2,\ \alpha = \beta = 1$. This profile shows a symmetric lump wave which is significant wave that can come into view in a range of physical systems. These waves are characterized by a swift increase in amplitude and a sluggish decline reverse to their early level.

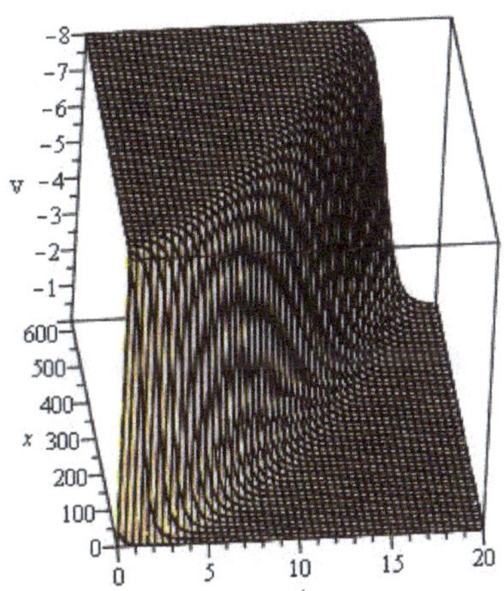

Figure 2. The 3D graph of the second equation in (80) is plotted in Figure 2 for $A = 0, B = 2, C = 1$, $\mu = e, H = 2 = k_2,\ \alpha = 0.5,\ \beta = 0.9$. This profile shows a symmetric kink wave which descends or ascends from one asymptotic state to another and at infinity it attains a constant velocity profile.

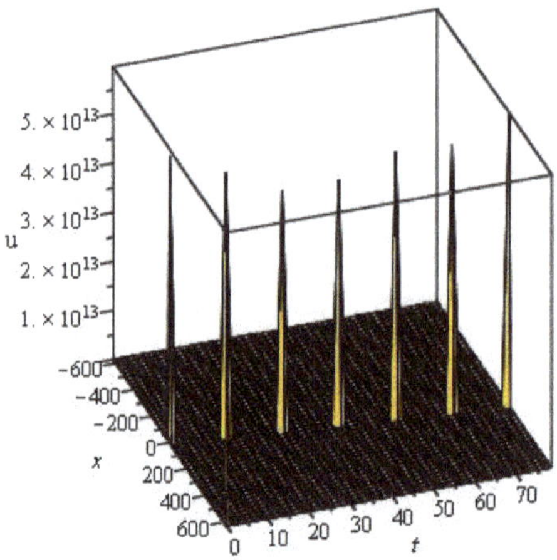

Figure 3. The 3D graph of first equation in (95) is illustrated in Figure 3 for $A = 2, B = 0, C = 4$, $\mu = 3, H = -5, k_2 = 2,\ r = p = q = 1, \alpha = \beta = 1$. This profile shows a symmetric solitary wave which has a fixed shape and constant speed which is asymptotically zero at large distance.

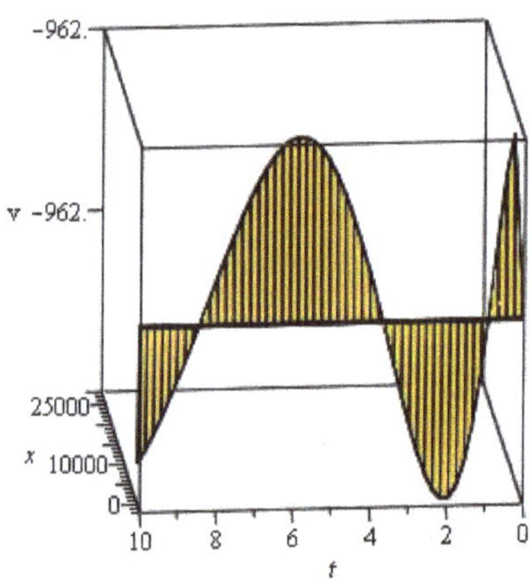

Figure 4. The 3D graph of the real part of the second equation in (107) is illustrated in Figure 4 for $A = 1, B = 0, C = 1, \mu = e, H = -2,\ k_2 = 109, r = 5,\ p = 2,\ q = 10,\ \alpha = 0.9,\ \beta = 0.5$. This profile shows a symmetric periodic wave which are travelling waves that show periodicity while propagating.

5. Conclusions

In this research work, FCKOS was addressed using two improved variants of EDAM. For the offered system of NODEs, the mEDAM and r+mEDAM approaches were able to discover a series form a solution, which was then distorted into a system of nonlinear algebraic equations to get verities of symmetric soliton solutions that are significant to the problem's physical interpretation. The existence of different travelling waves including kink waves, solitary waves, periodic waves, lump waves, etc., in soliton solutions were shown by depicting some 3D graphs. The article highlights the implication for several practical applications in different areas of science and demonstrate the potential of the EDAM in constructing families of soliton solutions for complex problems.

Author Contributions: Methodology, R.S.; Validation, A.M.S.; Resources, H.Y. and N.H.A.; Data curation, R.S.; Writing—original draft, H.Y. and N.H.A.; Writing—review & editing, A.M.S. All authors have read and agreed to the published version of the manuscript.

Funding: This work was supported by the Deanship of Scientific Research, the Vice Presidency for Graduate Studies and Scientific Research, King Faisal University, Saudi Arabia (Grant No. 3632).

Data Availability Statement: Data sharing is not applicable to this article as no new data were created or analyzed in this study.

Acknowledgments: This work was supported by the Deanship of Scientific Research, the Vice Presidency for Graduate Studies and Scientific Research, King Faisal University, Saudi Arabia (Grant No. 3632).

Conflicts of Interest: The authors declare no conflict of interest.

References

1. Abro, K.A.; Atangana, A. Dual fractional modeling of rate type fluid through nonlocal differentiation. *Numer. Methods Part. Differ. Equ.* **2022**, *38*, 390–405.
2. Shah, N.A.; Alyousef, H.A.; El-Tantawy, S.A.; Chung, J.D. Analytical investigation of fractional-order Korteweg-De-Vries-type equations under Atangana-Baleanu-Caputo operator: Modeling nonlinear waves in a plasma and fluid. *Symmetry* **2022**, *14*, 739. [CrossRef]
3. Tarasov, V.E.; Zaslavsky, G.M. Fractional dynamics of systems with long-range interaction. *Commun. Nonlinear Sci. Numer. Simul.* **2006**, *11*, 885–898. [CrossRef]
4. Su, N. Random fractional partial differential equations and solutions for water movement in soils: Theory and applications. *Hydrol. Process.* **2023**, *37*, e14844. [CrossRef]
5. Che, J.; Guan, Q.; Wang, X. Image denoising based on adaptive fractional partial differential equations. In Proceedings of the 2013 6th International Congress on Image and Signal Processing (CISP), Hangzhou, China, 16–18 December 2013; IEEE: Piscataway, NJ, USA, 2013; Volume 1, pp. 288–292.
6. Hamed, Y.S.; Abualnaja, K.M.; Chung, J.D.; Khan, A. A comparative analysis of fractional-order kaup-kupershmidt equation within different operators. *Symmetry* **2022**, *14*, 986.
7. Shah, N.A.; Wakif, A.; Yook, S.J.; Salah, B.; Mahsud, Y.; Hussain, K. Effects of fractional derivative and heat source/sink on MHD free convection flow of nanofluids in a vertical cylinder: A generalized Fourier's law model. *Case Stud. Therm. Eng.* **2021**, *28*, 101518. [CrossRef]
8. Alderremy, A.A.; Aly, S.; Fayyaz, R.; Khan, A.; Shah, R.; Wyal, N. The analysis of fractional-order nonlinear systems of third order KdV and Burgers equations via a novel transform. *Complexity* **2022**, *2022*, 4935809. [CrossRef]
9. Singh, J.; Kumar, D.; Kılıçman, A. Numerical solutions of nonlinear fractional partial differential equations arising in spatial diffusion of biological populations. *Abstr. Appl. Anal.* **2014**, *2014*, 535793. [CrossRef]
10. Kbiri, A.M.; Nonlaopon, K.; Zidan, A.M.; Khan, A. Analytical investigation of fractional-order Cahn-Hilliard and gardner equations using two novel techniques. *Mathematics* **2022**, *10*, 1643. [CrossRef]
11. Wang, Z.; Ahmadi, A.; Tian, H.; Jafari, S.; Chen, G. Lower-dimensional simple chaotic systems with spectacular features. *Chaos Solitons Fractals* **2023**, *169*, 113299. [CrossRef]
12. Jin, H.Y.; Wang, Z.A. Global stabilization of the full attraction-repulsion Keller-Segel system. *Discret. Contin. Dyn.-Syst.* **2020**, *40*, 3509–3527. [CrossRef]
13. Zhang, Y. A finite difference method for fractional partial differential equation. *Appl. Math. Comput.* **2009**, *215*, 524–529. [CrossRef]
14. Ford, N.J.; Xiao, J.; Yan, Y. A finite element method for time fractional partial differential equations. *Fract. Calc. Appl. Anal.* **2011**, *14*, 454–474. [CrossRef]
15. Elagan, S.K.; Sayed, M.; Higazy, M. An analytical study on fractional partial differential equations by Laplace transform operator method. *Int. J. Appl. Eng. Res.* **2018**, *13*, 545–549.
16. Mahor, T.C.; Mishra, R.; Jain, R. Analytical solutions of linear fractional partial differential equations using fractional Fourier transform. *J. Comput. Appl. Math.* **2021**, *385*, 113202. [CrossRef]
17. Jin, H.Y.; Wang, Z. Asymptotic dynamics of the one-dimensional attraction-repulsion Keller-Segel model. *Math. Methods Appl. Sci.* **2015**, *38*, 444–457. [CrossRef]
18. Lyu, W.; Wang, Z. Global classical solutions for a class of reaction-diffusion system with density-suppressed motility. *Electron. Res. Arch.* **2022**, *30*, 995–1015. [CrossRef]
19. Zhang, J.; Wang, X.; Zhou, L.; Liu, G.; Adroja, D.T.; da Silva, I.; Demmel, F.; Khalyavin, D.; Sannigrahi, J.; Nair, H.S.; et al. A Ferrotoroidic Candidate with Well-Separated Spin Chains. *Adv. Mater.* **2022**, *34*, e2106728. [CrossRef]
20. Chung, K.L.; Tian, H.; Wang, S.; Feng, B.; Lai, G. Miniaturization of microwave planar circuits using composite microstrip/coplanar-waveguide transmission lines. *Alex. Eng. J.* **2022**, *61*, 8933–8942. [CrossRef]
21. Song, J.; Mingotti, A.; Zhang, J.; Peretto, L.; Wen, H. Fast iterative-interpolated DFT phasor estimator considering out-of-band interference. *IEEE Trans. Instrum. Meas.* **2022**, *71*, 1–14. [CrossRef]

22. Dai, Z.; Xie, J.; Jiang, M. A coupled peridynamics-smoothed particle hydrodynamics model for fracture analysis of fluid-structure interactions. *Ocean Eng.* **2023**, *279*, 114582. [CrossRef]
23. Khan, H.; Baleanu, D.; Kumam, P.; Al-Zaidy, J.F. Families of travelling waves solutions for fractional-order extended shallow water wave equations, using an innovative analytical method. *IEEE Access* **2019**, *7*, 107523–107532. [CrossRef]
24. Momani, S.; Odibat, Z. Homotopy perturbation method for nonlinear partial differential equations of fractional order. *Phys. Lett. A* **2007**, *365*, 345–350. [CrossRef]
25. Odibat, Z.; Momani, S. The variational iteration method: An efficient scheme for handling fractional partial differential equations in fluid mechanics. *Comput. Math. Appl.* **2009**, *58*, 2199–2208. [CrossRef]
26. Guner, O.; Bekir, A. The Exp-function method for solving nonlinear space–time fractional differential equations in mathematical physics. *J. Assoc. Arab. Univ. Basic Appl. Sci.* **2017**, *24*, 277–282. [CrossRef]
27. Jabbari, A.; Kheiri, H.; Bekir, A. Exact solutions of the coupled Higgs equation and the Maccari system using He's semi-inverse method and (G′/G)-expansion method. *Comput. Math. Appl.* **2011**, *62*, 2177–2186. [CrossRef]
28. Manafian, J.; Foroutan, M. Application of $tan(\phi(\xi)/2)$-expansion method for the time-fractional Kuramoto-Sivashinsky equation. *Opt. Quantum Electron.* **2017**, *49*, 1–18. [CrossRef]
29. Younis, M.; Iftikhar, M. Computational examples of a class of fractional order nonlinear evolution equations using modified extended direct algebraic method. *J. Comput. Methods Sci. Eng.* **2015**, *15*, 359–365. [CrossRef]
30. Zhang, J.; Xie, J.; Shi, W.; Huo, Y.; Ren, Z.; He, D. Resonance and bifurcation of fractional quintic Mathieu-Duffing system. *Chaos: Interdiscip. J. Nonlinear Sci.* **2023**, *33*, 23131. [CrossRef]
31. Li, X.; Dong, Z.Q.; Wang, L.P.; Niu, X.D.; Yamaguchi, H.; Li, D.C.; Yu, P. A magnetic field coupling fractional step lattice Boltzmann model for the complex interfacial behavior in magnetic multiphase flows. *Appl. Math. Model.* **2023**, *117*, 219–250. [CrossRef]
32. Guo, C.; Hu, J. Fixed-Time Stabilization of High-Order Uncertain Nonlinear Systems: Output Feedback Control Design and Settling Time Analysis. *J. Syst. Sci. Complex.* **2023**, 1–22. [CrossRef]
33. Liu, X.; He, J.; Liu, M.; Yin, Z.; Yin, L.; Zheng, W. A Scenario-Generic Neural Machine Translation Data Augmentation Method. *Electronics* **2023**, *12*, 2320. [CrossRef]
34. Lu, S.; Liu, M.; Yin, L.; Yin, Z.; Liu, X.; Zheng, W. The multi-modal fusion in visual question answering: A review of attention mechanisms. *Peerj Comput. Sci.* **2023**, *9*, e1400. [CrossRef]
35. Lu, S.; Ding, Y.; Liu, M.; Yin, Z.; Yin, L.; Zheng, W. Multiscale Feature Extraction and Fusion of Image and Text in VQA. *Int. J. Comput. Intell. Syst.* **2023**, *16*, 54. [CrossRef]
36. Konno, K.; Oono, H. New coupled integrable dispersionless equations. *J. Phys. Soc. Jpn.* **1994**, *63*, 377–378. [CrossRef]
37. Mirhosseini-Alizamini, S.M.; Rezazadeh, H.; Srinivasa, K.; Bekir, A. New closed form solutions of the new coupled Konno–Oono equation using the new extended direct algebraic method. *Pramana* **2020**, *94*, 1–12. [CrossRef]
38. Elbrolosy, M.E.; Elmandouh, A.A. Dynamical behaviour of conformable time-fractional coupled Konno–Oono equation in magnetic field. *Math. Probl. Eng.* **2022**, *2022*, 3157217. [CrossRef]
39. Koçak, Z.F.; Bulut, H.; Koc, D.A.; Baskonus, H.M. Prototype traveling wave solutions of new coupled Konno–Oono equation. *Optik* **2016**, *127*, 10786–10794. [CrossRef]
40. Bashar, M.A.; Mondal, G.; Khan, K.; Bekir, A. Traveling wave solutions of new coupled Konno–Oono equation. *New Trends Math. Sci.* **2016**, *4*, 296–303. [CrossRef]
41. Naeem, M.; Yasmin, H.; Shah, R.; Shah, N.A.; Chung, J.D. A Comparative Study of Fractional Partial Differential Equations with the Help of Yang Transform. *Symmetry* **2023**, *15*, 146. [CrossRef]
42. Rehman, H.U.; Ullah, N.; Imran, M.A. Optical solitons of Biswas-Arshed equation in birefringent fibers using extended direct algebraic method. *Optik* **2021**, *226*, 165378. [CrossRef]

mathematics

MDPI

Article

Hopf Bifurcation, Periodic Solutions, and Control of a New 4D Hyperchaotic System

Yu Liu [1], Yan Zhou [1,2,*] and Biyao Guo [1]

[1] College of Mathematics Science, Inner Mongolia Normal University, Hohhot 010022, China; 20214015026@mails.imnu.edu.cn (Y.L.); 20214015014@mails.imnu.edu.cn (B.G.)

[2] Center for Applied Mathematical Science, Inner Mongolia Normal University, Hohhot 010022, China

* Correspondence: 20130022@imnu.edu.cn

Abstract: In this paper, a new four-dimensional (4D) hyperchaotic biplane system is designed and presented. The dynamical properties of this new system are studied by means of tools such as bifurcation diagrams, Lyapunov exponents and phase diagrams. The Hopf bifurcation and periodic solutions of this hyperchaotic system are solved analytically. In addition, a new hyperchaotic control strategy is applied, and a comparative analysis of the controlled system is performed.

Keywords: hyperchaotic system; Hopf bifurcation; periodic solutions; hyperchaos control; normal form theory

MSC: 37G35

1. Introduction

In 1979, Rössler discovered and studied the first hyperchaotic system—the Rössler system [1]. It is known that the minimum dimension of the phase space in which the hyperchaotic attractor is embedded should exceed three. It means that hyperchaos is a more complex dynamical phenomenon than chaos. Later, many four-dimensional hyperchaotic systems were discovered and studied [2,3], specifically four-dimensional hyperchaotic Lorenz-type systems [4,5]. Jia [6] constructed a hyperchaotic Lorenz-type system using state feedback control and studied its associated dynamics using Lyapunov exponents and bifurcation diagrams. Wang et al. [7] characterized a-new-uniform-four-dimensional-uniform-hyperchaotic-Lorenz-type system, employing a bifurcation method and Lyapunov stability theory. Compared to ordinary chaotic systems, hyperchaotic systems have more potential applications in information security [8–12], finance [13,14], lasers [15–17], and circuits [18–21]. Due to their higher dimensionality, hyperchaotic systems are accompanied by a vast amount of randomness and unpredictability. To the best of our knowledge, the complexity of the dynamics of hyperchaotic systems is yet to be fully grasped. There are only a few studies on the dynamics of hyperchaotic systems.

More effective methods must be used to analyze and study the complex dynamics of high-dimensional hyperchaotic systems. Moreover, it is necessary to study new high-dimensional hyperchaotic systems and investigate their hyperchaotic properties. Pecora [22] proposed that high-dimensional hyperchaotic systems are safer than chaotic systems because of their increased randomness and higher unpredictability. From a practical application and engineering point of view, hyperchaotic systems should have a higher level of complexity [23]. Although analytical tools and techniques are available in the literature for bifurcation and stability analysis [24,25], no such analytical tools are available for attractors, so we must rely on some graphical tools. Mahmoud et al. [26] constructed a new hyperchaotic complex Lorentz system by extending the idea of adding state feedback control and introducing complex periodic forces.

Similarly, a new 4D four-wing memristor hyperchaotic system was presented by incorporating a magnetron memristor with a linear memristor in the four-wing Chen system [27]. Moreover, a hyperchaotic system of a 4D generalized Lorenz first state equation was proposed by introducing a linear state feedback control [28]. Mezatio et al. proposed hyperchaos and the coexistence of infinite hidden attractors in a six-dimensional system [29]. In one study, the dynamical richness of the hyperchaotic systems and their increased complexity were recognized with the addition of nonlinear controllers [30]. Furthermore, some scholars succeeded in constructing hyperchaotic systems [31,32]. These systems have significantly broadened the study of hyperchaos and provided some control strategies and research methods.

It is difficult for mathematicians and engineers to fully understand the behavior of hyperchaotic systems because the associated dynamics of hyperchaotic systems exist in higher dimensions simultaneously. The main components of the hyperchaotic system are two positive Lyapunov exponents, Hopf bifurcation and the attractor. Hopf bifurcation and chaotic attractors are both richly developed on the basis of chaos theory [33–35]. Hopf bifurcation is critical in analyzing the stability of equilibrium points of the hyperchaotic system in high dimensions, and it is used to study the dynamical behavior of hyperchaotic systems [36–38] and to control hyperchaos [39–41] for various applications.

This paper is structured as follows. The first part of this work describes the numerical simulation results of the proposed new system. Then, the output of MATLAB codes is presented that graphically represents the system. In this study, the Runge–Kutta algorithm was mainly utilized for the numerical simulations. Moreover, the analysis of the system characteristics, such as chaos and hyperchaos, is numerically verified using a bifurcation diagram, Phase diagram, Lyapunov exponents spectrum, and Poincaré maps. The conditions for the Hopf bifurcation of the new chaotic system are obtained in the second part of this work. In the third part, the stability of the bifurcation period solution and the Hopf bifurcation direction formula of the system are calculated using the normal form theory [42]. In addition, two examples were used to test and verify the theoretical results. In the fourth part, hyperchaotic control is investigated [43]. The results show that the linear feedback control method can control the system reasonably if appropriate feedback coefficients are chosen. In Section 6, the outcomes of the study are summarized.

2. Description of the Model

In 1994, Sprott obtained 19 third-order quadratic systems that exhibit chaotic behavior via a computational search method [44]. This assumption is of great theoretical and practical significance for studying some systems. In 2010, Wei [45] obtained a new generalized Sprott C system and proposed methods to improve a similar system proposed by Zhang et al. [46] and Jafari et al. [47,48]. The new chaotic system proposed in this study is as follows:

$$\begin{cases} \dot{x} = a(y - x), \\ \dot{y} = cy - xz, \\ \dot{z} = -bz + y^2. \end{cases} \tag{1}$$

The following new four-dimensional hyperchaotic system is introduced by adding a linear controller to the system of equations given in (1):

$$\begin{cases} \dot{x} = a(y - x), \\ \dot{y} = cy - xz + p, \\ \dot{z} = -bz + y^2, \\ \dot{p} = -e(x + y). \end{cases} \tag{2}$$

where x, y, z and p are state variables, a, b, c and e are system parameters, and also e is the main control parameter of System (2).

In this subsection, some characteristics of System (2) are discussed, and more simulation results are present from the numerical methods. The dynamics of System (2) can be characterized by its Lyapunov exponents using the real constants $a = 40$, $b = 2$, $c = 22$. The corresponding bifurcation diagram is given in Figure 1. We apply the Jacobi method to calculate the Lyapunov exponent. The Lyapunov exponent spectrum of System (2) is shown in Figure 2.

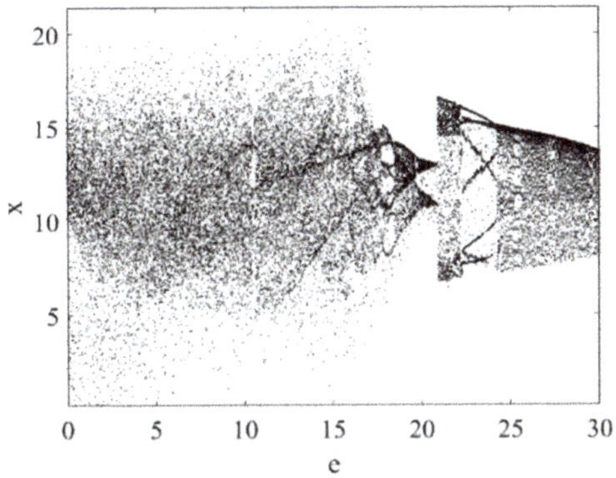

Figure 1. Bifurcation diagram of System (2) with $a = 40$, $b = 2$ and $c = 22$.

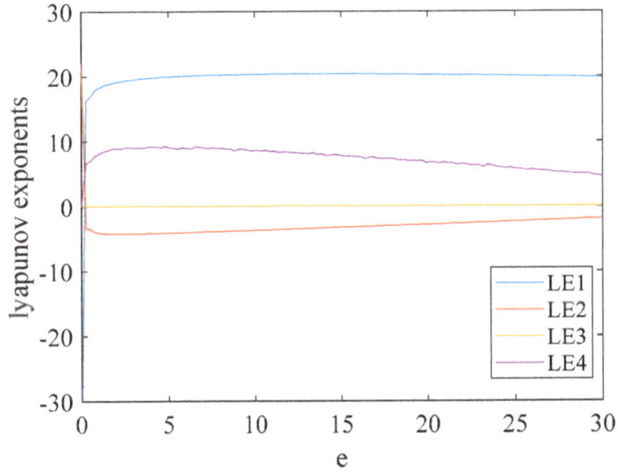

Figure 2. Lyapunov−exponent spectrum of System (2) with $a = 40$, $b = 2$ and $c = 22$.

According to the correspondence of Figures 1 and 2, when the parameter $e = 0.5$, the Lyapunov exponent of the new 4D System (2) is $L_1 = 16.9402$, $L_2 = -3.4133$, $L_3 = 0$, and $L_4 = 6.9890$. It can be seen that $L_1 > 0$, $L_4 > 0$ and $L_3 = 0$. Thus, System (2) is hyperchaotic at parameters $a = 40$, $b = 2$, $c = 22$ and $e = 0.5$. In this case, System (2) has a hyperchaotic attractor, as shown in Figure 3. Moreover, the Poincaré maps in the $x - y$ and $z - p$ planes are given in Figure 4.

In general, the above results show that System (2) has complex and interesting dynamical behavior, including hyperchaos and chaos.

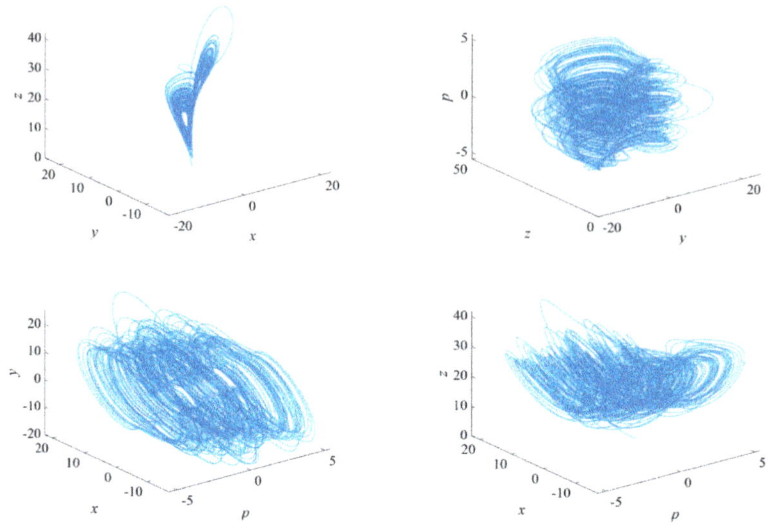

Figure 3. Phase diagram of System (2) with $a = 40$, $b = 2$, $c = 22$ and $e = 0.5$.

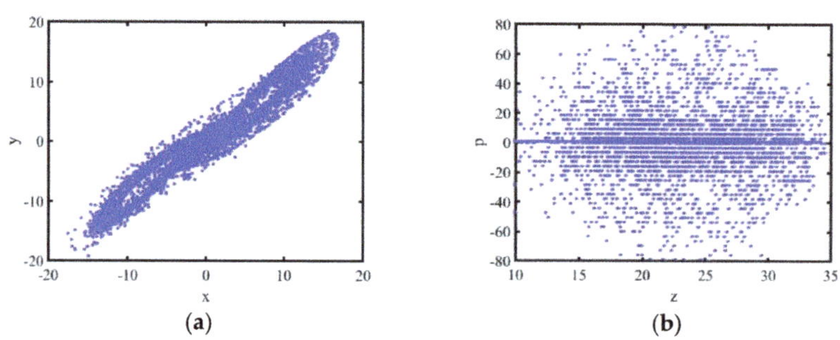

Figure 4. Poincaré maps (**a**,**b**) for the x−y and z−p planes at $a = 40$, $b = 2$, $c = 22$ and $e = 0.5$.

3. Stability Analysis and the Existence of Hopf Bifurcation

3.1. Equilibrium Stability

The equilibria of System (2) can be found by solving the following equations simultaneously:

$$\begin{cases} a(y-x) = 0, \\ cy - xz + p = 0, \\ -bz + y^2 = 0, \\ -e(x+y) = 0. \end{cases} \tag{3}$$

A simple analysis makes it easy to obtain the unique equilibrium at $E_0(0,0,0,0)$ for System (2).

The Jacobian matrix of System (2) at $E_0(0,0,0,0)$ is given by the following matrix:

$$J(E_0) = \begin{pmatrix} -a & a & 0 & 0 \\ 0 & c & 0 & 1 \\ 0 & 0 & -b & 0 \\ -e & -e & 0 & 0 \end{pmatrix}, \tag{4}$$

The following determinant can be obtained from the Jacobian matrix:

$$|\lambda E - J(E_0)| = \begin{vmatrix} \lambda + a & -a & 0 & 0 \\ 0 & \lambda - c & 0 & -1 \\ 0 & 0 & \lambda + b & 0 \\ e & e & 0 & \lambda \end{vmatrix}. \tag{5}$$

The characteristic equation is therefore given below:

$$\begin{aligned} f(\lambda) &= (\lambda + b)(\lambda^3 + (a-c)\lambda^2 + (e - ac)\lambda + 2ae) \\ &= \lambda^4 + (a + b - c)\lambda^3 + (e - ac - bc + ab)\lambda^2 + (2ae + be - abc)\lambda + 2abe = 0. \end{aligned} \tag{6}$$

The following relation can be obtained using the Routh–Hurwitz discriminant condition [49]:

$$f(\lambda) = P_0\lambda^4 + P_1\lambda^3 + P_2\lambda^2 + P_3\lambda + P_4 = 0. \tag{7}$$

A one-to-one correspondence between Equations (6) and (7) can be obtained by considering the following coefficients:

$$P_0 = 1,\ P_1 = a + b - c,\ P_2 = e - ac - bc + ab,\ P_3 = 2ae + be - abc,\ P_4 = 2abe.$$

The following determinant is obtained by substituting the P_0, P_1, P_2, P_3 and P_4.

$$D = \begin{vmatrix} P_1 & P_3 & 0 & 0 \\ P_0 & P_2 & P_4 & 0 \\ 0 & P_1 & P_3 & 0 \\ 0 & P_0 & P_2 & P_4 \end{vmatrix}. \tag{8}$$

It can be seen that the necessary and sufficient conditions for the real parts to be negative for all eigenvalues of the system are given in the following inequalities:

$$D_1 = P_1 = a + b - c > 0, \tag{9}$$

$$D_2 = \begin{vmatrix} P_1 & P_3 \\ P_0 & P_2 \end{vmatrix} = P_1P_2 - P_0P_3 > 0, \tag{10}$$

$$D_3 = P_3D_2 - P_4P_1^2 > 0, \tag{11}$$

$$D_4 = D = P_4D_3 > 0. \tag{12}$$

From Equations (9)–(12), we have the following conditions.

$$b > 0,\ e > ac,\ a > c,\ ae > 0,\ ac^2 - a^2c + ae - ce > 0$$

Therefore, the system will bifurcate when $e = \frac{ac(c-a)}{a+c}$. So, e is a critical value and is referred to as $e = e_0$.

3.2. Existence of a Hopf Bifurcation

Assume that System (2) of equations has a pure imaginary root $\lambda = \omega i$ ($\omega \in R^+$). From Equation (6), the following relation can be obtained:

$$\omega = \omega_0 = \sqrt{e - ac},\ e = e_0 = \frac{ac(c-a)}{a+c}.$$

Substituting $e = e_0$ into Equation (6), the following relationships are derived:

$$\lambda_1 = -b,\ \lambda_2 = c - a,\ \lambda_3 = i\omega_0,\ \lambda_4 = -i\omega_0.$$

Hence, System (2) satisfies the first condition of the Hopf bifurcation theorem. By differentiating the characteristic equations of the equilibrium point E_0 with respect to e, the following differential equation is acquired:

$$3\lambda^2\frac{d\lambda}{de}+2(a-c)\lambda\frac{d\lambda}{de}+(e-ac)\frac{d\lambda}{de}+2a+\lambda=0, \tag{13}$$

and

$$\lambda'(e)=\frac{d\lambda}{de}=-\frac{2a+\lambda}{3\lambda^2+2(a-c)\lambda+e-ac}. \tag{14}$$

Substituting the bifurcation value and eigenvalues into the above equation gives the following results:

$$\alpha'(0)=\mathrm{Re}(\lambda'(e_0))|_{\lambda=\sqrt{e-ac}i}=\frac{(a+c)^2}{4ac^2+2(a-c)^2(a+c)}>0, \tag{15}$$

$$\omega'(0)=\mathrm{Im}(\lambda'(e_0))|_{\lambda=\sqrt{e-ac}i}=\frac{2a^2-ac-c^2}{8ac^3+4c(a+c)(a-c)^2}\sqrt{2a(a+c)}\neq 0. \tag{16}$$

Hence, the second condition of the Hopf bifurcation theorem is satisfied.

The proposed chaotic system thus satisfies both conditions of the Hopf bifurcation theorem [50]. When $e=e_0$, the system shows Hopf bifurcations at the equilibrium point E_0.

4. Direction and Stability of Bifurcating Periodic Solutions

The primary purpose of this section is to find the direction and stability of the periodic solutions of the Hopf bifurcations in System (2). An approach based on the normal form theory and center manifold theorem is used [42].

First, the eigenvectors of the matrix are solved by setting the following solution equations:

$$\begin{cases}(\lambda+a)u_1-au_2=0,\\(\lambda-c)u_2-u_4=0,\\(\lambda+b)u_3=0,\\eu_1+eu_2+\lambda u_3=0.\end{cases} \tag{17}$$

Let v_1, v_2 and v_3 represent the eigenvectors that correspond to the eigenvalues $\lambda_1=-b$, $\lambda_2=c-a$ and $\lambda_3=i\omega_0$, respectively. It can be shown that the following relations hold:

$$v_1=\begin{pmatrix}0\\0\\1\\0\end{pmatrix},\ v_2=\begin{pmatrix}\frac{a}{c}\\1\\0\\-a\end{pmatrix},\ v_3=\begin{pmatrix}-\frac{ac}{e}+\frac{c}{e}\sqrt{e-ac}i\\1\\0\\-c+\sqrt{e-ac}i\end{pmatrix}.$$

A matrix Q can then be defined using the acquired expressions for the eigenvectors as follows:

$$Q=(\mathrm{Re}v_3,-\mathrm{Im}v_3,v_1,v_2)=\begin{pmatrix}-\frac{ac}{e}&-\frac{c}{e}\sqrt{e-ac}&0&\frac{a}{c}\\1&0&0&1\\0&0&1&0\\-c&-\sqrt{e-ac}&0&-a\end{pmatrix}. \tag{18}$$

Considering the following transformation,

$$\begin{pmatrix}x\\y\\z\\p\end{pmatrix}=Q\begin{pmatrix}x_1\\y_1\\z_1\\p_1\end{pmatrix}, \tag{19}$$

a relationship between x, y, z, p and x_1, y_1, z_1, p_1 can be obtained in the following manner:

$$\begin{pmatrix} x \\ y \\ z \\ p \end{pmatrix} = \begin{pmatrix} -\frac{ac}{e}x_1 - \frac{c}{e}\sqrt{e-ac}y_1 + \frac{a}{c}p_1 \\ x_1 + p_1 \\ z_1 \\ -cx_1 - \sqrt{e-ac}y_1 - ap_1 \end{pmatrix}. \tag{20}$$

By taking the derivative of Equation (20) and substituting the results into System (2), a new system expression is obtained, which is given below:

$$\begin{cases} \dot{x}_1 = -\sqrt{e-ac}y_1 + F_1(x_1, y_1, z_1, p_1), \\ \dot{y}_1 = \sqrt{e-ac}x_1 + F_2(x_1, y_1, z_1, p_1), \\ \dot{z}_1 = -bz_1 + F_3(x_1, y_1, z_1, p_1), \\ \dot{p}_1 = (c-a)p_1 + F_4(x_1, y_1, z_1, p_1). \end{cases} \tag{21}$$

where,

$$\begin{aligned} &F_1(x_1, y_1, z_1, p_1) = -k(\tfrac{ac}{e}x_1z_1 + \tfrac{c}{e}\sqrt{e-ac}y_1z_1 - \tfrac{a}{c}z_1p_1), \\ &F_2(x_1, y_1, z_1, p_1) = [(c-a)k - a](\tfrac{ac}{e}x_1z_1 + \tfrac{c}{e}\sqrt{e-ac}y_1z_1 - \tfrac{a}{c}z_1p_1), \\ &F_3(x_1, y_1, z_1, p_1) = {x_1}^2 + {p_1}^2 + 2x_1p_1, \\ &F_4(x_1, y_1, z_1, p_1) = (k+1)(\tfrac{ac}{e}x_1z_1 + \tfrac{c}{e}\sqrt{e-ac}y_1z_1 - \tfrac{a}{c}z_1p_1), \\ &k = \tfrac{ae+ac^2}{c^3-ae-2ac^2}. \end{aligned}$$

Then, using formulas reported in the literature [42], the following expressions related to the bifurcation at $e = e_0$ and $(x_1, y_1, z_1, p_1) = (0, 0, 0, 0)$ can be obtained:

$$\begin{aligned} g_{11} &= \tfrac{1}{4}[\tfrac{\partial^2 F_1}{\partial x_1^2} + \tfrac{\partial^2 F_1}{\partial y_1^2} + i(\tfrac{\partial^2 F_2}{\partial x_1^2} + \tfrac{\partial^2 F_2}{\partial y_1^2})] = 0, \\ g_{02} &= \tfrac{1}{4}[\tfrac{\partial^2 F_1}{\partial x_1^2} - \tfrac{\partial^2 F_1}{\partial y_1^2} - 2\tfrac{\partial^2 F_2}{\partial x_1 \partial y_1} + i(\tfrac{\partial^2 F_2}{\partial x_1^2} - \tfrac{\partial^2 F_2}{\partial y_1^2} + 2\tfrac{\partial^2 F_1}{\partial x_1 \partial y_1})] = 0, \\ g_{20} &= \tfrac{1}{4}[\tfrac{\partial^2 F_1}{\partial^2 x_1^2} - \tfrac{\partial^2 F_1}{\partial^2 y_1^2} + 2\tfrac{\partial^2 F_2}{\partial x_1 \partial y_1} + i(\tfrac{\partial^2 F_2}{\partial^2 x_1^2} - \tfrac{\partial^2 F_2}{\partial^2 y_1^2} - 2\tfrac{\partial^2 F_1}{\partial x_1 \partial y_1})] = 0, \\ G_{21} &= \tfrac{1}{8}[\tfrac{\partial^3 F_1}{\partial x_1^3} + \tfrac{\partial^3 F_1}{\partial x_1 \partial y_1^2} + \tfrac{\partial^3 F_2}{\partial x_1^2 \partial y_1} + \tfrac{\partial^3 F_2}{\partial y_1^3} + i(\tfrac{\partial^3 F_2}{\partial x_1^3} + \tfrac{\partial^3 F_2}{\partial x_1 \partial y_1^2} - \tfrac{\partial^3 F_1}{\partial x_1^2 \partial y_1} - \tfrac{\partial^3 F_1}{\partial y_1^3})] = 0. \end{aligned}$$

From the dimension $n = 4 > 2$, we calculate the following variables:

$$\begin{aligned} &h_{11}^1 = \tfrac{1}{4}(\tfrac{\partial^2 F_3}{\partial x_1^2} + \tfrac{\partial^2 F_3}{\partial y_1^2}) = \tfrac{1}{4},\ h_{11}^2 = \tfrac{1}{4}(\tfrac{\partial^2 F_4}{\partial x_1^2} + \tfrac{\partial^2 F_4}{\partial y_1^2}) = 0, \\ &h_{20}^1 = \tfrac{1}{4}(\tfrac{\partial^2 F_3}{\partial x_1^2} - \tfrac{\partial^2 F_3}{\partial y_1^2} - 2i\tfrac{\partial^2 F_3}{\partial x_1 \partial y_1}) = \tfrac{1}{4},\ h_{20}^2 = \tfrac{1}{4}(\tfrac{\partial^2 F_4}{\partial x_1^2} - \tfrac{\partial^2 F_4}{\partial y_1^2} - 2i\tfrac{\partial^2 F_4}{\partial x_1 \partial y_1}) = 0. \end{aligned}$$

By solving the following equations,

$$Dw_{11} = -h_{11},\ (D - 2i\omega_0 I)w_{20} = -h_{20},$$

where

$$h_{11} = \begin{pmatrix} h_{11}^1 \\ h_{11}^2 \end{pmatrix},\ h_{20} = \begin{pmatrix} h_{20}^1 \\ h_{20}^2 \end{pmatrix},$$

We obtain the following relations:

$$w_{11} = \begin{pmatrix} w_{11}^1 \\ w_{11}^2 \end{pmatrix} = \begin{pmatrix} \frac{b}{4} \\ 0 \end{pmatrix},\ w_{20} = \begin{pmatrix} w_{20}^1 \\ w_{20}^2 \end{pmatrix} = \begin{pmatrix} \frac{c-a}{4} - \frac{\sqrt{e-ac}}{2}i \\ 0 \end{pmatrix}.$$

Furthermore,

$$
\begin{aligned}
G^1_{110} &= \tfrac{1}{2}[\tfrac{\partial^2 F_1}{\partial x_1 \partial z_1} + \tfrac{\partial^2 F_2}{\partial y_1 \partial z_1} + i(\tfrac{\partial^2 F_2}{\partial x_1 \partial z_1} - \tfrac{\partial^2 F_1}{\partial y_1 \partial z_1})] \\
&= \tfrac{ack}{2e}(i-1) + \tfrac{c\sqrt{e-ac}}{2e}[k(c-a)-a](i+1), \\
G^2_{110} &= 0, \\
G^2_{101} &= 0, \\
G^1_{101} &= \tfrac{1}{2}[\tfrac{\partial^2 F_1}{\partial x_1 \partial z_1} - \tfrac{\partial^2 F_2}{\partial y_1 \partial z_1} + i(\tfrac{\partial^2 F_2}{\partial x_1 \partial z_1} + \tfrac{\partial^2 F_1}{\partial y_1 \partial z_1})] \\
&= \tfrac{ack}{2e}(-i-1) + \tfrac{c\sqrt{e-ac}}{2e}[k(c-a)-a](i-1), \\
g_{21} &= G_{21} + \sum_{n=1}^{2} (2G^n_{110} w^n_{11} + G^n_{101} w^n_{20}) \\
&= -\tfrac{2abc+ac(c-a)+2ac\sqrt{e-ac}}{8e}k + \tfrac{2bc-c^2+ac+2c}{8e}\sqrt{e-ac}[k(c-a)-a] \\
&+ \tfrac{(2bc+c^2-ac)\sqrt{e-ac}+2c(e-ac)}{8e}[k(c-a)-a]i \\
&+ \tfrac{2abc-ac(c-a)+2ac\sqrt{e-ac}}{8e}ki.
\end{aligned}
$$

Based on these calculations and analyses, we obtain the following results:

$$C_1(0) = \frac{i}{2\omega_0}[g_{20}g_{11} - 2|g_{11}|^2 - \frac{1}{3}|g_{02}|^2] + \frac{1}{2}g_{21} = \frac{1}{2}g_{21} \tag{22}$$

$$\mu_2 = -\frac{\mathrm{Re}C_1(0)}{\alpha'(0)}, \tag{23}$$

$$\beta_2 = 2\mathrm{Re}C_1(0), \tag{24}$$

$$\tau_2 = -\frac{\mathrm{Im}C_1(0) + \mu_2\omega'(0)}{\omega_0}. \tag{25}$$

The following conclusions can also be drawn:

(i) If $\mu_2 > 0 (< 0)$, the Hopf bifurcation is supercritical (subcritical), and for $e > e_0 (< e_0)$, the bifurcation has a periodic solution;
(ii) If $\beta_2 < 0 (> 0)$, the bifurcating periodic solutions are stable (unstable) on their orbits;
(iii) If $\tau_2 > 0 (< 0)$, the period of bifurcating periodic solutions increases or decreases.

For the verification of the above theoretical analysis, it is assumed that

$$a = 3,\ b = 2,\ c = -1$$

Then, $e_0 = 6$, and the following values are calculated:

$$\mu_2 = 5.13,\ \beta_2 = -0.54,\ \tau_2 \approx 0.35147$$

Therefore, when the parameter e is at its critical value, the Hopf bifurcation of the system at the equilibrium point $E_0(0,0,0,0)$ is supercritical. Moreover, the bifurcation direction is $e < e_0 = 6$. The bifurcation period solution of the system is stable, as shown in Figure 5. $e > e_0 = 6$ as shown in Figure 6.

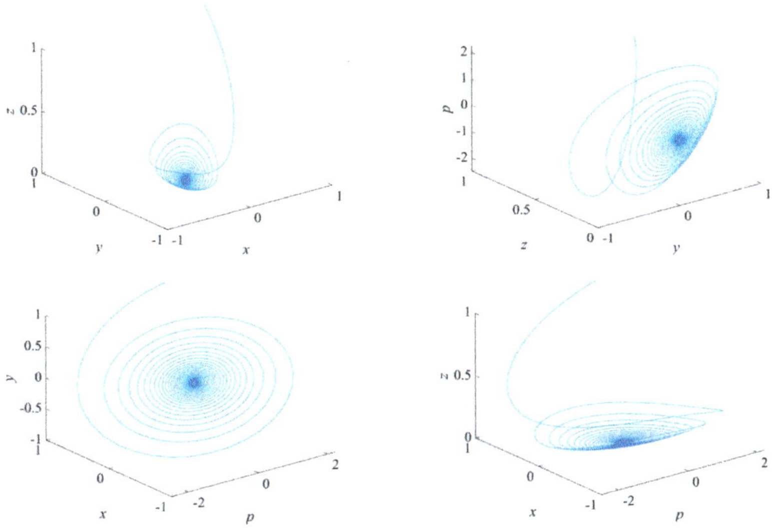

Figure 5. Phase diagram of System (2) with $a = 3$, $b = 2$, $c = -1$ and $e = 5$.

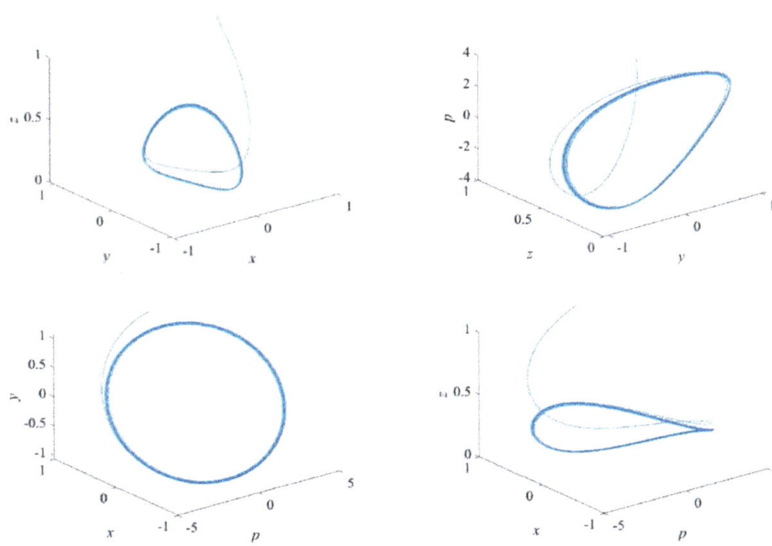

Figure 6. Phase diagram of System (2) with $a = 3$, $b = 2$, $c = -1$ and $e = 8$.

5. Hyperchaos Control

In many cases, chaos is generally harmful and needs to be suppressed. Therefore, scholars have paid extensive attention to controlling it. Scholars have developed many valuable methods for chaos control, such as the hybrid control c-strategy [51] and the ultimate boundedness [52]. The equation of the controlled system is as follows:

$$\begin{cases} \dot{x} = a(y - x) + r_1 x, \\ \dot{y} = cy - xz + p + r_2 y, \\ \dot{z} = -bz + y^2 + r_3 z, \\ \dot{p} = -e(x + y) + r_4 p, \end{cases} \tag{26}$$

where r_1, r_2, r_3 and r_4 are feedback coefficients. The Jacobian matrix of System (26) at the zero-equilibrium point is the following:

$$J_r = \begin{vmatrix} -a+r_1 & a & 0 & 0 \\ 0 & c+r_2 & 0 & 1 \\ 0 & 0 & -b+r_3 & 0 \\ -e & -e & 0 & r_4 \end{vmatrix}, \tag{27}$$

The following determinant can be obtained from the Jacobian matrix:

$$|\lambda E - J_r| = \begin{vmatrix} \lambda+a-r_1 & -a & 0 & 0 \\ 0 & \lambda-c-r_2 & 0 & -1 \\ 0 & 0 & \lambda+b-r_3 & 0 \\ e & e & 0 & \lambda-r_4 \end{vmatrix}. \tag{28}$$

The characteristic equation can be found in the following:

$$f_r(\lambda) = R_4\lambda^4 + R_3\lambda^3 + R_2\lambda^2 + R_1\lambda + R_0, \tag{29}$$

where,

$$\begin{aligned} R_0 &= 2abe + acr_4 - 2aer_3 - ber_1 + er_1r_3 + abr_2r_4 - bcr_1r_4 - acr_3r_4 \\ &\quad -ar_2r_3r_4 + br_1r_2r_4 + cr_1r_3r_4 - r_1r_2r_3r_4, \\ R_1 &= 2ae - be - abc - er_1 + er_3 + bcr_1 + bcr_4 - abr_2 - abr_4 + acr_3 + acr_4 + ar_2r_4 + ar_2r_3 \\ &\quad +ar_3r_4 + br_1r_2 + +br_1r_4 - cr_1r_3 - cr_1r_4 - cr_3r_4 + r_1r_2r_4 + +r_1r_2r_3 - r_1r_3r_4 - r_2r_3r_4, \\ R_2 &= ab - ac - bc - e - ar_2 - ar_3 - ar_4 - br_1 - br_2 - br_4 \\ &\quad +cr_1 + cr_3 + cr_4 + r_1r_2 + r_1r_3 + r_1r_4 + r_2r_3 + r_2r_4 + r_3r_4, \\ R_3 &= a + b - c - r_1 - r_2 - r_3 - r_4, \\ R_4 &= 1. \end{aligned}$$

According to the Routh–Hurwitz discriminant condition [49], the real parts of eigenvalues are negative if and only if,

$$R_3R_2 - R_1 > 0,\ R_3(R_1R_2 - R_3R_0) - R_1^2 > 0,\ R_3 > 0,\ R_0 > 0.$$

Case 1:

When $a = 40$, $b = 2$, $c = 22$ and $e = 1$, we assume $r_{1,2,3,4} = -25$. The corresponding Lyapunov exponents for System (2) are as follows:

$$L_1 = 18.2980,\ L_2 = -4.0706,\ L_3 = 0,\ L_4 = 8.0878.$$

Then, the corresponding Lyapunov exponents for System (26) are as follows:

$$L_1 = -3.2103,\ L_2 = -13.5230,\ L_3 = -23.3526,\ L_4 = -22.5437.$$

So, the zero-equilibrium point is asymptotically stable.

Case 2:

When $a = 40$, $b = 2$, $c = 22$ and $e = 3$, we assume $r_{1,2,3,4} = -30$. The corresponding Lyapunov exponents for System (2) are as follows:

$$L_1 = 19.5457,\ L_2 = -4.1972,\ L_3 = 0,\ L_4 = 8.9684.$$

Then, the corresponding Lyapunov exponents for System (26) are the following:

$$L_1 = -8.3379,\ L_2 = -16.6337,\ L_3 = -29.2114,\ L_4 = -27.8364.$$

Hence, the zero-equilibrium point is asymptotically stable.

For the two cases above, the time-domain waveforms of the hyperchaotic System (2) and the controlled System (26) are shown in Figures 7 and 8. By choosing appropriate feedback coefficients, the controlled System (26) is asymptotically stable at the zero-equilibrium point.

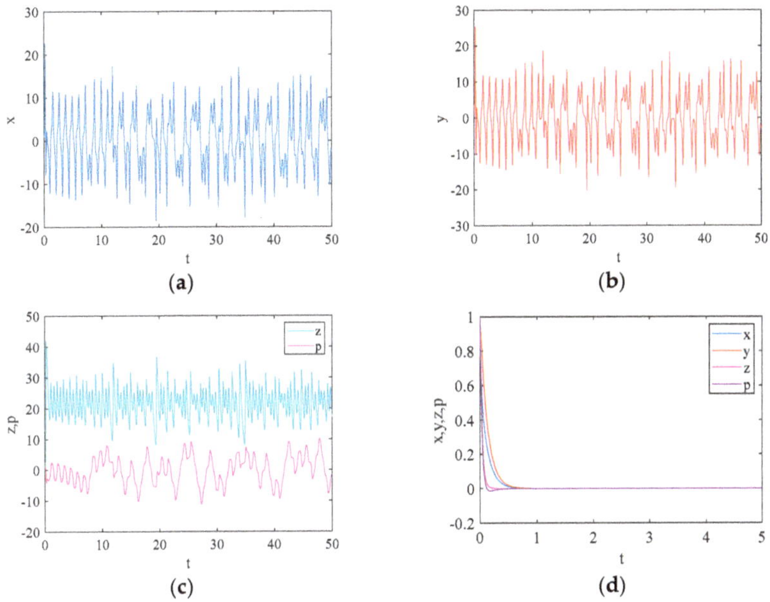

Figure 7. The time–domain waveform diagram for Case 1 with respect to Systems (2) for (**a–c**), and System (26) for (**d**).

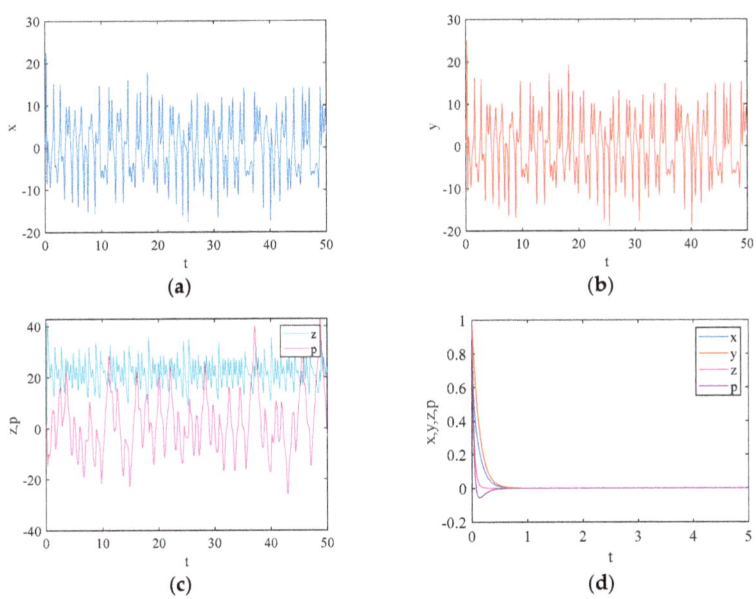

Figure 8. The time–domain waveform diagram for Case 2 with respect to Systems (2) for (**a–c**), and System (26) for (**d**).

6. Conclusions

This paper obtains a novel four-dimensional hyperchaotic system based on the generalized Sprott C system. This system has two nonlinear terms and seven linear terms. The system has Hopf bifurcation and can be solved to obtain explicit formulas for the direction and stability of the bifurcation periodic solutions. Additionally, we show the phase diagram of the bifurcation periodic solutions stability versus direction in Figures 5 and 6. We mainly use the Runge–Kutta algorithm for the numerical simulations in this paper. The results show that the new 4D hyperchaotic system has complex dynamical behavior.

In addition, we also performed linear feedback control on the new 4D hyperchaotic system. This new control strategy is novel and effective regarding hyperchaotic phenomena in control systems, as shown in Figures 7 and 8.

In the future, we will study more complex high-dimensional hyperchaotic systems and apply different methods. Five- and even six-dimensional hyperchaotic systems have rich and exciting properties and should be studied in depth.

Author Contributions: Conceptualization, Y.L. and Y.Z.; methodology, Y.L.; software, Y.L. and B.G.; formal analysis, B.G. and Y.Z.; investigation, Y.L.; data curation, Y.L.; writing—original draft preparation, Y.L.; writing—review and editing, B.G. and Y.Z.; supervision, Y.Z.; funding acquisition, Y.L. and Y.Z. All authors have read and agreed to the published version of the manuscript.

Funding: The authors gratefully acknowledge the support of the National Natural Science Foundation of China through grants No. 11962025 and 62161044, the Natural Science Foundation of Inner Mongolia Autonomous Region through grant No. 2019LH01002, the key project of the Natural Science Foundation of Inner Mongolia Autonomous Region through grant No. 2022ZD05, the Fundamental Research Funds for Inner Mongolia Normal University through grant No. 2022JBXC013, and the Graduate students' research & Innovation fund of Inner Mongolia Normal University through grant No. CXJJS22098.

Data Availability Statement: Not applicable.

Conflicts of Interest: The authors declare no conflict of interest.

References

1. Rössler, O.E. An equation for hyperchaos. *Phys. Lett. A* **1979**, *71*, 155–157. [CrossRef]
2. Vaidyanathan, S.; Volos, C.K.; Pham, V.T. Analysis, control, synchronization and SPICE implementation of a novel 4-D hyperchaotic Rikitake dynamo system without equilibrium. *J. Eng. Sci. Technol. Rev.* **2015**, *8*, 232–244. [CrossRef]
3. Yang, J.; Wei, Z.; Moroz, I. Periodic solutions for a four-dimensional hyperchaotic system. *Adv. Differ. Equ.* **2020**, *2020*, 198. [CrossRef]
4. Chen, Y.; Yang, Q. A new Lorenz-type hyperchaotic system with a curve of equilibria. *Math Comput. Simulat.* **2015**, *112*, 40–55. [CrossRef]
5. Leutcho, G.D.; Wang, H.; Fozin, T.F.; Sun, K.; Njitacke, Z.T.; Kengne, J. Dynamics of a new multistable 4D hyperchaotic Lorenz system and its applications. *Int. J. Bifurcat. Chaos* **2022**, *32*, 2250001. [CrossRef]
6. Jia, Q. Hyperchaos generated from the Lorenz chaotic system and its control. *Phys. Lett. A* **2007**, *366*, 217–222. [CrossRef]
7. Wang, H.; Zhang, F. Bifurcations, ultimate boundedness and singular orbits in a unified hyperchaotic Lorenz-type system. *Discret. Contin. Dyn. Syst. B* **2020**, *25*, 1791–1820. [CrossRef]
8. Lai, Q.; Lai, C.; Zhang, H.; Li, C. Hidden coexisting hyperchaos of new memristive neuron model and its application in image encryption. *Chaos Solitons Fractals* **2022**, *158*, 112017. [CrossRef]
9. Liu, L.; Tang, X.; Jiang, X.; Xu, Z.; Li, F.; Li, Z.; Huang, H.; Ni, P.; Chen, L.; Xi, L.; et al. Physical layer encryption scheme based on cellular automata and DNA encoding by hyper-chaos in a CO-OFDM system. *Opt. Express* **2021**, *29*, 18976–18987. [CrossRef]
10. Karmakar, J.; Pathak, A.; Nandi, D.; Mandal, M.K. Sparse representation based compressive video encryption using hyper-chaos and DNA coding. *Digit. Signal Process.* **2021**, *117*, 103143. [CrossRef]
11. Xiu, C.; Zhou, R.; Zhao, S.; Xu, G. Memristive hyperchaos secure communication based on sliding mode control. *Nonlinear Dyn.* **2021**, *104*, 789–805. [CrossRef]
12. Bian, Y.Y.; Yu, W.X. A secure communication method based on 6-D hyperchaos and circuit implementation. *Telecommun. Syst.* **2021**, *77*, 731–751. [CrossRef]
13. Rech, P.C. Hyperchaos and multistability in a four-dimensional financial mathematical model. *J. Appl. Nonlinear Dyn.* **2021**, *10*, 211–218. [CrossRef]

14. Li, X.; Rao, R.; Zhong, S.; Yang, X.; Li, H.; Zhang, Y. Impulsive control and synchronization for fractional-order Hyper-chaotic financial system. *Mathematics* **2022**, *10*, 2737. [CrossRef]
15. Yan, S.L. Study of an erbium-doped fiber three-ring laser guiding a hyperchaos series synchronization network link. *ICNCIS SPIE* **2022**, *12503*, 127–130.
16. Yan, S.L. Study of hyperchaos resulting from an erbium-doped fibre three-ring laser system. *Electron. Lett.* **2022**, *58*, 288–289.
17. Kingston, S.L.; Balcerzak, M.; Dana, S.K.; Kapitaniak, T. Transition to hyperchaos and rare large-intensity pulses in Zeeman laser. *Chaos* **2023**, *33*, 023128. [CrossRef]
18. Vaidyanathan, S.; He, S.; Simbas, A. A new multistable double-scroll 4-D hyperchaotic system with no equilibrium point, its bifurcation analysis, synchronization and circuit design. *Arch. Control Sci.* **2021**, *31*, 99–128.
19. Luo, J.; Qu, S.; Chen, Y.; Chen, X.; Xiong, Z. Synchronization, circuit and secure communication implementation of a memristor-based hyperchaotic system using single input controller. *Chin. J. Phys.* **2021**, *71*, 403–417. [CrossRef]
20. Vaidyanathan, S.; Sambas, A.; Azar, A.T.; Rana, K.; Kumar, V. A new 5-D hyperchaotic four-wing system with multistability and hidden attractor, its backstepping control, and circuit simulation. In *Backstepping Control of Nonlinear Dynamical Systems;* Academic Press: Cambridge, MA, USA, 2021; pp. 115–138.
21. Daum, H.H.; Tusset, A.M.; Ribeiro, M.A.; Balthazar, J.M.; Bueno, A.M.; Litak, G. Dynamics and control of a vibrating system with hyperchaotic behavior using an electronic circuit implementation. *Braz. J. Phys.* **2022**, *52*, 104. [CrossRef]
22. Pecora, L. Hyperchaos harnessed. *Phys. World* **1996**, *9*, 17. [CrossRef]
23. Ayub, J.; Aqeel, M.; Abbasi, J.N.; Sunny, D.A.; Rana, Z. Switching of behavior: From hyperchaotic to controlled magnetoconvection model. *AIP Adv.* **2019**, *9*, 125235. [CrossRef]
24. Fiaz, M.; Aqeel, M.; Marwan, M.; Sabir, M. Retardational effect and hopf bifurcations in a new attitude system of quad-rotor unmanned aerial vehicle. *Int. J. Bifurcat. Chaos* **2021**, *31*, 2150127. [CrossRef]
25. Panday, P.; Pal, N.; Samanta, S.; Chattopadhyay, J. Stability and bifurcation analysis of a three-species food chain model with fear. *Int. J. Bifurcat. Chaos* **2018**, *28*, 1850009. [CrossRef]
26. Mahmoud, G.M.; Ahmed, M.E.; Mahmoud, E.E. Analysis of hyperchaotic complex Lorenz systems. *Int. J. Mod. Phys. C* **2008**, *19*, 1477–1494. [CrossRef]
27. Yu, F.; Qian, S.; Chen, X.; Huang, Y.; Liu, L.; Shi, C.; Cai, S.; Song, Y.; Wang, C. A new 4D four-wing memristive hyperchaotic system: Dynamical analysis, electronic circuit design, shape synchronization and secure communication. *Int. J. Bifurcat. Chaos* **2020**, *30*, 2050147. [CrossRef]
28. Singh, J.P.; Roy, B.K. Hidden attractors in a new complex generalised Lorenz hyperchaotic system, its synchronisation using adaptive contraction theory, circuit validation and application. *Nonlinear Dyn.* **2018**, *92*, 373–394. [CrossRef]
29. Fonzin Fozin, T.; Megavarna Ezhilarasu, P.; Njitacke Tabekoueng, Z.; Leutcho, G.D.; Kengne, J.; Thamilmaran, K.; Mezatio, A.B.; Pelap, F.B. On the dynamics of a simplified canonical Chua's oscillator with smooth hyperbolic sine nonlinearity: Hyperchaos, multistability and multistability control. *Chaos* **2019**, *29*, 113105. [CrossRef]
30. Rahim, M.F.A.; Natiq, H.; Fataf, N.A.A.; Banerjee, S. Dynamics of a new hyperchaotic system and multistability. *Eur. Phys. J. Plus* **2019**, *134*, 499. [CrossRef]
31. Ouannas, A.; Grassi, G.; Ziar, T.; Odibat, Z. On a function projective synchronization scheme for non-identical fractional-order chaotic (hyperchaotic) systems with different dimensions and orders. *Optik* **2017**, *136*, 513–523. [CrossRef]
32. Vaidyanathan, S.; Azar, A.T.; Boulkroune, A. A novel 4-D hyperchaotic system with two quadratic nonlinearities and its adaptive synchronisation. *Int. J. Control Autom.* **2018**, *12*, 5–26. [CrossRef]
33. Wei, Z.; Pham, V.T.; Khalaf, A.J.M.; Kengne, J.; Jafari, S. A modified multistable chaotic oscillator. *Int. J. Bifurcat. Chaos* **2018**, *28*, 1850085. [CrossRef]
34. Wei, Z.; Zhu, B.; Escalante-González, R.J. Existence of periodic orbits and chaos in a class of three-dimensional piecewise linear systems with two virtual stable node-foci. *Nonlinear Anal. Hybrid Syst.* **2021**, *43*, 101114. [CrossRef]
35. Wei, Z.; Li, Y.; Moroz, I.; Zhang, W. Melnikov-type method for a class of planar hybrid piecewise-smooth systems with impulsive effect and noise excitation: Heteroclinic orbits. *Chaos* **2022**, *32*, 103127. [CrossRef]
36. Li, Y.; Wei, Z.; Aly, A.A. A 4D hyperchaotic Lorenz-type system: Zero-Hopf bifurcation, ultimate bound estimation, and its variable-order fractional network. *Eur. Phys. J. Spec. Top* **2022**, *231*, 1847–1858. [CrossRef]
37. Zhang, J.; Hou, J.; Xu, L.; Xie, Q. Dynamical analysis, circuit implementation, and simultaneous application of a novel four-dimensional hyperchaotic system based on cosine functions. *Microelectron. Eng.* **2023**, *271–272*, 111939. [CrossRef]
38. Liu, J.; Sun, Y.; Yao, M.; Ma, J. Stability Analysis and Nonlinear Vibrations of the Ring Truss Antenna with the Six-Dimensional System. *J. Vib. Eng. Technol.* **2022**, *11*, 899–920. [CrossRef]
39. Zhu, E.; Xu, M.; Pi, D. Anti-control of Hopf bifurcation for high-dimensional chaotic system with coexisting attractors. *Nonlinear Dyn.* **2022**, *110*, 1867–1877. [CrossRef]
40. Yan, S.; Wang, E.; Wang, Q.; Sun, X.; Ren, Y. Analysis, circuit implementation and synchronization control of a hyperchaotic system. *Phys. Scr.* **2021**, *96*, 125257. [CrossRef]
41. Al-Talib, Z.S.; Al-Azzawi, S.F. Projective synchronization for 4D hyperchaotic system based on adaptive nonlinear control strategy. *Indones J. Electr. Eng. Comput. Sci.* **2020**, *19*, 715–722. [CrossRef]
42. Hassard, B.D.; Kazarinoff, N.D.; Wan, Y.H. *Theory and Applications of Hopf Bifurcation*; CUP Archive: Cambridge, UK, 1981.
43. Cui, N.; Li, J. A new 4D hyperchaotic system and its control. *Aims Math* **2023**, *8*, 905–923. [CrossRef]

44. Sprott, J.C. Some simple chaotic flows. *Phys. Rev. E* **1994**, *50*, 647–650. [CrossRef] [PubMed]
45. Yang, Q.G.; Wei, Z.C.; Chen, G.R. An unusual 3D autonomous quadratic chaotic system with two stable node-foci. *Int. J. Bifurcat. Chaos* **2010**, *20*, 1061–1083. [CrossRef]
46. Zhang, Z.H. Hopf bifurcation analysis and control of a new Lorenz-like system. In Proceedings of the 26th Chinese Control and Decision Conference (2014 CCDC), Changsha, China, 31 May–2 June 2014; pp. 1597–1601.
47. Jafari, S.; Rajagopal, K.; Hayat, T.; Alsaedi, A.; Pham, V.-T. Simplest megastable chaotic oscillator. *Int. J. Bifurcat. Chaos* **2019**, *29*, 1950187. [CrossRef]
48. Jafari, S.; Ahmadi, A.; Khalaf, A.J.M.; Abdolmohammadi, H.R.; Pham, V.-T.; Alsaadi, F.E. A new hidden chaotic attractor with extreme multi-stability. *AEU Int. J. Elec. C* **2018**, *89*, 131–135. [CrossRef]
49. DeJesus, E.X.; Kaufman, C. Routh-Hurwitz criterion in the examination of eigenvalues of a system of nonlinear ordinary differential equations. *Phys. Rev. A* **1987**, *35*, 5288. [CrossRef]
50. Guckenheimer, J.; Homles, P. Nonliear oscillstions, Dynamical systems, and bifurcations of vector field. *Appl. Math. Sci.* **1983**, *42*, 117–156.
51. Cai, P.; Yuan, Z.Z. Hopf bifurcation and chaos control in a new chaotic system via hybrid control strategy. *Chin. J. Phys.* **2017**, *55*, 64–70. [CrossRef]
52. Chien, F.; Chowdhury, A.R.; Nik, H.S. Competitive modes and estimation of ultimate bound sets for a chaotic dynamical financial system. *Nonlinear Dyn.* **2021**, *106*, 3601–3614. [CrossRef]

mathematics

Article

Design of High-Dimensional Maps with Sine Terms

Othman Abdullah Almatroud [1], Viet-Thanh Pham [2], Giuseppe Grassi [3], Mohammad Alshammari [1], Sahar Albosaily [1] and Van Van Huynh [2,*]

[1] Department of Mathematics, Faculty of Science, University of Ha'il, Ha'il 2440, Saudi Arabia; o.almatroud@uoh.edu.sa (O.A.A.); dar.alshammari@uoh.edu.sa (M.A.); s.albosaily@uoh.edu.sa (S.A.)
[2] Modeling Evolutionary Algorithms Simulation and Artificial Intelligence, Faculty of Electrical and Electronics Engineering, Ton Duc Thang University, Ho Chi Minh City 758307, Vietnam; phamvietthanh@tdtu.edu.vn
[3] Dipartimento Ingegneria Innovazione, Universitá del Salento, 73100 Lecce, Italy; giuseppe.grassi@unisalento.it
* Correspondence: huynhvanvan@tdtu.edu.vn

Abstract: The use of the advancements in memristor technology to construct chaotic maps has garnered significant research attention in recent years. The combination of memristors and nonlinear terms provides an effective approach to proposing novel maps. In this study, we have leveraged memristors and sine terms to develop three-dimensional maps, capable of processing special fixed points. Additionally, we have conducted an in depth study of a specific example ($TDMM_1$ map) to demonstrate its dynamics, feasibility, and application for lightweight encryption. Notably, our general approach could be extended to develop higher-dimensional maps, including four- and five-dimensional ones, thereby opening up the possibility to create numerous higher-dimensional maps.

Keywords: chaos; sine term; memristor; high dimension; discrete map; lightweight encryption

MSC: 39A33; 39A60; 65P20

1. Introduction

A discrete map, also known as a discrete dynamical system, is a useful tool for the analysis of the behavior of chemical reactions and the spread of diseases [1]. Discrete maps can exhibit a variety of behaviors, including stability, periodicity, and chaos [2–5]. Fractional-order models and neural networks play a vital role in artificial intelligence and signal processing [6,7]. Discrete chaotic maps are particularly interesting because they exhibit complex and unpredictable behavior, even though they are deterministic and follow precise rules. Chaotic maps have important applications in fields such as cryptography, data encryption, and random number generation [8,9]. In this context, understanding and implementing the dynamics of discrete chaotic maps has become a crucial research topic [10,11].

The memristor is a fundamental electronic device that was proposed in 1971. However, it was not until 2008 that the first practical memristor was developed by a team of researchers at HP Labs. The development of the memristor has provided a new type of non-volatile memory that is faster, smaller, and requires less energy than existing technologies. Furthermore, memristors could be used in artificial intelligence, neuromorphic computing, and analog signal processing [12–14]. This has led to significant interest in the memristor from both the academic and industrial communities, with many researchers working to explore its full potential [15,16]

Memristors have been shown to be capable of generating chaotic behavior, and this property can be exploited to create new discrete chaotic maps [17–21]. Generally, authors explore 2D memristive maps due to their simplicity. However, recent research is also shifting towards investigating topics related to high-dimensional memristive maps, as they offer distinct advantages [22–24]. For instance, high-dimensional chaotic maps can store and process significantly more information compared to low-dimensional maps. Wang et al. conducted a study on a 3D memristive Lozi map [22], while another research group reported on a bi-memristor map in [23]. Additionally, a comprehensive list of 3D maps with memristors was introduced [24]. Researchers remain highly intrigued by the quest for an effective approach to designing high-dimensional maps.

This work considers another way to build high-dimensional maps with memristors and sine terms. The following are the primary advancements of this study. This work introduces a highly efficient method for the creation of high-dimensional memristive maps. These maps exhibit two distinct types of special fixed points, a plane of fixed points and the absence of any fixed points, categorizing them as unique maps with hidden dynamics [25]. By applying an extension of the suggested approach, the generation of even more intricate higher-dimensional maps, including 4D and 5D maps, becomes conveniently achievable. In Section 2, the general model and four example maps are introduced. Section 3 focuses on the specific map (called $TDMM_1$). Further examples of high-dimensional maps are discussed in Section 4. Section 5 presents the conclusions.

2. Model of 3D Maps

Chaotic discrete maps have intrigued scientists for decades due to their unpredictable and complex behaviors. These systems find application in various fields, from cryptography and secure communications to chaotic circuit design. With the discovery of memristors, a new dimension was introduced to the understanding and exploration of chaos in discrete maps. Memristors, the fourth fundamental circuit element, possess unique properties that offer novel possibilities in chaotic dynamics research. Recently, different 2D memristive maps have been proposed [20,26,27]. However, a few higher memristive maps have also been reported [22–24]. In this work, we develop a model of 3D maps, as shown in Figure 1. The main parts of the model are a sine function sin(.), a memristor, amplifiers (a_1, a_2, a_4, a_5), and a controller term a_3. The sine function is a popular function that was first applied to develop special discrete maps. Exploring further, additional functions could be employed in constructing high-dimensional maps. The effect of the sine term is indicated by a_1 and a_4. The memristor has an effect on the model through a factor a_2, while a_5 represents the feedback from $x(n)$ to $z(n+1)$. The term a_3 can be used to change the number of the model's fixed points.

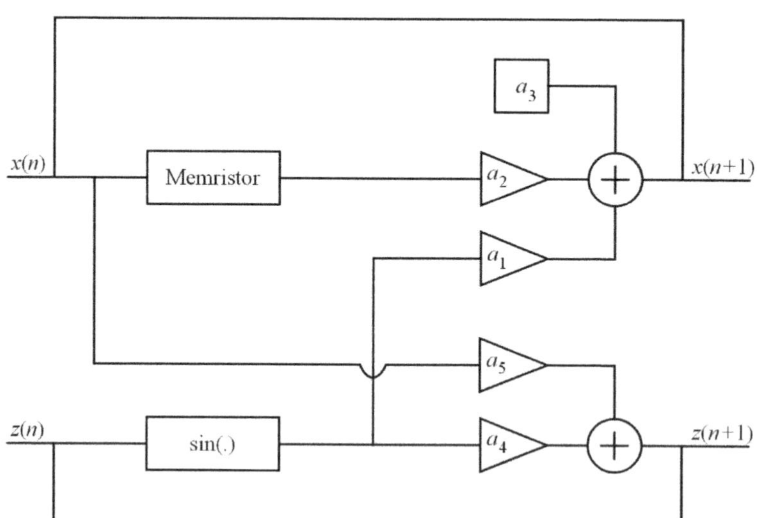

Figure 1. Diagram of 3D map using a sine function sin(.) and a memristor.

From Figure 1, the mathematical model is derived as

$$\begin{cases} x(n+1) = a_1 \sin(z(n)) + a_2 M(y(n))x(n) + a_3 \\ y(n+1) = y(n) + x(n) \\ z(n+1) = a_4 \sin(z(n)) + a_5 x(n) \end{cases} \tag{1}$$

with discrete memristance $M(y(n))$ and parameters $a_i, i = 1, \cdots, 5$. Here, x, y, and z are state variables. It is noted that x and z can be considered as the outputs of the model, while y is the internal state of the memristor.

The fixed point of (1) $P(x^*, y^*, z^*)$ is found by solving Equation (2)

$$\begin{cases} x^* = a_1 \sin(z^*) + a_2 M(y^*) x^* + a_3 \\ y^* = y^* + x^* \\ z^* = a_4 \sin(z^*) + a_5 x^* \end{cases} \tag{2}$$

We obtain

$$\begin{cases} x^* = 0 \\ \sin(z^*) = -\frac{a_3}{a_1} \\ z^* = -\frac{a_3 a_4}{a_1} \end{cases} \tag{3}$$

when $a_1 \neq 0$.

As shown in Equation (3), there is a plane of fixed points $P(0, y^*, 0)$ when $a_3 = 0$. When $a_3 \neq 0$, the fixed points depend on a_1, a_3, and a_4. In particular, the fixed points disappear for

$$\sin\left(\frac{a_3 a_4}{a_1}\right) \neq \frac{a_3}{a_1} \tag{4}$$

By selecting $M(y(n)) = (y(n))^2 - 1$, we obtain a three-dimensional memristive map (TDMM_1 map):

$$\begin{cases} x(n+1) = a_1 \sin(z(n)) + a_2 \left((y(n))^2 - 1\right) x(n) + a_3 \\ y(n+1) = y(n) + x(n) \\ z(n+1) = a_4 \sin(z(n)) + a_5 x(n) \end{cases} \tag{5}$$

The TDMM_1 map is chaotic for

$$\begin{cases} a_1 = a_3 = a_4 = 0.1 \\ a_2 = 1.65 \\ a_5 = 1 \end{cases} \tag{6}$$

and $(x(0), y(0), z(0)) = (0.01, 0.01, 0.01)$ (see Figure 2a). The maximum Lyapunov exponent (MLE) equals 0.2697.

Selecting different memristors, it is possible to obtain new 3D maps based on the general model (1). In Table 1, we report new maps, while their chaotic dynamics are illustrated in Figure 2. While we exclusively present a singular set of parameter values for each map, it is important to note that there exist various parameter values leading to the chaotic behavior of these maps.

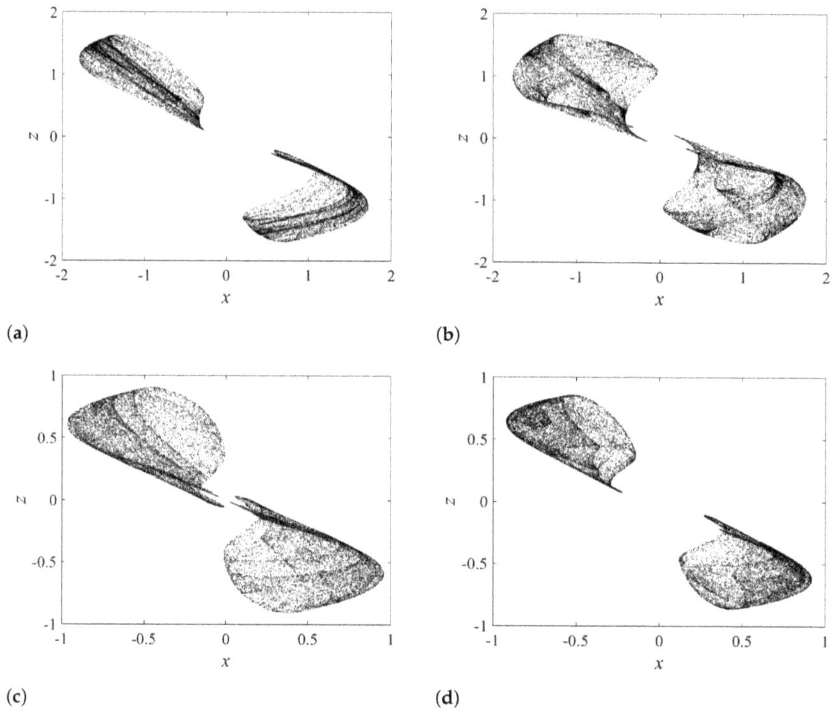

Figure 2. Iterative plots: (a) $TDMM_1$ map, (b) $TDMM_2$ map, (c) $TDMM_3$ map, (d) $TDMM_4$ map.

Table 1. List of new maps $(x(0), y(0), z(0)) = (0.01, 0.01, 0.01)$.

Name	Equations	Parameters	MLE
$TDMM_2$	$x(n+1) = a_1 \sin(z(n)) + a_2(\lvert y(n)\rvert - 1)x(n) + a_3$ $y(n+1) = y(n) + x(n)$ $z(n+1) = a_4 \sin(z(n)) + a_5 x(n)$	$a_1 = a_4 = 0.1$ $a_2 = 2.3, a_3 = 0.01$ $a_5 = 1$	0.2046
$TDMM_3$	$x(n+1) = a_1 \sin(z(n)) + a_2 \sin(\pi y(n))x(n) + a_3$ $y(n+1) = y(n) + x(n)$ $z(n+1) = a_4 \sin(z(n)) + a_5 x(n)$	$a_1 = a_4 = 0.1$ $a_2 = 1.8, a_3 = 0.01$ $a_5 = 1$	0.2415
$TDMM_4$	$x(n+1) = a_1 \sin(z(n)) + a_2\left(e^{-\cos(\pi y(n))} - 1\right)x(n) + a_3$ $y(n+1) = y(n) + x(n)$ $z(n+1) = a_4 \sin(z(n)) + a_5 x(n)$	$a_1 = a_4 = 0.1$ $a_2 = 2.5, a_3 = 0.01$ $a_5 = 1$	0.214

3. Study of $TDMM_1$ Map

The $TDMM_1$ map (5) has no fixed point when $a_1 = a_3 = a_4 = 0.1$ and $a_5 = 1$. We consider the effect of the memristor on the dynamics by changing a_2 from 1.3 to 1.7 (see Figure 3). Both chaotic and non-chaotic behaviors are observed in this range of a_2. Figure 3a shows a route from periodic dynamics to chaos.

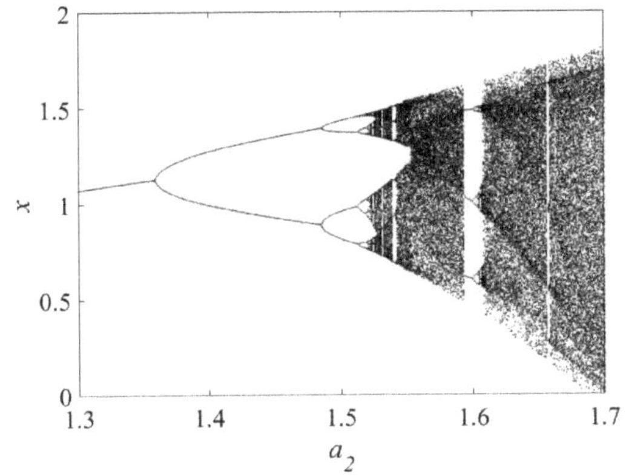

(**a**)

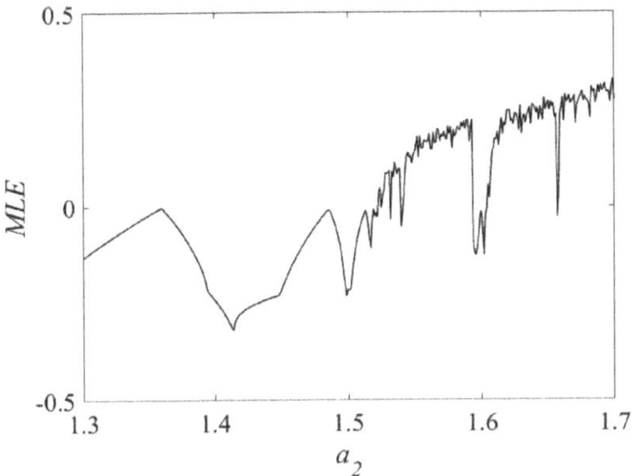

(**b**)

Figure 3. (**a**) Bifurcation diagram, (**b**) maximum Lyapunov exponents of the $TDMM_1$ map for $a_2 \in [1.3, 1.7]$.

The map is realized with a microcontroller via an Arduino Uno board. Signal x is displayed in Figure 4. The chaos of signal x verifies the map's feasibility with hardware.

The Internet of Things (IoT) has emerged as a groundbreaking technology that promises to connect and automate various physical objects and devices, transforming industries and enhancing our daily lives. However, along with its numerous benefits, the IoT shows security challenges. The rapid proliferation of IoT devices, which are often embedded with sensors, actuators, and other smart technologies, has created a complex and interconnected network of devices that can be vulnerable to security threats. Lightweight cryptography plays a crucial role in securing IoT environments, where resource-constrained devices require efficient and effective cryptographic solutions [28,29]. Its ability to provide strong security with minimal resource requirements makes it suitable for a wide range of IoT applications, including secure communication, device authentication, data protection, access control, and secure firmware updates. As the IoT ecosystem continues to grow, the importance of lightweight cryptography in protecting IoT devices cannot be overstated. We test a simple lightweight encryption proposed by Moysis et al. [8] using the $TDMM_1$ map. In this simple encryption, we generate random numbers from the $TDMM_1$ map, which are utilized to encrypt a small-sized image via XOR operation. The encryption algorithm comprises the following steps.

Step 1: Formation of a secret key through the utilization of initial values and map parameters.

Step 2: Generation of a random bit sequence (K), with each bit (k_i) being generated by the map's state variable, x

$$k_i = \begin{cases} 1, & \text{if} \quad \text{mod}\left(10^5|x(i)|, 1\right) \geq 0.5 \\ 0, & \text{if} \quad \text{mod}\left(10^5|x(i)|, 1\right) < 0.5 \end{cases} \quad (7)$$

Step 3: Conversion of the original image into a binary sequence (P).

Step 4: Application of the XOR operation to yield the encrypted data (C): $C = P \oplus K$.

Step 5: Utilization of the XOR operation to derive the decrypted data (P'): $P' = C \oplus K$, allowing for the reconstruction of the original image.

The original, encrypted, and decrypted images are displayed in Figure 5. A uniform histogram of the encrypted image protects it against statistical attacks (see Figure 6). The information entropy calculations of the encrypted and original images are 7.9974 and 7.4509, respectively. The information entropy closer to 8 protects encrypted data against entropy attacks. The obtained results illustrate the possibility of the $TDMM_1$ map for use in lightweight encryption.

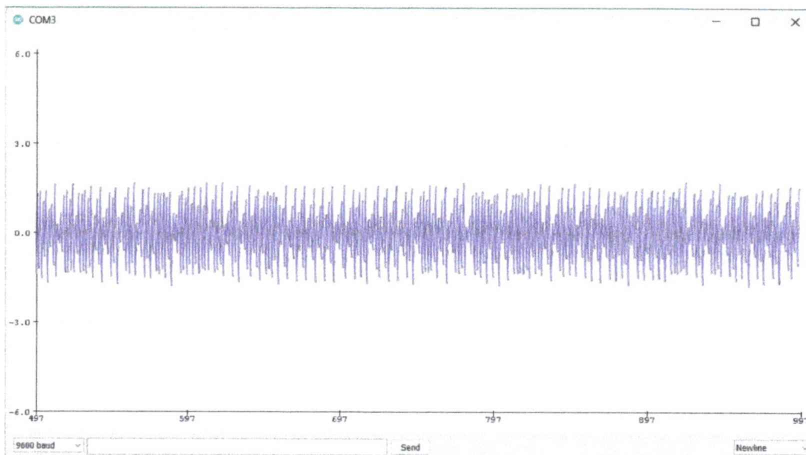

Figure 4. Experimental signal x captured by the Serial Plotter tool of Arduino.

Figure 5. Obtained results: original image (**left**), encrypted image (**middle**), and decrypted image (**right**).

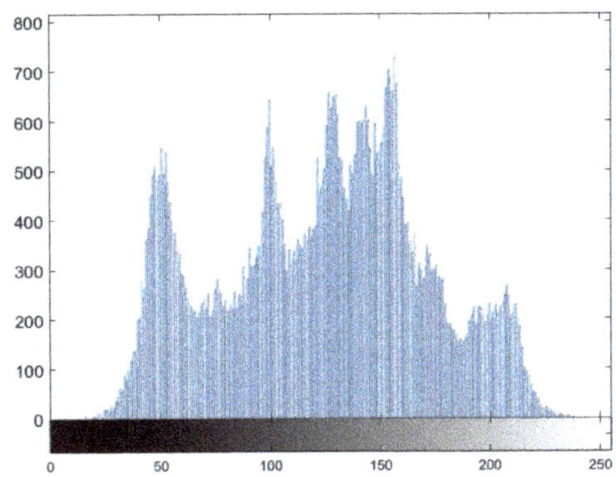

(**a**)

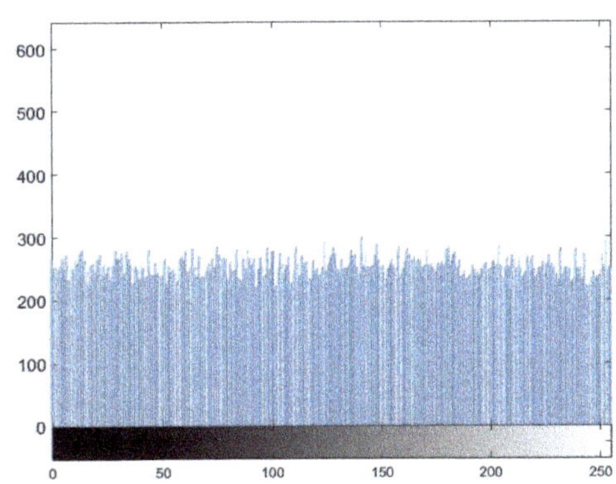

(**b**)

Figure 6. Histogram results of (**a**) original image and (**b**) encrypted image.

4. Discussion

High-dimensional chaotic maps, also known as multi-dimensional chaotic maps, are mathematical models that describe the dynamics of systems with many degrees of freedom. High-dimensional chaotic maps exhibit more complex and diverse behaviors than low-dimensional maps. By enlarging the model (1), higher-order dimensional maps are constructed easily.

Including an additional state $w(n)$ and $\sin(w(n))$, a 4D map is derived

$$\begin{cases} x(n+1) = a_1 \sin(z(n)) + a_2 \sin(w(n)) + a_3\Big((y(n))^2 - 1\Big)x(n) + a_4 \\ y(n+1) = y(n) + x(n) \\ z(n+1) = a_5 \sin(z(n)) + a_6 x(n) \\ w(n+1) = a_7 \sin(w(n)) + a_8 z(n) \end{cases} \tag{8}$$

with parameters $a_i, i = 1, \cdots, 8$. The chaos in the 4D map is shown in Figure 7 for

$$\begin{cases} a_1 = a_2 = a_4 = a_5 = a_7 = 0.1 \\ a_3 = 1.7 \\ a_6 = 1 \\ a_8 = 0.2 \end{cases} \tag{9}$$

The value of MLE is 0.3003, confirming the presence of chaos.

Similarly, when introducing two states $w(n)$, $v(n)$ and terms $\sin(w(n))$, $\sin(v(n))$, a 5D map is proposed as

$$\begin{cases} x(n+1) = a_1 \sin(z(n)) + a_2 \sin(w(n)) + a_3 \sin(v(n)) + a_4\Big((y(n))^2 - 1\Big)x(n) + a_5 \\ y(n+1) = y(n) + x(n) \\ z(n+1) = a_6 \sin(z(n)) + a_7 x(n) \\ w(n+1) = a_8 \sin(w(n)) + a_9 z(n) \\ v(n+1) = a_{10} \sin(v(n)) + a_{11} w(n) \end{cases} \tag{10}$$

with parameters a_i, $i = 1, \cdots, 11$. Figure 8 displays the chaos in the 5D map for

$$\begin{cases} a_1 = a_2 = a_3 = a_5 = a_6 = a_8 = a_{10} = 0.1 \\ a_4 = 1.7 \\ a_7 = a_9 = 1 \\ a_{11} = 0.2 \end{cases} \tag{11}$$

The value of MLE is 0.2849.

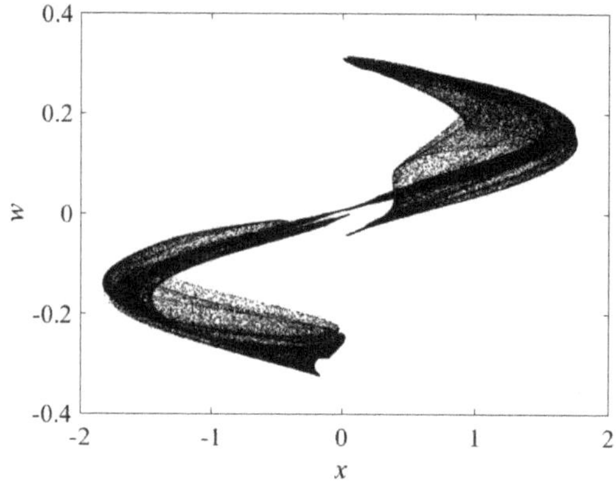

Figure 7. Iterative plots of the 4D map with $(x(0), y(0), z(0), w(0)) = (0.01, 0.01, 0.01, 0.01)$.

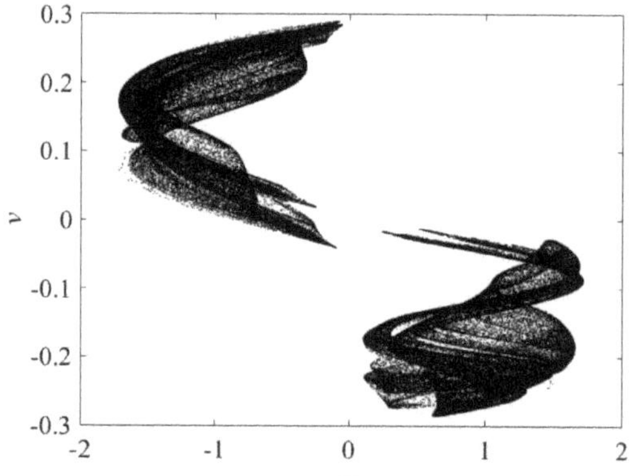

Figure 8. Iterative plots of the 5D map with $(x(0), y(0), z(0), w(0), v(0)) = (0.01, 0.01, 0.01, 0.01, 0.01)$.

5. Conclusions

We have conducted a study focusing on high-dimensional memristive maps, motivated by their potential application in various fields. In this research, we present a general approach to constructing these maps using memristors and sine terms. The resulting 3D model exhibits intriguing fixed points, making it particularly appealing. To illustrate the dynamics and practical applications of these maps, we specifically developed the $TDMM_1$ map, employing simulations and a microcontroller board. The $TDMM_1$ map generates chaotic signals, rendering it suitable for lightweight ciphers. Nevertheless, further investigations into the map's potential applications are planned for future work. In particular, the proposed approach is scalable and can be extended to create higher-dimensional maps, such as 4D and 5D maps.

Author Contributions: Conceptualization, G.G.; Investigation, O.A.A.; Methodology, V.-T.P.; Software, M.A.; Supervision, V.V.H.; Writing—original draft, S.A. All authors have read and agreed to the published version of the manuscript.

Funding: This research has been funded by the Scientific Research Deanship at the University of Ha'il, Saudi Arabia, through project number <<RG-23 087>>.

Data Availability Statement: No new data were created or analyzed in this study. Data sharing is not applicable to this article.

Conflicts of Interest: The authors declare no conflict of interest.

References

1. Pierre, C.; Jean-Pierre, E. *Iterated Map on the Interval as Dynamical Systems;* Springer: Berlin, Germany, 1980.
2. Dong, C.; Rajagopal, K.; He, S.; Jafari, S.; Sun, K. Chaotification of Sine-series maps based on the internal perturbation model. *Results Phys.* **2021**, *31*, 105010. [CrossRef]
3. Laskaridis, L.; Volos, C.; Munoz-Pacheco, J.; Stouboulos, I. Study of the dynamical behavior of an Ikeda-based map with a discrete memristor. *Integration* **2023**, *89*, 168–177. [CrossRef]
4. Zhu, W.; Sun, K.; He, S.; Wang, H.; Liu, W. A class of m-dimension grid multi-cavity hyperchaotic maps and its application. *Chaos Solitons Fractals* **2023**, *170*, 113370. [CrossRef]
5. Khennaoui, A.A.; Ouannas, A.; Bekiros, S.; Aly, A.A.; Jahanshahi, H.; Alsubaie, H. Hidden homogeneous extreme multistability of a fractional-order hyperchaotic discrete-time system: Chaos, initial offset boosting, amplitude control, control, and Synchronization. *Symmetry* **2023**, *15*, 139. [CrossRef]
6. Ali, Z.; Rabiel, F.; Hosseini, K. A fractal-fractional-order modified Predator-Prey mathematical model with immigrations. *Math. Comput. Simul.* **2023**, *207*, 466. [CrossRef]
7. Li, P.; Li, Y.; Xu, C.; Ren, J. Insight into Hopf bifurcation and control methods in fractional order BAM neural networks incorporating symmetric structure and delay. *Cogn. Comput.* **2023**, *preview*. [CrossRef]
8. Moysis, L.; Volos, C.; Jafari, S.; Munoz-Pacheco, J.; Kengne, J.; Rajagopal, K.; Stouboulo, I. Modification of the logistic map using fuzzy numbers with application to pseudorandom number generation and image encryption. *Entropy* **2020**, *4*, 474. [CrossRef]
9. Moysis, L.; Rajagopal, K.; Tutueva, A.; Volos, C.; Teka, B.; Butusov, D. Chaotic path planning for 3D area coverage using a pseudo-random bit generator from a 1D chaotic map. *Mathematics* **2022**, *9*, 1821. [CrossRef]
10. Garcia-Grimaldo, C.; Bermudez-Marquez, C.F.; Tlelo-Cuautle, E.; Campos-Canton, E. FPGA implementation of a chaotic map with no fixed point. *Electronics* **2023**, *12*, 444. [CrossRef]
11. Bao, H.; Li, H.; Hua, Z.; Xu, Q.; Bao, B. Sine-transform-based memristive hyperchaotic model with hardware implementation. *IEEE Trans. Ind. Inform.* **2023**, *19*, 2792. [CrossRef]
12. Ma, M.; Lu, Y.; Li, Z.; Sun, Y.; Wang, C. Multistability and phase synchronization of Rulkov neurons coupled with a locally active discrete memristor. *Chin. Phys. B* **2023**, *32*, 058701. [CrossRef]
13. Bao, B.; Zhao, Q.; Yu, X.; Wu, H.; Xu, Q. Three-dimensional memristive Morris–Lecar model with magnetic induction effects and its FPGA implementation. *Cogn. Neurodynamics* **2023**, *17*, 1079. [CrossRef] [PubMed]
14. Bao, H.; Hua, Z.; Li, H.; Chen, M.; Bao, B. Memristor-based hyperchaotic maps and application in auxiliary classifier generative adversarial nets. *IEEE Trans. Ind. Inform.* **2022**, *18*, 5297–5306. [CrossRef]
15. Ma, M.; Xiong, K.; Li, Z.; Sun, Y. Dynamic behavior anlysis and synchronization of memristor-coupled heterogeneous discrete neural networks. *Mathematics* **2023**, *11*, 375. [CrossRef]
16. Xu, Q.; Cheng, S.; Ju, Z.; Chen, M.; Wu, H. Asymmetric coexisting bifurcations and multi-stability in an asymmetric memristive diode-bridge-based jerk circuit. *Chin. J. Phys.* **2021**, *70*, 69–81. [CrossRef]
17. Bao, H.; Hua, Z.; Li, H.; Chen, M.; Bao, B. Discrete memristor hyperchaotic maps. *IEEE Trans. Circuits Syst. I Regul. Pap.* **2021**, *68*, 4534–4544. [CrossRef]

18. Zhao, Y.; Ding, J.; He, S.; Wang, H.; Sun, K. Fully fixed-point integrated digital circuit design of discrete memristive systems. *AEU-Int. J. Electron. Commun.* **2023**, *161*, 154522. [CrossRef]
19. Liu, X.; Sun, K.; Wang, H.; He, S. A class of novel discrete memristive chaotic map. *Chaos Solitons Fractals* **2023**, *174*, 113791. [CrossRef]
20. Wang, M.; An, M.; He, S.; Zhang, X.; Iu, H.H.C.; Li, Z. Two-dimensional memristive hyperchaotic maps with different coupling frames and its hardware implementation. *Chaos* **2023**, *33*, 073129. [CrossRef]
21. Sun, Q.; He, S.; Sun, K.; Wang, H. A novel hyperchaotic map with sine chaotification and discrete memristor. *Chin. Phys. B* **2022**, *31*, 120501. [CrossRef]
22. Wang, J.; Gu, Y.; Rong, K.; Xu, Q.; Zhang, X. Memristor-based Lozi map with hidden hyperchaos. *Mathematics* **2022**, *10*, 3426. [CrossRef]
23. Bao, H.; Gu, Y.; Xu, Q.; Zhang, X.; Bao, B. Parallel bi-memristor hyperchaotic map with extreme multistability. *Chaos Solitons Fractals* **2022**, *160*, 112273. [CrossRef]
24. Peng, Y.; He, S.; Sun, K. A higher dimensional chaotic map with discrete memristor. *AEU-Int. J. Electron. Commun.* **2021**, *129*, 153539. [CrossRef]
25. Zhang, L.; Liu, Y.; Wei, Z.; Jiang, H.; Bi, Q. Hidden attractors in a class of two-dimensional rational memristive maps with no fixed points. *Eur. Phys. J.-Spec. Top.* **2022**, *231*, 2173. [CrossRef]
26. Ramadoss, J.; Ouannas, A.; Tamba, V.K.; Grassi, G.; Momani, S.; Pham, V.T. Constructing non-fixed-point maps with memristors. *Eur. Phys. J. Plus* **2022**, *137*, 211. [CrossRef]
27. Bao, B.; Zhao, Q.; Yu, X.; Wu, H.; Xu, Q. Complex dynamics and initial state effects in a two-dimensional sine-bounded memristive map. *Chaos Solitons Fractals* **2023**, *173*, 113748. [CrossRef]
28. Gonzalez-Zapata, A.; Tlelo-Cuautle, E.; Cruz-Vega, I.; Leon-Salas, W. Synchronization of chaotic artificial neurons and its application to secure image transmission under MQTT for IoT protocol. *Nonlinear Dyn.* **2021**, *104*, 4581. [CrossRef]
29. Trujillo-Toledo, D.; Lopez-Bonilla, O.; Garcia-Guerrero, E.; Tlelo-Cuautle, E.; Lopez-Mancilla, D.; Guillen-Fernandez, O.; Inzunza-Gonzalez, E. Real-time RGB image encryption for IoT applications using enhanced sequences from chaotic maps. *Chaos Solitons Fractals* **2021**, *153*, 111506. [CrossRef]

mathematics

MDPI

Article

A Novel Eighth-Order Hyperchaotic System and Its Application in Image Encryption

Hanshuo Qiu [1], Xiangzi Zhang [2], Huaixiao Yue [3] and Jizhao Liu [1,*]

1 School of Information Science and Engineering, Lanzhou University, No.222, TianShui Road(south), Lanzhou 730000, China; qiuhsh21@lzu.edu.cn
2 School of Psychology, Northwest Normal University, No.967 Anning East Road, Lanzhou 730000, China; zhangxiangzi@nwnu.edu.cn
3 School of Computer Science, Nanjing University of Posts and Telecommunications, No.66 New Model Road, Nanjing 210003, China; b22040025@njupt.edu.cn
* Correspondence: liujz@lzu.edu.cn

Abstract: With the advancement in information and communication technologies (ICTs), the widespread dissemination and sharing of digital images has raised concerns regarding privacy and security. Traditional methods of encrypting images often suffer from limitations such as a small key space and vulnerability to brute-force attacks. To address these issues, this paper proposes a novel eighth-order hyperchaotic system. This hyperchaotic system exhibits various dynamic behaviors, including hyperchaos, sub-hyperchaos, and chaos. The encryption scheme based on this system offers a key space larger than 2^{2338}. Through a comprehensive analysis involving histogram analysis, key space analysis, correlation analysis, entropy analysis, key sensitivity analysis, differential attack analysis, and cropping attack analysis, it is demonstrated that the proposed system is capable of resisting statistical attacks, brute force attacks, differential attacks, and cropping attacks, thereby providing excellent security performance.

Keywords: chaos; hyperchaos; image encryption; information security; symmetric encryption

MSC: 37M25

1. Introduction

The increasing importance of digital images across various domains has been propelled by the rapid progress of information and communication technologies (ICTs). However, the widespread dissemination and sharing of digital images on a large scale have given rise to apprehensions surrounding issues of privacy and security. In order to mitigate these concerns, image encryption technology is widely employed to ensure the confidentiality and integrity of images on diverse devices [1], such as medical, military, satellite, and Internet of Things applications [2]. As a result, addressing these issues has become a critical and urgent challenge in these fields [3].

In recent decades, numerous symmetric image encryption methods have been proposed [4]. Specifically, image encryption techniques based on the Data Encryption Standard (DES) and Advanced Encryption Standard (AES) have been extensively researched and implemented in the field of symmetric encryption. Nevertheless, the security of traditional symmetric encryption algorithms is increasingly being challenged due to the continuous enhancement of computing power and the constant development of cryptanalysis technology. Research indicates that symmetric encryption suffers from drawbacks such as a limited key space and vulnerability to brute force attacks [5].

To overcome these limitations, researchers have turned to chaotic systems that exhibit desirable properties such as high ergodicity, aperiodicity, and sensitivity to initial values [3]. Due to the fact that it is crucial to deliver messages with complete security and to execute them online [6], it is possible to employ chaotic systems to safeguard the security of data transfer and advance the "industrial 4.0 revolution" being developed [7]. Chaotic systems have also been found to be efficient and effective in image encryption. For instance, the Lorenz chaotic system has been applied to image encryption [8], providing strong security and high resistance against common attacks [9]. Another example is the 2D-SCL map, which exhibits good ergodicity and hyperchaotic behavior [10]. However, most existing chaotic systems are traditional chaotic systems that encounter issues such as a small key space and a lack of capability to resist brute force attacks, statistical attacks, and differential attacks. Particularly in light of the developing deep learning landscape [11–13], the capacity to analyze complex issues has grown. Therefore, the pursuit of more secure and efficient encryption schemes is an appealing research direction [14].

A hyperchaotic system is characterized by having at least two positive Lyapunov exponents, indicating that its dynamics expand in more than one direction and give rise to a more complex attractor [15]. By increasing the system dimension and incorporating nonlinear terms, the dynamics of a hyperchaotic system become more complex and unpredictable. Compared to traditional chaotic systems, hyperchaotic systems exhibit higher key sensitivity, unpredictability, and pseudo-random properties [16].

In order to establish a more secure system, this work proposes an image encryption algorithm based on a novel eighth-order hyperchaotic system. Dynamic analysis demonstrates that the hyperchaostic system has extremely rich dynamical behaviors, including hyperchaotic, sub-hyperchaotic, chaotic, and limit cycle attractors. On this basis, the image encryption scheme based on this algorithm fully guarantees the confidentiality and integrity of the image by utilizing two different states of the hyperchaotic system [1]. Additionally, it incorporates steps such as row scrambling, column scrambling, and diffusion to enhance security at a higher level. Furthermore, through various analyses of the encryption scheme, including key sensitivity, key space, image histogram, pixel correlation, and other indicators, it has been demonstrated that the proposed algorithm possesses a high level of security and robustness.

The rest of this paper is organized as follows: Section 2 introduces the novel eighth-order hyperchaotic system and analyzes its dynamic characteristics. Section 3 provides an overview of the encryption and decryption schemes based on this system. The experimental results and detailed security analysis are presented in Section 4. Finally, Section 5 concludes the paper.

2. A Novel Eighth-Order Hyperchaotic System and Its Basic Properties

2.1. Equations of a Novel Eighth-Order Hyperchaotic System

Nowadays, some researchers propose low-dimensional chaotic systems to generate pseudo-random sequences to encrypt the original image [17], which means that the encrypted scheme has a small key space and is vulnerable to attacks. Therefore, a higher-dimensional chaotic system is required. Ref. [18] proposed an nth-order chaotic system with hyperbolic sine:

$$
\begin{cases}
\dot{x}_1 = x_2 - x_1 \\
\dot{x}_2 = x_3 - x_2 \\
\dots \\
\dot{x}_{n-3} = x_{n-2} - x_{n-3} \\
\dot{x}_{n-2} = x_{n-1} \\
\dot{x}_{n-1} = x_n \\
\dot{x}_n = -x_n - f(x_{n-1}) - nx_{n-2} - nx_{n-3} - \dots - \dfrac{1}{2n}x_1
\end{cases}
\tag{1}
$$

The nonlinear function in this system is $f(x_{n-1})$, which is defined by $f(x_{n-1}) = \rho \sinh(\phi x_{n-1})$, where $\rho = 1.2 \times 10^{-6}$ and $\phi = \frac{1}{0.026}$. Based on Equation (1), the eighth-order chaotic system with hyperbolic sine is described by

$$\begin{cases} \dot{x}_1 = x_2 - x_1 \\ \dot{x}_2 = x_3 - x_2 \\ \dot{x}_3 = x_4 - x_3 \\ \dot{x}_4 = x_5 - x_4 \\ \dot{x}_5 = x_6 - x_5 \\ \dot{x}_6 = x_7 \\ \dot{x}_7 = x_8 \\ \dot{x}_8 = -x_8 - \rho \sinh(\phi x_7) - 8(x_6 + x_5 + x_4 + x_3 + x_2) - \dfrac{x_1}{16} \end{cases} \tag{2}$$

where ρ, ϕ are control parameters. When $(\rho, \phi) = (1.2 \times 10^{-6}, \frac{1}{0.026})$ and the initial conditions are (0.1, 0.1, 0.1, 0.1, 0.1, 0.1, 0.1, 0.1), system (2) has a chaotic attractor, as shown in Figure 1 and the corresponding Lyapunov exponents of this chaotic attractor are (0.49, 0, − 0.60, −0.74, −0.99, −1.16, −1.38, −1.63). Moreover, system (2) has a unique stable equilibrium O(0, 0, 0, 0, 0, 0, 0, 0).

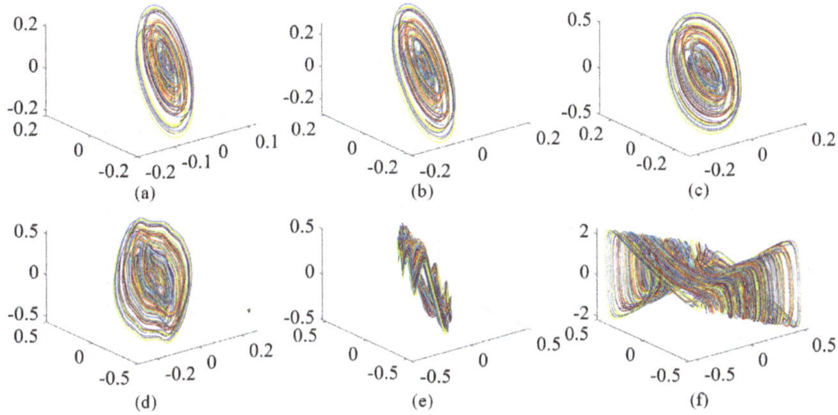

Figure 1. Chaotic attractor of system (2) with $(\rho, \phi) = (1.2 \times 10^{-6}, \frac{1}{0.026})$: **(a)** $x_1 - x_2 - x_3$ phase plane; **(b)** $x_2 - x_3 - x_4$ phase plane; **(c)** $x_3 - x_4 - x_5$ phase plane; **(d)** $x_4 - x_5 - x_6$ phase plane; **(e)** $x_5 - x_6 - x_7$ phase plane; **(f)** $x_6 - x_7 - x_8$ phase plane.

By coupling a few nonlinear terms, like trigonometric and exponential functions and system (2) to increase the complexity, the following 8D chaotic system is derived:

$$\begin{cases} \dot{x}_1 = x_2 - x_1 - \epsilon(\exp(\phi x_7)) + a\rho \tanh(x_8) \\ \dot{x}_2 = x_3 - x_2 + b\sin(x_1) \\ \dot{x}_3 = dx_4 - x_3 + \sin(x_5) \\ \dot{x}_4 = x_5 - x_4 + \sin(e(x_7 + x_8)) \\ \dot{x}_5 = x_6 - x_5 - \cos(x_3) + \sin(x_1) - \epsilon(\exp(\rho x_7)) \\ \dot{x}_6 = x_7 \\ \dot{x}_7 = x_8 + f\sin(x_5) \\ \dot{x}_8 = -cx_8 - \rho \sinh(\phi x_7) - 8(x_6 + x_5 + x_4 + x_3 + x_2) - \dfrac{x_1}{16} \end{cases} \tag{3}$$

where $c \in [0.65, 4]$; d is the constant parameter; a, b, e, and f are the coupling parameters; c, ρ, and ϕ are control parameters. When $(a,b,c,d,e,f,\rho,\phi) = (\frac{1}{2}, 3, 1, 2, \frac{1}{2}, 2, 1.2\times10^{-6}, \frac{1}{0.026})$, system (3) has a unique stable equilibrium O(−0.18, −0.18, −0.35, −0.01, −0.33, 0.43, 0, 0.65) and the corresponding eight Lyapunov exponents are (0.36, 0, −0.58, −0.93, −1.04, −1.16, −1.26, 1.39). The chaotic attractor of system (3) is shown in Figure 2.

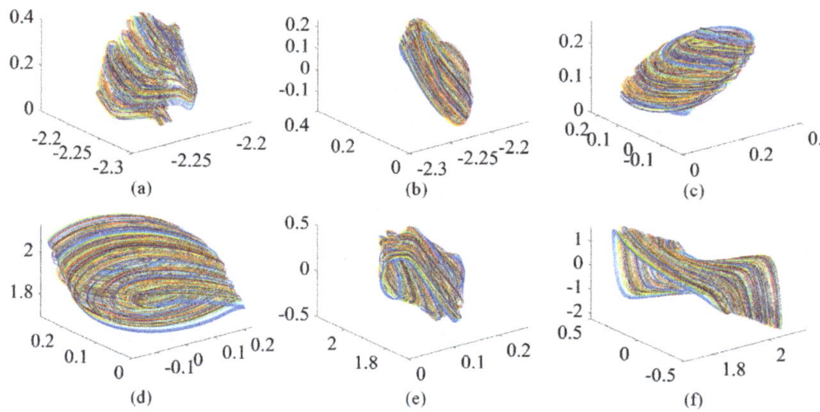

Figure 2. Chaotic attractor of system (3) with $(a,b,c,d,e,f,\rho,\phi) = (\frac{1}{2}, 3, 1, 2, \frac{1}{2}, 2, 1.2\times10^{-6}, \frac{1}{0.026})$: (**a**) $x_1 - x_2 - x_3$ phase plane; (**b**) $x_2 - x_3 - x_4$ phase plane; (**c**) $x_3 - x_4 - x_5$ phase plane; (**d**) $x_4 - x_5 - x_6$ phase plane; (**e**) $x_5 - x_6 - x_7$ phase plane; (**f**) $x_6 - x_7 - x_8$ phase plane.

By coupling a few linear terms and system (3) to control the scope of variables in the system and further improve the complexity [19], a novel eighth-order hyperchaotic system is proposed:

$$\begin{cases} \dot{x}_1 = x_2 - x_1 - \epsilon(\exp(\phi x_7)) + a\rho\tanh(x_8) \\ \dot{x}_2 = x_3 - x_2 + b\sin(x_1) - gx_1 \\ \dot{x}_3 = dx_4 - x_3 + \sin(x_5) + hx_7 \\ \dot{x}_4 = x_5 - x_4 + \sin(e(x_7 + x_8)) \\ \dot{x}_5 = x_6 - x_5 - \cos(x_3) + \sin(x_1) - \epsilon(\exp(\rho x_7)) + ix_7 \\ \dot{x}_6 = x_7 + ix_8 + jx_4 \\ \dot{x}_7 = x_8 + f\sin(x_5) + kx_5 + lx_6 \\ \dot{x}_8 = -cx_8 - \rho\sinh(\phi x_7) - 8(x_6 + x_5 + x_4 + x_3 + x_2) \end{cases} \tag{4}$$

where $c \in [0.65, 4]$; d is the constant parameter; $a, b, e, f, g, h, i, j, k$, and l are the coupling parameters; c, ρ, and ϕ are control parameters, determining the sub-hyperchaotic and hyperchaotic behaviors of the system [20]. Therefore, controllers c, ρ, and ϕ and coupling parameters $a, b, e, f, g, h, i, j, k$, and l cause the classical 8D chaotic system (2) to become a novel eighth-order hyperchaotic system (4) with two positive Lyapunov exponents [21], having eight Lyapunov exponents.

When $(a,b,c,d,e,f,g,h,i,j,k,l,\rho,\phi) = (\frac{1}{2}, 3, 0.75, 2, \frac{1}{2}, 2, -1, 1, -0.01, -3, 1, \frac{1}{2}, 1.2\times10^{-6}, \frac{1}{0.026})$ and the initial conditions are (0.1, 0.1, 0.1, 0.1, 0.1, 0.1, 0.1, 0.1), system (4) exhibits a hyperchaotic attractor in Figure 3, and the corresponding eight Lyapunov exponents are (0.34, 0.05, 0, −0.77, −0.96, −1.14, −1.32, −1.96).

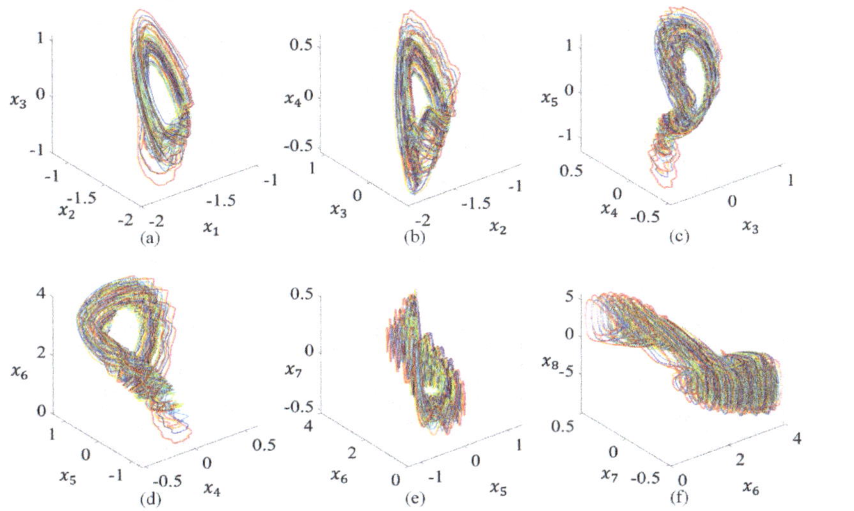

Figure 3. Hyperchaotic attractor observed from system (4) with $(a,b,c,d,e,f,g,h,i,j,k,l,\rho,\phi) = (\frac{1}{2}, 3, 0.75, 2, \frac{1}{2}, 2, -1, 1, -0.01, -3, 1, \frac{1}{2}, 1.2 \times 10^{-6}, \frac{1}{0.026})$: (**a**) $x_1 - x_2 - x_3$ phase plane; (**b**) $x_2 - x_3 - x_4$ phase plane; (**c**) $x_3 - x_4 - x_5$ phase plane; (**d**) $x_4 - x_5 - x_6$ phase plane; (**e**) $x_5 - x_6 - x_7$ phase plane; (**f**) $x_6 - x_7 - x_8$ phase plane.

When $(a,b,c,d,e,f,g,h,i,j,k,l,\rho,\phi) = (\frac{1}{2}, 3, 0.945, 2, \frac{1}{2}, 2, -1, 1, -0.01, -3, 1, \frac{1}{2}, 1.2 \times 10^{-6}, \frac{1}{0.026})$ and the initial conditions are $(0.1, 0.1, 0.1, 0.1, 0.1, 0.1, 0.1, 0.1)$, system (4) exhibits a sub-hyperchaotic attractor in Figure 4, and the corresponding eight Lyapunov exponents are $(0.25, 0, 0, -0.80, -0.96, -1.09, -1.36, -1.98)$.

When the novel eighth-order hyperchaotic system is applied to image encryption, it is necessary to define the default values of the constant parameter and the coupling parameters of the hyperchaotic system (a,b,d,e,f,g,h,i,j,k,l) as $(\frac{1}{2}, 3, 2, \frac{1}{2}, 2, -1, 1, -0.01, -3, 1, \frac{1}{2})$. The hyperchaotic system is as follows:

$$\begin{cases} \dot{x}_1 = x_2 - x_1 - \epsilon(\exp(\phi x_7)) + \frac{\rho}{2}\tanh(x_8) \\ \dot{x}_2 = x_3 - x_2 + 3\sin(x_1) - x_1 \\ \dot{x}_3 = 2x_4 - x_3 + \sin(x_5) + x_7 \\ \dot{x}_4 = x_5 - x_4 + \sin\left(\frac{x_7 + x_8}{2}\right) \\ \dot{x}_5 = x_6 - x_5 - \cos(x_3) + \sin(x_1) - \epsilon(\exp(\rho x_7)) + \frac{x_7}{2} \\ \dot{x}_6 = x_7 - x_8 \times 10^{-2} - 3x_4 \\ \dot{x}_7 = x_8 + 2\sin(x_5) + x_5 + \frac{x_6}{2} \\ \dot{x}_8 = -cx_8 - \rho\sinh(\phi x_7) - 8(x_6 + x_5 + x_4 + x_3 + x_2) \end{cases} \tag{5}$$

where the control parameters are $\rho = 1.2 \times 10^{-6}$, $\phi = \frac{1}{0.026}$, $\epsilon = 6 \times 10^{-9}$, $c \in [0.65, 4]$, and the initial conditions are $(0.1, 0.1, 0.1, 0.1, 0.1, 0.1, 0.1, 0.1)$.

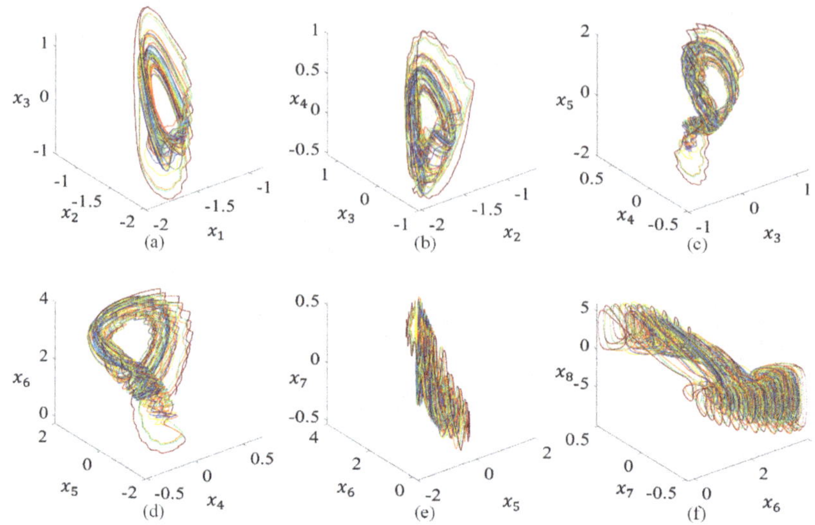

Figure 4. Sub-hyperchaotic attractor observed from system (4) with $(a, b, c, d, e, f, g, h, i, j, k, l, \rho, \phi) = (\frac{1}{2}$, 3, 0.75, 2, $\frac{1}{2}$, 2, −1, 1, −0.01, −3, 1, $\frac{1}{2}$, 1.2×10^{-6}, $\frac{1}{0.026})$: (**a**) $x_1 - x_2 - x_3$ phase plane; (**b**) $x_2 - x_3 - x_4$ phase plane; (**c**) $x_3 - x_4 - x_5$ phase plane; (**d**) $x_4 - x_5 - x_6$ phase plane; (**e**) $x_5 - x_6 - x_7$ phase plane; (**f**) $x_6 - x_7 - x_8$ phase plane.

2.2. Observation of Hyperchaos and Complex Dynamics

The Lyapunov exponent of a dynamical system is a quantity that characterizes the rate of separation of infinitesimally close trajectories. Over time, two sets of initially close conditions will gradually separate due to the chaotic nature of the system. The Lyapunov exponent quantifies this exponential separation [22]. By analyzing Lyapunov exponents, valuable insights can be gained regarding a system's sensitivity to its initial conditions, thereby aiding in the understanding and prediction of the behavior of complex systems [23].

Table 1 shows the properties of the Lyapunov exponent for an ordinary differential dynamical system.

The Lyapunov exponent spectrum of the system is shown in Figure 5 for $c \in [0.65, 4]$. Figure 5 shows a Lyapunov exponent spectrum, in which the eight colored lines represent the eight Lyapunov exponents, the red line represents the first Lyapunov exponent, and the green line represents the second Lyapunov exponent. When the first two Lyapunov exponents are greater than 0 and the third Lyapunov exponent is equal to 0, the system exhibits a hyperchaotic attractor. When the first Lyapunov exponent is greater than 0 and the second Lyapunov exponent is equal to 0, the system exhibits a chaotic attractor. The system exhibits hyperchaotic behavior, with the Lyapunov exponents having the signs (+, +, 0, − , −, −, −, −) when $c \in [0.65, 1]$ [24]. In individual intervals, a few sub-hyperchaotic regions such as $c \in [0.69, 0.695]$ and $c \in [0.94, 0.945]$ can be observed, which have the sign of Lyapunov exponents as (+, 0, 0, −, −, −, −, −). In the region of $c \in [1, 3.3]$, the system exhibits chaotic behavior, with the Lyapunov exponents having the signs (+, 0, −, −, −, −, −, −). In $c \in [3.3, 4]$, the majority of regions exhibit periodic behavior.

The complexity of the attractor can be described by the Kaplan–Yorke dimension, which can be calculated using the following formula:

$$D_{KY} = D + \frac{\sum_{i=1}^{D} LE_i}{|LE_D|} \tag{6}$$

In the hyperchaotic region, which is defined as $c \in [0.65, 1]$, the Kaplan–Yorke dimension falls within the approximate range of $[3.25, 4.5]$. However, for $c \in [1, 4]$, the Kaplan–Yorke dimension is mostly found within the range of $[1.75, 3.25]$.

Table 1. Properties of Lyapunov exponents for ordinary differential dynamical systems.

Dimension and Lyapunov Exponents	Symbol	State
1D (λ)	+	Divergent
1D (λ)	−	Stable fixed point
2D (λ_1, λ_2)	$(-, -)$	Stable fixed point
2D (λ_1, λ_2)	$(0, -)$	Limit cycle
3D ($\lambda_1, \lambda_2, \lambda_3$)	$(-, -, -)$	Stable fixed point
3D ($\lambda_1, \lambda_2, \lambda_3$)	$(0, -, -)$	Limit cycle
3D ($\lambda_1, \lambda_2, \lambda_3$)	$(0, 0, -)$	2D torus
3D ($\lambda_1, \lambda_2, \lambda_3$)	$(+, +, 0)$	Unstable limit cycle
3D ($\lambda_1, \lambda_2, \lambda_3$)	$(+, 0, 0)$	Unstable 2D torus
3D ($\lambda_1, \lambda_2, \lambda_3$)	$(+, 0, -)$	Chaos, strange attractor
4D ($\lambda_1, \lambda_2, \lambda_3, \lambda_4$)	$(+, 0, -, -)$	Chaos, strange attractor
4D ($\lambda_1, \lambda_2, \lambda_3, \lambda_4$)	$(+, 0, 0, -)$	Sub-hyperchaos, strange attractor
4D ($\lambda_1, \lambda_2, \lambda_3, \lambda_4$)	$(+, +, 0, -)$	Hyperchaos, strange attractor
…	…	…
8D ($\lambda_1, \lambda_2, \lambda_3, \lambda_4, \lambda_5, \lambda_6, \lambda_7, \lambda_8$)	$(0, -, -, -, -, -, -, -)$	Limit cycle
8D ($\lambda_1, \lambda_2, \lambda_3, \lambda_4, \lambda_5, \lambda_6, \lambda_7, \lambda_8$)	$(0, 0, -, -, -, -, -, -)$	2D torus
8D ($\lambda_1, \lambda_2, \lambda_3, \lambda_4, \lambda_5, \lambda_6, \lambda_7, \lambda_8$)	$(0, 0, 0, -, -, -, -, -)$	3D torus
8D ($\lambda_1, \lambda_2, \lambda_3, \lambda_4, \lambda_5, \lambda_6, \lambda_7, \lambda_8$)	$(+, 0, -, -, -, -, -, -)$	Chaos, strange attractor
8D ($\lambda_1, \lambda_2, \lambda_3, \lambda_4, \lambda_5, \lambda_6, \lambda_7, \lambda_8$)	$(+, 0, 0, -, -, -, -, -)$	Sub-hyperchaos, strange attractor
8D ($\lambda_1, \lambda_2, \lambda_3, \lambda_4, \lambda_5, \lambda_6, \lambda_7, \lambda_8$)	$(+, +, 0, -, -, -, -, -)$	Hyperchaos, strange attractor

Obtaining the equilibrium points is a crucial step in evaluating a new chaotic system, as it allows for the proper identification of the chaotic nature of the system [25].

Let $\dot{x}_1 = \dot{x}_2 = \dot{x}_3 = \dot{x}_4 = \dot{x}_5 = \dot{x}_6 = \dot{x}_7 = \dot{x}_8 = 0$, that is:

$$\begin{cases} 0 = x_2 - x_1 - \epsilon(\exp(\phi x_7)) + \frac{\rho}{2}\tanh(x_8) \\ 0 = x_3 - x_2 + 3\sin(x_1) - x_1 \\ 0 = 2x_4 - x_3 + \sin(x_5) + x_7 \\ 0 = x_5 - x_4 + \sin\left(\frac{x_7 + x_8}{2}\right) \\ 0 = x_6 - x_5 - \cos(x_3) + \sin(x_1) - \epsilon(\exp(\rho x_7)) + \frac{x_7}{2} \\ 0 = x_7 - x_8 \times 10^{-2} - 3x_4 \\ 0 = x_8 + 2\sin(x_5) + x_5 + \frac{x_6}{2} \\ 0 = -cx_8 - \rho\sinh(\phi x_7) - 8(x_6 + x_5 + x_4 + x_3 + x_2) \end{cases} \tag{7}$$

When $\rho = 1.2 \times 10^{-6}$, $\phi = \frac{1}{0.026}$, $\epsilon = 6 \times 10^{-9}$, $c = 0.75$, the given equilibrium point (0.14, 0.17, −0.11, 0.13, −0.87, −0.18, 0.40, 2.48) has been obtained, and the Jacobian matrix can be computed at these equilibrium points. The Jacobian matrix, denoted as $f'(x)$, represents the derivative of the multidimensional mapping:

$$f'(x) = \frac{\partial f}{\partial x} = \begin{bmatrix} \frac{\partial f_1}{\partial x_1} & \frac{\partial f_1}{\partial x_2} & \cdots & \frac{\partial f_1}{\partial x_8} \\ \frac{\partial f_2}{\partial x_1} & \frac{\partial f_2}{\partial x_2} & \cdots & \frac{\partial f_2}{\partial x_8} \\ \vdots & \vdots & \ddots & \vdots \\ \frac{\partial f_8}{\partial x_1} & \frac{\partial f_8}{\partial x_2} & \cdots & \frac{\partial f_8}{\partial x_8} \end{bmatrix} \tag{8}$$

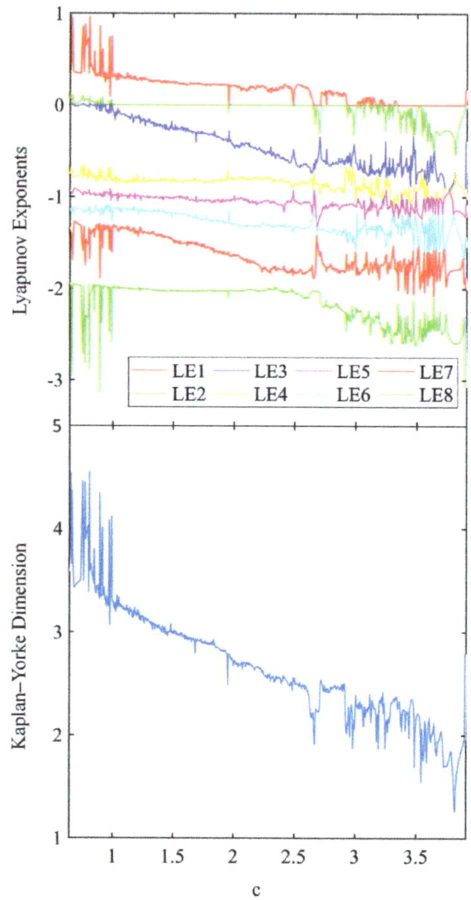

Figure 5. Lyapunov exponent map and Kaplan–Yorke dimension for a novel eighth-order hyperchaotic system.

The eight eigenvalues calculated based on the Jacobian matrix are

$$\begin{aligned} \lambda_1 &= (-0.36 + 13.15i), \\ \lambda_2 &= (-0.36 - 13.15i), \\ \lambda_3 &= 0.52, \\ \lambda_4 &= (0.02 + 1.18i), \\ \lambda_5 &= (0.02 - 1.18i), \\ \lambda_6 &= (-2.39 + 0.23i), \\ \lambda_7 &= (-2.39 - 0.23i), \\ \lambda_8 &= -0.80. \end{aligned} \tag{9}$$

The eigenvalues corresponding to λ_1 and λ_2, λ_4 and λ_5, and λ_6 and λ_7 exhibit a complex conjugate relationship, suggesting a characteristic oscillatory pattern. λ_3 has a positive real part, indicating divergence. λ_8 has a negative real part, indicating convergence.

Among the eight eigenvalues under consideration, it is observed that three of them exhibit instability due to the presence of eigenvalues with positive real parts. This implies that any perturbation introduced into the system will amplify over time, leading to a loss of stability at the equilibrium point. Conversely, the remaining five eigenvalues exhibit negative real components, indicating that any disturbance introduced into the system will gradually diminish, thereby preserving the stability of the equilibrium point [26].

The divergence formula for this system is as follows:

$$\nabla \cdot F = \frac{\partial \dot{x}_1}{\partial x_1} + \frac{\partial \dot{x}_2}{\partial x_2} + \cdots + \frac{\partial \dot{x}_8}{\partial x_8} \tag{10}$$

The divergence in this system is -5.74. Generally, the divergence of the hyperchaotic system is found to be negative, indicating that the system is a dissipative system.

3. Encryption and Decryption Scheme

The encryption scheme uses two chaotic sequences generated by the novel eighth-order hyperchaotic system Equation (5) when $c = 1.5$ and $c = 1.4$, which is used to enhance the security of images. The proposed scheme in this study involves row scrambling, column scrambling, and diffusing using chaotic sequence A ($c = 1.5$), as well as diffusing, column scrambling, and row scrambling using chaotic sequence B ($c = 1.4$). The encryption algorithm and decryption algorithm are shown in Algorithms 1 and 2.

Encryption Algorithm:

1. Calculate the chaotic sequence A according to the novel eighth-order hyperchaotic system when $c = 1.5$ and initial values are $(0.1, 0.1, 0.1, 0.1, 0.1, 0.1, 0.1, 0.1)$.
2. Calculate the *Key* by the average value of a matrix generated by original image.
3. Obtain the pixels of the original image and divide the original image into three channels of R, G, B.
4. Calculate the index s_A and c_A from the chaotic sequence A with different keys, where

$$\begin{cases} s_i = x_8(i) \times 10^8 - \lfloor x_8(i) \times 10^8 \rfloor \\ c_i = mod\left(x_3(i) \times 10^5 - \lfloor x_3(i) \times 10^5 \rfloor + \left| x_3(i) \times 10^8 - round(x_3(i) \times 10^8) \right|, 256\right) \end{cases} \tag{11}$$

5. Utilize the index s_A based on $2 \times Key$ to perform row scrambling on the output images of the three channels from Step 3.
6. Utilize the index s_A based on $3 \times Key$ to perform column scrambling on the output images of the three channels from Step 5.
7. Perform XOR operation on the index c_A and the image pixel value from Step 6.
8. Calculate the chaotic sequence B according to the novel eighth-order hyperchaotic system when $c = 1.4$ and initial values are $(0.1, 0.1, 0.1, 0.1, 0.1, 0.1, 0.1, 0.1)$.
9. Calculate the index s_B and c_B from the chaotic sequence B with the same formula from Step 4.
10. Perform XOR operation on the index c_B and the image pixel value from Step 7.
11. Utilize the index s_B based on $3 \times Key$ to perform column scrambling on the output images of the three channels in Step 10.
12. Utilize the index s_B based on $2 \times Key$ to perform row scrambling on the output images of the three channels in Step 11.
13. Merge the encrypted images of the three channels to generate the final encrypted image.

Algorithm 1 Encryption Algorithm

Input: Original Image (Org_Img), First initial conditions, Control parameters,
Output: Encrypted image (En_Img)

```
[m, n] ← size(Org_Img)
Avg_pixel_value ← mean2(Org_Img) × 10^-9    ▷ mean2 is a function that returns the average value of a matrix
paraset(x1, x2, x3, x4, x5, x6, x7, x8)    ▷ First round of encryption
function SEQ(x1, x2, x3, x4, x5, x6, x7, x8, Runge − Kutta, Avg_pixel_value)
    x1(1) ← x1(1) + Avg_pixel_value
    for i = 1 to 10 × m × n do
        [dx, dy, dz, du] ← Runge-Kutta(x(i), y(i), z(i), u(i))
        x1(i + 1) ← x1(i) + dx1
        x2(i + 1) ← x2(i) + dx2
        x3(i + 1) ← x3(i) + dx3
        x4(i + 1) ← x4(i) + dx4
        x5(i + 1) ← x5(i) + dx5
        x6(i + 1) ← x6(i) + dx6
        x7(i + 1) ← x7(i) + dx7
        x8(i + 1) ← x8(i) + dx8
        if mod(i, 10) = 0 then
            s_i = x8(i) × 10^8 − ⌊x8(i) × 10^8⌋
            t = |x3(i) × 10^8 − round(x3(i) × 10^8)|
            c_i = mod(x3(i) × 10^5 − ⌊x3(i) × 10^5⌋ + t, 256)
        end if
    end for
    return s, c
end function
s1 ← SEQ(x1, x2, x3, x4, x5, x6, x7, x8, m, n, Runge-Kutta1, 2 × Avg_pixel_value)    ▷ Using chaotic sequence A
s2 ← SEQ(x1, x2, x3, x4, x5, x6, x7, x8, m, n, Runge-Kutta1, 3 × Avg_pixel_value)
c ← SEQ(x1, x2, x3, x4, x5, x6, x7, x8, m, n, Runge-Kutta1, Avg_pixel_value)
S_index_1 ← Sort(s1)
S_index_2 ← Sort(s2)
Org_per_row ← confuse_row(Org_Img, S_index_1)
Org_per_col ← confuse_col(Org_per_row, S_index_2)
En_Img1 ← difuse(m, n, Org_per_col, c)

paraset(x1, x2, x3, x4, x5, x6, x7, x8)    ▷ Second round of encryption
x1(1) ← x1(1) + Avg_pixel_value
s1 ← SEQ(x1, x2, x3, x4, x5, x6, x7, x8, m, n, Runge-Kutta2, 2 × Avg_pixel_value)    ▷ Using chaotic sequence B
s2 ← SEQ(x1, x2, x3, x4, x5, x6, x7, x8, m, n, Runge-Kutta2, 3 × Avg_pixel_value)
c ← SEQ(x1, x2, x3, x4, x5, x6, x7, x8, m, n, Runge-Kutta2, Avg_pixel_value)
S_index_1 ← Sort(s1)
S_index_2 ← Sort(s2)
En_dif1 ← difuse(m, n, En_Img1, c)
En_per_col1 ← confuse(n, m, En_dif1, S_index_2)
En_per_row1 ← confuse(m, n, En1_per_col1, S_index_1)
```

Decryption Algorithm:

1. Calculate the chaotic sequence B according to the novel eighth-order hyperchaotic system when $c = 1.4$ and initial values are $(0.1, 0.1, 0.1, 0.1, 0.1, 0.1, 0.1, 0.1)$.
2. Obtain the pixels of the original image and divide the original image into three channels of R, G, B.
3. Calculate the index s_B and c_B from the chaotic sequence B with different keys.
4. Utilize the index s_B based on $2 \times Key$ to perform row recovery on the output images of the three channels from Step 2.
5. Utilize the index s_B based on $3 \times Key$ to perform column recovery on the output images of the three channels from Step 4.
6. Perform XOR operation on the index c_A and the image pixel value from Step 5.
7. Calculate the chaotic sequence A according to the novel eighth-order hyperchaotic system when $c = 1.5$ and initial values are $(0.1, 0.1, 0.1, 0.1, 0.1, 0.1, 0.1, 0.1)$.
8. Calculate the index s_A and c_A from the chaotic sequence A with different keys.
9. Perform XOR operation on the index c_A and the image pixel value from Step 6.
10. Utilize the index s_A based on $3 \times Key$ to perform column recovery on the output images of the three channels from Step 9.
11. Utilize the index s_A based on $2 \times Key$ to perform row recovery on the output images of the three channels from Step 10.
12. Merge the decrypted images of the three channels to generate the final decrypted image.

Algorithm 2 Decryption Algorithm

Input: Encrypted Image (En_Img), First initial conditions, Control parameters, Avg_pixel_value of (Org_Img)
Output: Original image (Org_Img)

$[m, n] \leftarrow \text{size}(En\_Img)$
$\text{paraset}(x_1, x_2, x_3, x_4, x_5, x_6, x_7, x_8)$ ▷ First round of decryption
$x_1(1) \leftarrow x_1(1) + Avg\_pixel\_value$
$s_1 \leftarrow \text{SEQ}(x_1, x_2, x_3, x_4, x_5, x_6, x_7, x_8, m, n, \text{Runge-Kutta2}, 2 \times Avg\_pixel\_value)$ ▷ Using chaotic sequence B
$s_2 \leftarrow \text{SEQ}(x_1, x_2, x_3, x_4, x_5, x_6, x_7, x_8, m, n, \text{Runge-Kutta2}, 3 \times Avg\_pixel\_value)$
$c \leftarrow \text{SEQ}(x_1, x_2, x_3, x_4, x_5, x_6, x_7, x_8, m, n, \text{Runge-Kutta2}, Avg\_pixel\_value)$
$S\_index\_1 \leftarrow \text{Sort}(s_1)$
$S\_index\_2 \leftarrow \text{Sort}(s_2)$
$En\_per\_row \leftarrow$ confuse_row(En_Img, S_index_1)
$En\_per\_col \leftarrow$ confuse_col(En_per_row, S_index_2)
$En\_Img1 \leftarrow$ difuse(m, n, En_per_col, c)

$\text{paraset}(x_1, x_2, x_3, x_4, x_5, x_6, x_7, x_8)$ ▷ Second round of decryption
$s_1 \leftarrow \text{SEQ}(x_1, x_2, x_3, x_4, x_5, x_6, x_7, x_8, m, n, \text{Runge-Kutta1}, 2 \times Avg\_pixel\_value)$ ▷ Using chaotic sequence A
$s_2 \leftarrow \text{SEQ}(x_1, x_2, x_3, x_4, x_5, x_6, x_7, x_8, m, n, \text{Runge-Kutta1}, 3 \times Avg\_pixel\_value)$
$c \leftarrow \text{SEQ}(x_1, x_2, x_3, x_4, x_5, x_6, x_7, x_8, m, n, \text{Runge-Kutta1}, Avg\_pixel\_value)$
$S\_index\_1 \leftarrow \text{Sort}(s_1)$
$S\_index\_2 \leftarrow \text{Sort}(s_2)$
$En\_dif1 \leftarrow$ difuse(m, n, En_Img1, c)
$En\_per\_col1 \leftarrow$ confuse_col(En_dif1, S_index_2)
$Org\_Img \leftarrow$ confuse_row(En1_per_col1, S_index_1)

The steps of the encryption and decryption scheme are shown in Figures 6 and 7.

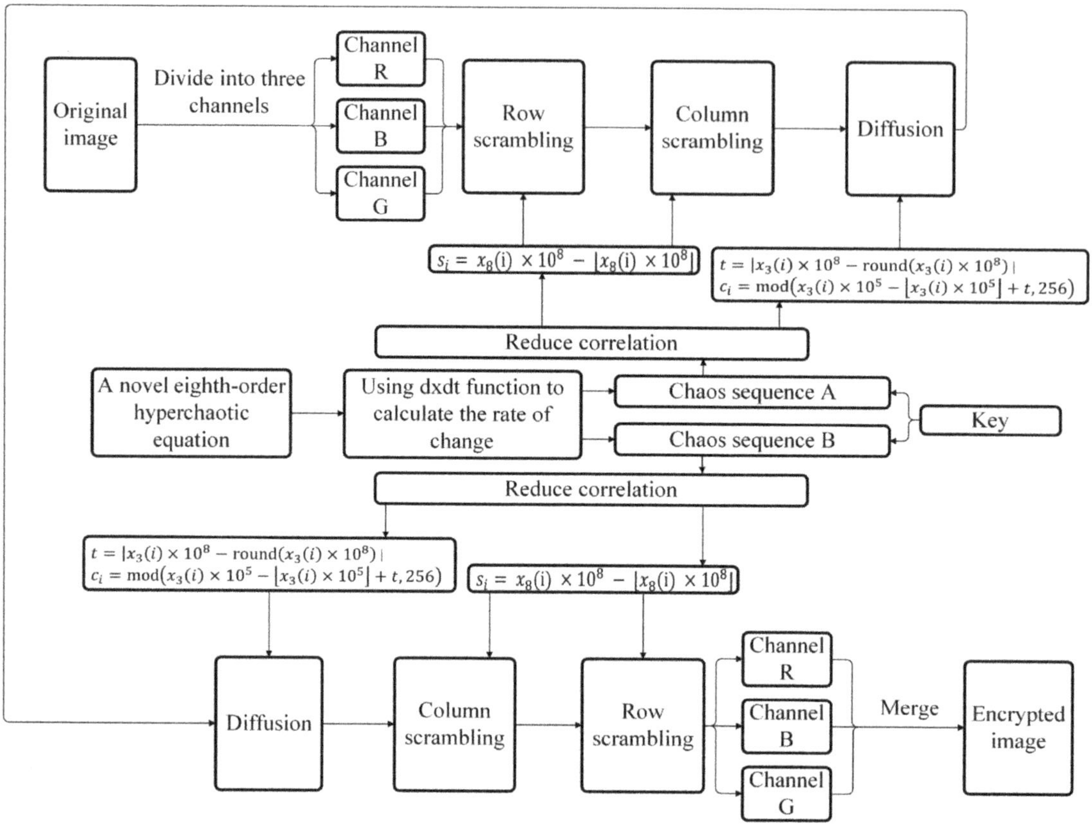

Figure 6. Scheme of image encryption.

Encryption time, particularly for chaos-based encryption algorithms, determines whether they can be employed in practice [27]. On a computer running Matlab 2022 and equipped with a 3.2 GHz Core R7-5800 U CPU, the speed of the proposed method is evaluated. This test uses a 512 × 512-pixel Lena image. Scrambling and diffusion have running times of 3.0608 and 3.1810 s, respectively. The chaotic sequence generation takes 3.0403 s to complete, while one round of encryption takes 9.5131 s. Since the proposed encryption scheme employs a serial encryption method and has a large key space, which takes longer than other references, a significant amount of effort is required to convert a serial approach to a parallel one and fully utilize the enormous processing power of GPUs [28]. The result of the experiment is that it is evident that there is still room for improvement in the encryption algorithm.

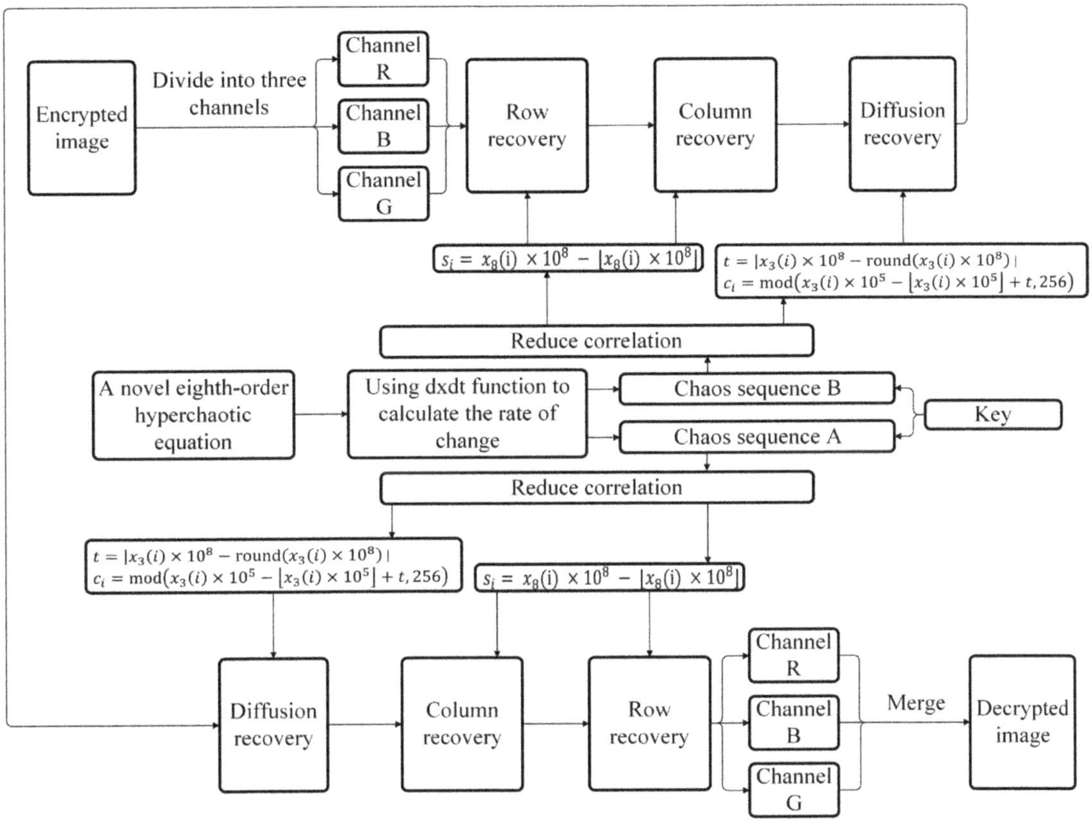

Figure 7. Scheme of image decryption.

4. Experiments with Related Security Analysis

4.1. Experimental Results

The following is an experimental analysis of the image encryption algorithm proposed in this paper. The experiment involves the use of eight color images, each consisting of 512 × 512 pixels, as depicted in Figure 8. The original images are shown in (a). The encrypted images are shown in (b)–(e), and the decrypted images are shown in (f)–(i).

The result of encrypting a gray image (512 × 512 Lena) is shown in Figure 9, indicating that the image encryption algorithm is also effective for gray images.

4.2. Histogram Analysis

A histogram is a visual representation that provides an estimation of the distribution of numerical data. It involves plotting the number of pixels at each intensity level to understand the distribution of pixels in an image [29]. To ensure resistance against statistical attacks, the histograms of both the original images and encrypted images need to be described [30].

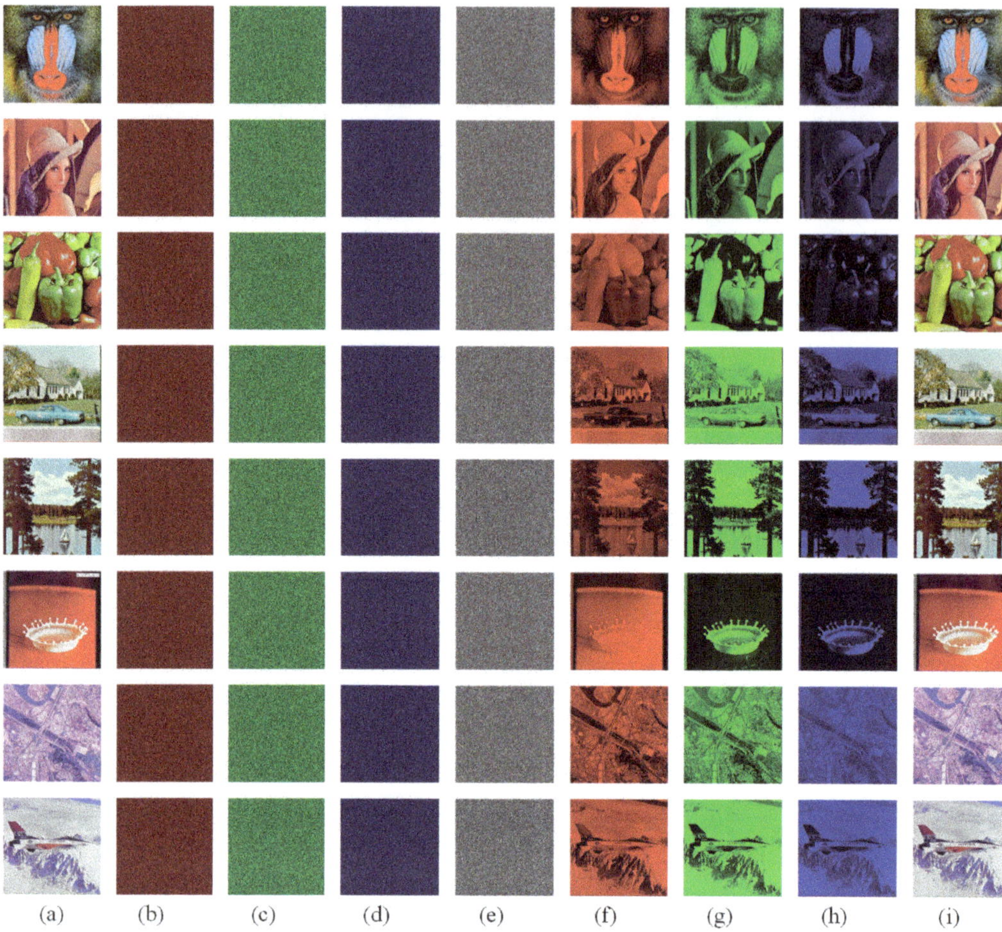

Figure 8. Image encryption and decryption results: (**a**) original image; (**b**–**d**) encrypted images of three channels of R, G, B; (**e**) encrypted images of three channels combined; (**f**–**h**) decrypted images of three channels of R, G, B; (**i**) decrypted images of three channels combined.

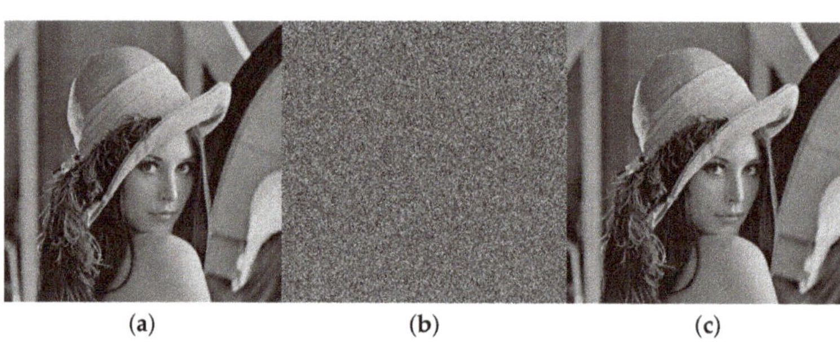

Figure 9. Gray image encryption and decryption results: (**a**) original image; (**b**) encrypted image; (**c**) decrypted image.

In order to quantitatively analyze histograms, the experiment uses variances of histograms to assess the uniformity of the encrypted images. Lower variance values indicate a higher level of uniformity in the encrypted images. The formula for calculating the variance of the histograms is as follows [22]:

$$\mathrm{var}(Z) = \frac{1}{n^2} \sum_{i=1}^{n} \sum_{j=1}^{n} \frac{1}{2}(z_i - z_j)^2 \tag{12}$$

where Z is the variance of the histogram, and z_i and z_j are the number of pixels i and j in a single channel. In the encryption experiment on the Lena image, the variance of the R channel of the plain image is 770811 and the variance of the R channel of the encrypted image is 262719; the variance of the G channel of the plain image is 490003 and the variance of the G channel of the encrypted image is 262718; the variance of the B channel of the plain image is 950821 and the variance of the B channel of the encrypted image is 262592, the variance of the gray channel of the plain image is 578833 and the variance of the gray channel of the encrypted image is 262698.

Figure 10 is the comparison of the original image and the encrypted image histogram.

Through the calculation of the variance and the analysis of the histogram, the histogram shows the distribution characteristics among the pixels. The encrypted image data of an ideal encryption scheme should be uniformly distributed, which can effectively prevent attackers from obtaining valid information from encrypted images [31], and effectively resist statistical attacks.

4.3. Key Space Analysis

The utilization of a substantial key space has the capability to effectively thwart brute force attacks, thereby mitigating the potential vulnerability of data decryption [32].

If the calculated resolution is 10^{15}, for variable x_1, the area of attraction domain is $x_1 \in [-1.88, -0.98]$, there are $0.89 \times 10^{15} = 0.89 \times 10^{15}$ kinds of choices. There are 1.17×10^{15} choices for x_2, 1.95×10^{15} choices for x_3, 1.16×10^{15} choices for x_4, 2.62×10^{15} choices for x_5, 3.78×10^{15} choices for x_6, 1.04×10^{15} choices for x_7, and 1.41×10^{16} choices for x_8. The size of the key space formed by the control variables is $0.89 \times 10^{15} \times 1.17 \times 10^{15} \times 1.95 \times 10^{15} \times 1.16 \times 10^{15} \times 2.62 \times 10^{15} \times 3.78 \times 10^{15} \times 1.04 \times 10^{15} \times 1.41 \times 10^{16} = 3.45 \times 10^{123}$. Consider only one control variable c in Equation (5), the key space of the system is $3.45 \times 10^{123} \times 2.7 \times 10^{15} = 9.32 \times 10^{138}$. When only the first-order term with a coefficient of 1 in the hyperchaotic equation is considered as the control variable, the key space of the system is 8.2×10^{351}. Additionally, the proposed encryption scheme involves two rounds of encryption based on the hyperchaotic system with different control variables, thus the key space is $8.2 \times 10^{351} \times 8.2 \times 10^{351} = 6.72 \times 10^{703} \approx 2^{2338}$. The actual key space of this scheme will be extremely larger than that value.

4.4. Correlation Analysis

Correlation refers to a statistical association, regardless of causality, between two random variables or sets of bivariate data. In the context of encryption algorithms, it is desirable for encrypted images with low-pixel correlation to be resistant to cryptographic attacks based on statistical analysis [33]. Therefore, a comprehensive understanding of correlations is essential in order to enhance the robustness and effectiveness of image encryption techniques [34].

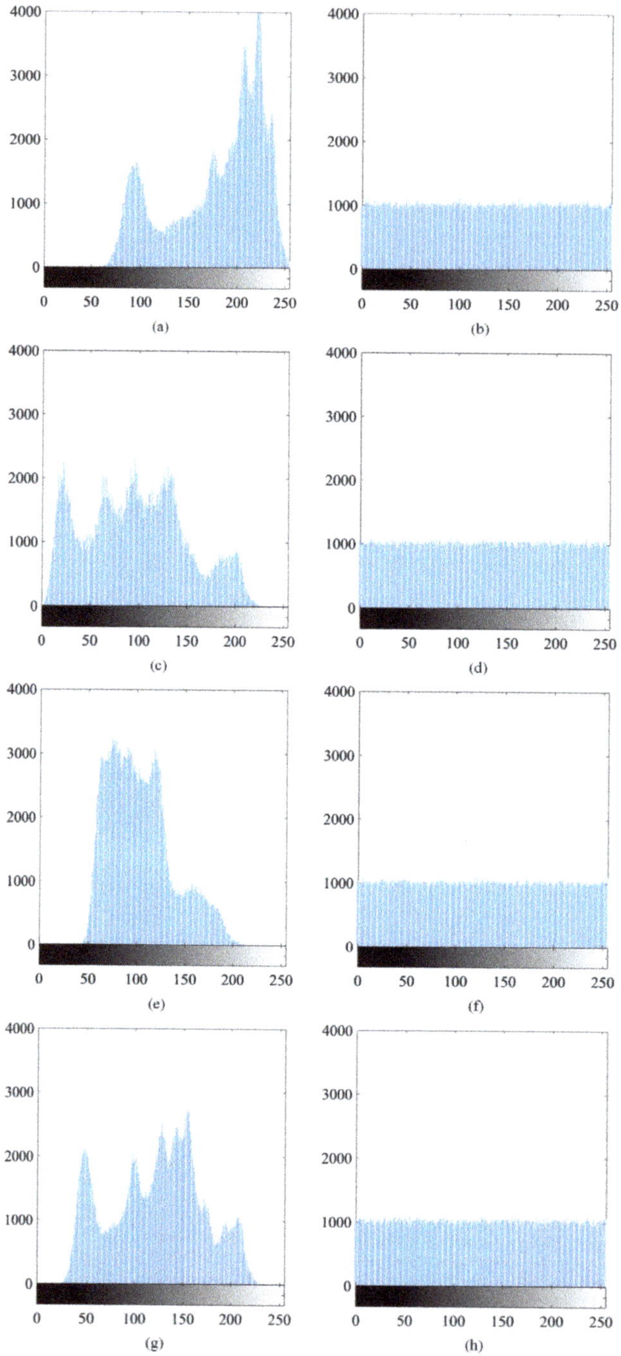

Figure 10. Comparison of the histograms of the original image and the encrypted image: (**a**,**c**,**e**,**g**) the histogram of the R, G, B, gray channel of the original image; (**b**,**d**,**f**,**h**) the histogram of the R, G, B, gray channel of the encrypted image.

To calculate the correlation, the following formula is used [35]:

$$\begin{cases} \mathrm{E}(u) = \dfrac{1}{N}\sum\limits_{i=1}^{N} u_i \\ \mathrm{D}(u) = \dfrac{1}{N}\sum\limits_{i=1}^{N} (u_i - E(u))^2 \\ \mathrm{cov}(u,v) = \dfrac{1}{N}\sum\limits_{i=1}^{N} (x_i - E(u))(y_i - E(v)) \\ \mathrm{r}_{xy} = \dfrac{\mathrm{cov}(u,v)}{\sqrt{\mathrm{D}(u)\cdot\mathrm{D}(v)}} \end{cases} \quad (13)$$

In order to present the importance of correlation more intuitively, Table 2 below will show the pixel value correlation analysis results of eight color images. Table 2 also displays the correlation to a gray house image, indicating that the encryption algorithm still works with gray images.

Table 2. Correlation coefficient of original images, the first round of encrypted images, and the second round of encrypted images.

Image	Original Image			First Round of Encrypted Image			Second Round of Encrypted Image		
	Horiz.	Vert.	Diag.	Horiz.	Vert.	Diag.	Horiz.	Vert.	Diag.
Mandrill	R 0.9123	0.8625	0.8505	0.0097	0.0084	0.0085	0.0079	0.0113	0.0122
	G 0.8628	0.7811	0.7496	0.0149	0.0108	0.0105	0.0097	0.0126	0.0126
	B 0.8965	0.8712	0.8314	0.0100	0.0135	0.0129	0.0123	0.0131	0.0110
Lena	R 0.9808	0.9898	0.9712	0.0093	0.0090	0.0140	0.0133	0.0103	0.0120
	G 0.9695	0.9827	0.9561	0.0140	0.0095	0.0145	0.0109	0.0089	0.0091
	B 0.9352	0.9591	0.9212	0.0109	0.0069	0.0153	0.0101	0.0107	0.0120
Peppers	R 0.9650	0.9677	0.9582	0.0090	0.0115	0.0101	0.0132	0.0083	0.0117
	G 0.9813	0.9819	0.9689	0.0106	0.0102	0.0098	0.0110	0.0127	0.0096
	B 0.9668	0.9667	0.9483	0.0137	0.0017	0.0082	0.0105	0.0136	0.0091
House	R 0.9552	0.9591	0.9252	0.0129	0.0098	0.0139	0.0118	0.0086	0.0136
	G 0.9405	0.9445	0.8951	0.0135	0.0061	0.0102	0.0107	0.0059	0.0109
	B 0.9728	0.9691	0.9456	0.0109	0.0090	0.0090	0.0136	0.0128	0.0112
Lake	R 0.9574	0.9557	0.9440	0.0105	0.0120	0.0156	0.0131	0.0132	0.0121
	G 0.9718	0.9666	0.9534	0.0140	0.0110	0.0129	0.0131	0.0119	0.0104
	B 0.9713	0.9697	0.9534	0.0117	0.0097	0.0117	0.0118	0.0148	0.0080
Splash	R 0.9938	0.9953	0.9898	0.0108	0.0077	0.0105	0.0103	0.0099	0.0090
	G 0.9812	0.9872	0.9713	0.0105	0.0054	0.0137	0.0114	0.0110	0.0129
	B 0.9826	0.9792	0.9653	0.0112	0.0029	0.0097	0.0137	0.0127	0.0115
San Diego	R 0.8539	0.8395	0.7770	0.0108	0.0072	0.0113	0.0132	0.0139	0.0092
	G 0.7933	0.7719	0.6943	0.0080	0.0098	0.0101	0.0108	0.0143	0.0086
	B 0.7930	0.7728	0.7055	0.0094	0.0069	0.0121	0.0118	0.0140	0.0096
Jetplane	R 0.9738	0.9593	0.9382	0.0132	0.0102	0.0112	0.0108	0.0126	0.0118
	G 0.9596	0.9691	0.9356	0.0137	0.0135	0.0115	0.0104	0.0117	0.0105
	B 0.9673	0.9431	0.9249	0.0121	0.0068	0.0139	0.0119	0.0110	0.0110
House (gray)	0.9503	0.9592	0.9172	0.0137	0.0086	0.0127	0.0100	0.0076	0.0104

It is evident that the correlation value of the original image is close to 1, while the horizontal, vertical, and diagonal correlations of the encrypted image are close to 0 [36]. These values indicate that the correlation between adjacent pixels of the encrypted image is very weak.

Figure 11, Figure 12, and Figure 13, respectively, show the original image, the first round of encrypted image, and the second round of encrypted image in the horizontal, vertical, and diagonal directions of pixel correlation sex. It can be seen from Figure 11 that, since the pixels of the original image are highly correlated, most points in these three directions align with the 45° line. Meanwhile, Figures 12 and 13 show that these points are distributed in the whole area, reflecting the weak pixel correlation in the encrypted image. Therefore, the algorithm proves that it is effective against attacks such as statistical attacks.

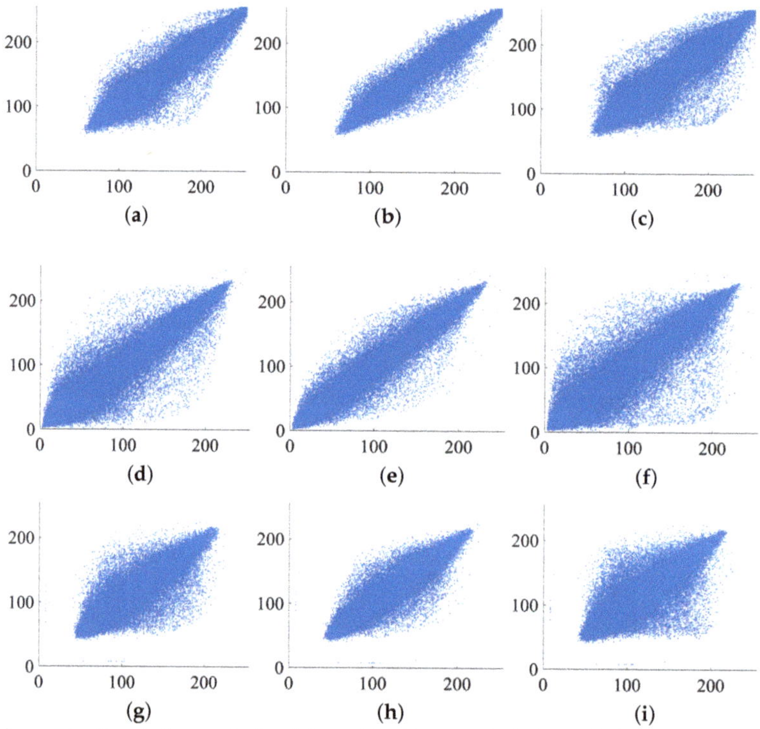

Figure 11. Correlation analysis of the original image: (**a**,**d**,**g**) correlation between pixels in the horizontal direction of the R, G, B channel of the original image; (**b**,**e**,**h**) correlation between pixels in the vertical direction of the R, G, B channel of the original image; (**c**,**f**,**i**) correlation between pixels in the diagonal direction of the R, G, B channel of the original image.

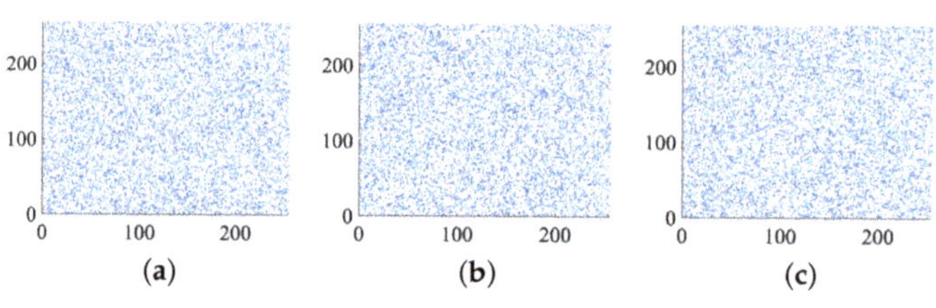

Figure 12. *Cont.*

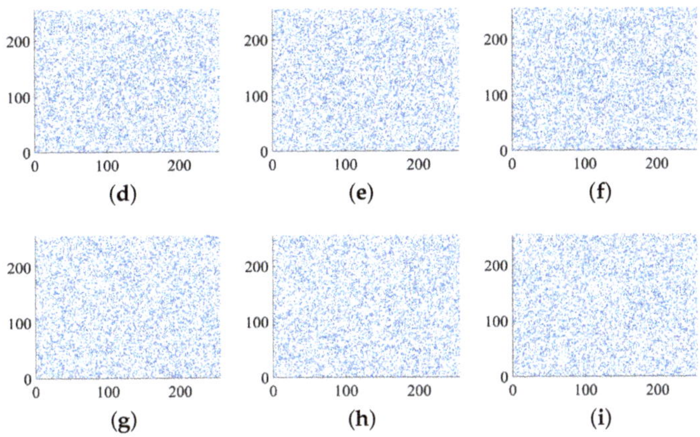

Figure 12. Correlation analysis of the first round of encrypted image: (**a**,**d**,**g**) correlation between pixels in the horizontal direction of the R, G, B channel of the first round of encrypted image; (**b**,**e**,**h**) correlation between pixels in the vertical direction of the R, G, B channel of the first round of encrypted image; (**c**,**f**,**i**) correlation between pixels in the diagonal direction of the R, G, B channel of the first round of encrypted image.

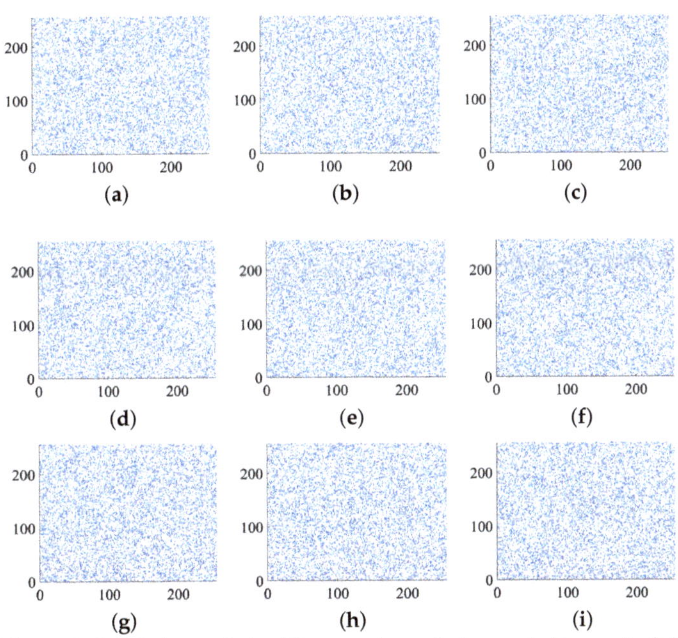

Figure 13. Correlation analysis of the second round of encrypted image: (**a**,**d**,**g**) correlation between pixels in the horizontal direction of the R, G, B channel of the second round of encrypted image; (**b**,**e**,**h**) correlation between pixels in the vertical direction of the R, G, B channel of the second round of encrypted image; (**c**,**f**,**i**) correlation between pixels in the diagonal direction of the R, G, B channel of the second round of encrypted image.

4.5. Entropy

To measure the expected value of a message and the unpredictability of information content, information entropy (IE) is usually taken to test the strength of a designed encryption algorithm [37], which is defined in Equation (14) for a received message m. The theoretical value of the information entropy is 8 [38].

$$IE(m) = \sum_{j=0}^{2^L-1} p(m_j)\log_2\left(\frac{1}{p(m_j)}\right) \tag{14}$$

where L is the length of pixel value in binary form (for images in this experiment, L = 9), $p(m_j)$ denotes the probability of the occurrence of the symbol m_j, and log_2 represents the base 2 algorithm. Table 3 is a comparison of the information entropy of the original image and the encrypted image of the eight color images and a gray house image.

Table 3. Entropy of original image, the first round of encrypted image, and the second round of encrypted image.

Image	Result		
	Original Image	First Round of Encrypted Image	Second Round of Encrypted Image
Mandrill	7.1073	7.9998	7.9998
Lena	7.7502	7.9998	7.9998
Peppers	7.6698	7.9997	7.9998
House	7.4858	7.9998	7.9998
Lake	7.7622	7.9997	7.9998
Splash	7.2428	7.9997	7.9997
San Diego	7.3311	7.9998	7.9998
Jetplane	6.6639	7.9997	7.9997
House (gray)	7.2334	7.9993	7.7993

4.6. MSE and PSNR Analysis

The most common metric for evaluating the effectiveness of lossy image compression codecs is PSNR. The correct determination of the spatial alignment and level offset between the encrypted picture sequence and the original image sequence is crucial to the PSNR calculation [39]. Given a noise-free m × n monochrome image I and its noisy approximation K, MSE and PSNR are defined as [40]

$$\text{MSE} = \frac{1}{mn}\sum_{i=1}^{m}\sum_{j=1}^{m}[I(i,j) - K(i,j)]^2 \tag{15}$$

$$\text{PSNR} = 10 \cdot \log_{10}\left(\frac{MAX_I^2}{MSE}\right) \tag{16}$$

where MAX_I is the maximum possible pixel value of the image. When samples are represented using linear PCM with B bits per sample, MAX_I is $2^B - 1$. In this paper, the pixels are represented using 8 bits per sample, and MAX_I is 255.

Table 4 shows the comparison of MSE and PSNR. To reduce the probability of assaults, a lower PSNR value and a higher MSE value are preferred [2]. As a result, it is clear that the PSNR values computed for encrypted pictures using the proposed scheme are comparable to or better than those obtained from other schemes in the literature [41].

Table 4. MSE and PSNR comparison.

Image	MSE	PSNR
Mandrill	8773	8.6994
Lena	8923	8.6256
Peppers	10129	8.0751
House	9252	8.4686
Lake	10099	8.0880
Splash	11252	7.6183
San Diego	8480	8.8469
Jetplane	10360	7.9772
House (gray)	8955	8.6103
Ref. [41]	8353	8.9272
Ref. [42]	7274	9.55
Ref. [43]	8332	8.9331

4.7. Ablation Analysis

The ablation analysis shows the improvement in encryption due to two rounds of encryption. The experiment can be divided into four cases and the result is demonstrated in Table 5.

Table 5. Ablation analysis.

Method	Key Space	Entropy	CC				NPCR (%)				UACI (%)			
			R	G	B	Cipher	R	G	B	Cipher	R	G	B	Cipher
Case 1	$> 2^{1169}$	7.9997	0.0107	0.0118	0.0105	0.0079	99.6391	99.6391	99.6391	99.6391	33.4310	33.4089	33.4219	33.4206
Case 2	$> 2^{1169}$	7.4858	0.0368	0.0446	0.0195	0.0079	99.3141	99.1238	99.2275	99.2218	22.0984	20.2759	27.1392	23.1712
Case 3	$> 2^{1169}$	7.9998	0.0107	0.0111	0.0105	0.0069	99.5838	99.6136	99.6048	99.6007	33.4498	33.4860	33.4681	33.4680
Case 4	$> 2^{1169}$	7.9998	0.0122	0.0099	0.0096	0.0067	99.6098	99.6238	99.6055	99.6131	33.4417	33.3564	33.2640	33.3541
Proposed	$> 2^{2338}$	7.9998	0.0113	0.0092	0.0125	0.0072	99.6162	99.6086	99.6048	99.6099	33.4552	33.4399	33.4081	33.4344

Case 1: Proposed method without scrambling.
Case 2: Proposed method without diffusion.
Case 3: Proposed method without the first round of encryption.
Case 4: Proposed method without the second round of encryption.

It can be seen from the table that, when encryption is performed without diffusion operation, the pixel correlation of the scheme is substantially higher than the proposed scheme, and the UACI is likewise far away from the theoretical value. Without scrambling operations or without one of the rounds being used for encryption, these data are within a respectable range, but the primary benefit of the proposed scheme with two rounds of encryption is the extremely large key space.

4.8. Key Sensitivity Analysis

Key sensitivity analysis is a cryptographic evaluation method that assesses the significance and security of an algorithm [35]. It ensures that even a slight modification to the key will render the original flat image irrecoverable [2].

This encryption system demonstrates a high level of sensitivity to the key. By maintaining constant control variables and initial conditions, a small increment of 10^{-14} is added to the key within the scheme. Consequently, the encrypted image exhibits significant differences between the two variables over time, displaying pseudo-random characteristics. This observation suggests that the system's key is highly sensitive to initial conditions. To illustrate this sensitivity, two similar images are encrypted using keys with minute differences. Figure 14 shows the waveform of x_1 and $x_1 + \Delta x$ over time and their difference.

After performing the subtraction of the encrypted images, it is clearly seen from Figure 15 that the resulting images exhibit significant dissimilarities.

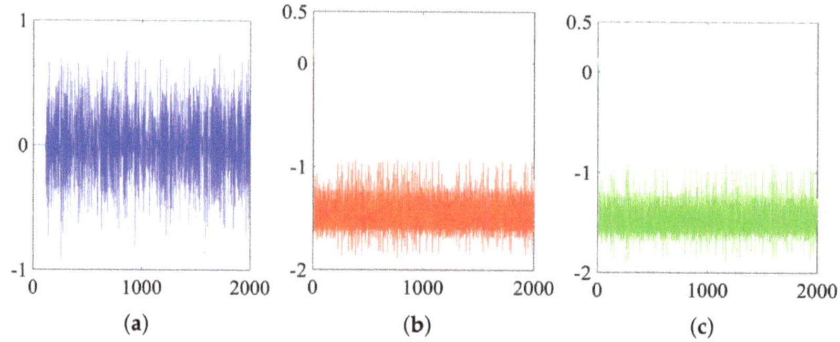

Figure 14. (**a**) The difference waveform of x_1 and $x_1 + \Delta x$ over time; (**b**) the values of $x_1 + \Delta x$ over time; (**c**) the values of x_1 over time.

Figure 15. Key sensitivity test: (**a**) the difference between the twice encrypted image of the R channel of images; (**b**) the difference between the twice encrypted image of the G channel of images; (**c**) the difference between the twice encrypted image of the R channel of images; (**d**) the difference between the twice encrypted images of three channels of images.

Key sensitivity analysis is usually performed based on the following two indicators: one is the number of pixels rate of change (NPCR), and the other is the uniform average intensity of change (UACI). These two indicators are defined as [44]

$$\text{NPCR} = \sum_{i=1}^{N}\sum_{j=1}^{M} \frac{D(i,j)}{M \times N} \times 100\% \quad (17)$$

$$\text{UACI} = \sum_{i=1}^{N}\sum_{j=1}^{M} \frac{|C_1(i,j) - C_2(i,j)|}{T \times M \times N} \times 100\% \quad (18)$$

$$\text{D(i, j)} = \begin{cases} 0, & \text{if } C_1(i,j) = C_2(i,j) \\ 1, & \text{if } C_1(i,j) \neq C_2(i,j) \end{cases} \quad (19)$$

where C_1 and C_2 are two encrypted images of size $M \times N$, and T denotes the largest allowed pixel intensity.

NPCR and UACI are theoretically 99.6043% and 33.4635% [45]. The data presented in Tables 6 and 7 demonstrates that the test value of the algorithm exhibits a high degree of proximity to the ideal value, indicating a strong level of key sensitivity. In summary, this scheme has high key sensitivity.

Table 6. NPCR of three channels in key sensitivity analysis.

Image	NPCR (%)		
	R	G	B
Mandrill	99.5930	99.6330	99.6113
Lena	99.5811	99.6162	99.6052
Peppers	99.6048	99.6021	99.6140
House	99.6162	99.6086	99.6048
Lake	99.6273	99.6307	99.6063
Splash	99.6078	99.5998	99.6201
San Diego	99.6117	99.6071	99.6025
Jetplane	99.6128	99.6227	99.6158
Lena (gray)		99.6017	

Table 7. UACI of three channels in key sensitivity analysis.

Image	UACI (%)		
	R	G	B
Mandrill	33.4605	33.4560	33.5050
Lena	33.3818	33.5105	33.4385
Peppers	33.4500	33.5263	33.5738
House	33.4552	33.4399	33.4081
Lake	33.5367	33.4740	33.3750
Splash	33.4298	33.4887	33.5137
San Diego	33.4646	33.4861	33.4083
Jetplane	33.5527	33.5670	33.5132
Lena (gray)		33.4496	

4.9. *Differential Attack*

To avoid differential attacks, a secure cryptosystem should be sensitive to plaintext [46], indicating that even minor alterations in the pixel values of a regular image can result in significant modifications in the corresponding encrypted image [47]. Figure 16 shows the results of differential attack experiments.

Tables 8 and 9 show the NPCR and UACI of the differential attack. The test results indicate a strong correlation between the system's value and the theoretical value, suggesting that the system is capable of effectively defending against differential attacks.

Table 8. NPCR of three channels in differential attack experiments.

Image	NPCR (%)		
	R	G	B
Mandril	99.6174	99.6136	99.6025
Lena	99.6105	99.6212	99.6162
Peppers	99.6204	99.6208	99.6262
House	99.5785	99.6117	99.6040
Lake	99.5979	99.6178	99.6166
Splash	99.6227	99.6246	99.6002
San Diego	99.6059	99.6071	99.5972
Jetplane	99.6254	99.6002	99.6227
Lena (gray)		99.6249	

Table 9. UACI of three channels in differential attack experiments.

Image	UACI (%)		
	R	G	B
Mandrill	33.4335	33.4402	33.4821
Lena	33.4898	33.4291	33.4875
Peppers	33.4562	33.4732	33.5182
House	33.4944	33.4663	33.5236
Lake	33.4197	33.5304	33.4407
Splash	33.4215	33.5089	33.4760
San Diego	33.4363	33.4986	33.4557
Jetplane	33.5001	33.4588	33.5305
Lena (gray)		33.4892	

Figure 16. Differential attack test: (**a**) the difference between the twice encrypted image of the R channel of images; (**b**) the difference between the twice encrypted image of the G channel of images; (**c**) the difference between the twice encrypted image of the R channel of images; (**d**) the difference between the twice encrypted images of three channels of images.

4.10. Cropping Attack

A robust cryptographic system should have the capability to resist potential data loss during transmission and storage [48]. The receiver wants to recover the plain image as much as possible from some of the information received in this case [33]. Thus, the analysis of cropping attacks is a valuable approach to assessing the robustness of encryption schemes [49].

For evaluating and comparing the performance of different encryption algorithms in the face of cropping attacks, a series of experiments is conducted, and the following comparative illustrations are produced. As shown in Figure 17, the images decrypted from the cipher images with data loss rates of 6.25, 12.5%, 23.44%, 25%, 43.75%, and 50% are very similar to the original images and can still provide valuable information about the input images' visual information.

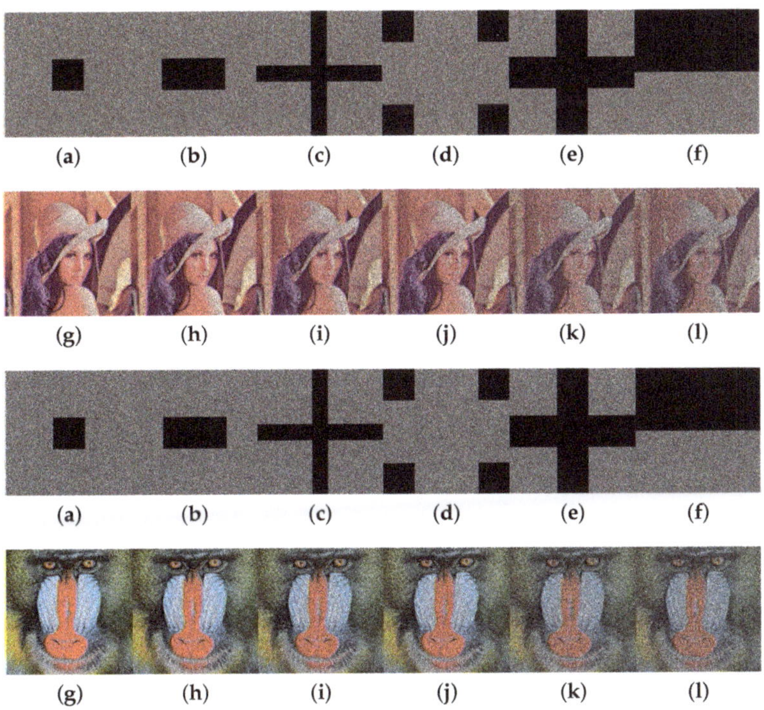

Figure 17. Cropping attack test [50]: (**a**) cropped 6.25% of the encrypted image; (**b**) cropped 12.5% of the encrypted image; (**c**) cropped 23.44% of the encrypted image; (**d**) cropped 25% of the encrypted image; (**e**) cropped 43.75% of the encrypted image; (**f**) cropped 50% of the encrypted image; (**g**) decrypted image based on the cropped 6.25% of the encrypted image; (**h**) decrypted image based on the cropped 12.5% of the encrypted image; (**i**) decrypted image based on the cropped 23.44% of the encrypted image; (**j**) decrypted image based on the cropped 25% of the encrypted image; (**k**) decrypted image based on the cropped 43.75% of the encrypted image; (**l**) decrypted image based on the cropped 50% of the encrypted image.

4.11. Randomness Tests for the Encrypted Image

In order to guarantee the security of the encryption system, the image should contain properties for further measurable investigation to distinguish between different designs [51]. For the DIEHARD test, which focuses on several types of potential randomness in the sequence [52], the value of each pixel of the encrypted image is transformed into binary.

The results of the DIEHARD test in Table 10 show that the proposed scheme exhibits highly random behavior.

Table 10. Result of DIEHARD tests suite.

Image	p-Value	Assessment
Birthday spacing	0.4381	PASSED
Overlapping permutation	0.8404	PASSED
Binary rank 32× 32	0.4542	PASSED
Binary rank 6×8	0.5309	PASSED
Bitstream	0.6567	PASSED
OPSO	0.1355	PASSED
OQSO	0.4506	PASSED
DNA	0.7073	PASSED
Count the ones 01	0.9588	PASSED
Count the ones 02	0.7266	PASSED
Parking lot	0.6397	PASSED
2DS sphere	0.0297	PASSED
3DS spheres	0.6735	PASSED
Squeeze	0.9060	PASSED
Overlapping sum	0.1625	PASSED
Runs	0.7672	PASSED
Craps	0.1105	PASSED

4.12. Comparison with Existing Methods

This section compares the scheme with existing encryption schemes by comparing the key space, entropy, CC, NPCR, and UACI. CC is the average value of the correlation of adjacent pixels in the horizontal, vertical, and diagonal directions of the image, and the formula is as follows:

$$CC = \frac{|C_h| + |C_v| + |C_d|}{3} \tag{20}$$

where C_h, C_v, and C_d are correlations of horizontal, vertical, and diagonal of encrypted images.

Table 11 shows the comparison of encrypted Lena images.

Table 11. Key space, entropy, CC, NPCR, and UACI comparison.

Method	Key Space	Entropy	CC				NPCR (%)				UACI (%)			
			R	G	B	Cipher	R	G	B	Cipher	R	G	B	Cipher
Proposed	$> 2^{2338}$	7.9998	0.0119	0.0096	0.0109	0.0070	99.5811	99.6162	99.6052	99.6062	33.3818	33.5105	33.4385	33.4623
Ref. [53]	$> 2^{160}$	7.9992	0.0320	0.0099	0.0221	-	100	100	100	100	33.6313	33.4737	33.6520	33.5857
Ref. [2]	2^{128}	7.9998	0.0020	0.0007	0.0018	0.0015	100	100	100	100	33.4877	33.3697	33.4629	33.4400
Ref. [54]	2^{233}	7.9967	0.0043	0.0035	0.0020	-	99.5865	99.2172	99.8480	-	33.4835	33.4640	33.2689	-
Ref. [55]	2^{626}	7.9998	-	-	-	0.0026	99.6296	99.6174	99.6473	-	33.6027	33.4997	33.5516	-
Ref. [56]	-	7.9956	0.0004	0.0004	0.0004	-	99.6420	99.5960	99.5290	99.5890	32.7630	30.0490	27.5670	30.1260
Ref. [57]	2^{170}	7.9998	0.0021	0.0025	0.00040	0.0013	-	-	-	99.6166	-	-	-	33.4476
Ref. [58]	2^{170}	7.9994	0.0034	0.0002	0.0028	0.0013	99.6099	99.6093	99.6101	-	33.4650	33.4637	33.4641	-
Ref. [59]	2^{711}	7.9978	-	-	-	0.0042	-	-	-	99.6090	-	-	-	33.4500
Ref. [60]	$> 2^{183}$	7.9994	0.0021	0.0009	0.0005	-	99.6089	99.6089	99.6085	-	33.4589	33.4598	33.4624	-
Ref. [61]	-	7.9998	-	-	-	0.0002	-	-	-	99.62	-	-	-	33.47
Ref. [62]	-	7.9997	-	-	-	0.0006	-	-	-	-	-	-	-	-
Ref. [41]	2^{554}	7.9989	0.0030	0.0015	0.0031	0.0036	99.6246	99.6246	99.6246	99.6246	33.0716	30.7640	27.8720	30.5681
Ref. [63]	2^{418}	7.9988	-	-	-	0.0022	-	-	-	99.6112	-	-	-	33.4254

5. Conclusions

The image encryption algorithm based on the novel eighth-order hyperchaotic system proposed in this paper performs a significant level of security in experiments. The algorithm effectively improves the randomness and unpredictability of encrypted images through multiple rounds of diffusion and scrambling operations. In contrast to the conventional chaotic system, the novel hyperchaotic system exhibits superior performance in terms of key space and resistance against attacks, while also demonstrating heightened sensitivity to keys. By comparing the results of other encryption algorithms, it can be seen that the key space of the proposed algorithm is significantly larger than those of other references; NPCR and UACI are closer to the theoretical values; and the pixel correlation is also lower than most references. Based on the aforementioned notable benefits, it is evident that the algorithm demonstrates exceptional performance in the encryption of images.

Author Contributions: Conceptualization, H.Q. and J.L.; methodology, H.Q. and J.L.; software, H.Q., J.L. and X.Z.; validation, H.Q., J.L. and H.Y.; formal analysis, H.Y.; investigation, H.Q.; resources, J.L.; data curation, H.Q.; writing—original draft preparation, H.Q.; writing—review and editing, J.L.; visualization, J.L.; supervision, H.Q.; project administration, J.L.; funding acquisition, J.L. All authors have read and agreed to the published version of the manuscript.

Funding: This research was funded by the Regional Project of the National Natural Science Foundation of China grant number 82260364, Gansu Provincial Science and Technology Department Youth Fund Project grant number 22JR5RA166, Gansu Higher Education Innovation Fund Project grant number 2022B-084.

Data Availability Statement: All experimental pictures in this article come from standard data sets, and all data are generated through algorithms.

Conflicts of Interest: The authors declare no conflict of interest.

References

1. Zheng, Q.; Wang, X.; Khurram Khan, M.; Zhang, W.; Gupta, B.B.; Guo, W. A Lightweight Authenticated Encryption Scheme Based on Chaotic SCML for Railway Cloud Service. *IEEE Access* **2018**, *6*, 711–722. [CrossRef]
2. Elias, E.P. Multichannel image encryption using dynamic substitution and JSMP map. *Optik* **2023**, *288*, 171183. [CrossRef]
3. Zhou, Y.; Bao, L.; Chen, C.P. A new 1D chaotic system for image encryption. *Signal Process.* **2014**, *97*, 172–182. [CrossRef]
4. Yassein, M.B.; Aljawarneh, S.; Qawasmeh, E.; Mardini, W.; Khamayseh, Y. Comprehensive study of symmetric key and asymmetric key encryption algorithms. In Proceedings of the 2017 International Conference on Engineering and Technology (ICET), Antalya, Turkey, 21–23 August 2017; pp. 1–7. [CrossRef]
5. Zhang, Y.-P.; Liu, W.; Cao, S.-P.; Zhai, Z.-J.; Nie, X.; Dai, W.-D. Digital image encryption algorithm based on chaos and improved DES. In Proceedings of the 2009 IEEE International Conference on Systems, Man and Cybernetics, San Antonio, TX, USA, 11–14 October 2009; pp. 474–479. [CrossRef]
6. Giap, V.N.; Nguyen, Q.D.; Pham, D.H.; Lin, C.M. Wireless Secure Communication of Chaotic Systems Based on Takagi–Sugeno Fuzzy Optimal Time Varying Disturbance Observer and Sliding Mode Control. *Int. J. Fuzzy Syst.* **2023**, 1–15. [CrossRef]
7. Giap, V.N. Text message secure communication based on fractional-order chaotic systems with Takagi–Sugeno fuzzy disturbance observer and sliding mode control. *Int. J. Dyn. Control* **2023**, *2023*, 1–15. [CrossRef]
8. Yu, Y.; Li, H.X.; Wang, S.; Yu, J. Dynamic analysis of a fractional-order Lorenz chaotic system. *Chaos Solitons Fractals* **2009**, *42*, 1181–1189. [CrossRef]
9. Zou, C.; Zhang, Q.; Wei, X.; Liu, C. Image Encryption Based on Improved Lorenz System. *IEEE Access* **2020**, *8*, 75728–75740. [CrossRef]
10. Chen, C.; Sun, K.; He, S. An improved image encryption algorithm with finite computing precision. *Signal Process.* **2020**, *168*, 107340. [CrossRef]
11. Dou, J.X.; Pan, A.Q.; Bao, R.; Mao, H.H.; Luo, L. Sampling through the lens of sequential decision making. *arXiv* **2022**, arXiv:2208.08056.
12. Dou, J.X.; Bao, R.; Song, S.; Yang, S.; Zhang, Y.; Liang, P.P.; Mao, H.H. Demystify the Gravity Well in the Optimization Landscape (student abstract). In Proceedings of the AAAI Conference on Artificial Intelligence, Washington, DC, USA, 7–14 February 2023.
13. Dou, J.X.; Mao, H.; Bao, R.; Liang, P.P.; Tan, X.; Zhang, S.; Jia, M.; Zhou, P.; Mao, Z.H. The Measurement of Knowledge in Knowledge Graphs.
14. Mobayen, S.; Vaidyanathan, S.; Sambas, A.; Kacar, S.; Cavusoglu, U. A Novel Chaotic System With Boomerang-Shaped Equilibrium, Its Circuit Implementation and Application to Sound Encryption. *Iran. J. Sci. Technol. Trans. Electr. Eng.* **2019**, *43*, 1–12. [CrossRef]

15. Sun, K.; Liu, X.; Zhu, C.; Sprott, J.C. Hyperchaos and hyperchaos control of the sinusoidally forced simplified Lorenz system. *Nonlinear Dyn.* **2012**, *69*, 1383–1391. [CrossRef]
16. Xiong, Z.; Qu, S.; Luo, J. Adaptive Multi-Switching Synchronization of High-Order Memristor-Based Hyperchaotic System with Unknown Parameters and Its Application in Secure Communication. *Complexity* **2019**, *2019*, 3827201. [CrossRef]
17. Li, Q.; Chen, L. An image encryption algorithm based on 6-dimensional hyper chaotic system and DNA encoding. *Multimed. Tools Appl.* **2023**, 1–18. [CrossRef]
18. Liu, J.; Ma, J.; Lian, J.; Chang, P.; Ma, Y. An Approach for the Generation of an Nth-Order Chaotic System with Hyperbolic Sine. *Entropy* **2018**, *20*, 230. [CrossRef]
19. Chen, H.; Bai, E.; Jiang, X.; Wu, Y. A Fast Image Encryption Algorithm Based on Improved 6-D Hyper-Chaotic System. *IEEE Access* **2022**, *10*, 116031–116044. [CrossRef]
20. Yang, Q.; Zhu, D.; Yang, L. A new 7D hyperchaotic system with five positive Lyapunov exponents coined. *Int. J. Bifurc. Chaos* **2018**, *28*, 1850057. [CrossRef]
21. Yang, Q.; Bai, M. A new 5D hyperchaotic system based on modified generalized Lorenz system. *Nonlinear Dyn.* **2017**, *88*, 189–221. [CrossRef]
22. Liu, J.; Ma, Y.; Li, S.; Lian, J.; Zhang, X. A new simple chaotic system and its application in medical image encryption. *Multimed. Tools Appl.* **2018**, *77*, 22787–22808. [CrossRef]
23. Koçak, H.; Palmer, K. Lyapunov Exponents and Sensitive Dependence. *J. Dyn. Differ. Equ.* **2010**, *22*, 381–398. [CrossRef]
24. Singh, J.P.; Roy, B. The nature of Lyapunov exponents is (+, +, -, -). Is it a hyperchaotic system? *Chaos Solitons Fractals* **2016**, *92*, 73–85. [CrossRef]
25. Yang, Y.; Gao, J.; Imani, H. Design, analysis, circuit implementation, and synchronization of a new chaotic system with application to information encryption. *AIP Publ.* **2023**, *13*, 075116. [CrossRef]
26. Vaidyanathan, S.; Tlelo-Cuautle, E.; Benkouider, K.; Sambas, A.; Ovilla-Martínez, B. FPGA-Based Implementation of a New 3-D Multistable Chaotic Jerk System with Two Unstable Balance Points. *Technologies* **2023**, *11*, 92. [CrossRef]
27. Lin, Z.; Liu, J.; Lian, J.; Ma, Y.; Zhang, X. A Novel Fast Image Encryption Algorithm for Embedded Systems. *Multimed. Tools Appl.* **2019**, *78*, 20511–20531. [CrossRef]
28. Lee, W.K.; Phan, R.C.W.; Yap, W.S.; Goi, B.M. SPRING: A Novel Parallel Chaos-Based Image Encryption Scheme. *Nonlinear Dyn.* **2018**, *92*, 575–593. [CrossRef]
29. Sankpal, P.R.; Vijaya, P.A. Image Encryption Using Chaotic Maps: A Survey. In Proceedings of the 2014 Fifth International Conference on Signal and Image Processing, Bangalore, India, 8–10 January 2014; pp. 102–107. [CrossRef]
30. Souyah, A.; Faraoun, K.M. An image encryption scheme combining chaos-memory cellular automata and weighted histogram. *Nonlinear Dyn.* **2016**, *86*, 639–653. [CrossRef]
31. Sang, Y.; Sang, J.; Alam, M.S. Image encryption based on logistic chaotic systems and deep autoencoder. *Pattern Recognit. Lett.* **2022**, *153*, 59–66. [CrossRef]
32. Mamlin, B.W.; Tierney, W.M. The Promise of Information and Communication Technology in Healthcare: Extracting Value from the Chaos. *Am. J. Med. Sci.* **2016**, *351*, 59–68. [CrossRef]
33. Ye, G.; Jiao, K.; Huang, X. Quantum logistic image encryption algorithm based on SHA-3 and RSA. *Nonlinear Dyn.* **2021**, *104*, 2807–2827. [CrossRef]
34. Anishchenko, V.; Vadivasova, T.; Okrokvertskhov, G.; Strelkova, G. Correlation analysis of dynamical chaos. *Phys. A Stat. Mech. Its Appl.* **2003**, *325*, 199–212. [CrossRef]
35. Liu, S.; Ye, G. Asymmetric image encryption algorithm using a new chaotic map and an improved radial diffusion. *Optik* **2023**, *288*, 171181. [CrossRef]
36. Pak, C.; Huang, L. A new color image encryption using combination of the 1D chaotic map. *Signal Process.* **2017**, *138*, 129–137. [CrossRef]
37. Ye, G.; Zhao, H.; Chai, H. Chaotic image encryption algorithm using wave-line permutation and block diffusion. *Nonlinear Dyn.* **2016**, *83*, 2067–2077. [CrossRef]
38. Zhen, P.; Zhao, G.; Min, L.; Jin, X. Chaos-based image encryption scheme combining DNA coding and entropy. *Multimed. Tools Appl.* **2016**, *75*, 6303–6319. [CrossRef]
39. Valandar, M.Y.; Ayubi, P.; Barani, M.J. A new transform domain steganography based on modified logistic chaotic map for color images. *J. Inf. Secur. Appl.* **2017**, *34*, 142–151. [CrossRef]
40. Li, X.; Yu, H.; Zhang, H.; Jin, X.; Sun, H.; Liu, J. Video encryption based on hyperchaotic system. *Multimed. Tools Appl.* **2020**, *79*, 23995–24011. [CrossRef]
41. Elkandoz, M.T.; Alexan, W. Image encryption based on a combination of multiple chaotic maps. *Multimed. Tools Appl.* **2022**, *81*, 25497–25518. [CrossRef]
42. Harun, S.W.; Zhang, X.; Wang, L.; Wang, Y.; Niu, Y.; Li, Y. An Image Encryption Algorithm Based on Hyperchaotic System and Variable-Step Josephus Problem. *Int. J. Opt.* **2020**, *2020*, 6102824. [CrossRef]
43. Alexan, W.; ElBeltagy, M.; Aboshousha, A. Lightweight Image Encryption: Cellular Automata and the Lorenz System. In Proceedings of the 2021 International Conference on Microelectronics (ICM), Nis, Serbia, 12–14 September 2021; pp. 34–39. [CrossRef]

44. Zhou, Y.; Hua, Z.; Pun, C.M.; Philip Chen, C.L. Cascade Chaotic System with Applications. *IEEE Trans. Cybern.* **2015**, *45*, 2001–2012. [CrossRef]
45. Wang, M.; Wang, X.; Zhang, Y.; Zhou, S.; Zhao, T.; Yao, N. A novel chaotic system and its application in a color image cryptosystem. *Opt. Lasers Eng.* **2019**, *121*, 479–494. [CrossRef]
46. Zhu, C. A novel image encryption scheme based on improved hyperchaotic sequences. *Opt. Commun.* **2012**, *285*, 29–37. [CrossRef]
47. Song, C.Y.; Qiao, Y.L.; Zhang, X.Z. An image encryption scheme based on new spatiotemporal chaos. *Opt. Int. J. Light Electron Opt.* **2013**, *124*, 3329–3334. [CrossRef]
48. Wang, L.; Song, H.; Liu, P. A novel hybrid color image encryption algorithm using two complex chaotic systems. *Opt. Lasers Eng.* **2016**, *77*, 118–125. [CrossRef]
49. Yan, X.; Wang, X.; Xian, Y. Chaotic image encryption algorithm based on arithmetic sequence scrambling model and DNA encoding operation. *Multimed. Tools Appl.* **2021**, *80*, 10949–10983. [CrossRef]
50. Gao, X.; Mou, J.; Xiong, L.; Sha, Y.; Yan, H.; Cao, Y. A fast and efficient multiple images encryption based on single-channel encryption and chaotic system. *Nonlinear Dyn.* **2022**, *108*, 613–636. [CrossRef]
51. Yasser, I.; Khalil, A.T.; Mohamed, M.A.; Samra, A.S.; Khalifa, F. A Robust Chaos-Based Technique for Medical Image Encryption. *IEEE Access* **2022**, *10*, 244–257. [CrossRef]
52. Mohammad Seyedzadeh, S.; Mirzakuchaki, S. A fast color image encryption algorithm based on coupled two-dimensional piecewise chaotic map. *Signal Process.* **2012**, *92*, 1202–1215. [CrossRef]
53. Basha, H.A.; Mohra, A.S.S.; Diab, T.O.M.; Sobky, W.I.E. Efficient Image Encryption Based on New Substitution Box Using DNA Coding and Bent Function. *IEEE Access* **2022**, *10*, 66409–66429. [CrossRef]
54. Wei, X.; Guo, L.; Zhang, Q.; Zhang, J.; Lian, S. A novel color image encryption algorithm based on DNA sequence operation and hyper-chaotic system. *J. Syst. Softw.* **2012**, *85*, 290–299. [CrossRef]
55. Kumar Patro, K.A.; Acharya, B. An efficient colour image encryption scheme based on 1-D chaotic maps. *J. Inf. Secur. Appl.* **2019**, *46*, 23–41. [CrossRef]
56. ul Haq, T.; Shah, T. 12×12 S-box Design and its Application to RGB Image Encryption. *Optik* **2020**, *217*, 164922. [CrossRef]
57. Huang, L.; Li, W.; Xiong, X.; Yu, R.; Wang, Q.; Cai, S. Designing a double-way spread permutation framework utilizing chaos and S-box for symmetric image encryption. *Opt. Commun.* **2022**, *517*, 128365. [CrossRef]
58. Huang, L.; Cai, S.; Xiong, X.; Xiao, M. On symmetric color image encryption system with permutation-diffusion simultaneous operation. *Opt. Lasers Eng.* **2019**, *115*, 7–20. [CrossRef]
59. Hamza, R.; Titouna, F. A novel sensitive image encryption algorithm based on the Zaslavsky chaotic map. *Inf. Secur. J. A Glob. Perspect.* **2016**, *25*, 162–179. [CrossRef]
60. Huang, L.; Cai, S.; Xiao, M.; Xiong, X. A Simple Chaotic Map-Based Image Encryption System Using Both Plaintext Related Permutation and Diffusion. *Entropy* **2018**, *20*, 535. [CrossRef] [PubMed]
61. Lin, C.M.; Pham, D.H.; Huynh, T.T. Synchronization of Chaotic System Using a Brain-Imitated Neural Network Controller and Its Applications for Secure Communications. *IEEE Access* **2021**, *9*, 75923–75944. [CrossRef]
62. Lin, C.M.; Pham, D.H.; Huynh, T.T. Encryption and Decryption of Audio Signal and Image Secure Communications Using Chaotic System Synchronization Control by TSK Fuzzy Brain Emotional Learning Controllers. *IEEE Trans. Cybern.* **2022**, *52*, 13684–13698. [CrossRef]
63. Wu, Y.; Zhang, L.; Berretti, S.; Wan, S. Medical Image Encryption by Content-Aware DNA Computing for Secure Healthcare. *IEEE Trans. Ind. Inform.* **2023**, *19*, 2089–2098. [CrossRef]

mathematics

MDPI

Article

Bifurcation, Hidden Chaos, Entropy and Control in Hénon-Based Fractional Memristor Map with Commensurate and Incommensurate Orders

Mayada Abualhomos [1], Abderrahmane Abbes [2,*], Gharib Mousa Gharib [3], Abdallah Shihadeh [4], Maha S. Al Soudi [5], Ahmed Atallah Alsaraireh [6] and Adel Ouannas [7]

1 Applied Science Research Center (ASRC), Applied Science Private University, Amman 11942, Jordan; abuhomos@asu.edu.jo
2 Laboratory of Mathematics, Dynamics and Modelization, Badji Mokhtar-Annaba University, Annaba 23000, Algeria
3 Department of Mathematics, Faculty of Science, Zarqa University, Zarqa 13110, Jordan
4 Department of Mathematics, Faculty of Science, The Hashemite University, P.O. Box 330127, Zarqa 13133, Jordan; abdallaha_ka@hu.edu.jo
5 Department of Basic Scientific Sciences, Applied Science Private University, Amman 11931, Jordan
6 Department of computer information systems, The University of Jordan, Amman 11942, Jordan
7 Department of Mathematics and Computer Science, University of Larbi Ben M'hidi, Oum El Bouaghi 04000, Algeria
* Correspondence: abderrahmane.abbes@univ-annaba.dz

Abstract: In this paper, we present an innovative 3D fractional Hénon-based memristor map and conduct an extensive exploration and analysis of its dynamic behaviors under commensurate and incommensurate orders. The study employs diverse numerical techniques, such as visualizing phase portraits, analyzing Lyapunov exponents, plotting bifurcation diagrams, and applying the sample entropy test to assess the complexity and validate the chaotic characteristics. However, since the proposed fractional map has no fixed points, the outcomes reveal that the map can exhibit a wide range of hidden dynamical behaviors. This phenomenon significantly augments the complexity of the fractal structure inherent to the chaotic attractors. Moreover, we introduce nonlinear controllers designed for stabilizing and synchronizing the proposed fractional Hénon-based memristor map. The research emphasizes the system's sensitivity to fractional-order parameters, resulting in the emergence of distinct dynamic patterns. The memristor-based chaotic map exhibits rich and intricate behavior, making it a captivating and significant area of investigation.

Keywords: Hénon-based map; memristor; discrete fractional calculus; chaotic dynamics; entropy; control

MSC: 37M20

1. Introduction

Discrete fractional calculus has emerged as a captivating research area that has grabbed the interest of mathematicians and scholars in various disciplines over the last decade. Its applications span diverse fields, including biology, ecology, and applied sciences, offering valuable insights into real-world challenges. Fractional systems have demonstrated the ability to describe complex nonlinear phenomena with greater accuracy compared to traditional integer-order systems [1], showcasing their unique properties, including long-term memory, viscosity, and flexibility. Recently, there has been a surge in published articles addressing this intriguing topic. Researchers have been offering various discrete-time fractional operators, conducting stability analyses, and presenting numerous theoretical findings [2–6]. Notably, Wu and Baleanu presented the first study that delves into the modeling of fractional chaotic maps using the left Caputo-like operator and investigates their chaotic characteristics [7]. As a result of these advances, this work paved the way for the emergence of more commensurate- and non-commensurate-order chaotic maps [8–13], in addition to exploring diverse control strategies and synchronization schemes that have been developed to synchronize the interactions between different fractional discrete chaotic systems [14–17]. These studies reflected that the system's behavior is highly dependent on the chosen fractional order, showcasing its non-linear and complex nature, which makes it a fascinating subject of study in the field of fractional dynamics.

A memory resistor, commonly known as a "memristor", has been widely recognized as the fourth fundamental circuit element that serves as a link between charge and magnetic flux. The theoretical concept of the memristor was initially forwarded by Chua in 1971 [18]. For an extended period, memristor research remained primarily theoretical until the first physical implementation of a memristor was achieved by HP laboratories in 2008. They successfully developed the first practical memristor using nanomaterials [19]. It has since become an essential component in various applications due to its unique properties and potential to revolutionize memory and computing technologies. Memristors have garnered significant attention and research interest, contributing to the advancement of various fields, including electronics [20], computing [21], nonvolatile memory [22], and neuromorphic systems [23].

In general, memristor-based chaotic systems are commonly designed using differential equations in the continuous-time domain [24]. However, until recent years, discrete-time memristive maps had not been extensively explored or discussed. In practice, discrete chaotic systems offer the advantage of avoiding parameter sensitivity issues present in continuous systems, making them easier to implement using digital hardware circuits [25]. Consequently, there has been a growing realization among researchers of the significance of exploring and understanding discrete memristive maps, leading to promising advancements in understanding the behavior of discrete memristor-based systems and their implications for various applications [26–30]. These studies contribute to exploring the interactions between memristive elements and mathematical functions, providing valuable insights into the dynamics of memristive maps and their potential applications in various fields.

The majority of the previous discrete memristors research has been focused on integer-order systems. Regrettably, the study of discrete fractional memristors remains inadequate, with relatively few studies dedicated to exploring their behavior and characteristics. For instance, Lu et al. [31] developed an innovative 2D discrete memristor map by incorporating a memristor into a 1D Rulkov neuron map. In [32], Peng et al. investigated the chaotic behaviors in the Caputo fractional memristive map, while in [33], the authors conducted an investigation into the multistability and synchronization of fractional maps resulting from the coupling of Rulkov neurons with locally active discrete memristors. Furthermore, Shatnawi et al. [34] recently explored the hidden attractors and multistability in a fractional non-fixed-point discrete memristor-based map. Additionally, the study of the fractional memristor-based discrete chaotic map based on the Grunwald–Letnikov operator and its implementation in digital circuits is presented in [35]. The studies highlight the intricate and rich behavior of the system, emphasizing the significance of fractional components in contributing to the complexity and versatility of memristor-based maps. The aforementioned papers have primarily concentrated on models with commensurate orders within discrete memristor-based maps. However, there appears to be a noticeable gap in the literature concerning the effect of the incommensurate-order case on the dynamics of such maps. This indicates an underexplored area in the field of discrete memristors, particularly in the context of incommensurate fractional memristors. Understanding the behavior and properties of incommensurate fractional memristors could lead to valuable insights and potential applications in various domains. Therefore, further investigation and research in this area are essential to uncovering the unique characteristics and potential benefits of incommensurate fractional memristors.

Inspired by the preceding discussion, the main innovations and contributions of this paper are summarized as follows:

1. A new 3D fractional-order Hénon-based memristor map is presented by establishing a connection between the 2D Hénon map and the discrete memristor.
2. The rich variety of complex nonlinear dynamical behavior is comprehensively explored, and some basic dynamical characteristics demonstrated by this map, such as phase portraits, bifurcation diagrams, and the maximum Lyapunov exponent, are investigated.
3. To measure the complexity and demonstrate the presence of chaos in the proposed memristor map, we give its sample entropy ($SampEn$) test results using a range of fractional values, encompassing both commensurate and incommensurate cases.
4. Chaos control and synchronization of the proposed 3D fractional Hénon-based memristor map are realized based on the stability theorem of fractional-order discrete-time linear systems.

The rest of this article is outlined as follows: In Section 2, we introduce essential preliminary concepts related to discrete fractional calculus and we introduce the mathematical model of the 3D fractional Hénon-based memristor map. In Section 3, we delve into an analysis of the dynamic characteristics of the fractional Hénon-based memristor map, focusing on both commensurate and incommensurate scenarios. This exploration is facilitated through phase portrait visualization, Lyapunov exponent analysis and bifurcation diagram plots. Section 4 involves the utilization of the sample entropy test ($SampEn$) to quantitatively measure the complexity and validate the presence of chaos within the map. In Section 5, we propose adaptive nonlinear controllers aimed at stabilizing and synchronizing the proposed 3D fractional Hénon-based memristor map. In conclusion, we provide a concise summary of the most noteworthy findings that we obtained during our study.

2. Preliminaries and Model Description

To elucidate our memristor framework, we first provide a specific overview within the domain of discrete fractional calculus. Then, we proceed to introduce the mathematical construct of the fractional Hénon-based memristor map, which incorporates the Caputo-left difference operator.

2.1. Discrete Fractional Calculus

Definition 1 ([2]). *The β-th fractional sum for a function Y can be expressed as*

$$\Delta_b^{-\beta}Y(v) = \frac{1}{\Gamma(\beta)}\sum_{l=b}^{b-\beta}(b-1-l)^{(\beta-1)}Y(l), \tag{1}$$

with $v \in \mathbb{N}_{b+\beta}$, $\beta > 0$.

Definition 2 ([4]). *The Caputo-like difference operator for a function $Y(v)$ can be stated as*

$${}^{C}\Delta_v^{\beta}Y(b) = \Delta_b^{-(m-\beta)}\Delta^m X(v) = \frac{1}{\beta(m-\beta)}\sum_{l=b}^{v-(m-\beta)}(v-l-1)^{(m-\beta-1)}\Delta^m Y(l), \tag{2}$$

where $v \in \mathbb{N}_{b+m-\beta}$, $\beta \notin \mathbb{N}$ and $m = \lceil\beta\rceil + 1$. $\Delta^m Y(v)$ and $(v-l-1)^{(m-\beta-1)}$ are the m-th integer difference operator and the falling factorial function, respectively, which are written as

$$\Delta^m Y(v) = \Delta(\Delta^{m-1}Y(v)) = \sum_{k=0}^{m}\binom{m}{k}(-1)^{m-k}Y(v+k), \qquad v \in \mathbb{N}_b, \tag{3}$$

and

$$(v-1-l)^{(m-\beta-1)} = \frac{\beta(v-l)}{\beta(v+1-l-m+\beta)}, \tag{4}$$

Remark 1. *For $m = 1$, we can define the Caputo-like operator by*

$$^{C}\Delta_b^{\beta}Y(v) = \Delta_b^{-(1-\beta)}\Delta Y(v) = \frac{1}{\beta(1-\beta)}\sum_{l=b}^{v-(1-\beta)}(v-1-l)^{(-\beta)}\Delta Y(l), \quad v \in \mathbb{N}_{b-\beta+1} \tag{5}$$

Theorem 1 ([7]). *The solution of the following fractional difference system*

$$\begin{cases} ^{C}\Delta_b^{\beta}Z(v) = Y(v+\beta-1, Z(v+\beta-1)) \\ \Delta^{j}Z(v) = Z_j, \quad m = \lceil\beta\rceil + 1, \end{cases} \tag{6}$$

is expressed by

$$Z(v) = Z_0(v) + \frac{1}{\Gamma(\beta)}\sum_{l=m-\beta}^{v-\beta}(v+1-l)^{(\beta-1)}Y(l-1+\beta, Z(l-1+\beta)), \quad v \in \mathbb{N}_{b+m}, \tag{7}$$

where

$$Z_0(v) = \sum_{j=0}^{m-1}\frac{(v-b)^j}{\Gamma(j+1)}\Delta^{j}Z(0). \tag{8}$$

2.2. Fractional-Order Hénon-Based Memristor Map

The original work of Hénon [36] introduced the 2D Hénon map, which is written as

$$\begin{cases} y_1(r+1) = 1 - \rho_1(y_1(r))^2 + y_2(r), \\ y_2(r+1) = \rho_2 y_1(r), \end{cases} \tag{9}$$

where ρ_1 and ρ_2 are adjustable parameters.

The memristor is a two-terminal nonlinear device that displays a pinched hysteresis in response to the application of any periodic voltage or current stimulation. Diverse memristors with discrete memristance values have been suggested through the use of differential modeling theory [37]. As per the concept presented in reference [38], the discrete memristor can be defined by

$$\begin{cases} v_r = M(q_r)i_r, \\ q_{r+1} = q_r + k\, i_r, \end{cases} \tag{10}$$

where v_r represents the output voltage, i_r is the input current, and q_r is the internal state of the discrete memristor at step r. $M(q_r)$ denotes the value of the discrete memristance function, which is equal, in this study, to

$$M(q_r) = \tanh q_r.$$

Thus, the mathematical model for the discrete memristor (10) is formulated by

$$\begin{cases} v_r = \tanh(q_r)i_r, \\ q_{r+1} = q_r + k\, i_r. \end{cases} \tag{11}$$

Rong et al. [26] expanded the dimension of the Ikeda map by incorporating the discrete memristor model (11) into the map (9), yielding the following 3D Hénon-based memristor map:

$$\begin{cases} y_1(r+1) = 1 - \rho_1 (y_1(r))^2 + y_2(r), \\ y_2(r+1) = \rho_2 y_1(r) + \mu \tanh(y_3(r)) y_2(r), \\ y_3(r+1) = y_3(r) + y_2(r). \end{cases} \tag{12}$$

where μ is the controller parameter. Figure 1 illustrates the bifurcation diagram and Lyapunov exponent, as well as the phase attractor of the 3D Hénon-based memristor map, while varying μ from 0 to 1. The evidence presented in Figure 1 provides that the model demonstrates chaotic dynamics for a significant range of values, specifically within the interval $\rho \in (0.448, 0.531) \cup (0.722, 0.986)$.

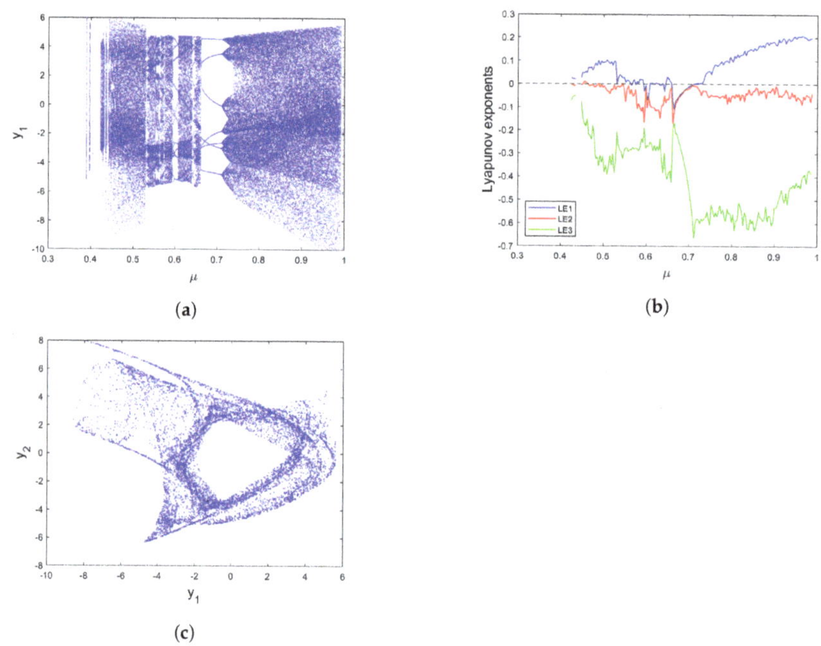

Figure 1. (**a**) Bifurcation diagram for μ ranging from 0 to 1. (**b**) The corresponding Lyapunov exponents. (**c**) Phase attractor of Hénon-based memristor map (12).

In this investigation, we extend the integer-order Hénon-based memristor map to generate the fractional-order Hénon-based memristor map by employing the Caputo difference operator. The formula representing the first-order difference of the Hénon-based memristor map is as follows:

$$\begin{cases} \Delta y_1(r) = 1 - \rho_1 (y_1(r))^2 + y_2(r) - y_1(r), \\ \Delta y_2(r) = \rho_2 y_1(r) + (\mu \tanh(y_3(r)) - 1) y_2(r), \\ \Delta y_3(r) = y_2(r), \end{cases} \tag{13}$$

where $\Delta y(r) = y(r+1) - y(r)$ is the standard difference operator. In the aforementioned system, if we substitute Δ with the Caputo-like operator ${}^c\Delta_b^\beta$ and replace r with $\varrho = v + \beta - 1$, the resulting system becomes a fractional-order difference system:

$$\begin{cases} {}^{c}\Delta_{b}^{\beta} y_1(v) = 1 - \rho_1 (y_1(\varrho))^2 + y_2(\varrho) - y_1(\varrho), \\ {}^{c}\Delta_{b}^{\beta} y_2(v) = \rho_2 y_1(\varrho) + (\mu \tanh{(y_3(\varrho))} - 1) y_2(\varrho), \\ {}^{c}\Delta_{b}^{\beta} y_3(v) = y_2(\varrho), \end{cases} \tag{14}$$

where $v \in \mathbb{N}_{b+1-\beta}$, b is the initial point, and $0 < \beta \leq 1$ represents the fractional order.

The fixed points of the fractional-order Henon-based memristor map (14) are the values of (y_1^*, y_2^*, y_3^*) that fulfill the following set of equations:

$$\begin{cases} 1 - \rho_1 (y_1^*)^2 + y_2^* - y_1^* = 0, \\ \rho_2 y_1^* + (\mu \tanh{(y_3^*)} - 1) y_2^* = 0, \\ y_2^* = 0. \end{cases} \tag{15}$$

It is clear that, from the third equation of (15), $y_2^* = 0$. Substituting y_2^* in the second equation, we obtain $y_1^* = 0$. Moreover, upon substituting y_1^* and y_2^* into the first equation of (15), it becomes apparent that the system (15) does not have a solution. This signifies that the fractional-order Henon-based memristor map (14) does not possess any fixed points. Consequently, as indicated in reference [39], all attractors produced by the fractional-order Henon-based memristor map (14) are hidden. This means that they are not visible in the traditional plots of the map's phase space.

3. Nonlinear Dynamics of the Fractional-Order Hénon-Based Memristor Map

In this section, we conduct an analysis of the behaviors of the 3D fractional-order Hénon-based memristor map (14). The analysis is carried out across commensurate and incommensurate orders. We employ a range of numerical tools, such as visualizing phase portraits, illustrating bifurcations, and estimating the maximum Lyapunov exponent (LE_{max}).

3.1. Commensurate-Order Fractional Hénon-Based Memristor Map

In this part, our focus is on elaborating on the different characteristics of the commensurate-order 3D fractional Hénon-based memristor map. It is important to recognize that a commensurate-order fractional system is comprised of equations that possess identical orders. To this end, we will now supply the numerical formula, which is presented in the following manner and is derived from Theorem 1:

$$\begin{cases} y_1(r) = y_1(0) + \sum\limits_{j=0}^{r-1} \frac{\Gamma(r-j-1+\beta)}{\Gamma(\beta)\Gamma(r-j)} \Big(1 - \rho_1 (y_1(j))^2 + y_2(j) - y_1(j)\Big), \\ y_2(r) = y_2(0) + \sum\limits_{j=0}^{r-1} \frac{\Gamma(r-j-1+\beta)}{\Gamma(\beta)\Gamma(r-j)} \Big(\rho_2 y_1(j) + (\mu \tanh{(y_3(j))} - 1) y_2(j)\Big), \\ y_3(r) = y_3(0) + \sum\limits_{j=0}^{r-1} \frac{\Gamma(r-j-1+\beta)}{\Gamma(\beta)\Gamma(r-j)} \Big(y_2(j)\Big), \end{cases} \tag{16}$$

Setting $y_1(0) = y_2(0) = t_3(0) = 0$ and the parameters $\rho_1 = 0.15$, $\rho_2 = -1.05$ and $\mu = 0.5$, the bifurcation diagram is used to show the variations in the behaviors of the commensurate 3D fractional Hénon-based memristor map (14), as the order β is varied from 0.8 to 1 with a step size of 0.0005. Figure 2 depicts the bifurcation and LE_{max}. By adjusting the commensurate-order β, we are able to explore a rich set of dynamic characteristics (hidden chaotic and regular) of the fractional map. In more detail, the system exhibits both chaotic and periodic oscillations in distinct regions of its phase space. More specifically, when $\beta \in (0.804, 0.855)$, the trajectories of the commensurate 3D fractional Hénon-based memristor map (14) exhibit hidden chaotic behavior, while as β transitions to the range of $\beta \in (0.855, 0.931)$, periodic windows with 7-period orbits appear, indicating the stability of the states of the map. However, when the commensurate-order β falls within the range of $\beta \in (0.932, 0.984)$, we can observe oscillations between the chaotic and regular trajectories in the states of the 3D fractional Hénon-based memristor map (14). During this range, the Lyapunov exponent (LE) also fluctuates between positive and negative values, indicating transitions between chaotic and non-chaotic behaviors in the system. Subsequently, for larger values of β, chaotic motions reappear, characterized by a positive maximum Lyapunov exponent (LE_max), indicating chaotic dynamics in the trajectories of the commensurate-order 3D Hénon-based memristor map. These described dynamic features are further confirmed by the Lyapunov exponent shown in Figure 2, providing additional evidence for the system's complex and diverse behavior and confirming the sensitivity of the map to changes in the commensurate-order parameter β. Furthermore, based on the observation of the maximum Lyapunov exponent, it can be concluded that when the maximum Lyapunov exponent is not positive, the commensurate 3D fractional Hénon-based memristor map exhibits regular oscillations. Conversely, the presence of chaotic oscillations is inferred when the exponent is positive.

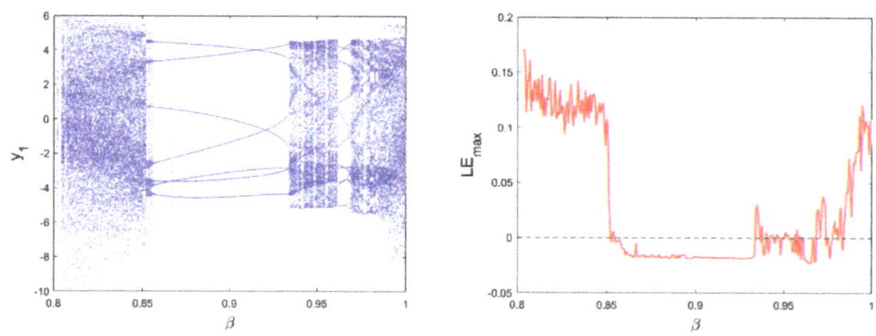

(a) **(b)**

Figure 2. (**a**) Bifurcation of commensurate-order Hénon-based memristor map (14) for $\beta \in (0.8, 1)$. (**b**) The corresponding LE_{max}.

Now, considering μ as the critical parameter, we plot three bifurcations of (14) associated with $\mu \in [0, 1]$ as shown in Figure 3, which correspond to the commensurate orders $\beta = 0.85$, $\beta = 0.9$ and $\beta = 0.95$. It is evident that both the parameter's system μ and the commensurate order β have an effect on the states of the commensurate fractional Hénon-based memristor map (14). Indeed, as the commensurate fractional-order β and parameter ρ increases, the commensurate 3D fractional Hénon-based memristor map (14) displays a more extended hidden chaotic region. This leads to the emergence of more complex oscillations and increased unpredictability in the system's behavior. The interplay between the fractional order and the system parameter has a significant impact on the dynamical behavior, and these changes can result in a richer range of chaotic patterns and intricate trajectories within the 3D Hénon-based memristor map (14). In order to achieve a comprehensive understanding of these characteristics, Figure 4 displays the discrete time evolution of the states y_1, y_2, and y_3 in the suggested commensurate map. We can observe that the trajectories are not regular or predictable. Instead, they display irregular patterns, which is a hallmark of chaotic behavior, where small differences in the initial conditions lead to vastly different trajectories. Additionally, Figure 5 illustrates the phase portraits for various values of the commensurate-order β ($\beta = 0.1$, $\beta = 0.4$, $\beta = 0.6$, $\beta = 0.9$, $\beta = 0.98$, and $\beta = 1$). From the figures, the observed trajectories in the proposed commensurate map switch between hidden chaotic oscillations and periodic behaviors as the commensurate-order β varies. This observation emphasizes the sensitivity of the system to changes in β and demonstrates the richness and complexity of the dynamical properties in the commensurate-order 3 D Hénon-based memristor map (14).

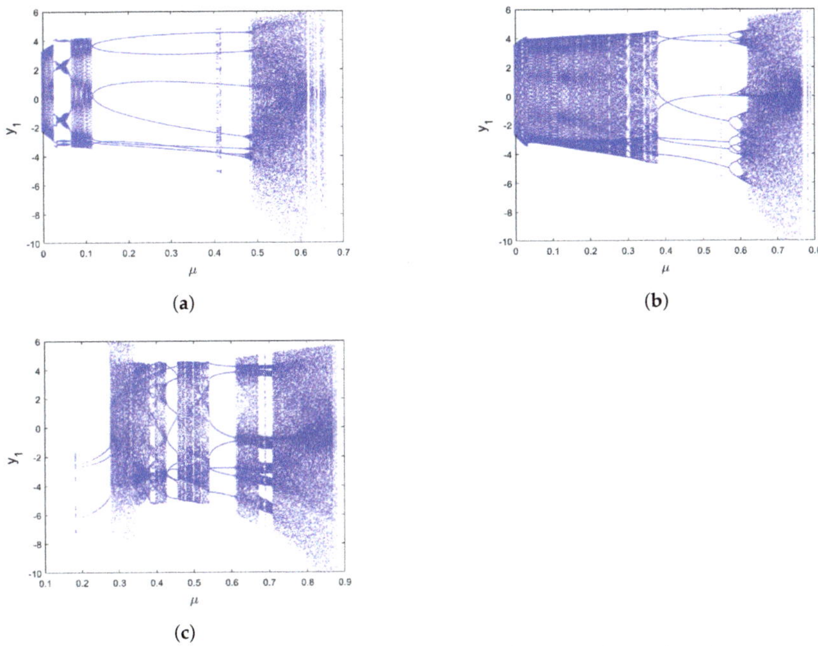

Figure 3. Three bifurcation diagrams of commensurate 3D fractional Hénon-based memristor map and their LE_{max} associated with μ, for (**a**) $\beta = 0.85$, (**b**) $\beta = 0.9$, and (**c**) $\beta = 0.95$.

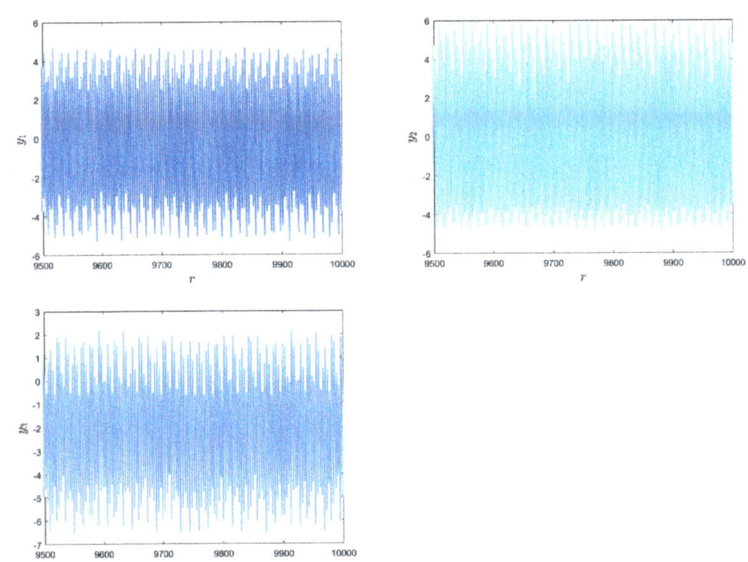

Figure 4. Time evolution of the commensurate 3D fractional Hénon-based memristor map (14) for $\beta = 0.98$.

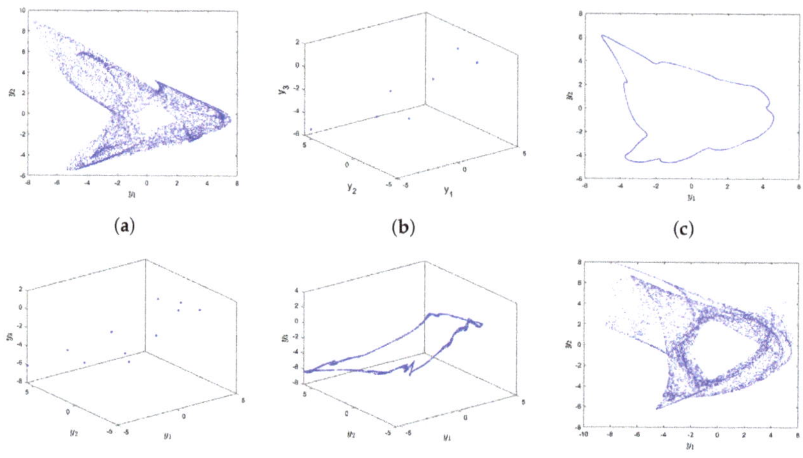

Figure 5. Phase portraits of (14) for different values of β (**a**) $\beta = 0.85$, (**b**) $\beta = 0.9$, (**c**) $\beta = 0.95$, (**d**) $\beta = 0.965$, (**e**) $\beta = 0.98$, (**f**) $\beta = 1$.

3.2. Incommensurate-Order Fractional Hénon-Based Memristor Map

In this section, we delve into the dynamics of the incommensurate-order fractional Hénon-based memristor map. The concept of the incommensurate order entails utilizing different fractional orders for each equation within the system. The representation of the incommensurate-order fractional Hénon-based memristor map is as follows:

$$\begin{cases} {}^{c}\Delta_{b}^{\beta_1} y_1(v) = 1 - \rho_1 (y_1(\varrho))^2 + y_2(\varrho) - y_1(\varrho), \\ {}^{c}\Delta_{b}^{\beta_2} y_2(v) = \rho_2 y_1(\varrho) + (\mu \tanh(y_3(\varrho)) - 1) y_2(\varrho), \\ {}^{c}\Delta_{b}^{\beta_3} y_3(v) = y_2(\varrho), \end{cases} \tag{17}$$

By utilizing Theorem 1, we can express the numerical representation of the incommensurate fractional 3D Hénon-based memristor map (17) as follows:

$$\begin{cases} y_1(r) = y_1(0) + \sum\limits_{j=0}^{r-1} \frac{\Gamma(r-j-1+\beta_1)}{\Gamma(\beta_1)\Gamma(r-j)} \Big(1 - \rho_1 (y_1(j))^2 + y_2(j) - y_1(j)\Big), \\ y_2(r) = y_2(0) + \sum\limits_{j=0}^{r-1} \frac{\Gamma(r-j-1+\beta_2)}{\Gamma(\beta_2)\Gamma(r-j)} \Big(\rho_2 y_1(j) + (\mu \tanh(y_3(j)) - 1) y_2(j)\Big), \\ y_3(r) = y_3(0) + \sum\limits_{j=0}^{r-1} \frac{\Gamma(r-j-1+\beta_3)}{\Gamma(\beta_3)\Gamma(r-j)} \Big(y_2(j)\Big), \end{cases} \tag{18}$$

We analyze the dynamics and characteristics of this map to understand its unique behavior and explore the implications of employing distinct fractional orders in the system's equations. These investigations offer a deeper understanding of how the fractional orders impact the system dynamics and underscore the importance of considering incommensurate orders in the analysis of the model's behavior. In Figure 6, we observe the variation of the order β_1 from 0.7 to 1 with a step size of $\Delta\beta_1 = 0.0005$. These figures illustrate the bifurcation and its corresponding Lyapunov exponent of the incommensurate-order 3D fractional Hénon-based memristor map (17) for $\beta_2 = 0.9$ and $\beta_3 = 1$, the parameters value $\rho_1 = 0.15$, $\rho_2 = -1.05$, $\mu = 0.5$, and the initial conditions $(y_1(0) = y_2(0) = y_3(0)) = 0$. From Figure 6a, it is evident that the state of the incommensurate Hénon-based memristor map (17) exhibits periodic behavior for larger values of β_1 as evidenced by negative Lyapunov exponents as shown in Figure 6b. On the other hand, as β_1 decreases, hidden chaotic behaviors emerge with positive values of LE_{max}. As the incommensurate-order β_1

decreases further, the trajectories undergo a transition state, and as β_1 drops below 0.745, the states of the fractional Hénon-based memristor map (17) exhibit a divergence towards infinity. In addition, the bifurcation chart and its corresponding largest Lyapunov exponent (LE_{max}), where the parameter β_3 is varied within the range $(0,1)$, are presented in Figure 7. In this analysis, we maintain the incommensurate orders as $\beta_1 = \beta_3 = 1$. From Figure 7, it is evident that, unlike the previous case, the trajectories of the incommensurate model exhibit hidden chaotic behavior when the order β_2 takes larger values as indicated by the positive values of LE_{max}. When β_2 decreases, the trajectories transition from chaotic to regular motion, where the states of the incommensurate-order fractional Hénon-based memristor map (17) become stable within the interval $\beta_2 \in (0.65, 0.78) \cup (0.897, 0.97)$. The Lyapunov exponent (LE_{max}) displayed in Figure 7b fluctuates between positive and negative values when β_1 lies within the region $\beta_2 \in (0.87, 0.897)$. This outcome indicates the presence of chaotic behavior with the emergence of periodic windows. Additionally, as β_2 decreases even further, the maximum Lyapunov exponent values increase until they reach their highest value, indicating that the fractional Hénon-based memristor map becomes chaotic. We also see that when the incommensurate-order β_3 continues to decrease, the map shows transition states, and the trajectories go to infinity. The observed changes in the largest Lyapunov exponent and the corresponding dynamic patterns illustrate the system's sensitivity to variations in the parameter β_2, highlighting the complexity and versatility of the incommensurate-order 3D fractional Hénon-based memristor map.

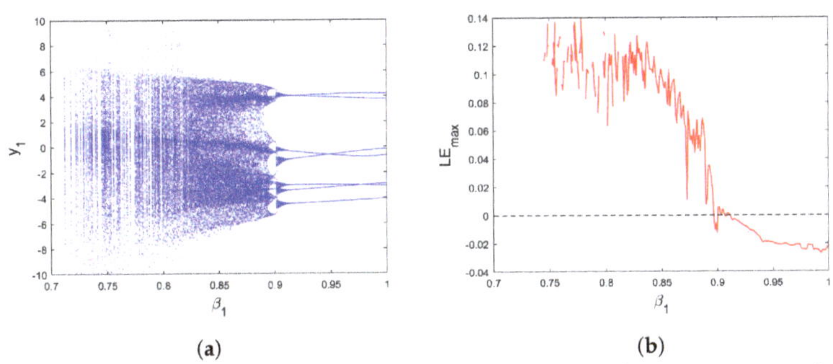

Figure 6. (**a**) Bifurcation of (17). (**b**) Corresponding LE_{max} versus the incommensurate fractional-order β_1 for $\beta_2 = 0.9$ and $\beta_3 = 1$.

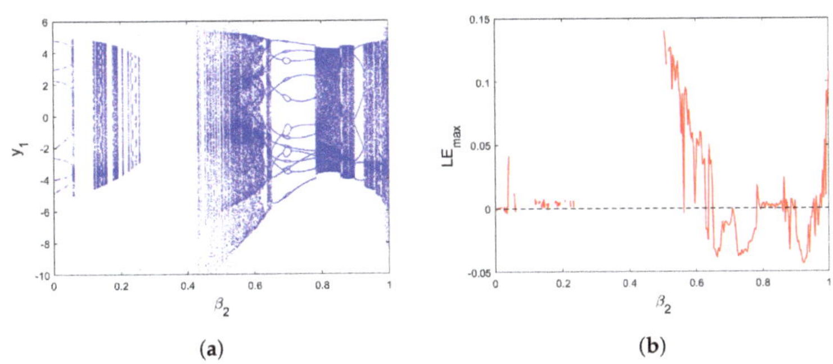

Figure 7. (**a**) Bifurcation of (17). (**b**) Corresponding LE_{max} versus the incommensurate fractional-order β_2 for $\beta_1 = \beta_3 = 1$.

Now, to provide a more detailed illustration of the influence of incommensurate orders on the behaviors of the Hénon-based memristor map, further investigation is carried out. These investigations offer a deeper understanding of how the fractional orders impact the system dynamics and underscore the importance of considering incommensurate orders in the analysis of the model's behavior. The three bifurcation diagrams presented in Figure 8 demonstrate the behaviors of the incommensurate Hénon-based memristor map (17) as the parameter μ varies within the range [0, 1]. The simulations are conducted with the value of parameters $\rho_1 = 0.15$ and $\rho_2 = -1.05$, and the initial conditions $(y_1(0) = y_2(0) = y_3(0)) = 0$. It is evident that these diagrams exhibit distinct patterns, indicating that the change in fractional orders $(\beta_1, \beta_2, \beta_3)$ significantly impacts the states of the incommensurate-order 3D fractional Hénon-based memristor map (17). For instance, when $(\beta_1, \beta_2, \beta_3) = (0.85, 0.9, 1)$, the system's states evolve from periodic to hidden chaotic behavior as the parameter μ increases. On the other hand, when $(\beta_1, \beta_2, \beta_3) = (1, 0.7, 1)$, oscillatory motion is observed, with trajectories remaining stable for small values of μ and becoming chaotic for large values of μ. In the case of $(\beta_1, \beta_2, \beta_3) = (1, 1, 0.9)$, a hidden chaotic region is evident throughout the interval, except for some periodic regions, where the model exhibits regular oscillations, especially when $\mu \in (0.66, 0.81)$. These results emphasize the sensitivity of the incommensurate 3D fractional Hénon-based memristor map (17) to changes in the orders β_1, β_2 and β_3, resulting in a diverse range of hidden dynamic behaviors, including hidden chaotic and periodic motion. This highlights the significance of incommensurate orders in shaping the system's dynamics. Additionally, the phase portraits of the state variables of the incommensurate fractional Hénon-based memristor map (17) as shown in Figure 9 further support the notion that incommensurate orders more accurately represent the system's behaviors. Overall, the study emphasizes the intricate and diverse nature of the incommensurate-order 3D fractional Hénon-based memristor map and the significance of the choice of fractional orders in modeling and characterizing its dynamics.

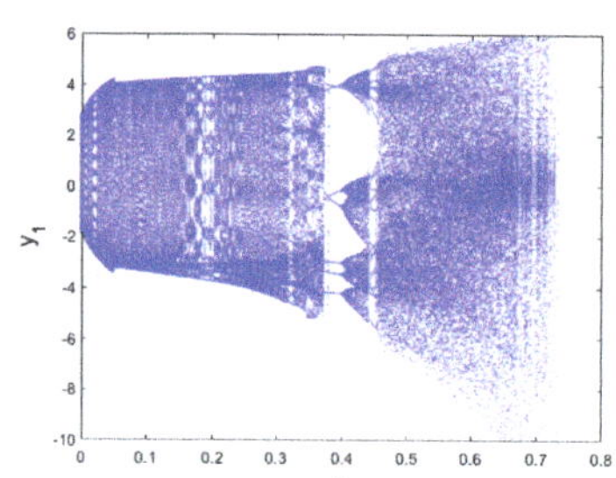

(a)

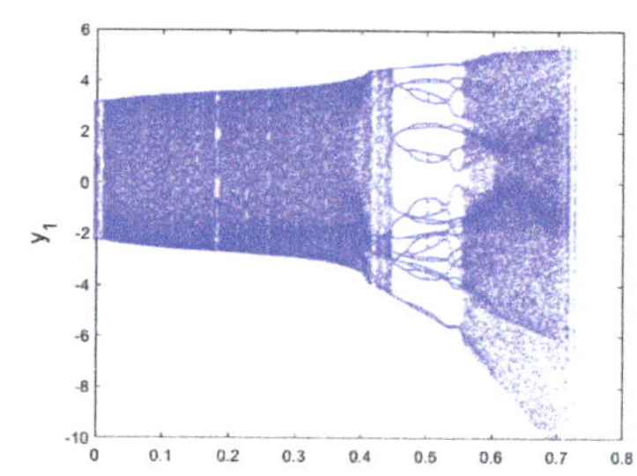

(b)

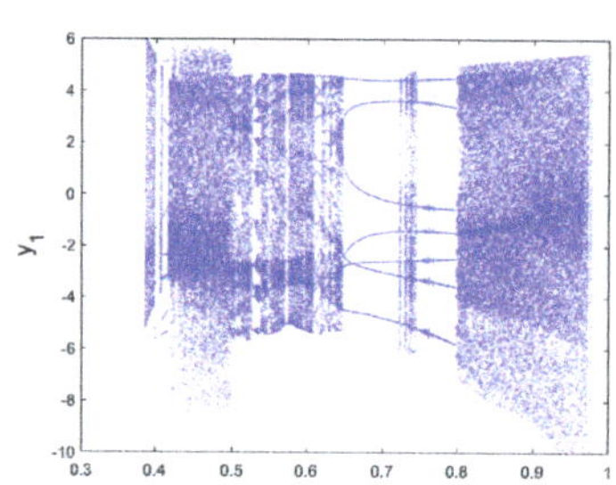

(c)

Figure 8. Bifurcations of (17) versus the parameter system μ for **(a)** $(\beta_1, \beta_2, \beta_3) = (0.85, 0.9, 1)$ **(b)** $(\beta_1, \beta_2, \beta_3) = (1, 0.7, 1)$ **(c)** $(\beta_1, \beta_2, \beta_3) = (1, 1, 0.9)$.

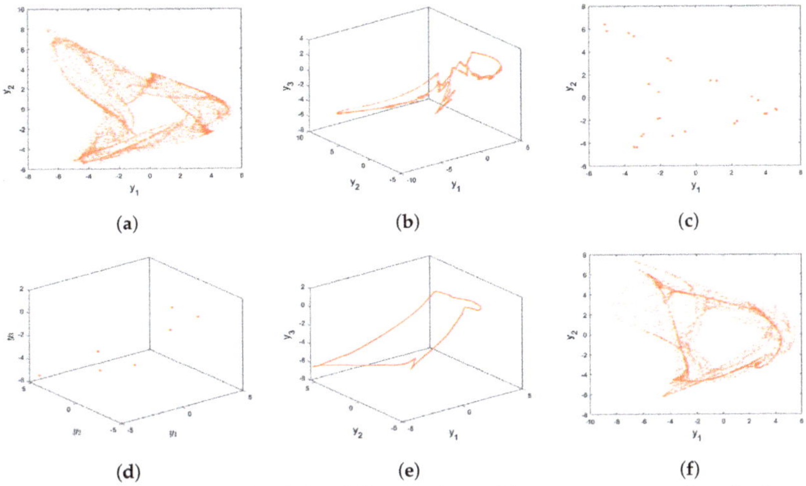

Figure 9. Phase portraits of (17) for different values of incommensurate orders β_1, β_2 and β_3 **(a)** $(\beta_1, \beta_2, \beta_3) = (0.85, 0.9, 1)$, **(b)** $(\beta_1, \beta_2, \beta_3) = (1, 0.6, 1)$, **(c)** $(\beta_1, \beta_2, \beta_3) = (1, 0.7, 1)$, **(d)** $(\beta_1, \beta_2, \beta_3) = (1, 0.9, 1)$, **(e)** $(\beta_1, \beta_2, \beta_3) = (1, 1, 0.7)$, **(f)** $(\beta_1, \beta_2, \beta_3) = (1, 1, 0.9)$.

4. The Sample Entropy Test (*SampEn*)

In this study, we employ the sample entropy (*SampEn*) method to assess the complexity of both the commensurate-order 3D fractional IHénon-based memristor map (14) and the incommensurate-order 3D fractional Hénon-based memristor map (17). Unlike approximate entropy (ApEn), SampEn can effectively measure the irregularity of time series regardless of the embedding dimension (m) and the similarity coefficient (r). Consequently, SampEn provides a more consistent and unbiased measure compared to ApEn [40]. The *SampEn* values indicate the complexity level of the time series, with higher values corresponding to higher complexity [41]. The calculation of *SampEn* is performed as follows:

$$SampEn = -\log \frac{\Psi^{j+1}(r)}{\Psi^{j}(r)}, \tag{19}$$

where $\Psi^{j}(r)$ is expressed as

$$\Psi^{j}(r) = \frac{1}{m-j+1} \sum_{i=1}^{m-j+1} \log C_i^j(r). \tag{20}$$

and $r = 0.2std(C)$ is the tolerance defined, and $std(C)$ represents the standard deviation.

The sample entropy results for the commensurate-order 3D fractional Hénon-based memristor map (14) and the incommensurate-order 3D fractional Hénon-based memristor map (17) are presented in Figure 10, with the initial conditions set as $(y_1(0), y_2(0), Y_3(0)) = (0, 0.0)$ and parameter values $\rho_1 = 0.15$ and $\rho_1 = -1.05$. The obtained *SampEn* values indicate the complexity levels of the time series, with larger values corresponding to higher complexity. The results demonstrate that both the commensurate and incommensurate fractional Hénon-based memristor maps exhibit higher complexity as indicated by their larger *SampEn* values. These findings align with the results obtained from the maximum Lyapunov exponent analysis, further confirming the chaotic nature of the dynamics in the proposed fractional map. The higher complexity and chaotic behavior support the significance of fractional orders in capturing the rich dynamics of the proposed fractional Hénon-based memristor map.

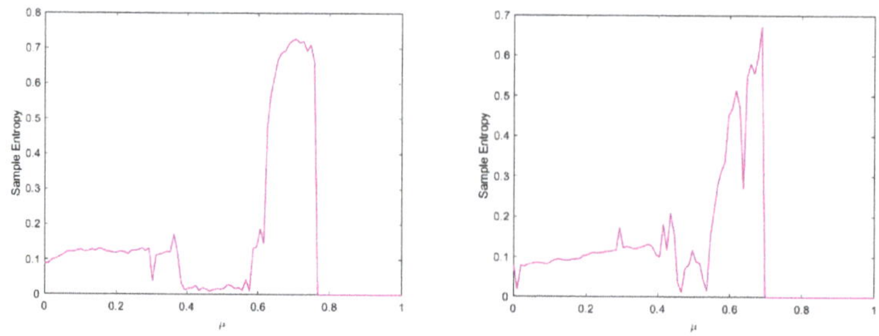

(**a**) (**b**)

Figure 10. The sample entropy results of the fractional Hénon-based memristor map versus the parameter μ for (**a**) $\beta = 0.9$, (**b**) $(\beta_1, \beta_2, \beta_3) = (1, 0.7, 1)$.

5. Control of Fractional Hénon-Based Memristor Map

In many real-world applications, it is essential to ensure that the system behaves in a stable and regulated manner. Control mechanisms are introduced to influence the system's dynamics, guiding it towards desired states or trajectories. This is particularly important in applications where maintaining a specific behavior or avoiding chaotic outcomes is a priority. Chaotic systems often undergo bifurcations, leading to unpredictable and undesirable behavior. By incorporating control parameters into the map, we can exert influence over these bifurcations, stabilizing the system or steering it towards specific regions of the phase space. This is vital for controlling and mitigating chaotic behavior.

Control is frequently used in synchronization and communication systems to ensure that different parts of a system remain coordinated. By introducing control into our map, we can explore its utility in synchronization tasks, making it relevant to applications in secure communications and information transfer. In this section, we introduce nonlinear controllers designed for stabilizing and synchronizing the proposed fractional Hénon-based memristor map's behavior, making it applicable to a wide range of practical scenarios.

5.1. Stabilization of Fractional Hénon-Based Memristor Map

Here, a stabilization controller is proposed to stabilize the suggested fractional Hénon-based memristor chaotic map. The main objective of the stabilization method is to design an effective adaptive controller that drives all states of the map towards zero asymptotically. To achieve this goal, we begin by revisiting the stability theorem for the fractional maps.

Theorem 2 ([42]). *Let $y(r) = (y_1(r), \ldots, y_n(r))^T$ and $B \in \mathcal{M}_n(\mathbb{R})$. The zero fixed point of the linear fractional-order map*

$$^{C}\Delta_b^{\beta} y(r) = B\, y(\varrho), \tag{21}$$

$\forall\, r \in \mathbb{N}_{b+1-\beta}$ is asymptotically stable if

$$\lambda_\iota \in \left\{ \gamma \in \mathbb{C} : |\gamma| \leq \left(2\cos\frac{|\arg\gamma| - \pi}{2-\beta} \right)^{\beta} \ \text{and} \ |\arg\gamma| \geq \frac{\beta\pi}{2} \right\}, \tag{22}$$

where λ_ι are the eigenvalues of the matrix B.

Now, the controlled fractional Hénon-based memristor map is given by

$$\begin{cases} ^{c}\Delta_b^{\beta} y_1(v) = 1 - \rho_1 (y_1(\varrho))^2 + y_2(\varrho) - y_1(\varrho) + C_1(\varrho), \\ ^{c}\Delta_b^{\beta} y_2(v) = \rho_2 y_1(\varrho) + (\mu \tanh(y_3(\varrho)) - 1) y_2(\varrho) + C_2(\varrho), \\ ^{c}\Delta_b^{\beta} y_3(v) = y_2(\varrho) + C_3(\varrho), \end{cases} \tag{23}$$

where $\varrho = v + \beta - 1$ and $C = (C_1, C_2, C_3)^T$ is the adaptive controller. The following theorem introduces control laws aimed at stabilizing the proposed novel fractional Hénon-based memristor map.

Theorem 3. *If suitable control laws are designed as follows,*

$$\begin{cases} C_1(\varrho) = -1 + \rho_1(y_1(\varrho))^2 - y_2(\varrho) - \alpha_1 y_1(\varrho), \\ C_2(\varrho) = -\rho_2 y_1(\varrho) - \mu y_2(\varrho)\tanh(y_3(\varrho)) - \alpha_2 y_2(\varrho), \\ C_3(\varrho) = -y_2(\varrho) - \alpha_3 y_3(\varrho), \end{cases} \tag{24}$$

where $-1 \leq \alpha_1 \leq 2^\beta - 1$, $-1 \leq \alpha_2 \leq 2^\beta - 1$ *and* $0 \leq \alpha_3 \leq 2^\beta$, *then the fractional Hénon-based memristor map can be stabilized at its equilibrium point.*

Proof. Substituting C_1, C_2 and C_3 into (23) yields the following linear system:

$$^C\Delta_b^\beta Y(r) = BY(\varrho), \tag{25}$$

where $Y = (y_1, y_2, q)^T$ and

$$B = \begin{pmatrix} -(1+\alpha_1) & 0 & 0 \\ 0 & -(1+\alpha_2) & 0 \\ 0 & 0 & -\alpha_3 \end{pmatrix}$$

Since $-1 \leq \alpha_1 \leq 2^\beta - 1$, $-1 \leq \alpha_2 \leq 2^\beta - 1$ and $0 \leq \alpha_3 \leq 2^\beta$, it is easy to see that the eigenvalues of the matrix B satisfy

$$|\lambda_j| \leq \left(2\cos\frac{|\arg\lambda_j| - \pi}{2-\beta}\right)^\beta \quad \text{and} \quad |\arg\lambda_j| = \pi \leq \frac{\beta\pi}{2}, \quad j = 1,2,3.$$

So, by employing Theorem 2, the controlled fractional Hénon-based memristor map is asymptotically stable. □

To validate the findings of Theorem 3, numerical simulations were performed. Figures 11 and 12 present the time series of the controlled fractional Hénon-based memristor map (23) for $\beta = 0.7$, $\alpha_1 = -0.2$, $\alpha_2 = 0.1$ and $\alpha_3 = 0.8$. It is evident from the figures that the system's states approach zero asymptotically, confirming the successful stabilization results.

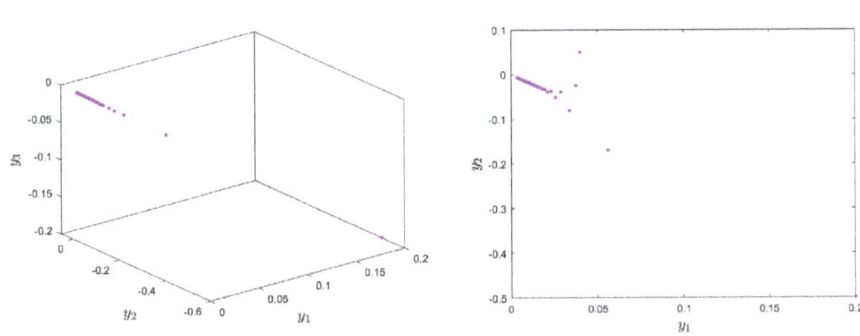

Figure 11. *Cont.*

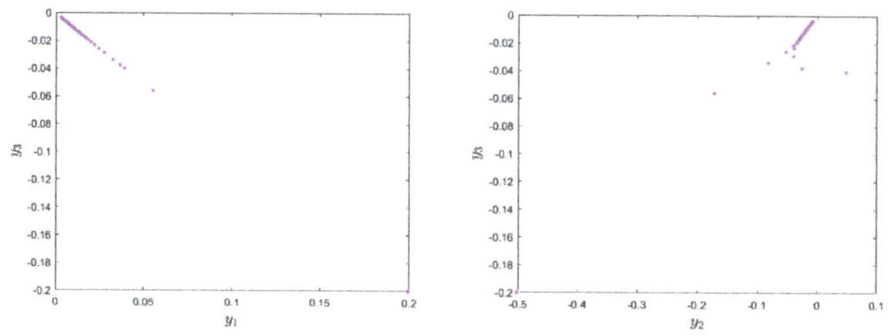

Figure 11. Attractors of the controlled fractional Hénon-based memristor map (23) for $\beta = 0.7$ and initial condition $(y_1(0), y_2(0), y_3(0)$ = $(0.2, -0.5, -0.2)$.

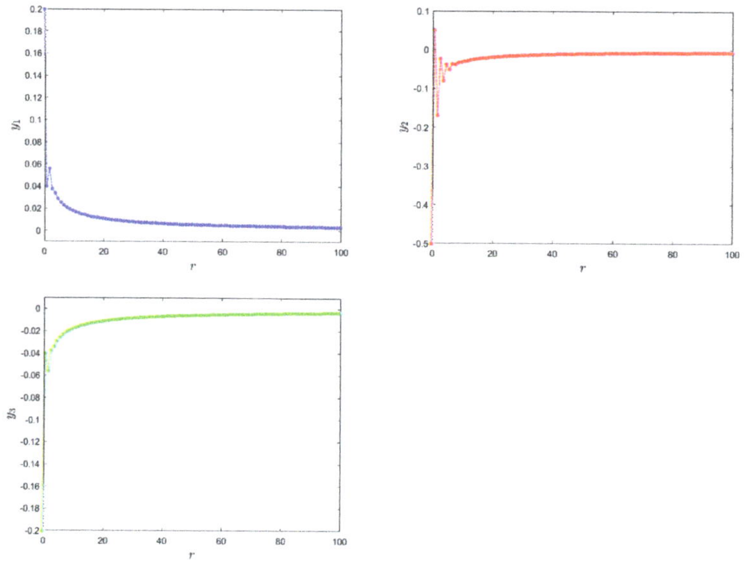

Figure 12. The stabilized states of the controlled fractional Hénon-based memristor map (23) for $\beta = 0.7$ and initial condition $(y_1(0), y_2(0), y_3(0)$ = $(0.2, -0.5, -0.2)$.

5.2. Synchronization Scheme of Fractional Hénon-Based Memristor Map

In the following, nonlinear controllers for achieving synchronization of the fractional Hénon-based memristor map are presented. The synchronization process aims to minimize the error between the master map and the slave map, forcing it to converge toward zero. The commensurate fractional Hénon-based memristor map, represented by Equation (14), is considered the master map, while the slave Hénon-based memristor map is defined as follows:

$$\begin{cases} {}^{c}\Delta_{b}^{\beta} y_{1s}(v) = 1 - \rho_1 (y_{1s}(\varrho))^2 + y_{2s}(\varrho) - y_{1s}(\varrho) + U_1(\varrho), \\ {}^{c}\Delta_{b}^{\beta} y_{2s}(v) = \rho_2 y_{1s}(\varrho) + (\mu \tanh(y_{3s}(\varrho)) - 1) y_{2s}(\varrho) + U_2(\varrho), \\ {}^{c}\Delta_{b}^{\beta} y_{3s}(v) = y_{2s}(\varrho) + U_3(\varrho). \end{cases} \tag{26}$$

U_1, U_2 and U_3 represent the synchronization controllers. The fractional error map is defined as follows:

$$\begin{cases} {}^C\Delta_b^\beta e_1(v) = -e_1(v)(\rho_1(y_{1s}+y_1)+1)+e_2(v)+U_1(\varrho), \\ {}^C\Delta_b^\beta e_2(v) = \rho_2 e_1(v)+\mu(y_{2s}\tanh(y_{3s})-y_2\tanh(y_3))-e_2(v)+U_2(\varrho), \\ {}^C\Delta_b^\beta e_3(v) = e_2(\varrho)+U_3(\varrho) \end{cases} \tag{27}$$

The control rule proposed to establish this synchronization scheme is outlined in the theorem presented below.

Theorem 4. *Subject to*

$$\begin{cases} U_1(\varrho) = e_1(v)(\rho_1(y_{1s}+y_1)-\gamma_1)-e_2(v), \\ U_2(\varrho) = -\rho_2 e_1(v)-\mu(y_{2s}\tanh(y_{3s})-y_2\tanh(y_3))-\gamma_2 e_2(\varrho), \\ U_3(\varrho) = -e_2(\varrho)-\gamma_3 e_3(\varrho) \end{cases} \tag{28}$$

where $0 \le 1+\gamma_i \le 2^\beta$ *(*$i=1,2$*) and* $0 \le \gamma_3 \le 2^\beta$*, the master Hénon-based memristor map* (14) *and slave Hénon-based memristor map* (26) *are synchronized.*

Proof. Substituting the control law (28) into the fractional error map (27), we obtain

$${}^C\Delta_d^\beta(e_1(v),e_2(v),e_3(v))^T = B\times(e_1(\varrho),e_2(\varrho),e_3(\varrho))^T, \tag{29}$$

where

$$B = \begin{pmatrix} -(1+\gamma_1) & 0 & 0 \\ 0 & -(1+\gamma_2) & 0 \\ 0 & 0 & -\gamma_3 \end{pmatrix}$$

The eigenvalues of the matrix B are $\lambda_1 = -(1+\gamma_1)$, $\lambda_2 = -(1+\gamma_2)$ and $\lambda_3 = -\gamma_3$. It is easy to see that for $0 \le 1+\gamma_i \le 2^\beta$ ($i=1,2$) and $0 \le \gamma_3 \le 2^\beta$, the eigenvalues satisfy the stability condition stated in Theorem 2, demonstrating that the zero solution of the fractional error map (27) is asymptotically stable, leading to the achieved synchronization of the master Hénon-based memristor map (14) and the slave Hénon-based memristor map (26). □

To confirm the validity of this result, numerical simulations are conducted using MATLAB. The values of the specific parameters chosen are $\beta = 0.98$, $\gamma_1 = 0.1$, $\gamma_2 = -0.3$, $\gamma_3 = 1$, and the initial values $(e_1(0),e_2(0),e_3(0)) = (-0.1,0.1,0.2)$. Figure 13 presents the time evolution of the states of the fractional error map (27). The figure clearly illustrates that the errors tend to zero, validating the effectiveness of the earlier discussed synchronization process.

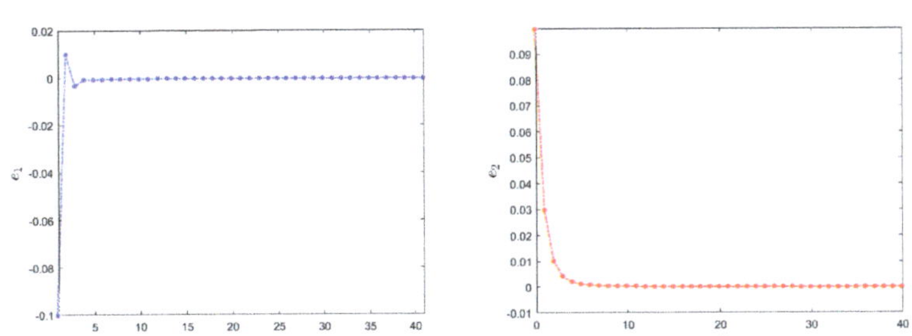

Figure 13. *Cont.*

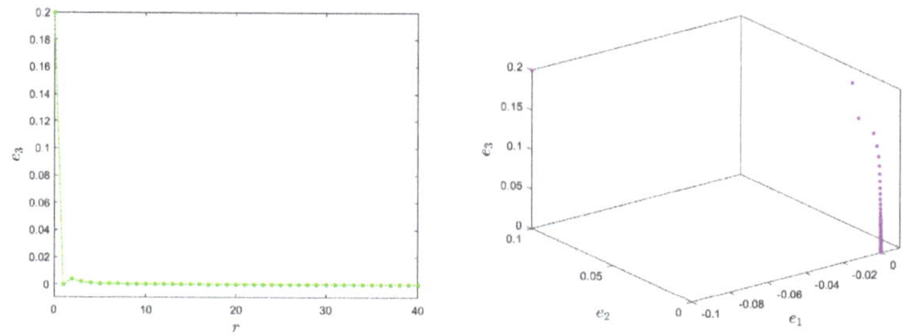

Figure 13. Synchronization states of the fractional error map (27).

6. Conclusions

The presented article introduced a novel 3D fractional Hénon-based memristor map and thoroughly investigated its behavior under commensurate and incommensurate fractional orders. The analysis of the map revealed the absence of any fixed points, revealing that the map can exhibit intricate and diverse complex hidden dynamical behaviors. By employing a range of analytical methods, such as Lyapunov exponent calculations, bifurcation analysis, and phase portraits, the distinct behaviors of the proposed fractional Hénon-based memristor map are thoroughly explored across various scenarios. Furthermore, the sample entropy algorithm is utilized to quantitatively assess the model's complexity. The results highlight the substantial influence exerted by the system parameters and fractional-orders on the states of the fractional Hénon-based memristor map. These parameters play a crucial role in shaping the system's hidden dynamics and behavior, causing variations in trajectories within the map's state space. Ultimately, the paper introduces effective control laws that ensure the stabilization and synchronization of the proposed map, driving its states towards asymptotic convergence to zero. Through the numerical simulations conducted, this research offers an extensive understanding of the system's dynamics, revealing numerous intriguing and diverse hidden chaotic behaviors. These findings hold significant value in elucidating the implications of fractional memristive maps, further enriching the field of chaotic dynamics and nonlinear systems.

Author Contributions: Conceptualization, A.A., A.S., A.A.A. and A.O.; Methodology, M.A., A.A., G.M.G., A.S., M.S.A.S., A.A.A. and A.O.; Software, M.A., A.A., G.M.G. and M.S.A.S.; Validation, A.A., M.S.A.S., A.A.A. and A.O.; Formal analysis, M.A., A.A., G.M.G., A.S. and M.S.A.S.; Investigation, A.A., G.M.G., A.S., A.A.A. and A.O.; Writing—original draft, A.A. and A.O.; Writing—review & editing, M.A., A.A., A.S. and M.S.A.S.; Visualization, M.A., A.A., G.M.G., A.S., M.S.A.S., A.A.A. and A.O.; Funding acquisition, M.A., G.M.G., A.A.A. and A.O. All authors have read and agreed to the published version of the manuscript.

Funding: This research received no external funding.

Institutional Review Board Statement: Not applicable.

Informed Consent Statement: Not applicable.

Data Availability Statement: All data that support the findings of this study are included within the article.

Conflicts of Interest: The authors declare no conflict of interest.

References

1. Hilfer, R. (Ed.) *Applications of Fractional Calculus in Physics*; World Scientific: Singapore, 2000.
2. Atici, F.M.; Eloe, P. Discrete fractional calculus with the nabla operator. *Electron. J. Qual. Theory Differ. Equ. [Electron. Only]* **2009**, *2009*, 1–12. [CrossRef]
3. Anastassiou, G.A. Principles of delta fractional calculus on time scales and inequalities. *Math. Comput. Model.* **2010**, *52*, 556–566. [CrossRef]
4. Abdeljawad, T. On Riemann and Caputo fractional differences. *Comput. Math. Appl.* **2011**, *62*, 1602–1611. [CrossRef]

5. Wu, G.C.; Song, T.T.; Wang, S. Caputo–Hadamard fractional differential equations on time scales: Numerical scheme, asymptotic stability, and chaos. *Chaos Interdiscip. J. Nonlinear Sci.* **2022**, *32*, 093143. [CrossRef]
6. Majhi, S.; Perc, M.; Ghosh, D. Dynamics on higher-order networks: A review. *J. R. Soc. Interface* **2022**, *19*, 20220043. [CrossRef]
7. Wu, G.C.; Baleanu, D. Discrete fractional logistic map and its chaos. *Nonlinear Dyn.* **2014**, *75*, 283–287. [CrossRef]
8. Abbes, A.; Ouannas, A.; Shawagfeh, N.; Khennaoui, A.A. Incommensurate fractional discrete neural network: chaos and complexity. *Eur. Phys. J. Plus* **2022**, *137*, 235. [CrossRef]
9. Shatnawi, M.T.; Abbes, A.; Ouannas, A.; Batiha, I.M. A new two-dimensional fractional discrete rational map: Chaos and complexity. *Phys. Scr.* **2022**, *98*, 015208. [CrossRef]
10. Hamadneh, T.; Abbes, A.; Falahah, I.A.; AL-Khassawneh, Y.A.; Heilat, A.S.; Al-Husban, A.; Ouannas, A. Complexity and Chaos Analysis for Two-Dimensional Discrete-Time Predator–Prey Leslie–Gower Model with Fractional Orders. *Axioms* **2023**, *12*, 561. [CrossRef]
11. Abbes, A.; Ouannas, A.; Shawagfeh, N. An incommensurate fractional discrete macroeconomic system: Bifurcation, chaos, and complexity. *Chin. Phys. B* **2023**, *32*, 030203. [CrossRef]
12. Abbes, A.; Ouannas, A.; Shawagfeh, N.; Grassi, G. The effect of the Caputo fractional difference operator on a new discrete COVID-19 model. *Results Phys.* **2022**, *39*, 105797. [CrossRef] [PubMed]
13. Dababneh, A.; Djenina, N.; Ouannas, A.; Grassi, G.; Batiha, I.M.; Jebril, I.H. A new incommensurate fractional-order discrete COVID-19 model with vaccinated individuals compartment. *Fractal Fract.* **2022**, *6*, 456. [CrossRef]
14. Khennaoui, A.A.; Ouannas, A.; Bendoukha, S.; Grassi, G.; Lozi, R.P.; Pham, V.T. On fractional–order discrete–time systems: Chaos, stabilization and synchronization. *Chaos Solitons Fractals* **2019**, *119*, 150–162. [CrossRef]
15. Saadeh, R.; Abbes, A.; Al-Husban, A.; Ouannas, A.; Grassi, G. The Fractional Discrete Predator–Prey Model: Chaos, Control and Synchronization. *Fractal Fract.* **2023**, *7*, 120. [CrossRef]
16. Ouannas, A.; Khennaoui, A.A.; Batiha, I.M.; Pham, V.T. Synchronization between fractional chaotic maps with different dimensions. In *Fractional-Order Design*; Academic Press: Cambridge, MA, USA, 2022; pp. 89–121.
17. Abbes, A.; Ouannas, A.; Shawagfeh, N.; Jahanshahi, H. The fractional-order discrete COVID-19 pandemic model: stability and chaos. *Nonlinear Dyn.* **2023**, *111*, 965–983. [CrossRef]
18. Chua, L. Memristor-the missing circuit element. *IEEE Trans. Circuit Theory* **1971**, *18*, 507–519. [CrossRef]
19. Strukov, D.B.; Snider, G.S.; Stewart, D.R.; Williams, R.S. The missing memristor found. *Nature* **2008**, *453*, 80–83. [CrossRef]
20. Ma, X.; Mou, J.; Liu, J.; Ma, C.; Yang, F.; Zhao, X. A novel simple chaotic circuit based on memristor–memcapacitor. *Nonlinear Dyn.* **2020**, *100*, 2859–2876. [CrossRef]
21. Lin, T.C.; Huang, F.Y.; Du, Z.; Lin, Y.C. Synchronization of fuzzy modeling chaotic time delay memristor-based Chua's circuits with application to secure communication. *Int. J. Fuzzy Syst.* **2015**, *17*, 206–214. [CrossRef]
22. Sun, J.; Kang, K.; Sun, Y.; Hong, Q.; Wang, C. A multi-value 3D crossbar array nonvolatile memory based on pure memristors. *Eur. Phys. J. Spec. Top.* **2022**, *231*, 3119–3130. [CrossRef]
23. Bao, B.; Rong, K.; Li, H.; Li, K.; Hua, Z.; Zhang, X. Memristor-coupled logistic hyperchaotic map. *IEEE Trans. Circuits Syst. Regul. Pap.* **2021**, *68*, 2992–2996. [CrossRef]
24. Itoh, M.; Chua, L.O. Dynamics of memristor circuits. *Int. J. Bifurc. Chaos* **2014**, *24*, 1430015. [CrossRef]
25. Li, C.; Feng, B.; Li, S.; Kurths, J.; Chen, G. Dynamic analysis of digital chaotic maps via state-mapping networks. *IEEE Trans. Circuits Syst. I Regul. Pap.* **2019**, *66*, 2322–2335. [CrossRef]
26. Rong, K.; Bao, H.; Li, H.; Hua, Z.; Bao, B. Memristive Hénon map with hidden Neimark–Sacker bifurcations. *Nonlinear Dyn.* **2022**, *108*, 4459–4470. [CrossRef]
27. Almatroud, O.A.; Pham, V.T. Building Fixed Point-Free Maps with Memristor. *Mathematics* **2023**, *11*, 1319. [CrossRef]
28. Lai, Q.; Lai, C.; Zhang, H.; Li, C. Hidden coexisting hyperchaos of new memristive neuron model and its application in image encryption. *Chaos Solitons Fractals* **2022**, *158*, 112017. [CrossRef]
29. Lin, H.; Wang, C.; Sun, J.; Zhang, X.; Sun, Y.; Iu, H.H. Memristor-coupled asymmetric neural networks: Bionic modeling, chaotic dynamics analysis and encryption application. *Chaos Solitons Fractals* **2023**, *166*, 112905. [CrossRef]
30. Liu, X.; Sun, K.; Wang, H.; He, S. A class of novel discrete memristive chaotic map. *Chaos Solitons Fractals* **2023**, *174*, 113791. [CrossRef]
31. Lu, Y.M.; Wang, C.H.; Deng, Q.L.; Xu, C. The dynamics of a memristor-based Rulkov neuron with the fractional-order difference. *Chin. Phys. B* **2022**, *31*, 060502. [CrossRef]
32. Peng, Y.; He, S.; Sun, K. Chaos in the discrete memristor-based system with fractional-order difference. *Results Phys.* **2021**, *24*, 104106. [CrossRef]
33. Ma, M.; Lu, Y.; Li, Z.; Sun, Y.; Wang, C. Multistability and phase synchronization of Rulkov neurons coupled with a locally active discrete memristor. *Fractal Fract.* **2023**, *7*, 82. [CrossRef]
34. Shatnawi, M.T.; Abbes, A.; Ouannas, A.; Batiha, I.M. Hidden multistability of fractional discrete non-equilibrium point memristor based map. *Phys. Scr.* **2023**, *98*, 035213. [CrossRef]
35. Peng, Y.; Liu, J.; He, S.; Sun, K. Discrete fracmemristor-based chaotic map by Grunwald–Letnikov difference and its circuit implementation. *Chaos Solitons Fractals* **2023**, *171*, 113429. [CrossRef]
36. Hénon, M. A two-dimensional mapping with a strange attractor. *Commun. Math. Phys.* **1976**, *50*, 69–77. [CrossRef]

37. Bao, H.; Hua, Z.; Li, H.; Chen, M.; Bao, B. Discrete memristor hyperchaotic maps. *IEEE Trans. Circuits Syst. I Regul. Pap.* **2021**, *68*, 4534–4544. [CrossRef]
38. Bao, B.C.; Li, H.; Wu, H.; Zhang, X.; Chen, M. Hyperchaos in a second-order discrete memristor-based map model. *Electron. Lett.* **2020**, *56*, 769–770. [CrossRef]
39. Leonov, G.A.; Kuznetsov, N.V.; Mokaev, T.N. Hidden attractor and homoclinic orbit in Lorenz-like system describing convective fluid motion in rotating cavity. *Commun. Nonlinear Sci. Numer. Simul.* **2015**, *28*, 166–174. [CrossRef]
40. Richman, J.S.; Moorman, J.R. Physiological time-series analysis using approximate entropy and sample entropy. *Am. J.-Physiol.-Heart Circ. Physiol.* **2000**, *278*, H2039–H2049. [CrossRef]
41. Li, Y.; Wang, X.; Liu, Z.; Liang, X.; Si, S. The entropy algorithm and its variants in the fault diagnosis of rotating machinery: A review. *IEEE Access* **2018**, *6*, 66723–66741. [CrossRef]
42. Čermák, J.; Győri, I.; Nechvátal, L. On explicit stability conditions for a linear fractional difference system. *Fract. Calc. Appl. Anal.* **2015**, *18*, 651–672. [CrossRef]

MDPI AG
Grosspeteranlage 5
4052 Basel
Switzerland
Tel.: +41 61 683 77 34

Mathematics Editorial Office
E-mail: mathematics@mdpi.com
www.mdpi.com/journal/mathematics

www.ingramcontent.com/pod-product-compliance
Lightning Source LLC
Chambersburg PA
CBHW061522210926
51850CB00008B/2010